Have women made any significant contribution to our traditionally male-dominated Christian church? Here is a book that replies with a resounding "Yes!" - and offers proof in 121 brief biographies of women who lived from the first century right into the present. Its 400 pages are packed with an astonishing array of fascinating and exciting spiritual biographies. Names we know and names we have never heard of are here, names of women high-born and wealthy, names of women born to poverty and obscurity. Queens and peasants, noblewomen and serving maids, all are outstanding servants of the Christian church, united in their selfless devotion to Jesus Christ.

ISBN 0-916441-46-6

90000

9 780916 441463

GREAT WOMEN
OF THE
CHRISTIAN FAITH

THE CHRISTIAN LIBRARY has been designed and produced for the discerning book lover. These classics of the Christian faith have been printed and bound with beauty, readability, and longevity in mind. Great care has gone into the selection of these volumes, with the hope that you will not only find books that are a joy to read, but books that will stir your faith and enlighten your daily walk with the Lord.

GREAT WOMEN
OF THE
CHRISTIAN FAITH

• • •

EDITH DEEN

A BARBOUR BOOK

This edition is reprinted by arrangement with Harper and Row, Publishers, Inc.

ISBN 0-916441-46-6

Published by   Barbour and Company, Inc.
P.O. Box 719
Uhrichsville, OH 44683

Printed in the United States of America

GENERAL CONTENTS

◆ ◆ ◆

CONTENTS BY SECTIONS

✦ ✦ ✦

[ix]

CONTENTS BY SECTIONS

CHAPTER 3. WOMEN OF A TIME OF AWAKENING

SECTION II

SPIRITUAL BIOGRAPHIES OF CHRISTIAN WOMEN FROM
THE EIGHTEENTH TO THE TWENTIETH CENTURY
CHAPTER 4. WOMEN WHO PIONEERED

CONTENTS BY SECTIONS

CHAPTER 5. WOMEN WHO BUILT

CHAPTER 6. WOMEN WHO ADVANCED

SECTION III

VIGNETTES OF OTHER CHRISTIAN WOMEN
THROUGH NINETEEN CENTURIES

CONTENTS BY SECTIONS

CONTENTS BY SECTIONS

[xiv]

CONTENTS BY SECTIONS

To my sister
Jane Alderman Lewis
whose love ever surrounds me

❖ ❖ ❖

O woman, great is thy faith:
be it unto thee even as thou
wilt. MATTHEW 15:28

SPIRITUAL BIOGRAPHIES
OF CHRISTIAN WOMEN FROM THE
SECOND TO THE SEVENTEENTH CENTURY

✦ ✦ ✦

CHAPTER I

Women of the Early Centuries

VIBIA PERPETUA—
EARLY CHRISTIAN MARTYR
(181?-203)

• • •

Perpetua, the mother of an infant son, suffered persecution and death with her maidservant Felicitas and four other Christians under a Roman edict against Christianity. Hers is an authentic record of early Christian martyrdom.

HER BLOOD BECAME THE SEED OF THE CHURCH

VIBIA PERPETUA WAS in her early twenties when, singing a psalm, she went forth with joyful, radiant countenance to a martyr's death. She and her Christian companions were condemned to be thrown into the arena among wild animals and then to be killed by a gladiator's sword. But Perpetua had caught a glimpse of Christ's sufferings on the Cross, and she was not afraid.

Perpetua lived in North Africa, at Carthage, where Christians from Rome had brought the Gospel and where vigorous Christian churches were springing up. Her ties with the world were strong. The devoted mother of an infant son, she was young, beautiful, of noble birth and well educated. Yet she was willing to sacrifice her life for her faith.

The Roman emperor Septimius Severus, fearing the rising power of Christianity, issued an edict prohibiting Christians from teaching or making converts. Perpetua and her companions were among the first victims of this

[3]

edict. The five others who suffered martyrdom with Perpetua—her maid-servant Felicitas, her teacher, the deacon Saturus, and three fellow Christians, Revocatus, Secundulus and Saturninus—had all been condemned for being converts to the new religion.

They knew the story of how Paul's own conversion nearly two centuries earlier had followed soon after Stephen's martyrdom. Paul had said: "And when the blood of thy martyr Stephen was shed, I also was standing by" (Acts 22:20). They were confident that their martyrdom would win many in the pagan city of Carthage to Christianity, for they were aware that the blood of these earliest martyrs had become the seed of the Church.

Perpetua had been baptized only a short time before she was condemned. As she came out of the water, she said: "The Holy Spirit has inspired me to pray for nothing but patience under bodily pains." Though she was very young, she must have known other kinds of suffering earlier, for there is no record of her husband, and it is assumed that he was either dead or had deserted her because she was a Christian.

While she and her five companions awaited arrest, her aged father came and pleaded with her to renounce her faith. "Father," she said to him, "do you see this vessel lying there? Can one call anything by any other name than what it is? So neither can I call myself anything else than what I am, a Christian." Though her father raged and threatened to beat her, she remained calm and firm.

The next day she and her companions were put in prison. "I was very much afraid," she wrote, "because I had never experienced such gloom. O terrible day! Fearful heat because of the crowd and from the jostling of the soldiers! Finally I was racked with anxiety for my infant."

Two church deacons succeeded in getting Perpetua and her maidservant Felicitas into a better part of the prison. Here they brought her infant son to her. She wrote:

I suckled my child, who was already weak from want of nourishment. In my anxiety for him I spoke to my mother, and comforted my brother and commended to their care my son. And I pined excessively because I saw them pining away because of me. These anxieties I suffered for many days; and I then obtained leave that my child should remain with me in the prison. Immediately I gained strength and being relieved from my anxiety about the child, my prison suddenly became to me a palace, so that I preferred to be there rather than anywhere else.

Strengthened in spirit, even in prison, she became more conscious of her closeness to God, "a God whose blessings were so well proved," she said. Uncertain of her fate and that of her fellow prisoners, she asked God to reveal it to her in a vision. The next day she told her companions:

Last night in a vision, I saw a golden ladder of wondrous size reaching up to heaven; so narrow that only one could go up at once. On its sides were every kind of iron instrument, swords, lances, hooks, daggers. If one went up carelessly, one's flesh would be torn, and pieces would be left on the iron implements. Under the ladder was a dragon of wondrous size, which laid snares for those climbing it, and frightened them from the ascent.

Now Saturus went up first. He had given himself up voluntarily after our arrest on our account, because he had taught us the faith, and he had not been present on the occasion of our trial. When he had reached the top of the ladder he turned and said to me, "Perpetua, I am waiting for you; but take care that the dragon does not bite you." And I said, "In the name of Jesus Christ he shall not hurt me." The dragon, as if afraid of me, slowly thrust his head underneath the ladder and I trod upon his head, as if I were treading on the first step.

Perpetua also told of seeing nearby a large garden, in which sat an old shepherd milking ewes. Around him stood a multitude of persons clad in white. "He gave us some cheese," she said, "and as we tasted it, the multitude of those who were clad in white said 'Amen.' Through the sound of their voices I was awakened."

Her prison companions interpreted this dream to mean that all of them were certain to suffer martyrdom. It was their own worthiness, not their pain or torture, which now became their first concern.

Before they were summoned before the tribunal, Perpetua's father entered the prison a second time and pleaded with his daughter: "Do not cut us off entirely; for not one of us will ever hold up his head again if anything happens to you." And with tears in his eyes he kissed her hands and fell at her feet. Distressed at his sadness, she tried to comfort him, saying: "This will be done on that scaffold which God has willed; for know that we have not been placed in our own power but in God's."

The next day she and her companions were questioned by Hilarian, Procurator of Carthage.

"Art thou a Christian?" he asked.

"I am," she answered. "I cannot forsake my faith for freedom."

When her father heard these words he knew that Perpetua and the others with her would be thrown to the beasts, and he tried to rescue his daughter. Hilarian commanded that he be beaten with a rod, and Perpetua suffered as much as if she had received the blows herself.

When the day of her execution drew near, her father, worn out with much suffering, came for the last time and cast himself down before her. She grieved for his unhappy old age. Her child was brought to her for the last time, and she confessed: "God so ordered it that it was no longer required to suck, nor did my milk inconvenience me."

Felicitas, eight months with child, feared she might be left behind to suffer in the company of strangers, instead of with her companions in faith, for a woman with child was not punished in public. Three days before they were to march into the arena of wild beasts, Perpetua and her companions prayed that Felicitas might be delivered of her child. Her labor pains came upon her a month early. A prison attendant mocked her, saying: "If you cry out now, what will you do when you are thrown to beasts in the arena?"

Felicitas replied: "I myself suffer not, but then another shall be in me who shall suffer for me, because I am to suffer for Him." The daughter who was born to her in prison was brought up by her sister.

Three days later she and Perpetua prepared for death. For their last meal, instead of the feast usually given to condemned prisoners, they celebrated an agape, a religious meal partaken of by early Christians in token of love and kindness. In the early Church it was looked upon with the same reverence as was the Eucharist.

On the day of their execution, the condemned Christians walked to the arena. Perpetua's face was radiant, and she sang a psalm. Wearing a simple tunic and with her lovely hair falling softly over her shoulders, she made her way toward the arena with easy grace. Behind her marched Felicitas with Saturus and the three other Christian men.

As she and her companions passed the Procurator, they spoke boldly: "You may judge us, but God will judge you." This remark infuriated the people and they demanded that Perpetua and her companions be given extra scourges. Walking confidently to their death, as Christ had walked to Calvary, they rejoiced that they could now enter more fully into His suffering and bear witness to their faith in Him.

The Christian men faced the beasts first. They were attacked by a leopard, a bear and a wild boar. Saturus, the teacher, was so covered with blood that the spectators cried out in scorn: "He is well baptized!"

Perpetua and Felicitas were thrown into the arena with a savage steer, which attacked Perpetua first. Discovering her tunic had been torn, she modestly hastened to gather it about her. When she saw Felicitas had been tossed by the infuriated animal, she went to her aid. Together they waited for another attack from the same beast, but the spectators thundered: "Enough!" Then she looked at herself and saw marks of injury on her body and her dress, but she felt no pain. She had been given victory over her senses and a consciousness of oneness with God. She knew that God was more powerful than her persecutors, who might destroy only her body, not her spirit. She dwelt in God, and He in her.

During a moment of rest Perpetua asked for her brother and when he appeared begged him to stand fast in the faith. The message she asked him to take back to her family was that they must love one another and not allow "our suffering to keep them from the faith."

Again she walked valiantly into the arena, this time to be beheaded. The gladiator was unskilled and gave her only slight wounds. After a cry of pain, she herself directed the gladiator's sword to her throat and died.

Perpetua and her companions met their death in the arena on a day in March, 203 A.D., but they live on in early Christian history as noble martyrs. Because of their courageous spirit and sublime faith, the Church grew and many others were attracted to a religion which produced such heroes.

Perpetua recorded her own story until the day before her death. The church father Tertullian added this postscript to her life: "O most brave and blessed martyrs, you have gone out of prison rather than into one. Your dungeon is full of darkness, but you yourselves are light. Your dungeon has bonds, but God has made you free."

HELENA—

MOTHER OF CONSTANTINE

(255-330)

◆ ◆ ◆

The first Christian empress-mother in history, she was also the first woman to enshrine places in the Holy Land. Her son Constantine named the ancient city of Helenopolis for her, and had gold medals struck bearing her effigy.

SHE ENSHRINED HOLY PLACES OF CHRIST

HELENA WAS among the first pilgrims to the Holy Land and there she discovered the places made holy by Christ's life and death. She built the Church of the Nativity at Bethlehem and the Church of the Holy Sepulchre at Jerusalem, and according to legend, she found the true Cross on which Christ had been crucified. For this the Church canonized her.

Helena was the mother of the first Christian emperor, Constantine, whose reign from 306-337 A.D. saw the emergence of Christianity from a persecuted sect to the powerful State Church of the Roman Empire.

Owing to the scantiness of ancient sources, much in Helena's life is open to question. Some historians claim that she was a Christian during Constantine's youth and influenced him to revolt from paganism. Others believe that neither Helena nor her son was converted to Christianity until after Constantine's victory in 312 over Maxentius, the ruler of Italy and North Africa. It was just before this crucial battle that Constantine saw above the setting sun the sign of Chi-Rho, the first two Greek letters of the word Christos, outlined in rays of light and with it the words: "In this sign thou shalt conquer." Because Constantine's soldiers were outnumbered two to one by those of his enemy Maxentius, Constantine attributed his victory to the Christian God. From that time on he praised the blessings that Christ had conferred on him and described himself as belonging to the Christian Church. He legalized the church calendar and designated Sunday as a holy day. Furthermore, he appointed Christians in ever-increasing numbers to the higher administrative posts of the Empire.

Helena's early years before and during her marriage to the Roman Emperor Constantius I, surnamed Chlorus, are obscure. Some authorities contend that she was a British princess, the daughter of Coel or Coelus, the British king of Colchester immortalized in the Mother Goose rhyme of "Old King Cole, the merry old Soul." John Leland, whom King Henry VIII appointed as his Antiquary in 1533, journeyed six years through England, making exhaustive researches. He claims that Helena was King Coel's daughter. If so, she may well have been a Christian from birth, for at Colchester about the time of her birth in 255 A.D. Leland says there was a Christian church with a Christian bishop. Colchester residents later boasted that the great Empress Helena was born there, and took for the arms of their town the cross she is said to have discovered. A number of churches in Britain are dedicated to Helena. At Bishopgate is the Church of St. Helena, which dates from 1210 A.D. and contains many curious old monuments dedicated to her. Her name appears often on the streets and buildings in the vicinity of this church.

There is another theory that Chlorus did not visit Britain until 296 A.D. and had then long been married to Helena. According to this account, Helena's father had been an innkeeper at the ancient town of Drepanum, situated in Asia Minor on an arm of the Sea of Marmara. In honor of his mother, Constantine later renamed Drepanum for her, calling it Helenopolis. It is identified today with the modern village of Hersek.

After Helena had been married to Chlorus at least nineteen years, he divorced her in 293 A.D. for political reasons. He was given the title of

Caesar, made ruler of Gaul, Spain and Britain, but in return was required to marry Theodora, the daughter of Maximian, his patron.

Helena's son Constantine remained faithful to his mother after her divorce. When his father died and Constantine became emperor in 306 A.D., he called her out of obscurity to the imperial court and ordered that all honor be paid her as the mother of the sovereign.

In this period as empress-mother, Helena resembles Bath-sheba, who quickly gained a commanding influence at court when her son Solomon became king. She also suggests another Bible woman, the Queen of Sheba, who went on a long journey from her kingdom in southwest Arabia to Jerusalem to test the wisdom of Solomon. Helena went to Jerusalem to discover the places where Jesus had been. It took courage to make such a journey in those days.

After Constantine became master of the East, he assembled Christianity's first general council at Nicaea and the next year wrote to Macrius, Bishop of Jerusalem, ordering the building of a magnificent church upon Mount Calvary. Helena, though now probably in her late seventies, superintended this pious work. She also hoped to discover the Cross on which Jesus had died. Other chroniclers say that Helena was directed by dreams to go to Jerusalem and search for the Holy Sepulchre.

Helena found the place where she believed the tomb to have been, but it was covered with earth, and a temple of Venus had been erected upon it. She had this pagan temple destroyed, and ordered her workmen to excavate for the sacred cave. One can imagine the emotion Helena felt as she stood at the spot where Mary Magdalene had seen Christ's empty tomb and the place from which she had gone to report to the disciples the miracle of the Resurrection.

Helena found here too, adjacent to the garden of Joseph of Arimathea in whose "new tomb" Jesus was laid (John 19:38-42), what she believed to be the true Cross of Calvary. Ambrose, one of the early church fathers, writes that when Helena discovered His Cross she "adored not the wood but He who had been nailed to the wood and burned with an earnest desire to learn the secret of immortality."

In the area where the Cross of Calvary and the tomb were found, Helena in 325 A.D. built the Church of the Holy Sepulchre. It still stands among a group of many buildings, which have been added to the original structure built more than sixteen centuries ago. The feet of generations of pilgrims have worn the steps leading to the spot where Helena believed she found the Cross. The heart of this church is the marble chapel of the Holy Sepulchre, perpetually lighted by forty-three lamps provided by various religious bodies.

Helena also built the Church of the Nativity at Bethlehem. Today thousands come to Manger Square at the head of a road sweeping up from the Jerusalem-Hebron highway and enter the ancient gray church begun by Helena above a hillside grotto, believed by many to be over the site of the manger. In no other church have Christians worshiped for so many centuries.

So great was Helena's devotion that she not only built these two churches, says Eusebius, but assisted individuals and entire communities in the Holy Land. The poor were special objects of her charity. The ecclesiastical historian Sozomen says that "during her residence at Jerusalem, Helena assembled virgins at a feast, ministered to them at supper, presented them with food, poured water on their hands and performed other similar services customary to those who wait upon guests."

Undoubtedly, the problems of her last years caused Helena to turn to Christianity for spiritual strength. Her daughter-in-law Fausta is said to have induced Constantine, by false accusations, to kill Crispus, his eldest son by a former marriage. Constantine in turn has been accused of ordering his wife Fausta suffocated to death in a heated bath, when he learned that his son was innocent of Fausta's accusations.

When Helena died in 330 A.D. Constantine was with her, as were his sons, Constantine, Constantius and Constans. The emperor ordered that his mother be buried with utmost pomp and soon thereafter he had coins struck in her honor. Her body was later brought from Rome to Constantinople, which Constantine had rebuilt and made the capital of the Roman Empire. There she was laid to rest in the imperial vault of the Church of the Apostles near the sarcophagus which Constantine had prepared for himself. Since the ninth century, however, the Abbey of Hautvilliers, near Reims, where a special devotion to Helena developed, has claimed to be in possession of her body.

Helena continues to be revered, for in the seventy-five-year span of her life she brought to God the homage and tribute of her devotion. She used the power and privileges of her royal position to further the Christian cause throughout the known world.

MACRINA—FOUNDER OF A RELIGIOUS COMMUNITY
FOR WOMEN IN THE EASTERN CHURCH
(327-379)

✦ ✦ ✦

With her brother Gregory, one of the church fathers, she was a pioneer in the monastic life. She healed, prophesied, and spread the faith.

THE "GREAT SISTER" OF BASIL AND GREGORY

MACRINA WAS reared in the land of Pontus, a strong Christian center and one of the areas to which the First Letter of Peter is written. The people of Pontus are addressed as "the elect according to the foreknowledge of God the Father, through sanctification of the Spirit."

Macrina's story, told by her brother Gregory, has become one of the classics of the early Church. W. K. Lowther Clarke, its translator, says: "Had the story been written in the Greek of the Fourth Century B.C. instead of that of the Fourth Century A.D., it would probably have been one of the world's classics."

Her family, for about a century or more, had played a leading role in Christianity. Her grandmother, Macrina the Elder, was influenced by Gregory the Illuminator, the "Apostle of Armenia," and her husband was a Christian of considerable property in both Pontus and Cappadocia.

During the persecution of Christians under Galerius and Maximianus, Macrina's grandparents were compelled to conceal themselves with a few devoted servants in a forest on the mountains of Pontus, where they endured great privations for seven years.

Macrina's father, a very learned man, became a distinguished lawyer and a professor of rhetoric in Cappadocia. Her mother Emmelia was a godly woman. Though the mother of ten, she found time to develop a love for the things of the soul in the hearts of her children. She succeeded so well that three of them, Gregory, Peter and Basil, became bishops, and these three, together with their sister Macrina, were later declared saints. Emmelia's home has fittingly been called "a nursery of bishops and saints."

Through her distinguished brothers, Macrina was in touch with the great Christian issues of her time. Her brothers, Basil the Great, and Gregory, Bishop of Nyssa, became strong supporters of orthodox Christian faith as spelled out in the Nicene Creed. After her mother's death, she helped to rear and educate her younger brother Peter, who became Bishop of Sebaste. An older brother was a distinguished jurist.

In 358 Basil journeyed to Egypt to visit the religious communities which Pachomius and his sister had founded in 320 A.D., one for men and the other for women. These were at Tabennisi on the right bank of the Nile. Basil spoke in glowing terms to Macrina of the spiritual progress of these religious communities and together they decided to found monasteries on a plan similar to the brother-and-sister communities in Egypt. Macrina was well fitted for this work, for, according to John Chrysostom, "she was a great organizer, an independent thinker, and as well educated as Basil himself."

They chose a place of much natural beauty in a mountainous region of Pontus. Their rock-hewn religious houses, on the edge of the Iris River, overlooked an inspiring view of plains, valleys and wooded mountains.

These religious houses became a community for those wholly devoted to the Christian life. Here Macrina taught other women the Scriptures in which she was so well versed. Here she established a hospital described as so large that it was "like a walled city or the pyramids in size."

Her brother Gregory tells the story of a child brought to her with an eye disease. The parents discovered that "all disease had been purged away by the divine drug" which Macrina administered to the child. They returned home with their child well and whole again and praised the Gospel of Christ as taught by Macrina.

Though Gregory was drawn away from monastic life into the general life of the Church, during which time he became a bishop, his "great sister" successfully continued her religious community until the end of her life. She set an example of "no anger, jealousy, hatred, pride, luxuries or honors." She and the women around her prayed and sang unceasingly and "grew purer with the discovery of new blessings."

His sister's resignation to the will of God, Gregory records, equaled her self-denial. Though she had inherited great wealth, she shared it with others, and when she died she had nothing. So real was her poverty that her brother Gregory threw his own episcopal cloak over her body as it was borne to the grave.

She also ministered to her own family, persuading her mother to give up her ostentatious way of life. When Emmelia lost one of her favorite sons, Nautcratius, in a hunting accident, Macrina, teaching her mother to be brave, helped her overcome her grief.

Eight years after Gregory had been elected Bishop of Nyssa, and probably while he was on his way to the Council of Antioch, he visited Macrina's monastery at Pontus, where, as he explains, he found his "great sister" ill and near death. Though she was weak when he arrived, she lifted her hand Heavenward and said: "This favor also Thou hast granted me, O God."

As they talked, she showed her brother the divine purpose behind sorrows and disasters. She also spoke of their parents, recalling their divine blessings.

As she lay dying, she gave her brother a vision of the great role he could play in the spread of Christianity. "Churches summon you as an ally and director. Do you not see the grace of God in all this?" she asked him. "Do you fail to recognize the cause of such great blessings, that it is your parents' prayers that are lifting you up so high, that you have little or no equipment within yourself for your success?"

"So sweet were her words to my ears," continues Gregory, "that I longed that she might never cease delighting my ears with her sweetness."

After their conversation, she prayed all night. Of her last hours her brother writes: "She seemed to be hurrying toward Him whom she desired, that she might speedily be loosed from the chains of the body."

Finally she asked that her couch be turned toward the East, and, whispering in a low voice, prayed:

Thou, O Lord, hast freed us from the fear of death. Thou hast made the end of this life the beginning to us of true life. Thou for a season rest our bodies in sleep and wake them again. Thou givest our earth, which Thou hast fashioned with Thy hands, to the earth to keep in safety. One day Thou will take again what Thou hast given, transfiguring with immortality and gracing our mortal remains. Thou hast saved us from the curse and from sin, having become both for our sake.

Thou hast shown us the way of resurrection, having broken the gates of hell, and how to overcome him who had the power of death—the Devil. Thou hast given a sign to those that fear Thee in the symbol of the Holy Cross, to destroy the adversary and save our life. O God eternal to whom I have been attached from my mother's womb, whom my soul has loved with all its strength, to whom I have dedicated both my flesh and my soul from my youth up until now—do Thou give me an angel of light to conduct me to the place of refreshment, where is the water of rest, in the bosom of the holy Father.

Thou didst break the flaming sword and didst restore to Paradise the man that was crucified with Thee and implored Thy mercy. Remember me, too, in Thy kingdom; because I, too, was crucified with Thee, having nailed my flesh to the cross for fear of Thee. And of Thy judgments have I been afraid. Let not the terrible chasm separate me from Thy elect. Nor let the slanderer stand against me in the way; nor let my sin be found before Thine eyes, if in anything I have sinned in word or deed or thought, or been led astray by the weakness of our nature.

O Thou who hast power on earth to forgive sins, forgive me, that I may be refreshed and may be found before Thee when I put off my body, without defilement on my soul. But may my soul be received into Thy Hands spotless and undefiled, as an offering before Thee.

When she had finished praying, a lamp was brought to her. Looking toward its light, she repeated the song of praise sung in the convents at the early eventide festival of the Lighting of Lamps.

Two women, Vastiana, daughter of a senator, and Lampadia, a deaconess, kept a vigil during her last hours. Soon the entrance hall could not hold the stream of mourners whom she had so lovingly inspired during her long service. As her nuns kept watch through the night preceding her funeral, they sang this song:

> The light of our eyes has gone out.
> The light that guided our souls has been taken away.
> The safety of our life is destroyed.
> The seal of immortality is removed,
> The bond of restraint has been taken away,
> The support of the weak has been broken,
> The healing of the sick removed.
> In thy presence the night became to us as day,
> Illuminated with pure life,
> But now even our day will be turned to gloom.

NONNA—

MOTHER OF GREGORY THE DIVINE

(329?-374)

❖ ❖ ❖

A mother of rare qualities, she acknowledged but one kind of beauty: that of soul; the only form of noble birth she recognized was goodness.

SHE WAS WIFE, MOTHER AND GRANDMOTHER OF BISHOPS

"What a woman she is! Not even the Atlantic Ocean, or if there be a greater one, could meet her drafts upon it, so great and so boundless is her love of liberality." In such terms Gregory of Nazianzus speaks of his mother Nonna in his famous orations. Gregory tells how, like Hannah of the Bible, she promised him to God before his birth, dedicated him to God immediately afterward, and consecrated his hands by making him touch the Bible.

There is no exact date for Nonna's birth, but she lived until about 374 A.D. She was the wife, mother and grandmother of bishops. Her home was in Nazianzus, which seems to have been in Cappadocia, one of the areas to which First Peter is addressed. Her famous son was born at Arianzus, his father's country estate in the neighborhood of Nazianzus.

Nonna, the child of Christian parents, was responsible for the conversion to Christianity of her husband, Gregory the Elder. When she met him he was a member of the Hypsistarians, a fourth-century sect which refused to worship God as Father, revering Him only as "All Ruler and Highest." Soon after Gregory the Elder was baptized, he was consecrated Bishop of Nazianzus, an office he held for forty-five years. Gregory the Younger tells how his father was stimulated by his mother in deed and word to attain the highest excellence.

Nonna had two other children, a daughter Gorgonia, probably somewhat older than Gregory, and a son Caesarius, a distinguished and trusted court physician in Constantinople.

Gregory speaks of his sister's two sons, who also became bishops, and tells of how well Gorgonia herself was reared by his mother. He calls her a sister "who excelled in modesty, presented herself to God as a living temple, opened her house to those who lived according to God, and who was eyes to the blind, feet to the lame and a mother to orphans."

Nonna sent her two sons, Gregory and Caesarius, to a famous school at Caesarea, the capital of Cappadocia. Here began the friendship between Basil of Caesarea, sometimes called St. Basil the Great, and Gregory—a friendship which greatly affected the development of the theology of their age.

From his school in Caesarea in Cappadocia, Gregory first went to Caesarea in Palestine, where he studied rhetoric, and then to Alexandria, where he studied theology.

On one occasion, setting out from Alexandria for Athens, Gregory was all but lost in a great storm at sea. In the oration, delivered at the death of his father, which is the main source of information about Nonna, he tells of the part his mother played in saving him in this tempest. She learned of his danger in a vision, and she and his father "soothed the waves" by prayer. One of his shipmates, he declares, saw "mother walk upon the sea, and seize and drag the ship to land with no great exertion. We had confidence in the vision, for the sea began to grow calm, and we soon reached Rhodes. We ourselves became an offering in consequence of that peril; for we promised ourselves if we were saved, we would give ourselves to God."

He relates how his mother and father shared their wealth with others, "rivalling each other in their struggle after excellence." Because his mother was such "a trusty steward with money," his father entrusted to her the greater part of their bounty.

Gregory compares his mother to King Hezekiah of Judah, who prayed in the midst of his sickness and was restored to health. When Nonna, who had always been strong, vigorous and free from disease, became sick and was for many days in danger, God sustained her in an unusual way, as Gregory recounts:

> She thought she saw me, who was her favorite, coming up to her suddenly at night, with a basket of pure white loaves, which I blessed and crossed as I was wont to do, and then fed and strengthened her, and she became stronger. . . . Next morning, when I paid her an early visit, I saw at once that she was brighter, and when I asked, as usual, what kind of a night she had passed, and if she wished for anything, she replied, "My child, you most readily and kindly fed me, and then you ask how I am. I am very well and at ease."

While others have been "honored and extolled for natural and artificial beauty," Gregory proclaims that his mother "has acknowledged but one kind of beauty, that of the soul, and the preservation or the restoration as far as possible of the Divine Image." He says that the only form of noble birth she recognized was goodness, and that "she applied herself to God and Divine things as closely as if absolutely released from household cares, allowing neither branch of her duty to interfere with the others, but rather making each of them support the other."

MARCELLA—FOUNDER OF THE
FIRST RELIGIOUS COMMUNITY FOR WOMEN
IN THE WESTERN CHURCH
(325-410)

♦ ♦ ♦

In the oratory of her palace in Rome, Jerome taught the Bible to Roman women.
Later Marcella established the first convent for women in the Western Church.
When the Goths sacked Rome, they beat her, attempting to make her reveal the
hiding place of her fortune, but she had already given it to the poor.

HER "CHURCH OF THE HOUSEHOLD" WAS FAMOUS IN ROME

MARCELLA, a wealthy and beautiful woman of Rome, and a descendant of
the old and noble family of Marcelli, is famous not for her fine clothes,
carriages or marble palace with its gold ceiling, but for her love of the
Scriptures and her leadership of the fourth-century community of Christian
women.

Her most lasting fame is as the founder of the first convent in the
Western Church. She received her inspiration for this as a little girl, when
her mother Albina extended hospitality to Athanasius, Patriarch of Alexandria, who was then in exile. She listened spellbound while this venerable
prelate told of the monks living in the Egyptian desert. The memory of
their example never left her and when, many years later, she was widowed
by the premature death of her husband, she was inspired by the devotion
of these ascetic Christians of the desert to turn her sumptuous palace on
the Aventine in Rome into a Christian retreat from the frivolity and corruption of the capital. She set apart an oratory for Christian worship.

The noblest women of Rome came to her home to hear discourses on
the Bible by Jerome, Father and Doctor of the Church. He had arrived in
Rome from Constantinople in 382 to attend a church council. He was
assigned as a guest to the hospitality of Marcella. She persuaded him to
hold the classes for some of Rome's most distinguished women.

Never before had the city witnessed such enthusiasm in the study of the
Scriptures and never before was there assembled for such study so dis-

tinguished and intelligent a group of women. They listened avidly to the great Bible authority, for he was translating the original Hebrew and Greek texts into a Latin version called the Vulgate, which was to become the Bible of Christendom for a thousand years. Jerome remained in Rome for three years, working on his translation, instructing his hostess and her friends and profiting by their criticism.

During this time Marcella asked him questions concerning the Bible and he found in her much virtue and ability, much intuition and spiritual insight. "What had come to me as the fruit of long study and constant meditation," he writes, "she learned and made it her own."

So important were Jerome's Bible classes that he later refers to Marcelia's palace as the Ecclesia Domestica or The Church of the Household, an institution which, during the close of the fourth and beginning of the fifth century, was the glory of the Church not only in the West but also in the East.

Marcella's Church of the Household was more than a house of study and prayer. It became a center for deeds of Christian charity and sacrifice. Fabiola received inspiration there to establish the first hospitals in Rome, later spending her immense fortune for the relief of the sick and the dying. There, also, Paula and her daughter Eustochium made their decision to aid Jerome in his Latin translation of the Bible. Marcella was herself inspired to establish on the outskirts of Rome the first religious retreat for women.

"That holy woman Marcella, who set before us a life worthy of the gospels" is the way Jerome describes her in one of the nineteen epistles he wrote to and about Marcella.

After Jerome's departure from Rome for Bethlehem, he frequently advised friends that Marcella could supply copies of Bible material they requested. Once, when a dispute arose in Rome concerning the meaning of the Scriptures, he asked Marcella to settle it.

When Jerome first met Marcella, she doubtless had been a widow for some time. He relates that her husband had died seven months after her marriage. She never remarried. For this reason Jerome frequently compares her to Anna of Jerusalem, mentioned in Luke 2:36-38; and describes Marcella as an example of Christian widowhood, commending her in this manner:

Anna lived with her husband seven years from her virginity; Marcella seven months. Anna looked for the coming of Christ; Marcella held fast the Lord whom Anna received in her arms. Anna sang His praise when He was still a wailing infant; Marcella proclaimed His Glory now that He had won His triumph. Anna spoke of Him to all those who waited for the redemption of Israel; Marcella cried out with the nations of the redeemed. [Epistle 54]

In Jerome's Memorial Epistle 127, written two years after Marcella's death to her friend Principia, he describes Marcella as young, highborn, and distinguished for her beauty and her self-control. He notes her aristocratic descent from a line of consuls and prefects, but he enlarges more on her virtues than on her birth.

Jerome narrates that the illustrious and aged Senator Cerealis paid court to Marcella after the death of her husband and offered to make over his fortune to her. Her mother Albina had worked hard to get this wealthy husband for her daughter. But Marcella said to her: "Had I a wish to marry, rather than to dedicate myself to perpetual chastity, I should look for a husband and not for an inheritance." This rejection convinced others that they had no hope of winning Marcella's hand.

At that time Rome was a city of wickedness in which it was almost impossible to attain a stainless reputation. Marcella made this verse her guide: "Blessed are the undefiled in the way, who walk in the law of the Lord" (Ps. 119:1). In order to guard her reputation, she was extremely discreet. She went nowhere in public without her mother as her companion and would receive no one in her house, not even monks or the clergy, unless others were present. Her companions were virgins and widows, all of them serious rather than frivolous, for she knew that a woman's character is judged by her choice of friends.

Rebelling against the immense weight of splendid clothing then in fashion and the hours devoted to painting the face and curling the hair before a mirror, she adopted a coarse brown dress. Her appearance marked her as consecrated to a religious and self-denying life.

Gradually Marcella attracted a group of women who also aspired to dedicated Christian living. They too were women of refinement and education who gave up their frivolities and adopted her manner of dress. She soon became the center of a circle of the most influential women in Rome.

Marcella lived an ascetic life for many years. She and Principia, whom she had brought up and loved as a daughter, found a place in the suburbs of Rome where they and other women could live in monastic seclusion. "I had the joy of seeing Rome transformed into another Jerusalem," writes Jerome. Religious homes for women who longed to live a deeply Christian life soon became numerous. Here women devoted themselves to prayer, to the study of the Scriptures, to the singing of the Psalms in Hebrew, and to the relief of the poor.

Marcella lived a life of prayer so completely that she spent much time in the churches dedicated to the apostles and martyrs. There she escaped from the throngs in the streets and the distractions of the city.

She spent much time, too, studying the Scriptures, and often when she did not understand their meaning, she would write Jerome in Bethlehem, asking him to enlighten her. Her delight in the Scriptures, writes Jerome, was incredible. She was forever singing: "Thy words have I hid in mine heart that I might not sin against thee" (Ps. 119:11). She also would sing the Psalm describing the perfect man: ". . . his delight is in the law of the Lord; and in his law doth he meditate day and night" (Ps. 1:2). This meditation on the law, Jerome says, Marcella understood not as a mere review of written words but as something requiring action. In one letter she asked him: "What are the things which an 'eye hath not seen nor ear heard'?" (I Cor. 2:9). Jerome answered that these are spiritual things which can be only spiritually discerned.

He frequently wrote to her about the things of the spirit. Word of a friend's death came to her while Marcella and Jerome were studying the 73rd Psalm. Later in the day he wrote her a letter, praising her dead friend and concluding with: "We must not seek to possess both Christ and the world. No. Things eternal must take the place of things transitory."

At another time Jerome wrote to Marcella about Paula's daughter Blaesilla, who had been criticized for her austerities: "A person who cavils at lives like hers has no claim to be considered a Christian."

Most of Jerome's letters to Marcella were written from the Holy Land. He described the charms of the sacred places and urged her to leave Rome and come to Bethlehem to join her old companions, among whom were Paula and her daughter Eustochium. But Marcella never went to the Holy Land.

When Alaric and his Goths sacked the city of Rome, some of the blood-stained victors found their way into Marcella's religious house. She received them without any appearance of alarm. When they asked her for gold, she pointed to her coarse dress to show them that she was poor and had no buried treasure. Not believing that a woman of her station would have chosen poverty, they beat her with whips. Marcella is said to have felt no pain at this brutal treatment, but to have thrown herself at their feet, pleading tearfully that her younger friend Principia be spared what she, an old woman of eighty-five, did not fear. Jerome relates that Christ softened the men's hearts, for they sent Marcella and her friend to the Basilica of St. Paul, then used as a sanctuary for the poor and afflicted. She thanked God for delivering them unharmed and rejoiced that the victors had found her poor, not made her so, for she had already given all her wealth away.

A few days after these events, the aged Marcella died. She had named Principia the heir to her poverty, thus showing a real understanding of Paul's exhortation to the Corinthians: "For you know the grace of our

Lord Jesus Christ, that though he was rich, yet for your sake he became poor, so that by his poverty, you might become rich" (II Cor. 8:9). True wealth, Marcella knew, is of the spirit.

MONICA—
MOTHER OF AUGUSTINE
(331-387)

♦ ♦ ♦

One of the most prayerful mothers in history, Monica helped to save her erring son and he became one of the greatest men in the Church.

THE MODEL OF CHRISTIAN MOTHERS

MONICA'S TEARS over her son's evil ways and her prayers for him during eighteen years saved Augustine for the Church. It was Augustine who, as Bishop of Hippo, saved Christianity when the Roman Empire was falling apart and who gave hopeless and bewildered men confidence in the eternal "City of God."

Augustine records in his *Confessions* that his mother was born of Christian parents in 331 A.D. at Tagaste, an ancient Roman town about one hundred and fifty miles from Carthage. Her husband Patricius, a burgess of Tagaste, though a pagan by birth, became a Christian later in his life. In 354 A.D., when Augustine was born, Monica was twenty-three years old. She had another son, Naviguus, and a daughter. Though Augustine does not give his sister's name, other sources say that it was Perpetua. In naming her daughter, Monica may have been familiar with the story of one of the first Christian women martyrs, Vibia Perpetua.

Monica maintained loving relationships with her family, even with her mother-in-law, who was at first prejudiced against her by the whisperings of malicious servants. Monica won over her mother-in-law by her patience and humility, so that not only was domestic peace established between them, but they learned to live together with what Augustine calls "a wonderful sweetness of mutual good-will."

With her husband, who was an irritable man, Monica exercised the same patience. When her friends marveled that she endured her husband's fury, and asked what remarkable rule she used, she confided her secret. In his moments of violent temper she held her peace, for she had learned that "an angry husband should not be resisted, neither in deed, nor even in word." But as soon as he was calm and tranquil again, she would quietly tell him her feelings and opinions.

Monica showed herself "such a peacemaker between differing and discordant spirits," says her son, that when she had heard on both sides the most bitter things, she would disclose nothing about the one to the other, save what might bring about peace between them.

She won her husband over so completely that when he died in 371 A.D., when she was forty, he too had become a servant of God. At her husband's death she turned to the wearing of her distinctive emblem, a widow's dress with a black robe and a white or gray veil.

Monica has inspired many great works of art and literature. Ary Scheffer, in his painting of Monica and Augustine, which hangs in the National Gallery in London, depicts her in this attire. She is gazing Heavenward with her hands clasped. In the church of Sancto Spirito, at Florence, the painting by Filippo Lippi shows her seated on a throne on each side of which stands a group of Christian women. In this church there is also a picture of Monica with her son. Vandyck depicts her kneeling, and looking up to Augustine, who, in an ecstatic vision, is borne up by angels and beholds the opening heavens and Christ the Lord. Matthew Arnold bases his sonnet, "Monica's Last Prayer," on the moving scene at her deathbed when she tells her son: "This only I ask, that you will remember me at the Lord's altar, wherever you be."

Francis de Sales, seventeenth-century Bishop of Geneva, says that Monica, like Hannah, consecrated her son to God before his birth. Augustine relates that his father "did not trouble himself with how I grew toward God, or how chaste I was, so long as I was skillful in my studies." But of his mother he writes: "In her breast Thou hadst even begun Thy temple, and the commencement of Thy holy habitation." He speaks of her as God's handmaid who poured into his ears much about God, none of which sank into his heart until he was older. "For she despised, and I remember privately warned me with a great solicitude not to commit fornication; but above all things never to defile another man's wife." These appeared to the youthful Augustine as "womanish counsel," which, he says, "I would blush to obey." Later, Augustine confesses that these words of counsel were God's and not just his mother's. "But this I knew not," he says, "and rushed on headlong into such blindness, that amongst my equals I was ashamed to be less shameless."

As Augustine walked what he called the streets of his Babylon, reveling in its moral filth, "as in cinnamon and precious ointments," his mother continued to pray for him. In his sixteenth year, he committed theft and enjoyed the company of his fellow sinners who stole with him. He said that it was a pleasure to him to laugh when seriously deceiving others. Through all this period his faithful mother did not cease praying for him.

At seventeen Augustine left his birthplace for the great city of Carthage, where, as he expressed it, "a cauldron of unholy loves bubbled up all around me." At sixteen he took a mistress and had a son by her. Later he joined the Manicheans, an heretical group. These and other excesses he records in his *Confessions*, the most intimate and soul-searching of all autobiographies. At last he tells how God "drew his soul out of the profound darkness," because of his mother who, he says, wept on his behalf more than most mothers weep when their children die. "For she saw that I was dead by that faith and spirit which she had from Thee, and Thou heardest her, O Lord. Thou heardest her, and despisedst not her tears, when pouring down, they watered the earth under her eyes in every place where she prayed; Yea, Thou heardest her."

In a dream Monica was consoled when she saw herself standing on a wooden rule symbolizing the rule of faith. A bright youth was advancing toward her, joyous and smiling, while she was grieving and bowed down with sorrow. The youth inquired of her the cause of her sorrow and she answered that it was her son's destruction she was lamenting. But the youth asked her to see that "where she was, there was I also." Then she saw in the dream her son Augustine standing near her on the same rule.

Monica related this dream to her son and he tried to interpet it as meaning that she would become a Manichean as he was. But his devout mother replied: "No, for it was not told me that 'where he is, there shalt thou be, but where thou art, there shall he be.' "

Though the dream allayed her anxiety, her son did not change immediately. For nearly nine years he "wallowed in slime, striving often to rise, but being all the more heavily dashed down." When Monica asked a certain bishop to talk to her son, the bishop refused, saying that he was still unteachable. "Leave him alone for a time," the bishop said to Monica, "only pray God for him; he will of himself, by reading, discover what that error is, and how great its impiety." Monica still was not satisfied and repeated her entreaties, until the bishop exclaimed: "Go thy way, and God bless thee, for it is not possible that the son of these tears should perish." Monica accepted the bishop's words as though they were "a voice from heaven."

Augustine left Carthage for Rome. When he moved on to Milan, Monica decided to follow him. Though it was dangerous for a widow to travel alone, "my mother felt secure in Thee," Augustine later commented. Even the sailors came to her for comfort in a storm and she assured them of a safe arrival because God had foretold it to her in a vision.

When Monica arrived at Milan, she found to her great joy that her son was no longer a Manichean. Though he was not yet a Christian, the good news was more than she had expected at this moment. Monica had mourned her son as one dead—dead to the spirit—but now she had renewed confidence that he would be raised up to God. Augustine says that his mother remembered the words of Jesus to the son of the Widow of Nain: "Young man, I say unto thee, Arise" (Luke 7:14). Monica, a widow too, had a son who was virtually dead. But as she repeated these words of Jesus to herself she knew that her son, too, would arise.

In Milan, she listened to the counsel of Bishop Ambrose, who said that the "fountain of living water" (John 4:10) of which Jesus had spoken to the Woman of Samaria would spring up into everlasting life in her son also. Ambrose and Monica became friends because of their mutual interest in Augustine and because Ambrose was impressed with Monica's fervency of spirit and her loyalty to the Church. He often praised her to her son and congratulated Augustine that he had such a mother.

Monica urged her son to take a wife and she thought he had heeded her advice when he sent his mistress of some fifteen years back to Africa. Instead of marrying, however, Augustine dismissed this mistress only to choose another.

Augustine's spirit had a long struggle with the flesh until a turning point came one day when he went into a garden. He flung himself down under a fig tree and cried out to God: "How long, Lord? Wilt Thou be angry forever? Why is there not this hour an end to my uncleanness?" Suddenly he heard the voice of a child singing in the garden: "Take up and read; take up and read." Quickly he took up a volume of St. Paul's Epistles and read Romans 13:13, 14: "Not in rioting and drunkenness, not in chambering and wantonness, not in strife and envying; but put ye on the Lord Jesus Christ, and make not provision for the flesh, to fulfill the lusts thereof." He read no further, for instantly "all the gloom of doubt vanished away."

Augustine hurried to Monica to tell her what had happened. Monica's grief was turned into gladness, "much more plentiful than she had desired and much dearer and chaster than she used to crave."

Acknowledging his own wickedness, Augustine now praised God, the author of safety, and Jesus Christ, the Redeemer. "O Lord, truly am I Thy servant and the son of Thy handmaiden," he said. On Easter Day in 387, Augustine and his son Adeodatus were baptized by Bishop Ambrose of

Milan. With his conversion he lost all desire for fame, marriage or riches.

Augustine, his mother and a handful of devoted friends now decided to return to Africa. En route they stopped at Ostia, at the mouth of the Tiber River, to rest. Augustine records the conversation he had there with his mother by a window overlooking the garden of the house they occupied. Each heart opened to the other, and they talked for hours of God and His works. With the tumult of the flesh silenced, Augustine remembered: "We created not ourselves but were created by Him who abideth forever." Turning to her son, Monica spoke:

Son, for myself, I have no longer any pleasure in this life. What I want here further, and why I am here, I know not, now that my hopes in this world are satisfied. There was indeed one thing for which I wished to tarry a little in this life, and that was that I might see thee a Catholic Christian before I died. My God has exceeded this abundantly, so that I see thee despising all earthly felicity. . . . What do I here?

Five days later, while they were still in Ostia, Monica became ill and, calling Augustine to her, said: "Here shall you bury your mother." Her son Naviguus had expressed the wish that she might die in her own country, but when Monica heard this she told Augustine: "Lay this body anywhere, let not the care of it trouble you at all. This only I ask, that you will remember me at the Lord's altar, wherever you be." Then, as Augustine records, "she receded silently into her pain." She did not dread being buried far from home, for as she herself had once said: "Nothing is far to God; nor need I fear lest He should be ignorant at the end of the world of the place when He is to raise me up."

In 387 A.D., on the ninth day of her illness and at the age of fifty-six, Monica died. Of his mother's funeral Augustine writes:

We did not consider it fitting to celebrate it with tearful plaints and groanings; for on such wise are they who die unhappy, or are altogether dead, wont to be mourned. But she neither died unhappy, nor did she altogether die. For of this were we assured by the witness of her good conversation, her faith unfeigned and other sufficient grounds.

ANTHUSA—
MOTHER OF JOHN CHRYSOSTOM
(347?-407?)

* * *

She devoted her life to her son, who became one of the great preachers of Christianity. She was a resident of Antioch in Syria.

SHE GUIDED HER SON TO GREATNESS

"HEAVENS! What women these Christians have!" the great pagan orator Libanius exclaimed in admiration when he learned about the self-sacrifice and purity of Anthusa. She was a contemporary of Nonna and lived in Antioch, the starting point of Paul's three missionary journeys. Anthusa's son John became a great Christian leader, so renowned for his preaching that he earned the name Chrysostom, meaning "Golden-Mouthed."

The Antioch of Anthusa's time was one of the four chief cities of the Roman Empire. Of its population of about two hundred thousand, half were Christian. Its streets were lined with covered colonnades of marble, beneath which the people could walk protected from the scorching sun of summer and the rains of winter. From the mountains to the south, massive stone aqueducts, whose solid masonry remains to this day, brought copious streams of water to its numerous baths and fountains. Splendid villas set in beautiful gardens adorned its suburbs, and there were many groves and parks.

We can picture Anthusa living in one of these villas. Her husband Secundus, an illustrious man in the Imperial Army of Syria, died when their son John was an infant, leaving her widowed when she was about twenty years old.

Although she had the means to give her son a good education, she dreaded bringing him up amid the corruptions of Antioch. But the burden of rearing him, she later declared, was lightened for her by God's support and the joy of seeing her husband's image reproduced in her child.

All her love, care, wealth and energies were concentrated on her son, who showed high intelligence and a love for the beautiful even in childhood. Her chief endeavor was to nurture in him the highest qualities of Christian character. In his formative years she taught him to love the Bible, and he later spoke of the influence of an early and intimate acquaintance with the Scriptures. From this, he said, came his enthusiasm for the good, his moral energy, his aversion to ostentation, his zeal for justice and truth and his steadfast faith. The spiritual interpretations and the practical applications found in his great homilies on Genesis, Matthew, John, Romans, Galatians, Corinthians, Ephesians, Timothy and Titus owe much to his mother's early teachings. Anthusa did not marry again, for she felt her child must come before her own happiness.

The fact that Anthusa sent her son to the celebrated orator Libanius to study is further evidence of her good sense. She had inherited the literary spirit of the Greek philosophers and poets and transmitted much of her classical knowledge to her son. It was also her guidance that started him on his career as a preacher and expositor of the Bible, for she inspired him to study theology under the noted Diodore of Tarsus. Later John said that "the Bible was the fountain for watering the soul." Though he reveled in his classical education, he drank still more deeply of the things of the spirit from his mother at home.

After finishing his formal education, John began the practice of law. His court speeches attracted wide attention and were highly commended by his old master Libanius. A brilliant career as a lawyer lay open to him, but he strongly disapproved of the fraud and avarice which marked the transactions of businessmen in Antioch.

One day when he had decided to retire to a remote hermitage in Syria, his mother led him into her room, made him sit by her on the bed on which he was born, and said to him:

I was not long permitted to enjoy the virtue of thy father, my child; so it seemed good to God. My travail pangs at your birth were quickly succeeded by his death, bringing orphanhood upon thee, and upon me an untimely widowhood. Which only those who have experienced them can fairly understand.

I implore you this one favor only—not to make of me a second time a widow, or to revive the grief which time has lulled. Wait for my death—perhaps I shall soon be gone! When you have committed my body to the ground, and mingled my bones with your father's bones, then you will be free to embark on any sea you please.

John yielded to his mother's entreaties and remained in her home, living the life of a monk and withdrawing himself from all worldly occupations and amusements. He strengthened his mind by study and prayer, and grew in wisdom and devotion. In later years he became one of the greatest reformers and ascetics in the Church.

PAULA—

JEROME'S INSPIRER

(347-404)

• • •

This noble Roman woman aided Jerome in his translation of the Bible. She also built a hospice and monasteries in Bethlehem and is herself buried there. Her daughter Eustochium and her granddaughter Paula also aided Jerome.

SHE SHARED HER WEALTH FOR GOOD CAUSES

PAULA WAS a Roman Christian woman remembered for several important contributions. She was a friend and disciple of the famous scholar Jerome, who dedicated many of his Bible translations and several of his commentaries to her. Her pilgrimage through the Holy Land was probably the first extensive trip to the holy places made by a Christian woman. She gave generously of her great wealth to build and maintain Christian churches, hospitals and monasteries. Finally she was buried in Bethlehem near the reputed birthplace of Jesus where today stands the Church of the Nativity.

Paula gave Jerome inspiration and intellectual stimulus while he labored on his Biblical material, revising and correcting some of the Latin translations then being used and making new Latin translations from the original Hebrew and Greek texts. His Latin Bible became the basis of most of the Roman Catholic translations into modern languages.

So highly did Jerome value the assistance given to him by Paula and her daughter Eustochium that he dedicated his version of Job, Isaiah, Samuel, Kings, Esther, Galatians, Philemon, Titus and the twelve minor prophets to them. Some people criticized Jerome for dedicating his books to his two spiritual daughters, but he simply commented: "There are people, O Paula and Eustochium, who take offense at seeing your names at the beginning of my works. These people do not know that while Barak trembled, Deborah saved Israel; that Esther delivered from supreme peril the children of God. I passed over in silence Anna and Elizabeth and the other holy women of the Gospel, but humble stars compared with the luminary, Mary. Is it not to women that our Lord appeared after His Resurrection? Yes, and the men could then blush for not having sought what women had found."

Paula not only aided Jerome in the translation of the Bible but she obtained, at her own expense, books and rare manuscripts essential to his work. In the Bethlehem convents she later established, there originated the copying of manuscripts which became a universal practice in the monasteries of succeeding centuries. Jerome read many of his translations and commentaries to her. She in turn questioned him keenly on the Scriptures, and led him to study more deeply.

Jerome's friendship with Paula and Eustochium suggests the friendship of Jesus with Mary and Martha of Bethany. This kind of friendship was not common in the ancient world and was made possible only by the "love which radiated from the cross." Paula had not only Jerome's strength of character but also the womanly virtues of sympathy and understanding. Their friendship was cemented by a common desire to extend the cause of Christianity.

Jerome's respect for the understanding of Paula and her daughter is reflected in the topics of prefaces addressed to them in several of his translations. In his rendition of the Book of Esther, for example, he assures them that he is acting as "a faithful translator, adding nothing of my own." He explains to them further that the book has been "drawn from all kinds of perplexing entanglements of language."

In speaking to them of his Isaiah translation, Jerome says he used the polished speech suitable for a man of rank and refinement. Jerome perceived that Isaiah was more an evangelist than a prophet, more a poet than a prose writer. In his translation of Job, he states that "the blessed Job, as far as the Latins are concerned, was till now lying amidst filth and swarming with worms of error, but is now whole and fresh again." Not only for the Book of Job, but for the entire Bible, Jerome presented Latin-speaking Christians with a "whole and fresh" version in the language they spoke.

In his preface to Titus he tells Paula and her daughter that this epistle should be of special interest to them, as it was written "from Nicopolis, near Actium, where their property lay."

These words are a clue to the source of Paula's wealth which she gave so willingly to the work of the Church. She probably received a large part of her vast income from the city of Nicopolis, which she owned. In Bethlehem she built four religious houses, three for women and one for men. She served as the head of the nunneries, while Jerome presided over the monastery. With these were connected a chapel and a hospice. The latter served as a shelter for pilgrims, the sick, the poor, orphans, the old, travelers and destitute of every kind. Like the Biblical Dorcas, she helped the needy and the sick wherever she found them.

Paula was a woman of rank as well as of wealth. Her father, says Jerome, traced his ancestry to the Gracchi and the Scipios, families that had given to Rome her most outstanding generals, orators and statesmen. Jerome adds that she was "heir and representative of that celebrated Paula in Roman history whose name she bore." She was married at seventeen to Toxotius of the patrician Julian family whose most illustrious member was Julius Caesar.

Her house on the Aventine Hill in Rome has been described as a palace glittering with gold. Here she entertained members of the highest rank of society. Here, too, she reared her four daughters, Blaesilla, Paulina, Eustochium and Rufina, and her son Toxotius.

Jerome records that at her husband's death, when she was in her early thirties, Paula's grief was so great that she nearly died herself. At this time, her friend Marcella won her to Christianity. When Jerome came to Rome and was persuaded to teach the Bible class organized by Marcella, Paula enrolled herself and her eldest daughters.

Soon after she became a Christian, she desired to follow more completely Christ's humble way of life. Like other early Christians, she protested against the materialism which was undermining Roman society. The consecration and asceticism of Paula and other Christians emphasized the difference between Christianity and paganism.

The early Christians tried to relieve misery and poverty. In her great pity for the suffering and dying, Paula's kindness was boundless. Many of Rome's poor, as they lay dying, were wrapped in her blankets. Many of the bedridden were supported from her purse. She gave so much to charity in Rome and buried so many paupers that relatives began complaining about her expenditures and asking what inheritance she would leave her children. She wisely answered: "I shall leave them the mercy of God."

Before her conversion, Paula had dressed in rich silks and decked herself in the finest jewels. Like other women of her rank, she painted her face, darkened her eyes and plaited her dark hair with false yellow tresses. She wore gold shoes and was carried in a litter, a row of eunuchs walking in front of her.

When she became a Christian, she began to adopt many austerities. This discipline prepared her for her later trip to the Holy Land, when she exchanged her litter for an ass, her fine foods for a little bread and oil, her handsome couch for a pallet of woven goat's hair laid on the bare ground. She began to pray longer than she slept.

Yet the woman in her was never lost in the saint. When her constitutionally frail daughter Blaesilla died of the austerities she practiced soon after she became a Christian, Paula grieved greatly. To console her in the loss of her daughter, Jerome reminded her that none of us is born to live forever, that Abraham, Moses, Isaiah, John, Paul and even the Son of God Himself had all experienced death. He pardoned Paula's tears as a mother but asked her to restrain her grief. "When I think of the parent I cannot blame you for weeping but when I think of the Christian, the mother disappears from my view."

When Jerome had returned to the Holy Land, he urged Paula and her daughter Eustochium to leave Rome for Bethlehem and Jerusalem that they might see where Jesus was born and where He suffered death on the Cross. Paula had by this time been a Christian for five years. In order to make this trip, she had to leave her house, her other children, her servants, her property and everything connected with her high position in the world.

She embarked at Portus, an ancient harbor of Italy. Rufina, Paula's youngest daughter, stood on the shore sobbing and begged her mother to remain at home until Rufina should be married. Her son Toxotius also entreated her not to leave. But Paula, Jerome writes, "overcame her love for her children by her love of God. She knew herself no more as a mother that she might approve herself as a handmaid of Christ. Yet she wrestled with her grief, as though she were being forcibly separated from parts of herself."

Paula's affection for her children was great, and she had to turn her eyes away so that she might not see what she could not behold without agony.

Jerome describes in detail Paula's journey, which took her first to Cyprus, where she and her daughter, and probably a group of Roman maidens in their party, joined Jerome. She met again Bishop Epiphanius, whom she had entertained in her home in Rome. She also visited monasteries on the island, and then went on to Antioch, where she was welcomed by Paulinus, the bishop there.

After this she entered Elijah's town on the shore at Zarephath, and next she passed over the sands of Tyre on which Paul had once knelt. She went on to the humble abode of Philip and his daughters "which did prophesy." Paula also visited Jacob's well, where Christ talked with the Samaritan

Woman. At Bethlehem she saw Rachel's tomb and went to the place where Jesus was born. Seeing this sacred spot, she was so overcome with emotion that she declared: "This is my dwelling place, because it was the country chosen by my Lord for Himself."

Everywhere Paula journeyed she meditated on Bible passages. She also distributed money to the poor. Her first home, until she built her monastery in the rock hills, was a mud hut.

Jerome writes that after Paula built the monasteries, chapel and hospice, she directed her nuns to recite the Psalms at dawn, when they went in a body to the chapel and when they made garments for the poor. Jerome began to regard Paula as "one of the marvels of the Holy Land."

In Jerome's Letter 23, written to Paula's daughter Eustochium, and perhaps the most famous of all his letters, he discusses at great length the motives which ought to guide those who devote themselves to a life of virginity and the rules by which they ought to regulate their daily conduct. The letter contains a vivid picture of the luxury, immorality and hypocrisy then prevalent in Roman society.

Paula's daughter-in-law Laeta wrote from Rome asking Jerome how she ought to bring up her infant daughter, also named Paula, as a virgin consecrated to Christ. Jerome replied in Letter 107, dated 403 A.D., giving advice as to the child's training and education. Feeling some doubt, however, that his plan would be practicable in Rome, he advised Laeta in case of difficulty to send the child Paula to Bethlehem, where she could be educated under the watchful care of her grandmother and her aunt Eustochium.

"A soul which is to be the temple of God must be educated in the temple," Jerome wrote to Laeta, who accepted his advice and sent the girl to Bethlehem. This child eventually succeeded Eustochium as head of the nunnery founded by Paula. Thus three generations of this devoted family served Christianity in the Holy Land. In this letter Jerome refers to Paula, the child's grandmother, as a "holy, venerable woman" and tells the child's mother that Christians are born, not made. He reminds her that Hannah vowed Samuel to God's service before his birth (I Sam. 1:1). Recounting how Hannah's son Samuel had been nurtured in the temple at Shiloh, he urges Laeta to do as much for her little Paula.

In his memorial Letter 108 praising the elder Paula, Jerome explains that, as she lay dying, it seemed as though she were leaving strangers to go home to her own people. She whispered the verse of the Psalmist: "Lord, I have loved the habitation of thy house, and the place where thine honour dwelleth" (Ps. 26:8).

"We do not grieve that we have lost her," continues Jerome. "We thank God that we have had her, and that we have her still, for," he adds in words based on Luke 20:38, "all live unto God."

Jerome further consoles Paula's daughter: "Be not fearful: you are endowed with a splendid heritage. The Lord is your portion, and to increase your joy, your mother has now after a long martyrdom won her crown. Now that she has ascended from her little Bethlehem to the heavenly realm, she can say to the true Naomi, 'Thy people shall be my people, and thy God my God.'"

Bidding a final farewell to Paula's memory, Jerome counsels her daughter: "Your faith and your works unite you to Christ; thus standing in His presence you will the more readily gain what you ask. Be like Mary, mother of Jesus; prefer the food of the soul to that of the body. Mary's surpassing purity made her worthy to be the Mother of Christ." "In her example," he says, "is life. In Eve's example, on the other hand, is death."

So greatly revered was Paula that when she was buried near Jesus' birthplace, six bishops bore her body to the grave. During the three days preceding the funeral, choirs of virgins chanted in Greek, Latin and Syriac. People from all parts of Palestine came to her funeral and the poor showed garments which they had received from her.

So lasting was her memory that more than ten centuries later Domenichino, in his magnificent painting of Jerome, depicted Paula ministering to him. This picture is one of the treasures of the Vatican.

Jerome was too much grieved to preach Paula's funeral sermon but he wrote her epitaph, saying that she was the first Roman woman to choose the hardship of life in Bethlehem as a service to Christ.

HILDA—
ANGLO-SAXON ABBESS OF WHITBY
(614-680)

• • •

Her monastery at Whitby was an important Christian center. She inspired the first English Christian poet, Caedmon, and educated five of England's bishops, as well as the king's daughter, her successor as abbess.

"ALL WHO KNEW HER CALLED HER MOTHER"

HILDA'S ABBEY at Whitby in Yorkshire was the most celebrated religious house in the northeast of England in the seventh century. It stood like a beacon on a rocky headland three hundred feet above the North Sea. Beneath it flowed the River Esk, and nearby was a fishing village. The view from the rock-bound promontory was one of solemn grandeur.

The lofty tower of the church almost certainly had a bell which sounded out across the stormy sea, reminding those who sailed that prayers were being said for them on the high cliffs. A light was kindled in the tower at night to warn ships of the peril near the shore. Thus the abbey was originally called Streaneshalch, an Anglo-Saxon word meaning "light of the beacon."

The abbey itself, a cluster of buildings including dormitories, schools, a refectory and a church, must have looked like a small village. Probably wooden structures with roofs of striking colors, they broke the bleakness of the gray cliffs in the winter and enhanced their beauty in the warm summer sun.

Candelabra shed light down long, dark corridors furnished with plain benches. To the church at daybreak fishermen and women and children from the village below came to praise God. Here, too, journeyed Christian pilgrims, some in humble garments, some on foot and some with trains of horsemen.

Hilda was the head and the heart of this Christian center. For more than two decades she ruled as administrator, teacher and spiritual guide. To fishermen and kings alike, she was "mother" in the most inspiring meaning of the term.

A woman of commanding appearance and noble character, she exercised a profound influence over many, for people recognized her innate wisdom and great love of God. Cultured, gifted, serene, one can picture her quietly going about her many duties. She probably wore the flowing white robes and dark headdress of the early Christians of Bible times. Like them, she inspired people with her apostolic zeal, as she aided the sick and needy, and brought knowledge to the ignorant and new faith to the disheartened and the weary. Christianity flourished in her abbey, and history honors her as the most distinguished churchwoman of Anglo-Saxon times.

Hilda's greatness emerges in the lives and works of her disciples. Five of the monks at Whitby became bishops: Bosta, Bishop of York; Aetta, Bishop of Colchester; Ottfor, Bishop of Worcester; Wilfred II, Bishop of York; and John, Bishop of Beverley. The latter was the most famous among them, both for his holiness and for his learning.

Among the serfs attached to the abbey was the uneducated herdsman Caedmon. One evening, while lying in the straw of an ox's crib, he thought he heard a voice say: "Sing something." "How can I sing?" he asked. "Sing nevertheless," the voice answered. The surprised Caedmon asked: "What can I sing about?" This time the voice commanded: "Sing the story of the world's birth."

Then an inspiration came, and Caedmon began to sing the story of the Creation in crude but heart-warming verse. To people of Anglo-Saxon times, this sudden burst of song seemed of divine origin.

Hearing of the marvelous story of the birth of song in an ox's crib, Hilda must have been reminded of the birth of Christianity in a stable. She sent for Caedmon and asked him to recite his poem for her. She was so impressed that she brought him into her monastery, taught him Bible stories and encouraged him to compose verses about them.

Up to this time, only those who knew Latin could understand the Bible. Now Caedmon began to compose metrical paraphrases of Genesis and other parts of the Bible in Anglo-Saxon, the language of the people. This helped to make the Christian faith intelligible and interesting to the common people. Some scholars regard his Genesis verses as the germ of Milton's *Paradise Lost*. For fostering Caedmon's gift, Hilda holds an honored place as a mother of English letters.

Hilda's years span an eventful epoch in the early history of Christianity in England. She was born in 614, just seventeen years after Augustine of Canterbury and his monks passed through that famous city in southeast

England singing their pathetic litany: "Turn from this city, O Lord, this anger and wrath, for we have sinned."

Before Hilda's birth, her mother, Berguswida, dreamed that she was searching for her husband, Hereric, but could not find him. However, under her garment she found a precious jewel that shed light over all Northumbria. Her baby Hilda, precious as a gem, later diffused light over Northumbria.

Driven in her childhood from their home, Hilda's parents took refuge in Yorkshire, where her father was poisoned by the petty King Cedric. Hilda's great uncle, King Edwin of Northumbria, deposed Cedric and annexed his territory to avenge his nephew's death. He also brought Hilda to his court where she was reared a Christian by Queen Ethelberga, who had brought her Christian priest with her when she came from her homeland in Kent to become Edwin's bride.

Ethelberga was a daughter of Bertha and of Ethelbert, first Christian king of Kent and founder of the See of Canterbury. From her mother, who established the first place of Christian worship at Canterbury, Ethelberga had learned to draw close to God. She was instrumental in converting her husband and many members of his family to Christianity.

On Easter Eve in 627, in a wooden church at York, the king was baptized, and Hilda was evidently baptized at the same time. After this event, thousands of people in once pagan Northumbria accepted Christianity.

Six years later, Edwin was killed in battle, fighting to spread his faith, and Hilda was brought face to face with a Christian's willingness to die for Christ. Now she wanted to live for Christ. During the invasion and rebellion that followed Edwin's death she joined her aunt Ethelberga when the queen took refuge with relatives at Kent.

One of the first decisions of Oswio, Edwin's successor as king of Northumberland, was to send to Iona for Bishop Aidan and ask him to start religious centers throughout the kingdom. Aidan asked Hilda to help him, and when she was thirty-three, she opened her first monastery on the banks of the Wear River. The next year she was made head of the monastery of Hartlepool. About nine years later, when the king gave her land at Whitby for an abbey, she started her work there.

King Oswio had made a vow to God that if he won the battle against the Mercians, he would give his daughter to God and also set aside land for a Christian monastery. His enemies incautiously put the river at their back, and when the rains came they were in panic. Oswio and his men attacked and were victorious. After the victory, King Oswio took his daughter Aelfled, then about a year old, to the monastery at Hartlepool.

When Hilda built and organized Whitby the king sent his daughter there to be brought up as a child of Christ. Twenty-two years later, at Hilda's death, the princess became her successor.

Eminent early abbesses like Hilda ruled wide territories and exercised rights like those of barons, sitting on governing bodies and furnishing soldiers to the king in time of war. With the king's backing, Hilda's monastery developed into an important religious center. In 664, less than a decade after it was established, King Oswio, probably at the suggestion of Hilda, convoked an important Synod there. Anglo-Saxons were not observing Easter on the same day as Roman Catholics elsewhere, and this was a constant source of dissension. The king, for example, observed the Easter of the Anglo-Saxon Church, while his queen, Eanfleda, observed the Easter of the Roman Church. When the majority of those meeting at Whitby favored the Roman date, Hilda seems to have given up her personal preference for the Anglo-Saxon custom and introduced the Roman practice at her monastery.

The facts of Hilda's life have been affectionately told by the Venerable Bede in his *Ecclesiastical History*. He calls Whitby "The Bay of the Lighthouse," indicating what a beacon of light she set up there on the North Sea. Bede, who was baptized by one of her bishops, John of Beverley, had personal contact with her. He writes: "All who knew her called her mother, on account of her piety and grace. She lived thirty-three years with her family very nobly, and then resolved to go into religious service. . . . She never failed to return thanks to her Maker or publicly or privately to instruct the flock committed to her charge." She died in 680, as she was admonishing her people to preserve harmony within the Church.

CHAPTER 2

Women of the Middle Centuries

CLARE—FOUNDER OF THE

FRANCISCAN ORDER OF POOR CLARES

(1194-1253)

* * *

A co-worker with Francis of Assisi, she took the vow of poverty and organized the Poor Clares, a religious order for women that spread throughout the world.

SHE BECAME POOR IN THINGS BUT RICH IN SPIRIT

LIKE A BRIGHT STAR, Clare of Assisi has taken an honored place beside a brighter star, Francis of Assisi, one of the most beloved saints in history. She was co-founder with Francis of the Franciscan Order of Poor Clares, barefooted nuns in ash-colored habits who have walked these last seven hundred years beside Francis' brown-robed friars. These Franciscans began their Christian work against a lurid background of war and shameless church corruption, but the little company of Poor Clares and Friars are illumined in an atmosphere of light, love and peace.

The Franciscans attempted to walk in Jesus' footsteps, especially obeying his words: "Sell all thou hast and give to the poor" (Matt. 19:21). They sought to imitate as nearly as possible at Assisi, the Italian town on the south slope of olive-clad Mount Subasio, the life led by Jesus and his disciples eleven hundred years earlier in Palestine. Their shelter was meager and they begged their food as alms. The Franciscans lived in sheds, cabins or cells made of wattle and daub, and their churches were small and simple.

Renunciation of possessions was to them no more than a preliminary step to receiving the more inspiring inheritance of spiritual joy, which opened the treasures of the kingdom of Heaven. Detachment of mind and heart from material things—and such detachment is what Francis meant by poverty—gave the Franciscans delight in natural beauty and a sense of comradeship not only with man, but with bird and beast, with rock and stone, with vines and grass, with fire and water.

Clare and Francis enjoyed a spiritual friendship of which there is no more beautiful example in history. Their love for each other was a love radiating from the Cross. Tenderness was here, illumination, and above all, courage. She developed under his influence into a rare, exquisite, individual woman. In her maturer years she became known for her brilliance, her inflexible will, her power to draw others to her.

Like Francis, she knew there was spiritual danger in prosperity and in the ownership of property. Francis, according to tradition, forbade his friars to own so much as a psalter, for he said that if a friar owned a psalter he would wish for a breviary. If he owned a breviary he would soon be haughtily commanding one of his fellows to bring it to him. These, he said, were among the dangers of even a few possessions.

"Poverty is the way to salvation, the nurse of humility and the root of perfection," he taught. "Its fruits are hidden but they multiply themselves in infinite ways."

The Franciscans carried out Jesus' command to the rich young man: "Go thy way, sell whatsoever thou hast, and give to the poor, and thou shalt have treasure in heaven; and come, take up the cross, and follow me" (Mark 10:21; also Matt. 19:21, Luke 18:22). Clare, like Francis, sought to do as Jesus bade.

During her lifetime she founded branches of the Order in Italy, France and Germany. The Italian houses were at Assisi, Rome, Venice, Siena, Pisa, Mantua, and elsewhere. In later years, England alone had sixty-five houses of Poor Clares.

Clare gave up many earthly possessions when she entered the Franciscan Order. She was born in 1194 of a noble family and spent her girlhood in an atmosphere of wealth and culture. Her father Favorino Sciffo was the Count of Sasso-Rosso. He owned a large palace in Assisi and a castle up the slope of Mount Subasio. Her mother Artolena belonged to the noble family of Fiumi, and was conspicuous for her consecration. At her father's death, when Clare inherited considerable property, she took nothing for herself or her Order, but gave it all to hospitals and to the poor.

Clare was sixteen when she first heard Francis preach in the Church of St. George at Assisi. She was uplifted by his message, which stressed the adoration of God, repentance, love for one's enemies, humility, and the celibate life. After she heard Francis her life had one goal: to be more like the devout Franciscans.

Accompanied by a single trusted companion, she went to consult Francis about her desire to live the religious life. Not long after this, she committed herself wholly to his guidance, considering him to be, after God, the director of her steps.

Their meetings probably took place at St. Mary of the Angels, also called St. Mary of the Little Portion, the first home of the Franciscans, which stood some two miles outside the gates of Assisi and half a mile from the Church of St. Damian, a small edifice which Francis had rebuilt with his own hands.

It was arranged that on the night of Palm Sunday, 1211, Clare would divorce herself from the world. At this time she was nearly eighteen, a tall girl with almond-shaped eyes, broad forehead and small chin.

When the day came, she first went with her parents to the Cathedral to hear Mass. Then she made ready to leave her parents' home to enter a cloister, to throw aside her beautiful clothes and don an ash-colored robe with a black hood and girdle of rope. Though her family had dreamed of an important marriage for her, she made a vow of perpetual virginity.

That night she went with a mature woman companion through the unused postern gate of her parents' home and sped through the wood. She found her way in the darkness to the Church of St. Mary of the Little Portion, on the left bank of the river Chiagio, in a grove of ancient cypress trees. Here she joined a small community of Benedictine nuns until Francis could prepare a house for her.

Later, she was sent to St. Angelo di Panzo, near Assisi, where her sister Agnes joined her. Afterward Francis gave Clare and her sister a little house adjoining the Chapel of St. Damian, outside the walls of Assisi, and installed them as the first two nuns of the Second Order of Franciscans. Here Clare began her great work. Soon she was joined by her mother and other wealthy friends.

Among the many princesses who became members of the Order was Agnes, daughter of King Ottokar I of Bohemia, and niece of the king of Hungary. This Bohemian princess, who was sought in marriage by two kings, consulted Clare about entering a nunnery. Some years later Clare sent five of her nuns from Italy to Prague. There Agnes, with seven young Bohemian women of the nobility, joined the Poor Clares, exchanging their jeweled gowns for rough, ash-colored robes.

For the remaining forty years of her life Clare never left her cloister. Within this monastery, in the center of a garden covering seven acres and surrounded by high walls and deep woods, she lived a consecrated life and helped others to live according to the same ideals.

The Poor Clares at St. Damian became the mother house of a great religious order whose members co-operated in Francis' work of evangelization. Until 1219 Clare followed the oral counsel of Francis, but that year rules for the Order were set in writing. At Clare's request these rules were severe.

Her life of service with him is lighted with a kind of radiance. Self had no part in their co-operation. Only the rarest natures, such as they both possessed, could rise to such heights. Early he had heard a voice say to him: "Francis, seest thou not that My house is in ruins? Go and restore it for me." Clare encouraged him in this restoration. She was thirty-two when Francis died at the age of forty-four. She survived him nearly thirty years, and during that time heroically struggled to uphold his rule of absolute poverty.

Clare has been pictured going around the nunneries putting warm covering on the sleeping sisters on cold winter nights, gently nursing the ill and washing the feet of poor travelers, but her main roles were praying and teaching. She passed from oratory to choir and into the terrace garden and back to her spinning, her face lighted by an inner joy.

Gifted with the needle, she taught the sisters of her Order to sew. Like the wise-hearted women of Exodus 35:25, she and these other devout women spun "both of blue, and of purple, and of scarlet, and of fine linen" for the Church.

During the last twenty-eight years of her life, probably because of the austerities of her youth, she was deprived of the use of her legs, and spent hours sitting on a bench, spinning flax of wonderful fineness.

Because of her physical infirmities, she advised others in her Order not to practice too many austerities. To Agnes of Bohemia, when she first became a member of the Poor Clares, she wrote: "Since our bodies are not of brass and our strength is not that of stone, but instead we are weak and subject to infirmities, I implore you vehemently in the Lord to refrain from exceeding rigors of abstinence which I know you practice."

About 1249, when she was unable to walk, her cloister was attacked by a group of Saracens, nomads from the Syro-Arabian desert, who were ransacking, plundering and burning towns in Italy. Unafraid even in the presence of such danger, she bade the sisters carry her to the door of the monastery. With stout heart she addressed the Saracens and then she prayed:

"Doth it please thee, O my God, to deliver the defenseless children whom I have nourished with Thy love into the hands of these beasts? Protect them, Good Lord, I beseech Thee, whom I am this hour not able to protect." She heard a voice answer: "I will always have them in my keeping."

Turning to the sisters she spoke with authority: "Fear not." At this moment the Saracen invaders scrambled down the walls of the cloister, routed by the words of a valiant woman.

To the end of her life Clare endeavored to live by Christ's example. When Pope Gregory IV advised her to modify her rule of absolute poverty and accept a yearly revenue for her Order at St. Damian's, he explained: "If your vow prevents you, I will release you from it." Her answer was: "Holy Father, I have no wish to be released from amongst the followers of Christ."

A medieval chronicler tells of Clare's last days, during which a Franciscan brother consoled her in her infirmities and exhorted her to patience. Her answer to him was: "Believe me, dearest brother, that ever since the day I received the grace of vocation from our Lord through His servant Francis, no suffering hath ever troubled me, no penance too hard, no infirmity too great."

From her sickbed in San Damiano she saw and heard a solemn midnight Mass celebrated in the Basilica of St. Francis, two miles away. For her ability to receive images and sounds over a distance, she was in 1958 proclaimed by Pope Pius XII the patron saint of television. This choice had been proposed at the end of ceremonies in Assisi on the seventh centenary of her death.

During her last illness, Pope Innocent IV visited her twice and heard her confession. He is reported to have said as he absolved her: "Would to God I had so little need of absolution."

In her last will and testament, she inserted a prophecy that Francis had made years earlier. While begging alms to repair the Church of St. Damian, he used to say: "Assist me to finish this building. Here will one day be a monastery of devout women, by whose good fame our Lord will be glorified over the whole Church." In Clare he found the devout woman for whom he had been waiting.

In her last testament she called herself "The Little Flower of St. Francis," an image expressing the spirituality of their friendship. She was in truth the flower of Francis' inspiration. Francis said of her: "She is the way of salvation, the nurse of humility and the root of perfection."

She has been immortalized in the religious art of the world. She appears in Simone Martini's fresco in the Convent of St. Clare of Assisi, where her body rests. Massari paints the scene in which she confronted the Saracens and they fled from her cloister. Murillo shows her on her death-bed, surrounded by nuns and friars while a company of virgin martyrs approaches her.

The meaning of her life is, perhaps, best expressed, not so much in her portraits, nor even in Francis' words about her, but in Paul's words: "For ye know the grace of our Lord Jesus Christ, that, though he was rich, yet for your sakes he became poor, that ye through his poverty might be rich" (II Cor. 8:9).

ELIZABETH OF HUNGARY—
HELPER OF THE POOR
(1207-1231)

♦ ♦ ♦

Daughter of a king, wife and mother of princes, Elizabeth used her royal revenue for the distressed. During a famine she fed nine hundred at her palace gate. She built a hospital and cared for the sick.

SHE LAY NOT UP FOR HERSELF TREASURES UPON EARTH

THE LIFE OF Elizabeth of Hungary was like a luminous ray lighting the thirteenth century. Although she died when she was only twenty-four, the story of her consecration to God and her noble acts of charity has con-tinued to inspire many to a higher way of life for more than nine centuries.

She was the daughter of a king and the wife of a prince, but she wore her regal honors humbly. When she entered a church to meditate on Christ's Passion, she removed her crown jewels, for she had seen Christ crowned with thorns and could not bear to appear in a sacred place wearing precious gems. She gave up her fine clothes for a plain gray Franciscan robe and wore it with such grace that others were uplifted by her queenliness. Al-though she could have had the finest food, her meals frequently consisted only of bread and honey or a dry crust with the smallest cup of wine. She lived in a troubled time of cultural confusion, but she brought freshness and poise wherever she appeared.

Elizabeth was born in 1207 in the royal castle of Pozsony (today Bratislava). She was reared in Wartburg Castle, a gray structure that rose from the mist and snowy pines of a Thuringian forest near the medieval town of Marburg in Hesse. The castle with its thick stone walls, heavy iron gates and watchtowers, drawbridge, parapets, and dark, damp cellars was surrounded by meadows and gardens. At Wartburg she spent a very happy childhood. But when Elizabeth was seven her mother died, and she learned as a young girl to take her perplexities into the Wartburg Chapel.

She came from a deeply religious family. Her mother, Gertrude, daughter of Berchtold, Duke of Meran, belonged to a long line of Christians. Her mother's sister, Hedwig, wife of Henry VI, Duke of Silesia, founded a convent for lepers after rearing her six children. Her mother's brother, Egbert, was Bishop of Bamberg, and two other uncles were also clergymen. Her father, Andrew II, was famous for his wars against the infidel nations on the frontier, but still more noted for his generosity toward the Church and the poor.

When she was only four years old, Elizabeth was betrothed to Louis IV, Prince of Thuringia. Having played together as children, Elizabeth and Louis continued throughout their lives to call each other "Brother" and "Sister." As Louis grew to manhood he developed the highest virtues of the Christian knight and sovereign and lived up to his motto: "Piety, Chastity, Justice."

In the spring of 1221, when she was fourteen and he was twenty-one, they were married in St. George's Church in Eisenach. The ceremony was a deeply religious experience for Elizabeth who became aware of her mystical union with Christ. She and her husband agreed to rule their people justly and to welcome religious orders to their castle.

When Elizabeth went to live in her husband's castle, she took with her garments of fine broadcloth or brocade as well as fur-trimmed capes and long, pointed brocade slippers. Her dresses with their round necklines had embroidered strips of gold or silver cloth falling straight down from the collar over the bodice and skirt. The sleeves, narrow to the elbow, widened until they fell in full folds halfway to the edge of the skirt.

She wore her flowing garments well, for she was tall and of graceful carriage. She had softly molded features and, though she was a daughter of the North, possessed the clear olive complexion of a southern maiden. Her face was framed by hair of the darkest hue.

The castle that she went to as a bride stood on a plateau two hundred and seventy feet above the Danube River. There for six years she lived an idyllic life, riding often at her husband's side on his journeys through his territories. When she could not go with him, she greeted him at his return dressed in her gayest Hungarian silks, her brilliantly colored wimple, and her jeweled necklace. "This I do not for pride of heart," she said. "I wish to be comely in my dress for God purely, for I would not give my husband any occasion of sin by having anything in me to displease him." The life of Elizabeth and Louis has been described as a heaven on earth.

As Louis' wife, Elizabeth had her choice of four or five homes and has been referred to as "Elizabeth of the Many Castles." When her first child, Herman, was born, she moved to Kreutsberg Castle on the Werra River. Here also were born her other three children: Gertrude, who became an abbess, and her two Sophias.

After the birth of each child, she took the infant in her arms and walked barefoot over the rough roads from the Wartburg heights to St. Katherine's Chapel. Before the priest and altar she thanked God for the delivery of her child and recited the Psalm: "Children are a heritage of the Lord; and the fruit of the womb is his reward. As arrows are in the hand of a mighty man, so are children of the youth" (Ps. 127:3, 4).

Elizabeth's life of devotion and good works had roots in her early training. In her childhood she had heard from her father the story of Francis of Assisi. The secret of his life became the secret of hers. Like him, she was sustained by a double joy—the joy of love and the joy of suffering for love.

Her father also told Elizabeth the story of the young noblewoman, Clare of Assisi, who with the encouragement of Francis had founded the Order of Poor Clares. Among Elizabeth's most prized gifts was a beautiful copy of Clare's Prayer to Christ, one verse of which read: "Do Thou, by Thy most bitter death, give me a lively Faith, firm Hope, a perfect Charity." This motto became the motivating influence in Elizabeth's life. As Clare and Francis had done, she nursed the sick, cared for newborn babies and saw that the aged had food and fire.

Among the miseries of the age was leprosy, introduced into Europe by Crusaders returning from the East. The lepers in their coarse gray gowns were dreaded and loathed, and many were forced to wander till they died. Elizabeth, remembering that Christ ate in the house of a leper and that He bade His disciples to heal the sick and cleanse the lepers, devoted herself to the most menial service for these poor creatures.

One day she brought a weakened leper home and laid him on her husband's couch. When Louis' mother heard of this, she said: "Come my son, and you shall see one of the wonders which your Elizabeth works and

I cannot prevent. . . . Outcasts are laid in your bed, and that troubles me, lest you should be smitten with infection. Look for yourself, dear son." According to the legend, Louis, pulling the coverlet from the bed, saw not the form of a leper but the form of Jesus of Nazareth.

Deeply moved, Louis granted his wife her request to build a home for lepers, halfway up the steep slope toward Wartburg Castle. There the wretched wanderers who could not climb as far as the castle were given relief. He was as eager as she to relieve suffering, and he took pride in his wife's many benefactions to the poor and needy in his kingdom.

A severe famine brought disease and crime to Thuringia in the summer of 1226. Elizabeth's husband was with the Emperor Frederick II in Italy, and most of his soldiers had accompanied him. Elizabeth felt herself responsible for order in the land. She feared an uprising, for the people were so hungry that they went into the fields and forests seeking nuts and berries, gathering herbs and mosses, grubbing roots and stripping bark from dead pines to grind into meal. When they gathered at her castle gate crying, "Bread, we want bread"—unlike Marie Antoinette who cried out during the French Revolution: "If the people have no bread, give them cake"—she ordered all bakers to work night and day baking bread, and she gave them flour from her own reserves. She also had great kettles of soup prepared. Monks and nuns worked with her, distributing bread and hot soup to the hungry.

Soup kitchens were also opened throughout the land. Granaries were emptied. Wood was cut and distributed. Churches and chapels were opened for the homeless. Elizabeth relieved hundreds who might have died during the dreadful famine.

She no longer felt herself a princess but His humble servant. She took all the ready money in the royal treasury and distributed it among the sick and suffering. In order to raise even larger funds she sold her most precious jewels and the massive silver cradle in which she had been placed as an infant. Though her husband's agents and treasurers accused her of squandering money, she was not dismayed. Believing the first duty of a prince to be the preservation of his people, she increased her efforts among the needy.

Her husband, hearing of the heavy burden that had fallen upon his young wife, obtained the emperor's leave to return from Italy. Long before he arrived at the palace, his treasurers and stewards met him and said that his wife had impoverished the land by opening the coffers and barns and distributing money and food to the needy. But his reply to their criticism was: "Let her do good and give to God whatever she will, so long as she leaves me Wartburg and Nurnberg. Alms will never ruin us."

During his happy reunion with his wife, he gently asked her: "Dear sister, what became of your poor people during this weary winter?" Grateful that hundreds of them had been fed at the palace gate, she calmly answered: "I gave God what was His, and God has kept for us what was yours and mine."

All through the summer and autumn of 1227, the states of Germany, of which Thuringia was one, prepared to send men on a Crusade to the Holy Land. Louis had been put in charge of the Central German contingent of the Crusaders. Elizabeth and her husband had never known happier days than those of the summer before his departure, but their joy was short-lived. As he was about to leave for the Holy Land, Louis consoled his wife, saying: "What I am doing is for the love of Jesus Christ." She pleaded with him: "Stay with me, if it be not against the will of God." But he answered her: "Give me leave to go, for so I have vowed." Elizabeth replied: "I would not keep you against God's own liking. May God grant you ever to do as He would have you." Then, as the soldiers began to march away, singing one of the Crusaders' songs, she tore herself from her husband and turned homeward.

In his concern for his wife, who was several months with child, and for his children, Louis left them in the care of his brother, Henry Raspe IV. Elizabeth's enemies, who had accused her of squandering the kingdom's funds to feed the poor, began to criticize her to her husband's brother.

She had a premonition that she would never see her husband again and began to wear the dark robes of widowhood. When September drew to a close, her fourth child, Gertrude, named for her mother, was born. Meanwhile, her premonition about Louis came true. His ship put into Otranto, Italy, because of bad weather, and there he was stricken with fever and died in 1227, about the time of Gertrude's birth in Thuringia. Elizabeth's mother-in-law did not tell her of her husband's death until after the birth of their child. When she heard the news, Elizabeth said: "The world is dead to me and all that was pleasant in the world."

A year later, evil counselors suggested to her husband's brother Henry that, under an old Thuringian law, the principalities belonged to him as the oldest living male member of the family. Henry assumed full power and sent Elizabeth from the palace, an outcast. On the plea that the treasury had been depleted by her lavish giving to the poor, the allowance assigned to her by her husband was stopped.

In the falling dusk of a midwinter day, Elizabeth, barely twenty years old, the daughter of a long line of kings, made her way alone down a rugged path from the castle gate. As she trudged along, she forgave her husband's relatives for her suffering. She entered Eisenach, where the townspeople had been forbidden to give her assistance. In this town where she had built a hospital and prepared a home for children, not a door was opened to her. She went on to the Convent of St. Catherine and from there to an inn, but was turned away each time. She rested that night in the courtyard where the innkeeper kept empty casks and jars.

The next day a few faithful ladies of her court brought her four small children to her. Drawing them close, she said: "May God so love me, I know not whither to turn, or where to rest your little bodies, though all the lordship of this town is yours, dear son." Her ladies then reassured her: "Where you go, madam, we also shall go; and where your Highness is, there shall we be."

Elizabeth answered them cheerfully: "Since the people will not be our hosts today we shall ask God to take us for His guests." She led them all into a church, where they took shelter that day. A poor priest invited them under his roof, and Elizabeth bought food for her children and her ladies with the small jewels she wore. A few days later they were fortunate enough to find refuge in a crowded corner of the home of a wealthy townsman.

Elizabeth learned to accept all of her trials by thinking only of Christ's suffering and of how people had mocked Him too. In her extremity she prayed: "Lord, if Thou wouldest be with me, I would be with Thee, and I wish never to be parted from Thee!" She had a vision and heard Him answer: "If thou dost wish to be with Me, I desire to be with thee." When she was questioned about this vision, she was wise enough not to reveal it, but answered: "What I saw there it is not fitting to tell; but know that I was in great felicity and I beheld marvelous secrets of God."

Soon Mechthild, abbess of a convent in Kitzlinger, who may have been Elizabeth's aunt, heard of her plight and persuaded Elizabeth's uncle, Egbert, Bishop of Bamberg, to send for her. He offered her a house adjoining his palace.

En route to Bamberg, she met the procession bearing her husband's bier. As she stood beside the uncovered coffin, she was overcome with sorrow. But remembering God, she conquered her anguish, and prayed:

I give Thee thanks, O Lord, that Thou hast been pleased to grant Thy handmaid the great desire I had to behold the remains of my beloved, and in Thy compassion to comfort my afflicted soul. I do not repine that he was offered up by himself and by me for the relief of Thy Holy Land, although with all my heart I love him. Thou knowest, O God, that I would set his presence—most delightful to me—before all the joys and enchantments of this world, had Thy graciousness yielded him to me. But now I lay at Thy disposal him and me, as Thou wilt. Nay, though I could call him back at the cost of the smallest hair of my head, I would not call him back against Thy will.

The Thuringian Crusaders who had gone forth with Louis now became Elizabeth's defenders. They told Henry Raspe that he had angered God by mistreating her and her children and that divine vengeance would overtake the land unless he offered conciliation to so saintly a lady.

When the Crusaders told Elizabeth that they had appealed to her brother-in-law in her behalf, she answered: "Castles, cities, burgs, domains which would involve and harass me, I will have none of. But the revenues of my dowry which are my due, these I beg my brother to give me with good will, to have and to use and to spend freely for the welfare of my beloved and my own." Not only was Elizabeth's dowry restored to her, but the rights of her son to succeed his father were recognized and she returned with her children to Wartburg Castle.

It was not long, however, before her brother-in-law ignored his agreements with the Crusaders and Elizabeth found herself in disfavor once again. It was at this time that Pope Gregory, with all the solicitude of a father, wrote her a letter encouraging her in her choice of the things that do not pass away. He appointed Conrad of Marburg as her protector.

She moved to Marburg Castle, which was hers by marriage settlement. But her relative remained unfriendly, so she soon left and went with her family to live in a humble little cottage. In the spring she frequently went to pray under the open sky in a beautiful spot beside a bubbling stream. Although the church she longed to build there was never erected, she did found a guest-house and a small chapel nearby.

On Good Friday, 1228, Elizabeth took the vows of the Third Order of St. Francis and became the first Franciscan tertiary in Germany. Placing her hands upon a bare altar, she renounced her children, her parents, her kinsfolk and the pomp of the world, for she wished to follow Christ in poverty and love. The formation of the Third Order is regarded as one of the most important events in the spiritual life of the Middle Ages. Elizabeth is honored in the stained-glass windows of the Lower Church of St. Francis in Assisi, where she is portrayed standing between Francis and Clare of Assisi.

After her renunciation of material things—in her heart she had long before abandoned them—she found greater spiritual fulfillment. Again she served the lepers, the aged, the poor. Twice a day she attended those in the hospital suffering from the worst diseases.

Daily she spun wool for a livelihood. Though often ill, she continued to work, and while her hands were busy she talked with God. A nobleman said to her one day: "Never was a king's daughter seen spinning wool before." She was a royal princess who sought to be "glorious within" (Ps. 45:13).

In 1231, as winter was drawing near, Elizabeth died at the age of twenty-four, apparently of exhaustion. To the little chapel where her body was laid came the blind and the dumb, the deaf and the lame, demoniac and leper. Four years later, when Elizabeth was declared a saint, two hundred thousand persons gathered near her grave at Marburg to do her honor.

Around the small chapel there arose the memorial Church of St. Elizabeth, which has been called the greatest Christian monument to a woman in the world. In 1848 Charles Kingsley wrote a moving poetic drama, *The Saint's Tragedy,* based on her life of self-renunciation, alms-giving, and compassion for all who suffer.

CATHERINE OF SIENA—
REVITALIZED THE CHURCH
(1347-1380)

♦ ♦ ♦

She spent three years in silence and solitude preparing for her Christian Service. During the Black Death she walked among the sick and dying, ministering to them. Later she devoted herself to the Church, and was influential in having the Papacy returned from Avignon, France, to Rome. Her Book of Divine Doctrine *expresses the union of the soul with God.*

LOVE WAS CENTRAL IN HER LIFE

No WOMAN in history understood church matters better than the four-teenth-century saint, Catherine of Siena, who was born at a time of nearly unequaled church corruption. No woman was more uncompromising or more relentless in carrying out what she felt was the will of God. She influenced kings and queens and popes alike, and her last six years were a long martyrdom of service to the Church. Her prayers, miracles, heal-ings, writings, and her life—all place her among the great women saints of history.

God was at the center of Catherine's life, which was marked by many achievements. In a storm at sea she relied on Him, telling the sailors "to turn over the rudder in God's name and sail with the wind Heaven sends us." In the Black Death that swept Europe, when her own Siena lost one-third of its population, her presence brought courage and hope as she ministered to the sick and dying. She inspired a weak Pope with new confidence in God. In the Great Schism that divided Christendom for nearly forty years she was a powerful force for peace.

Her message to the world was simple. She taught that there are two realms: One includes egoism, sin, darkness, death, hell; the other is love, self-denial, devotion to duty, light, life, Heaven. The door to the kingdom of God is Jesus. He who abides in self trusts in that which perishes, but he who abides in Jesus rests in the eternal.

Catherine of Siena's life story, says the distinguished Norwegian writer Sigrid Undset in her biography *Catherine of Siena*, "represents one of the most fascinating ever told of a woman's life, the life of a rich and radiant talent developing in an exceptional way under the influence of divine grace."

Catherine Benincasa was born in 1347 in Siena, an important city in Tuscany, Italy, filled with beautiful churches and public buildings and surrounded by wooded valleys, pleasant lanes, olive gardens and sheep meadows. She was the twenty-third child of her parents. Her twin lived but a few days, and Catherine, the youngest child, became the darling of her family and neighbors. Her mother, Lapa Piagenti, was a cherished companion throughout Catherine's life, and often traveled with her in later years, shielding her from the increasing demands upon her time and strength. Catherine inherited her energy from her mother, but her spirit-uality and gentleness were a legacy from her father, Giacomo Benincasa, a dyer by trade. Love and deep faith are reflected in his words to her when she decided to give her life to prayer and penitence: "May God preserve us, dearest daughter, from trying in any way to set up ourselves against the will of God. We have long seen that it was no childish whim of thine, and now we know clearly that it is the spirit of God that con-strains thee. Keep thy vow therefore, and live as the spirit tells thee, we will no longer hinder thee. We ask thee only for one thing, always to intercede for us in prayer."

It was in her father's house, rather than in a convent, that Catherine sought the Lord. Like so many others in Siena, her home was built on the slope of a hill. Her father's dye rooms were on the basement level, and the bedrooms on the next floor adjoined a terrace laid out like a garden. In the large kitchen which also served as a dining room the family gathered around the fire for meals, and after supper the women spun and sewed.

Catherine became a capable homemaker. One Christmas she sent to the Pope at Rome oranges, which she had candied herself and decorated in gold leaf. Oranges were then a great novelty in Italy.

The hill above her home was dominated by the austere red brick church of St. Dominic, the saint who founded the Order to which she later belonged. Above the roof of this church she saw, as a child of seven, the vision that was the beginning of her spiritual life. She beheld Christ enthroned in a sky of radiant colors and sublime shapes looking straight at her and blessing her. During the next twenty years Catherine experienced similar visions while walking toward this church. Both in church and in her father's house, she enjoyed a spiritual communion that was the source of her greatness.

Soon after her first vision Catherine set out alone one day to find a place where she might lead a solitary life. Stories of saints who dwelt alone in the desert with God had captured her imagination. Passing through the city gate, she came upon a little cave. Feeling that God had guided her feet, she went in and knelt down and prayed.

When she was twelve, her parents urged her to marry, but she chose the celibate way of life. She took no vows and was under no rule or direction, but she sought a place in the house where she could draw closer to God. Near his own dye quarters her father gave her a room, fifteen feet long and nine feet wide. In this small dark spot she had a plank for a bed and a log of wood for a pillow. A lamp hanging from the crucifix on the wall gave the only light. Here Catherine drew as close to God as any who had ever gone into the desert to be alone with Him. Her underground cell-like chamber later became a sacred place to men and women who came to listen to her. Secretaries, sometimes three at a time, came here and took down the inspired words spoken while she was in ecstasy. These were later compiled and included in her books.

For three years, from the ages of fourteen to seventeen, Catherine lived in silence and solitude in her father's house. At first she imitated the penitential exercises of the old Anchorites of the desert, fasting rigorously and eating only herbs and bread and water. Later she subsisted on the Sacrament alone. She allowed herself less and less sleep, until at last she slept scarcely two hours out of twenty-four. She sought this solitude so that her soul could be free to raise itself to the presence of God and become the instrument of His Holy Spirit.

Prayer was the staff that sustained her. When she prayed, everything vanished around her and she seemed to float in a world of light. She left her underground room only to go to church, and when she returned she began her prayers again. Her one object was to have her prayers rise continuously to God. Her only recreation during this period was weaving her favorite flowers—roses, lilies and violets—into wreaths and crosses, singing gently as she wove them. God said to her in the quiet of her cell: "In self-knowledge humble thyself, see that in thyself thou dost not even exist; for thy very being, as thou wilt learn, is derived from Me, since I have loved both thee and others before thou wert in existence."

Catherine tried to free herself from material concerns and she succeeded so well in bringing her body into absolute subjection to her will that later, when she went among those with the Black Death and other loathsome diseases, she had no consciousness of her own physical being and no fear for herself. Material things held no attraction for her. She discovered that even though a man owned the whole world it could not satisfy him, for the things in the world are of less value than a man and therefore cannot bring him lasting happiness. In her difficult task of finding and understanding God, she learned that one must presevere long, and endure sustained self-denial and untiring diligence. As she expressed it, she built "an inner cell in her soul." This inner cell became her private sanctuary when she journeyed in later years over the roads and seas of the world, serving wherever her fellow men needed her.

She achieved profound humility, and later revealed to others that "eternal truths are like the stars—they can best be seen from the depth of the well of humility." She knew that only in making self little may one become great; only in silence may one discover the soul. The revelations and visions she received were a vital part of Catherine's faith. She frequently heard a voice which she identified with Christ. When she was seventeen she heard Him say: "Do manfully, my daughter, and without hesitation those things will be put into thy hand, for now being armed with the fortitude of the Faith, thou wilt happily overcome all thine adversaries." In obedience to these words, Catherine gave up her solitary life in the underground cell and took her normal place once more at the family dining table. She also swept the floors, cooked, washed the dishes and laundered the family linens, often working at these tasks all night.

Before long the voice spoke to her once more, saying: "Open for Me the gates of souls that I may enter them. The soul that loves My Truth never leaves herself any rest, but ever seeks to serve others. It is impossible for you to give Me the love that I ask, but I have given you a neighbor that ye may do for him that which ye cannot do for Me. Love him without any worldly thought, without looking for any gain or return. That which ye do for him, then I look upon as done for Me."

In 1363, her sixteenth year, Catherine felt herself called to join the Dominican Tertiaries. After three years of solitary communion with God she began her period of active service to the Church and her fellow men.

She put on her veil of white, representing purity of body and soul, and her cape of black, a symbol of humility and death to the world. She became a familiar figure in the streets of Siena. She was a woman of delicate features, pale face, piercing gray eyes and a contagious smile, and she brought all under the spell of her Tuscan charm.

Calm and gay and patient, she rapidly came to understand practical affairs; and yet there dwelt in her frail body a genius for spiritual things that was to change the course of church history.

When the voice spoke to her, calling her "daughter" and again telling her she should become more closely united to Him in her deeds of charity toward her neighbors, she questioned: "Who am I, a woman, to go into public service?" And the voice replied:

"The word impossible belongeth not to God; am not I He who created the human race, who formed both man and woman? I pour out the favor of My spirit on whom I will. Go forth without fear, in spite of reproach. . . . I have a mission for Thee to fulfill. Wheresoever thou goest I will be with thee. I will never leave thee but will visit thee and direct all thy actions."

Catherine's tasks in Siena multiplied. She served the sick and needy with firm courage and smiling countenance. She entered prisons and attended public executions to comfort the accused with prayer and song. One of her most famous letters was written in protest over the execution of a young nobleman who had uttered some unguarded half-jesting words against the government of Siena. He was condemned to death, and Catherine visited him before and at the time of the execution. She brought her radiance into this scene of injustice and prison ugliness and brutality, ministering to the doomed man and arousing the conscience of the city.

In 1368, when revolution broke out in Siena and bands of armed men paraded the streets, people were afraid to leave their houses, but Catherine passed bravely among the combatants and as she did so they saluted her.

Soon there gathered about her a group of disciples from all classes, nobility and clergy, scholars and artisans, the wicked and the good. As she went about her missions of mercy, the band of followers grew larger. Often a thousand or more men and women came down from the surrounding mountains to see and hear her. Some were attracted by her spirituality; some came from idle curiosity to gaze upon one who healed and who spoke in a new way of spiritual things.

In 1374—when she was twenty-seven—she returned from a visit to Florence to find Siena in the grip of the Black Death, a plague then sweeping Europe. Hundreds of people died daily, and carts made daily rounds to collect the bodies for burial. While the plague raged she was the leader of an untiring little band that nursed the sick. Eighty thousand people died in Siena and Catherine herself lost a sister, a brother, eight nephews and nieces.

During the outbreak she met Raymond of Capua, who was later elected General of the Dominican Order. He became her chief spiritual friend and biographer. Catherine probably learned from him much of the theology on which her teaching is based, but she was also his counselor. When he suffered terrible inner strife she strengthened him by asking: "What has become of your conviction that everything that happens is according to God's Providence, not only in great matters but in the smallest trivialities?"

When the Black Death subsided, Catherine turned to the greatest work of her life, purification and reformation of the Church. Once more she heard a voice say to her: "Sweetest Daughter, thou seest how she [the Church] has soiled her face with impurity and self-love and become swollen with pride and avarice of those who feed at her bosom."

Catherine was no longer afraid to speak out, even against such powerful churchmen as the Papal legates who oppressed the cities of Italy. She criticized the Church's vast expenditures for luxuries which were paid for by the offerings of the poor. She condemned the unnatural vice that prevailed in many monasteries. "Those who should be the temples of God," she wrote, "are the stables of swine. They carry the fires of hatred and vengeance and evil will in their souls. . . . Those who rule must above all be able to rule themselves."

For hours each day Catherine prayed for nothing less than the restoration of the Church to its original purity. She had undertaken a task beyond mortal capacity, and she often suffered great physical distress herself. But she renewed her inner strength by spending as much as six hours at a time in prayer at St. Dominic's Church, long after others had left the services. On more than one occasion, her opponents came while she was in prayer and threw her from the church onto the walk outside. Evil tongues spoke against her with attacks on her character, but she prayed and worked on unafraid.

First she suggested a crusade to serve a spiritual and political need. She asked that the marauding bands of mercenaries who were ravishing Europe be enrolled under the Cross. In 1374, Pope Gregory XI proclaimed such a crusade from Papal headquarters in Avignon, France, and Catherine flung herself into the cause.

She often kept three secretaries busy, dictating rapidly to each of them in turn. She wrote to nobles and private citizens, kings and queens and the Pope himself. To Queen Joan of Naples she wrote: "Rise up manfully, sweet sister. It is no longer the time for sleep, for time sleeps not, but ever passes like the wind. For love's sake, lift up the standard of the most holy cross in your heart." Charles V of France she addressed in these terms: "No more of such folly and blindness. I tell you, on behalf of Christ crucified, that you delay no longer to make this peace."

Seeking to strengthen the Church, Catherine turned to the practical task of moving the Papacy from Avignon, where it had been for almost three-quarters of a century, back to Rome.

She wrote stirring messages to Pope Gregory XI, who was small in stature and weak in resolve, but noble in intention. She reminded him that if a serious wound is treated only with ointment, when it needs to be cauterized or cut out with steel, it fails to heal and infects everything, and death may follow. "Why does that shepherd of the Church go on using so much ointment?" she asked. "Since God has given you authority and you have assumed it you should use your virtue and powers; and if you are not willing to use them, it would be better for you to resign what you have assumed; more honor to God and health to your soul it would be," she declared. Surprisingly, the Pope listened with an attentive ear to her requests, although he took no immediate action. Meanwhile, Catherine became involved in a dispute between the Pope and the Papal states of Italy. When the Pope sent hated French officials to Florence and excommunicated the entire city, religious life there became paralyzed, trade was ruined, and the city began to die. The Florentines felt that they had no alternative but to declare war against the Pope, and other Papal states joined them. Catherine urged forbearance on Pope Gregory and the rebels to submit in order to avoid war.

The Florentines recognized her greatness and inspiration, and as leaders of a league of eighty cities, they summoned her to their city. After many conferences with them, she was induced by leaders of the moderate party to go to France and present their case to the Pope. They promised to send an embassy to ratify peace on the terms she arranged.

After long prayer she was bidden, in a vision, to take an olive branch in her hand, and bearing the cross upon her shoulders, go forth and bring peace between the Pope and his rebellious children.

Catherine set out from Siena on June 18, 1376, for France, traveling on a donkey or on foot over rutted country roads. With her went a little band of disciples, including Brother Raymond of Capua, Stephen Maconi, a son of a Siena senator, and three beloved women friends.

Gregory XI was the sixth pope to reside in France. His palace, built on the summit of the Rock of Domes in Avignon, commanded a view of the Rhone River and the surrounding country. Froissart, the French chronicler of the period, called it the "finest and strongest building in the world, a great fortress of stone." Within were all the luxuries of the age, and the Pope lived here like a feudal lord, surrounded by his princely cardinals. Catherine's contemporary, Petrarch, had said of the Avignon palace: "I know by experience that there is no piety there, no charity, no faith, no reverence for God, or any fears of Him, nothing holy, nothing just, nothing worthy of man. Love, purity, decency, candor are banished from it."

Though she was without education, wealth or rank, Catherine confidently entered the great palace at Avignon, dressed in her white serge habit and patched black mantle. In her first audience with the Pope, he could not understand her Tuscan language, and she could not interpret his Latin, but her spiritual adviser Raymond served as interpreter. On behalf of the Florentines she exhorted the Pope to fight for the Church's spiritual riches, not its temporal possessions. She reminded him of the Church's great mission of salvation.

Catherine's work might have been crowned with immediate success had the Florentines sent the embassy they had promised. Weeks and months passed while she remained in Avignon but still the delegation did not arrive. "The Florentines are mocking both you and me," the Pope said to Catherine. "Either they will not send any envoys at all, or when they do come, they will not have the powers to act." He was right. When the envoys finally arrived, they refused to consult Catherine or to acknowledge her as their emissary.

During her four months in Avignon, Catherine turned again to the task of fighting the selfishness and self-interest which kept the center of the Church at Avignon. She aroused the Pope's sense of duty to move the Papacy back to Rome, sustaining his wavering resolution and soothing his fears.

The Pope's cardinals had frightened him, saying that he would be poisoned if he returned to Rome, or that he might die there of malaria. But Catherine cleverly reminded him that if it was poison he was afraid of, there was probably as much poison at Avignon as in Rome. "Do not be a boy, be a man. I beseech your Holiness in the name of Christ Crucified to make haste," she urged him. "Adopt a holy deception; let it seem that you are going to delay for a time, and then do it swiftly and suddenly, for the more quickly it is done, the sooner will you be freed from these torments and troubles."

So great was the opposition to the move back to Rome that the Pope no longer dared talk with Catherine but communicated with her by letters and messengers. After weeks of delay, the Pope left his palace at Avignon and sailed from Marseilles to Genoa, where Catherine and her disciples had paused on their journey home to Siena.

The Pope wanted to talk with Catherine in Genoa, but he did not dare to send for her openly. Like Saul of old when he sought out the woman of Endor under cover of darkness, the Pope disguised himself before making his way to Catherine. There is no record of what words passed between them, but the Pope regained his courage and proceeded to Rome. Catherine had accomplished the first of her great missions: Rome was again the center of the Church. She now turned to the task of gaining support for the Roman Pope.

The Pope then summoned Catherine to go as his emissary to Florence, which for seventeen months had suffered under the rule of his French officials. When she arrived there she spoke before three bodies of magistrates. A mob, incensed against the Pope, set out to murder her. While she waited with her disciples in a little house on a hillside outside Florence, the crowd came and found her in the garden. There she kneeled before them, bared her throat and spoke fearlessly: "I am Catherine. Do to me whatever thou wilt. But I charge you, in the name of the Almighty, to hurt none of these who are with me." The mob left in confusion. Later Catherine persuaded the rulers of the city to listen to her counsel, and peace between the rebellious people and the Pope was finally signed. Pope Gregory died soon thereafter.

Confident of Catherine's great power, the new Italian Pope, Urban VI, summoned her to Rome. Though she was ill, her will and courage never wavered. She went there with forty of her disciples. Citizens in authority visited her. Chiefs of the army sought her advice. The sick and wounded looked to her for help.

While in Rome she continued her fiery correspondence until she had helped to win Germany, Hungary and Sweden to the claims of the new Pope. After she spoke before Urban and his cardinals, he turned to exclaim: "Behold my brethren, how contemptible we are before God, when we give way to fear. This poor woman puts us to shame, whom I call so, not out of contempt, but by reason of the weakness of her sex, which should make her timid, even if we were confident. It is she who now encourages us."

Catherine turned to the humble Christian hermits who lived in scattered cells around Rome, for she saw that she was not achieving her purpose with the scheming churchmen, who lacked spirituality. Among the hermits she hoped to find the help needed to achieve righteous church government. Calling them forth after their years of solitude and prayer, she besought them to support her program. Only a few came to her aid. Catherine addressed the others scornfully: "Now really, the spiritual life is quite too lightly held if it is lost by change of place. Apparently God is an accepter of place, and is found only in a wood, and not elsewhere in time of need."

In the space of four days, shortly before her death, while in ecstasy, she dictated her "Dialogue," parts of which ring like the words of the ancient prophets. This is the best known of her works and is entitled *The Book of Divine Doctrine*. It has a significant place in Italian literature, ranking with Dante's *Divine Comedy* as an outstanding attempt to express the union of the soul with God.

Catherine's prayers, twenty-six in all, comprise a second volume. Her nearly four hundred letters addressed to kings, popes, cardinals, bishops, conventual bodies, political corporations and individuals comprise a third volume. The style, historical importance and spiritual quality of these letters are of a very high order.

Like Jesus, she chose pain, affliction and persecution. She was only thirty-three when she died, slightly older than Christ Himself when crucified, and yet in those few years she accomplished the impossible, because she was daily in contact with the Divine Power.

Catherine possessed deep mystical knowledge. One of her favorite statements was that "a soul cannot live without loving." It must have something to love for it was created in love," she explained. The essence of Jesus' being was a fullness of love. Love, she emphasized, carried the soul as the feet carry the body.

One of her basic contributions to mystical knowledge was her understanding of self-love, which she declared to be the source of every evil. It has poisoned the entire world, and brought disease into the mystical body of the Church. The fire of God's love, Catherine knew, "must burn up self-love and self-will and let the soul appear, beautiful and full of grace, as it was meant to be when God created us."

Salvation, she says, "consists in passing from this dark, restless and tormented Existence in which the worldly man lives, to life in truth, to that in which it is really worth living. This change of spirit becomes possible through experience, the bitter experience that everything is transient. Everything rushes on, everything flies away."

One of her most famous prayers expresses her desire for eternal communion with His Spirit:

> Oh, Holy Spirit, come into my heart.
> Draw it by Thy power to Thee, true God,
> Grant me love with fear of Thee.
> Guard me from all evil thought.
> Warm me and inflame me with Thy love.
> Holy my Father and sweet my Lord,
> Help me now in all my labors,
> Christ who art Love, Christ who art Love.

No Christian woman has surpassed Catherine of Siena in sacrifice and devotion. No one has borne more flaming witness to the Unseen, to its inexhaustible fountains of Love. No one has fought against vice, disease and death with greater courage. No woman has attacked church corruption with such vigor. Catherine of Siena's life reveals an extraordinary blend of mystical faith and practical Christian service.

JOAN OF ARC—
THE DEBORAH OF FRANCE
(1412-1431)

• • •

Guided by her "voices," she led France to victory during the latter part of the Hundred Years' War. She was burned at the stake on charges of witchcraft and heresy but was declared innocent nineteen years later.

SHE GAVE HEROISM TO THE SOUL OF CHRISTIANITY

BECAUSE SHE WAS sensitive to divine voices unheard by others, the marvelous entered Joan of Arc's destiny. She seems to have been born for two purposes, one to save her beloved France, which she envisioned as a holy kingdom, and the other to have the Dauphin of France (later Charles VII) crowned king. She takes her place among the noble figures in history, not only because she accomplished these purposes, but because she displayed courage and faith and later great fearlessness when condemned to be burned at the stake.

Early in her life she heard voices coming from the angel Michael and the martyred saints Margaret and Catherine. She looked upon these voices as God's special agents or messengers. As she conversed with them, she was filled with an inner radiance. Her voices continued for almost four years, until, at the age of sixteen, she began her great mission for France. She heard them at many times and places—while she watched her father's flocks, while she was in the old oak woods, beside the fountain, before the shrine, in the chapel, or in her own little chamber.

It was God's voice that came to her most often and most vividly during her period of preparation. She lovingly referred to Him as Messire, and He was as real to her as if she stood beside Him. The simplicity and directness of her relationship to Him are conveyed in her own words:

Whenever I am sad because what I say be command of Messire is not readily believed, I go apart and to Messire I make known my complaint, saying that those to whom I speak are not willing to believe me. And when I have finished my prayer, straightway I hear a voice saying unto me, "Daughter of God, go, I will be thy helper." And this voice fills me with so great a joy, that in this condition I will forever stay.

Joan was born in 1412 at Domrémy on the Meuse River near the forest of the Vosges in northeast France. Her village, which then had less than fifty houses, lay in an area of broad valleys and low hills crowned with oaks, maples and birches. Joan, sometimes called The Maid of Orléans, was the youngest of four children. One of her brothers was a parish priest, another a tiler.

Her father, Jacques d'Arc, was a good Christian and an industrious farmer who occupied a position in the village comparable to that of mayor. Her mother, Isabelle Romée, the sister of a priest and beloved for her consecrated way of life, taught Joan to pray, as well as to spin and weave and cook. In her biography *Saint Joan of Arc*, V. Sackville-West says of Isabelle: "One cannot help feeling that she was a mother worthy to engender the daughter she did engender, and that perhaps justice has never been wholly done to her."

For several generations Europe had been oppressed by war. When Joan was born the Hundred Years' War was in its seventy-fifth year, and the troubles of her own Domrémy made her familiar with the sufferings caused by armed conflict.

The English and their allies, the Burgundians, were masters of France north of the Loire. It seemed to the French just a matter of time before they would occupy the entire land.

The heir to the French throne, the Dauphin Charles, had been disinherited and proscribed by the English king, Henry VI, and even by the queen mother, Isabella of France, who favored Henry VI in opposition to the Dauphin.

When she was about sixteen, Joan's voices told her that succor would come to the Dauphin of France before mid-Lent. She felt herself called to serve as Heaven's answer to her country's cries of distress. In company with an older relative who understood the meaning of her voices, she made her way in May 1428 from Domrémy to Vaucouleurs, a distance of about fifteen miles, to appear before Robert de Baudricourt, the military governor. He attached no importance to the first visit of this maid who told him that she was sent by the Lord. She asked him to write to the Dauphin and say that, by the will of God, she was to lead him to his crowning. Refusing what seemed to him a ridiculous request, the governor sent her back to her parents in Domrémy. Like other mystics, she was obedient to spiritual guidance, and now waited for further direction from her voices.

Toward the end of October, word reached Domrémy that the English were about to take Orléans. If they succeeded, it seemed certain that southern France would surrender. Sensing it was time for her to make a second appeal to Baudricourt, Joan went before him with the plea: "My Lord captain, God has commanded me many times to go to the gentle Dauphin who must be and who is the true King of France, and he shall grant me men-at-arms with whom I shall raise the siege of Orléans and take him to his anointing at Reims."

Baudricourt, realizing that an army was being raised for the conquest of the Dauphin's territory south of the Loire, decided that she might really be inspired, and he opposed her no longer. Granting her a letter of introduction, he told her to go to Chinon where the Dauphin lived.

Joan changed her red dress for the uniform of a soldier and had her long, dark hair cut in page-boy fashion. Criticized for wearing men's clothing, she replied that "the matter of clothes is scarcely worth bothering about. That is the least important thing. This, and everything I have done, was at the behest of God and His angels." Her attire enabled her to ride a horse more easily and to mingle with soliders. Walking among the roughest of them, the miracle was that she retained her purity. She told hard-drinking, foul-mouthed men whom she led that God would give victory only to a moral army. Sensing her innocence and her indefinable strength, many followers sought to mend their ways.

She passed through the English lines unrecognized as she made her way to Chinon. Historians describe the Dauphin as incompetent, bored, clumsy, ugly. When he heard of her arrival, he refused to see her. "Who is this girl with this fantastic claim who seeks an audience with me?" he inquired. Finally Joan was admitted to the palace and led into the throne room lighted by fifty torches. Three hundred people were gathered there, but with meekness and simplicity she walked past them all and up to the Dauphin.

"Most noble Dauphin," she said, "my voices have told me to come to help you and your kingdom."

"Why don't the voices come to me?" retorted the Dauphin.

"They do come to you," she replied, "but you do not hear them. You have not stayed in the field in the evening listening for them. If you prayed with your heart and listened, you too would hear the voices as well as I do." The Dauphin took her aside and talked to her privately. "I am God's messenger," she informed him, "sent to tell you that you are the king's son and the true heir to France. And France is to be a Holy Kingdom."

The sluggish, unimaginative Dauphin was unimpressed with this young peasant girl who called herself a messenger of God. He could not understand what she meant when she said France was to be a holy kingdom. How could he, its Dauphin, have a holy mission to fulfill?

In order to see if she were a true daughter of the Church, he had her examined by a group of clergymen. When one of them asked her if she believed in God, she surprised him with the ready answer: "Yes, more than you do." When they scoffed at her inner illumination, she told them that "in the books of our Lord is written much more than in all your books." To some of the examiners, this was heresy.

Growing impatient after three weeks of questioning, Joan requested that they lead her to the army. It was finally decided that she should be allowed to lead an expedition to Orléans. She said as she departed: "I thank our Lord that He has freed me from the tortures of the narrow-minded clerics."

From a church Joan acquired a sword on which were five crosses. Like other company commanders, she carried a banner sprinkled with holy water. Charles had her clothed in glistening armor. She mounted a horse and led the French troops into battle against the English who were fighting to capture the French throne.

At the head of her company marched a body of priests, chanting psalms and hymns. In her address to the rough warriors before the Battle of Orléans, she asked them to renounce their sins and to join her in receiving the sacrament. Suddenly, as if a miraculous change had come over them, the soldiers shook off their lethargy and were swept by a mood of confidence and courage.

When they arrived near Orléans, the wind changed as she had predicted and the French troops could make their way across the Loire River in their small boats. The crossing was on April 28, 1429.

During the battle that followed, she heard a voice say: "In God's name go down against them, for they shall fall and shall not stay and shall be utterly discomfited; and you shall lose scarce any men. Arise and pursue them."

On May 8, 1429, the French captured Orléans, the English stronghold. The townspeople surged forth to see Joan in her shining armor, for they believed that God, who struck down Goliath with a stone from a shepherd's sling, had raised up the daughter of a peasant farmer for their deliverance.

After taking Orléans, Joan led the French army to victory over the English in four other battles and she prevailed upon the Dauphin to march on to Reims. Her victories enabled him to enter this city where the kings of France were traditionally crowned and consecrated with oil. Joan realized perhaps better than anyone else that the anointing was the sign of power and victory, for the Book of Samuel says: "Then Samuel took a vial of oil, and poured it upon [Saul's] head, and kissed him, and said, Is it not because the Lord hath anointed thee to be captain over his inheritance?" (I Sam. 10:1). "The Gentle Dauphin," as she called him, crowned and anointed, was now King Charles VII of France.

A few days after the Dauphin was crowned, Joan marched again at the head of the army and made an assault on Paris. This failed and she was wounded in the thigh by an arrow. The Burgundians captured her on May 24, 1430, and sold her to the English for a sum slightly more than three thousand dollars, but the English, even while they held her in prison, were uneasy because the French people loved her so much.

She was tried as a witch and a heretic before a tribunal of forty theologians and jurists at Rouen, as Jesus had been tried before the chief priests, elders and scribes. Among her judges were ten members of the University of Paris, which was strongly Burgundian and intolerant, twenty-two canons of Rouen, and a group of monks and friars.

Joan's steadfast courage during her trial equaled her bravery on the battlefield. Her voices advised her "to accept everything willingly" and not to fear martyrdom nor despair. She spoke boldly in her own defense to the court. "I come from the side of God and have nothing to do here. Leave me to God, from whom I come." To the president of the Tribunal, she defiantly declared: "Sir, you wish to be my judge. Take heed what you do, for I am truly sent from God; and that places you yourself in the very greatest danger."

Her inquisitors, sensing her spiritual quality and her stamina, asked her if she would submit to the decision of the Church. Her answer was: "I hold that our Lord and the Church are indivisible; therefore it is wrong for you to make difficulties for me in this connection. Why do you make these difficulties when everything is as one?" Then they asked her if she knew the difference between the Church Militant and the Church Triumphant. She did not understand, for she had not studied theology. Unperturbed, however, she told them: "I came to the King of France in the name of God, and of the Victorious Church above us; and at their bidding, to that Church, do I submit all my good deeds, and everything else which I have done, or shall do in the future. When you ask me if I submit to the Church Militant, there is nothing for me to say. . . . With regard to myself, I submit through my acts solely to the Church in Heaven: and that means God."

Joan loved the Church and longed to serve it, but she declared: "If the Church demands something of me which goes against God's bidding, I shall not do it under any circumstances. . . . My voices did not command me not to obey the Church, but first to obey God."

So great was the prejudice of the judges against her that what she answered in her defense was hardly considered. Toward the end of the trial she was led into the torture chamber and shown all the horrible instruments there. Resolute even in the midst of these threats, she told her accusers: "Even if you tear my limbs from each other, and part my soul from my body, I shall not say anything different; and even though I did say something different, I would make it clear that you had forced me to do so by violent means. . . . I have asked my voices whether I should submit to the Church, and to the clergy who have constrained me so violently. The voices told me that God would help me when I wished; and that therefore I must entrust all my deeds to Him."

She was tricked into signing a revocation. A brief, unimportant paper was read to her, which she could sign without treason to her voices or her soul. She signed what she supposed was this paper, but another document had been craftily substituted for it, and what she actually signed was a long, humiliating, traitorous recantation. A few days later she declared to her accusers that as for the scrap of paper which contained her recantation, she had not understood it at all. This declaration was further evidence in the mind of the court that she was guilty of heresy and witchcraft. The final judgment against her was based on twelve points. Among others it cited the worthlessness of her vision, denied her gift of prophecy and censured her masculine dress.

On May 30, 1431, the morning after the verdict was pronounced, she was told by two priests that she was to die at the stake in two hours. She wore a black garment, and, instead of the crown of thorns, they placed on her head a pointed paper hat bearing the inscription, "Apostle, Backslider, Heretic, Idolator."

Looking down upon the town of Rouen, where the trial had been held, she cried out: "Rouen, Rouen, O Thou, my last dwelling place!" Her last request was for a cross from the neighboring church, and she kissed it as she was chained to the stake, her fiery Calvary.

In a few minutes, as the smoke and flames enveloped her, she cried: "Jesus." Her ashes were thrown into the Seine from the bridge of Rouen. The English returned to their camp muttering: "We are Lost! We have burned a saint!"

A trial ordered by King Charles VII in 1450 reversed the verdict of the earlier court, though it was not until 1456 that her sentence was finally annulled. She was canonized in 1920 and made patroness of France in 1922.

Joan of Arc has been represented in many paintings and statues, and her life has inspired many poets and writers. She appears notably in Shakespeare's *Henry VI*, Voltaire's *La Pucelle d'Orléans* (1738), Schiller's *Maid of Orléans* (1801), Mark Twain's *Personal Recollections of Joan of Arc* (1896), Maxwell Anderson's *Joan of Lorraine,* and George Bernard Shaw's *Saint Joan.* A statue in the market place of Rouen marks the place where she was burned at the stake. Another beautiful statue of her is in the Place des Pyramides in Paris. In the Metropolitan Museum of Art in New York there is a painting of her by Bastien Le Page, and a great canvas of her by Boutet De Monvel hangs in the Art Institute in Chicago. On Riverside Drive in New York City there is a statue of her riding her horse.

Many biographies have been written about her. Among the authors are V. Sackville-West, Anatole France and Lucien Fabre. To some writers she is a militant Amazon, to others a pathological case. But to most she was a saint who showed that God was in the midst of the historical events of the fifteenth century, as He had been in Israel's history. God chose her to liberate France and to crown the Dauphin.

The quality of her courage and the strength of her belief in God is beautifully expressed in Shaw's play, in which she says:

My loneliness shall be my strength, too; it is better to be alone with God; His friendship will not fail me nor His counsel, nor His love. In His strength I will dare and dare and dare, until I die.

ISABELLA OF CASTILE—
FIRST TO AID THE CHURCH IN THE NEW WORLD
(1451-1504)

❖ ❖ ❖

Religious reasons prompted her to finance Columbus' first voyage to America. On his second voyage, she sent clergymen and equipment for the first church in the New World. Her ten-year Crusade against Moslem Moors had a Christian objective.

HER FAITH CHANGED THE COURSE OF
CHRISTIAN CIVILIZATION

FROM HER BIRTH in Madrigal in 1451, destiny seemed to have set Isabella apart for high purposes. Her mother, Doña Isabel, was a deeply religious woman who, after her husband's death, devoted herself to her children, and was especially zealous in implanting strong religious principles in her serious-minded daughter.

Though her spiritual beauty would have made an unattractive woman attractive, Isabella was also blessed with physical charm. She had hair the color of molten copper, clear, fresh skin, light blue eyes. She was of medium height, well proportioned, and had an intelligent, lofty expression. In dress she followed the prevailing fashions. Her queenly robe, with its full skirt, tight bodice and girdle tied in a looped knot at the front, fell over her ankles, revealing the tips of square-toed shoes. In royal outdoor ceremonies she appeared in a robe of woven cloth of gold, and a riding hood of black velvet.

Prayer sustained Isabella throughout her career. As a young girl, she spent a long time each day beseeching God to keep her and her young brother Alfonso safe. At fifteen, when her degenerate half-brother Enrique, at that time King of Castile, was plotting to marry her off to a forty-three-year-old scoundrel, she also turned to prayer. The marriage was circumvented by the death of the bridegroom on his journey to claim his bride, so Isabella felt that her fervent prayers had been answered.

When her beloved brother Alfonso, heir to the throne, died suddenly in his teens, Isabella, although heartbroken, harbored no bitterness. Immediately after the funeral, she hastened to a Cistercian convent at Avila where she spent several days alone in meditation and prayer.

In the political crisis following the death of Alfonso, Isabella became the hope of Castile, which was at that time the largest of the Spanish kingdoms. The revolutionary party urged her to usurp the throne from Enrique, who had treated her so badly, but she let it be known that she would never seek power as a means of retaliation.

When suitors asked for her hand, she sent her chaplain to observe them at close range. Ferdinand, heir to the throne of Aragon, became the most likely prospect. When the time for their betrothal approached, she prayed for the good both of Ferdinand's kingdom of Aragon and of her Castile. She declared: "Before all things I shall beg God in all my affairs, and especially this one which touches me so nearly, that He will show me His will, and raise me up for whatever may be for His service and for the welfare of these kingdoms." During this time of decision, when the jealous and unprincipled Enrique added to her burdens, Isabella again and again knelt in prayer.

When Isabella wed Ferdinand in 1469, she was the acknowledged heir to the domain of Castile, although she did not assume the throne until five years later when Enrique died. The marriage between Isabella and Ferdinand united the kingdoms of Aragon and Castile, creating a strong Spain which for the next century was a leading power in Europe.

After being crowned queen in 1474, Isabella, then only twenty-three years old, left the ceremony and walked immediately to the cathedral. Humbly calling herself a handmaiden of the Lord and prostrating herself before the high altar, she gave thanks to God for bringing her safely through so many perils to such a high honor. She asked for grace to rule according to God's will and to use the authority He had given her with justice and wisdom.

Intricate problems awaited her as queen, but she had supreme confidence that God would guide her. Her godliness soon brought the clergy and common people to her side, and their loyalty became her main support during her reign of three decades.

When Juana, unacknowledged daughter of Isabella's half-brother Enrique, tried to usurp her throne, Isabella went to her chapel and prayed: "My Lord Jesus Christ, in your hands I place all my affairs and I implore your protection and aid." A queen of action as well as of prayer, she put on a breastplate of steel and mounted her horse to ride to the Archbishop of Toledo to enlist his support, which was essential to her success.

When King Alfonso V of Portugal threatened war in defense of his niece Juana's claim to the throne, Isabella rode valiantly among the towns of her kingdom, soliciting their help. Often she ended her appeal with this prayer:

Thou O Lord, who knowest the secret of the heart, of me Thou knowest that not by any unjust way, not by cunning or by tyranny, but believing truly that these realms of the King my father belong to me rightfully, have I endeavored to obtain them, that what the kings my forebears won with so much bloodshed may not fall into the hands of an alien race. Lord, in whose hands lies the sway of kingdoms, I humbly beseech Thee to hear the prayer of Thy servant, and show forth the truth, and manifest Thy will with Thy marvelous works: so that if my cause is not just, Thou give me wisdom and courage to sustain it with the aid of Thine arm, that through Thy grace we may have peace in these kingdoms, which till now have endured so many evils and destructions.

Sometimes called a mystic, Isabella was also a stern realist. She never permitted her life of contemplation to draw her away from her practical duties. In every crisis, she appealed to God, and then proceeded to act with energy. To her the Church was like a blockaded city, hated by her enemy, the Moslem Moors, but unconquerable. She was willing to make any sacrifice for it, and to engage in a ten-year Crusade against the Moors.

She insisted upon clean living and clean speech among her soldiers. Frequently she appeared on the field of battle, and in a soul-stirring speech, stressed the religious character of the war against the Moslems. Breathing new courage into the hearts of her soldiers, she reminded them that they were soldiers of the Cross.

Despite her piety, Isabella did not simply leave everything to God. "In all human affairs," she said, "there are things both certain and doubtful, and both are equally in the hands of God, who is accustomed to guide to a good end the causes that are just and are sought with diligence."

Like the Biblical Deborah, Isabella sometimes took command of several thousand men herself. History's most vivid picture of her is not in queenly robe but as a warrior riding a high-spirited white horse on the battlefield. Never sparing herself, she rode over icy mountain passes, through deserts in the burning heat, through dust six inches deep. Sometimes she did this when she was with child. Wherever she went, victory almost invariably followed.

Ever mindful of the suffering of her soldiers, she was the first ruler to introduce movable camp hospitals. When she visited the wounded in camp, she often dressed the wounds herself. She also promoted church services for the soldiers and sent many priests and friars to the camp to perform church ceremonials.

Material possessions were never as important to Isabella as Christian ideals. After she started her Crusade against the Moors, she needed funds to carry it through. Asking the Church for half of its silver treasure to melt into money, the clergy voted to make the loan for three years. She suffered acutely at the thought of melting religious treasures, some a thousand years old, but she knew that peace among her people was more essential than candlesticks in a church.

With money thus provided by the Church, she began her Christian Crusade in earnest. Troops were paid. New recruits enlisted. The tramp of soldiers, the neighing of horses, and the creaking of artillery were heard, as Spanish armies began to march, and the Moors were forced to retreat.

When other funds to finance the war became necessary, Isabella pawned her gold and silver, her priceless heirlooms, her pearl necklace, her balas rubies, even her jeweled crown.

She was stimulated by the impossible. Once she virtually moved a mountain that was in the way of her army. She put six thousand men to work digging and blasting a new road on the mountainside. They broke rocks, cut down trees, filled in valleys and leveled a large area. Nine days later Isabella's heavy military engines, drawn by great oxen, drove slowly through a gap in the mountain and made a surprise attack on the Moors.

The fall of Granada in 1492 marked the end of the war with the Moors. This occurred in January. Church bells rang from the Mediterranean to the North Sea to celebrate Isabella's final victory. She quickly had the Moslem mosques prepared for use as Christian churches and cathedrals, sending them bells, missals and communion vessels. "Let us rejoice," she declared, "for the exaltation of our faith as well as for the augmentation of our temporal prosperity, in which not only Spain but all Christendom shall participate."

Bearing a giant crucifix, a cardinal rode from the camp to take possession of Granada, the beautiful capital which for seven hundred years had been embellished and enriched by Moorish rulers. As Queen Isabella and King Ferdinand entered the city, a vast gathering of clergy raised a triumphant hymn and the whole army knelt to give thanks to the Almighty.

Queen Isabella, in her religious fervor and ambition to extend Christianity, made some grievous mistakes. In her support of the merciless Inquisition, directed chiefly against the Jews because they did not believe in Christ, and against the Moors who believed only in Mohammed, she felt she could rid the country of heretics and that Christianity would gain a stronger foothold. In this decision she relied too heavily on some of her religious advisers.

Most historians are lenient with Isabella for her role in the Inquisition. William H. Prescott, in his *Ferdinand and Isabella*, written in 1837, makes this point:

It will be difficult to condemn her, indeed, without condemning the age; for these very acts are not only excused, but extolled by her contemporaries, as constituting her strongest claims to renown, and to the gratitude of her country. They proceed from the principle, openly avowed by the court of Rome, that zeal for the purity of the faith could atone for every crime. . . . It was not to be expected that a solitary woman, filled with natural diffidence of her own capacity on such subjects, should array herself against those venerated counsellors, whom she had been taught from her cradle to look to as the guides and guardians of her conscience.

The English historian Martin Hume accounts for Isabella's support of the Inquisition in this manner: "Her saintly devotion to her Faith blinded her eyes to human things, and her anxiety to please the God of Mercy made her merciless to those she thought His enemies."

Spain now entered the most memorable epoch in its history. Why was Isabella so successful as a ruler? She appointed able and trustworthy men to the principal offices. Confident of her backing, they ousted imposters and executed justice. She abolished the bribing of officials and set up courts of justice, hearing doubtful cases and appeals herself. She organized her government into five departments, a Council of Justice, a Council of State, a Supreme Court of the Holy Brotherhood, a Council of Finance and a council for matters dealing purely with Ferdinand's kingdom of Aragon. She also saw that the bishops appointed were men of good character.

Columbus, introduced to the court by her former confessor, Father Juan Perez, appeared for the first time in 1484 and asked for money to finance his voyage to the New World. At that time Isabella's army was still fighting the Moors and she was with child, her fifth, but she said: "Send Columbus to Cordova and we shall hear what he has to say when we return."

Later, when he explained that his plan would be an advantage to all Christendom, she listened more attentively. When he said he wanted to bring "a vast mystery into the limits of actual knowledge," she was enthralled. She understood the heroic imagination of one who dreamed of accomplishing the impossible, for she herself liked to tackle difficult tasks. She was impressed with his Biblical answers to the objections of churchmen who believed that the earth was flat.

The war with the Moors now having ended, Isabella and Ferdinand, by April 1492, made an agreement with Columbus that he was to begin his enterprise. Before dawn on August 3, after he and his men had partaken of the Sacrament, Columbus gave the command to set sail, and the voyage began "in the name of Jesus." On October 12, a day big with destiny for civilization, he sighted land off San Salvador.

When Queen Isabella sponsored Columbus' voyage to the New World, her ultimate aim was to extend Christianity. She thought of Columbus primarily as a missionary explorer whose discoveries would make it possible for Christianity to enter new areas. Columbus' given name, Christopher, meaning "Christ-Bearer," was a fitting one.

On Columbus' first voyage he was amazed at the response of the natives at Puerto Gibara in Cuba as he and his men sang *Ave Maria* and *Salve Regina* at sundown. Columbus wrote in his journal for Isabella and Ferdinand:

> I maintain, Most Serene Princess, that if they had access to devout religious persons knowing the language, they would all turn Christian, and so I hope in our Lord that Your Highnesses will do something about it with much care, in order to turn to the Church so numerous a people and to convert them.

When Isabella delegated Columbus to make a second voyage in 1493, it was not only to make further discoveries and to colonize but to spread the Gospel. This time she sent along a number of the clergy, to whom was entrusted the conversion of pagans in the new lands. The clergymen carried as a special gift from Queen Isabella complete equipment, such as bells and communion plate, for the first Christian church in the New World, built in the now ruined town of Isabella, on the north coast of the present Dominican Republic.

On his second voyage Isabella stocked his ships with seeds of wheat, barley, oranges, lemons, melons and other fruits, as well as with cows, bulls, goats, horses, pigs, hens and rabbits. The New World, rich in soil but poor in products, profited from her practical knowledge of agriculture as well as from her Christianity.

Isabella was among the greatest of the Christian queens. So humane was her attitude that she would not allow the Indians, brought back to Spain by Columbus' men, to be kept in slavery. Ordering that they be returned to their own lands, she made it plain there must be no more slaves. Declaring the Indians a free people, she asked that the Indians in the new country be treated with kindness and gentleness, that their wrongs be rectified, and that the sacred work of converting them to Christianity be carried on.

The great explorer, Isabella's junior by only a few months, shared her religious turn of mind, and like her, believed that God is with those who put their trust in Him. "This conviction that God destined him to be an instrument for spreading the faith was far more potent than the desire to win glory, wealth and worldly honors, to which he was certainly far more indifferent," declares Samuel Eliot Morison in his life of Columbus, *Admiral of the Ocean Sea.*

Not only did Isabella aid in the discovery of America and achieve final victory over the Moors in Spain, but she accomplished many other things for her country. She encouraged learning and established printing presses. Spain published the first polyglot Bible, known as the *Complutensian Polyglot,* containing the Old Testament in Hebrew, Greek (the Septuagint) and Latin (the Vulgate) together with Aramaic translations of the first five books of the Old Testament, and the Greek New Testament.

Isabella erected hospitals and churches, endowed monasteries and was a generous patron of all the arts and sciences. The study and practice of medicine flourished in her reign. When she became queen there was only one university in Spain, at Salamanca. Before her death there were several, endowed by her or by men whom she raised to power.

Humble at heart, she never considered any task too lowly if it could serve a good purpose. When she heard that discipline was lax in a convent, she set an example by taking her own spinning wheel there and spending a day at work. She gave beautiful pieces of her own embroidery to Spanish churches and the Church of the Holy Sepulchre in the Holy Land.

Toward her family Isabella showed a thoughtful Christian spirit. She tenderly watched over her mother in her declining years. Her love for her husband Ferdinand was the strongest of all her personal affections. She acted with him as if they were one and was as solicitous of his royal position as of her own, although they differed on some matters.

Their marriage agreement gave her the right to be undisputed sovereign of Castile, and her husband could make no appointments there, either civil or military, without her consent. She was deeply wounded when early in their marriage she learned that he regarded her title to Castile as a mere formality and had tried to usurp her power, although she accepted the knowledge in good grace and loved him through this and other difficulties.

Ferdinand and Isabella had a son and four daughters, and she was as far-sighted for them as for her nation. When her first child, Isabel, was conceived, she thanked God. Two years later when her son Juan was born, she took him to the cathedral to be baptized. A month later, like Hannah and Mary of old, she presented him at the temple. She spared no pains in molding his character that he might one day embody her ideal of kingship. At seventeen, he was killed by a fall from his horse while hunting and his death was a national calamity. Though overcome by the tragedy, she could still say: "God gave him and God has taken him away. Blessed be his Holy Name."

Tragedy stalked the lives of three of her daughters. Isabel, her eldest, was married first to Don Alfonso, heir to the throne of Portugal, who died within a few months. Later she married his brother Emmanuel, but died at the birth of their son Miguel. Little Miguel, himself heir to the thrones of Portugal, Castile and Aragon, died in his first year.

Next in succession was Isabella's third child, Joanna, or Joan, as she is also called. At Isabella's death, Ferdinand declared his daughter insane —though she was not—in order that he might inherit Castile. Joanna's husband, Philip the Handsome of Burgundy, permitted this deception in order to use Joanna's Spanish heritage for his European schemes.

In recent years letters of her son Charles V, guarded as a Spanish secret for three and a half centuries, have revealed the tragedy of her life. Isabella's third daughter, Catherine of Aragon, as she is best known in England, or Catalona as she was called in Spain, married Prince Arthur of England. At his death she married Henry VIII; she was the first of his six wives. She lived with him eighteen years and bore him one daughter, Mary Tudor, who became a reigning queen of England. When she did not bear Henry VIII a son, the marriage, by a degree of nullity, was declared void from the beginning.

Maria, Isabella's fourth daughter, was more fortunate than the others. She married her sister Isabel's husband, Emmanuel of Portugal, and bore him six sons and two daughters.

The loss of her children and grandchildren and their afflictions hastened Isabella's death, which occurred two weeks before Columbus returned from his fourth and last voyage.

Realizing that death had taken his best friend, Columbus wrote to his son Diego:

The principal thing is to commend affectionately and with great devotion the soul of the Queen our lady to God. Her life was always Catholic and holy and prompt in all things in His Holy service; for this reason we may rest assured that she is received in His Glory, and beyond the care of this rough and weary world.

It was Queen Isabella's wish to be buried in a coarse Franciscan robe. This was in keeping with her proclamation against costly and ostentatious funerals. Believing in the immortality of the soul, she argued that it was inconsistent for Christians to waste too much money on "vain and transitory things."

VITTORIA COLONNA—
INSPIRER OF MICHELANGELO
(1490-1547)

◆ ◆ ◆

She increased Michelangelo's religious faith and inspired this great artist with an ideal of womanhood. Together they worked for reform within the Church, she with her pen and he with his brush. She is the first woman in history to turn her talents to writing religious verse.

SHE LED A GREAT ARTIST CLOSER TO GOD

VITTORIA COLONNA, one of the greatest spirits of the Italian Renaissance, had the power of making goodness attractive and religion interesting. The master painter Michelangelo was attracted by her faith, which stimulated his own. He said that her conversation, and above all the pure and beautiful life she led in the midst of the luxury and immorality of the Rome of the Renaissance, helped to make him a Christian. Michelangelo "saw the Godhead in Vittoria's face, till he took on a more Godlike grace," commented Algernon Swinburne.

There was everything in the great artist to appeal to a noblewoman: his integrity, his high sense of honor, his many-sided genius. Their friendship was the glory of their lives and the edification of the Church. The character of that friendship, in an age known for its corruption, is indicative of the high religious idealism of Vittoria Colonna.

They met in Rome probably while he was painting "The Last Judgment" on the wall behind the altar in the Sistine Chapel, the Popes' private chapel. Twenty-four years earlier, in the same chapel, he had completed the monumental frescoes depicting "The Creation," "The Fall of Man" and "The Flood."

The earlier paintings had required more than four years of toil. He spent even longer on "The Last Judgment." He was convinced, he said, that "good painting is nothing less than a copy of the perfection of God and a reminder of His painting." In the Sistine Chapel, Michelangelo delineated the human form and face in unmatched variety and grandeur.

Though their meeting could have been earlier, their first recorded visit took place in the convent chapel in Rome, probably in 1538, when he was sixty-three and she was forty-seven. Vittoria was then living in a religious center on Monte Silvestro. The convent garden joined that of the Colonna palace, which had been her family's home for generations. Fra Ambrogio of Siena, a famous Dominican, was giving a series of lectures on St. Paul's Epistles in the Church of San Silvestro de Monte Cavallo. Vittoria Colonna often remained at the church or in the convent garden after these lectures to discuss art and poetry with her friends.

After one of these gatherings she sent Michelangelo this note: "It is cool and fresh and pleasant here. Come and lose a part of the day with us." The great master accepted her invitation.

Their meeting has been immortalized in art by the Portuguese painter of miniatures, Francis of Holland, in his "Dialogues on Art," thought to have been painted in Rome in 1538. It depicts Vittoria Colonna, Michelangelo and others meeting in the chapel. Adjoining are the convent gardens with the city of Rome lying below. It shows Vittoria receiving her guest with dignified courtesy. Her golden hair is covered by a veil, her widow's dress of black velvet falls softly about her feet, and her expression is one of charity and humility. She was a beautiful woman with delicately molded classical features, large bright eyes and a high forehead.

Michelangelo's drawing of a "Deposition from the Cross," in which the dead body of Christ is supported by two angels, and a "Crucifixion," which he painted with so much devotion for Vittoria, mark their friendship. When the first of the drawings reached her, she wrote him:

I have received your letter and examined the "Crucifixion," which truly has crucified in my memory every other picture I ever saw. Nowhere could one find another figure of our Lord so well executed, so living and so exquisitely finished.

Later, when Michelangelo sent Vittoria Colonna the second drawing, she wrote:

Your works forcibly stimulate the imagination of all who look at them. My study of them made me speak of adding goodness to things perfect in themselves, and I have seen now that "all is possible to him who believes." I had the greatest faith in God, that He would bestow upon you supernatural grace for the making of this Christ, and when I saw it, it was so wonderful that it surpassed all my expectations in every way.

Then she goes on to make a graceful little play of words upon Michelangelo's name.

I tell you that it rejoices me greatly that the angel on the right hand should be so much the most beautiful, because Michael will place you, Michelangelo, at the right hand of the Lord in the last day.

Vittoria Colonna understood that Michelangelo's work was a divine calling requiring consecration. He himself said:

In order to represent in some degree the adored image of our Lord, it is not enough that a master should be great and able; I maintain also that he must be a man of good conduct, and more or less, if possible, a saint, in order that the Holy Ghost may rain down inspiration on his understanding.

Vittoria Colonna's sequence of sonnets on *The Triumph of Christ* shows that God had also "rained down inspiration" on her "understanding" of Christ. One of these sonnets follows:

> Stretched naked on the Cross the Lord, I see,
> With pierced side and nailed hands and feet,
> Upon whose head the thorny crown is set,
> By vilest men assailed with injury.
> The heavy weight of the world's sin doth lie,
> Upon his shoulders, and in such a plight
> The heart that only is with love alight
> O'ercometh death and every enemy.
> Patience, obedience, truth and humbleness,
> There were the stars, with other virtues high,
> That did adorn His son of charity.
> Therefore in that sharp fight did these appear
> After His lovely death to make more clear
> The glory of His everlasting grace.

A letter to her written by Michelangelo in 1538 indicates his reliance on her appreciation and counsel.

I am going in search of truth with uncertain step. My heart, floating unceasingly between vice and virtue, suffers and finds itself failing, like a weary traveler wandering on in the dark. Ah, do thou become my counselor. Thy advice shall be sacred. Clear away my doubts. Teach me in my wavering how my unenlightened soul may resist the tyranny of passion unto the end. Do thou thyself, who has directed my steps toward Heaven by ways of pleasantness, prescribe a course for me.

Vittoria's deep perception and sympathy with the message Michelangelo was striving to express through his painting is revealed in one of her letters to him:

Painting, better than any other means, enables us to see the humility of the saints, the constancy of the martyrs, the purity of the virgins, the beauty of the angels, the love and charity with which the seraphim burns. It raises and transports mind and soul beyond the stars, and leaves us to contemplate the eternal sovereignty of God.

These and other writings and conversations between them stress the simplicity of the Christian Gospel. To Vittoria Colonna, religion was the keynote of existence, the meaning and explanation of life. She desired to carry the ideal of Christian perfection from the monastery into everyday practice. Michelangelo reveled in the religious atmosphere that surrounded her, for it soothed his irritated nerves and gave him peace. Their religious spirit is essentially the same—a spirit of contrition, humility and unwavering faith.

He found himself talking to Vittoria as he had never talked to a woman before. She represented to him the best of the Renaissance, its learning, intelligence, enthusiasm. There was also a trace in her of the mysticism of a simpler age. The common tie of the same religious aspirations, the same longings for a purified Church—these bound them together. Each worked for reform within the Church, he with his brush, she with her pen.

Vittoria belonged to the Order of the Oratory of Divine Love, a society whose aim was to purify the Roman Church from within, keeping its unity intact. She worked to bring purer morals and evangelical simplicity to the Catholic Church. What leisure time she had from prayer, meditation and writing she gave to letters. Their theme was the perplexing and all-important one of the purification of the Church. Her closest friends, in addition to Michelangelo, were others who aspired to the same goals.

Among these was Queen Margaret of Navarre, elder sister of Francis I, King of France, whose salon became the stronghold of religious reforms. Another was the Duchess Renée of Italy, an avowed Protestant and friend of John Calvin. Vittoria also was a friend of Bembo, Italian cardinal and man of letters, who in his *Eclogues and Elegies* said of Vittoria Colonna that she has "illuminated the ages with rays of her virtue." She was also close to the Pope.

Vittoria Colonna was born in 1490, two years before Columbus discovered America. Her birthplace was the ancient walled city of Marino, nestling among the Alban hills, not far from the Lake of Albano. She was a daughter of the ancient Roman family of Colonna. Her mother was a niece of a saintly man. Her father was Grand Constable for King Ferdinand II of Naples. The king, to secure the faithfulness of her father, betrothed her at the age of four to Ferrante Francesio d'Avalos, the only son of the Marquis of Pescara. Most of her letters are signed "The Marchesa of Pescara," though history knows her best by her maiden name of Vittoria Colonna.

Her marriage in 1509, when she was nineteen, was celebrated with much festivity. She enjoyed what has been called a "two-year honeymoon" with her husband on the beautiful island of Ischia, where mountains and valleys, sea and sky, and the luxuriant vegetation of its tropical climate combine to make it a poet's dream.

Early in 1512, war broke out between the King of France and the King of Naples, and Vittoria's husband was placed in command of the army of Naples. Alone on Ischia, Vittoria spent her time in study, perfecting herself in the art of poetry, communing with God, and finding solace in all the lovely sights of nature.

Her husband was wounded in battle and returned to Ischia for a little while but was called again to join the allied armies in Lombardy. Vittoria resumed her studies. In 1515 she persuaded her husband to adopt his nephew, and there grew a tie between Vittoria and the nephew as strong as that of a mother and son.

Vittoria and her husband were separated by his military duties for long periods of time. However, the fact that he recognized her fine qualities is shown in a poetic tribute written to her while he was a prisoner of war.

During these separations Vittoria remained a loyal wife and a devout follower of the spiritual life. Her husband, however, did not find it so easy to resist temptation, and his flirtation with a prominent lady of the court caused considerable scandal. Reports of his behavior doubtless reached Vittoria, but she continued to admire him as a talented general and a courageous soldier.

At one time her husband was offered the crown of Naples if he would betray Italy and join the cause of the French. He must have been tempted by this offer, and it is possible that a letter from Vittoria encouraging him to live up to higher ideals contributed much to his decision not to sacrifice his honor. He could hardly decide otherwise in the face of her firm words:

Titles and kingdoms do not add to true honor; virtue and truth, these alone enable a man's name to descend untarnished to posterity. I do not desire to be the wife of a king, but I desire to be the wife of that great general who shows his bravery in war, and his magnanimity in peace; he surpasses the greatest kings.

At the end of her husband's active military service his battle wounds failed to heal and he fell seriously ill. He made his will, leaving his property to Vittoria, under the care of their adopted son. This son not long afterward vanished with his ship at sea.

At her husband's death, Vittoria Colonna went to a convent and spent many days in prayer and meditation on his passing. She survived him twenty years.

Vittoria soon turned to writing sonnets. There were more than a hundred about her husband's greatness as a commander and his bravery in battle. Afterward she wrote sincere and dignified religious poetry which reveals that she had achieved serenity of soul, had learned some of the meaning of the Eternal Mystery, and had something to unfold to all those who will wait and listen.

Ten years after the death of her husband, Vittoria met Michelangelo. One of the most beautiful women in Italy and one of the most celebrated, she had refused many offers of marriage. She had turned to religion for solace until it became her one absorbing love. Friendship, touched with loving understanding, was what the great painter brought into the last decade of Vittoria Colonna's life.

In this sonnet to her, Michelangelo defines the quality of his love:

> Seeking at least to be not all unfit
>> For thy sublime and boundless courtesy,
>> My lowly thoughts at first were fain to try
>> What they could yield for grace so infinite.
> But now I know my unassisted wit
>> Is all too weak to make me soar so high,
>> For pardon, lady, for this fault I cry,
>> And wiser still I grow remembering it.
> Yea, well I see what folly 'twere to think
>> That largess, dropped from thee like dews from heaven,
>> Could e'er be paid by work so frail as mine.
> To nothingness my art and talent sink;
>> He fails who from his mortal stores hath given
>> A thousand fold to match one gift divine.

Michelangelo wrote eight sonnets and three madrigals to Vittoria Colonna. In one of the madrigals he tells of God speaking through her and of his being saved by her.

In the last years of her life, she gave up all her elegance of the past and was often seen in public in the simplest attire. Many of her poems, like these three lines, express her humble, holy thoughts:

> Spirit in Paradise, Pray thee plead
> That I may follow thy fair, humble way,
> In thought, in wish, in every holy deed.

As a girl and a bride, she had been surrounded with luxuries. She often wore a dress trimmed with cloth of gold, a crimson satin cap with halo of wrought gold, and a golden girdle. Among her wedding gifts preserved in the archives are diamond crosses, gold chains, and a bed covered with crimson satin and blue taffeta fringed with gold. Her home at Ischia was a castle. But toward the end, in the years when she knew Michelangelo best, she chose to live simply in a convent.

During her final illness Michelangelo came to her bedside every day. She died in the convent of the Caesarian Palace in Rome in 1547. At her request, there is neither stone nor tablet to mark the place where her body rests.

Michelangelo saved for posterity one hundred and forty-three of her sonnets and some of her letters. As he said later of her: "Her love kept my old tired heart, so near the point of death, alive." He lived to the age of eighty-nine, almost seventeen years longer than Vittoria Colonna.

Her immortal prayer, which at her request Michelangelo repeated to her in her last hours, must have strengthened him in his remaining years, just as it has strengthened other Christians:

Grant, I beseech Thee, Lord, that I may always adore Thee with that abasement of soul which befits my humbleness, and with that exaltation of mind which Thy Majesty demands, and let me ever live in the fear which Thy justice inspires and in the hope which Thy mercy allows, and submit to Thee as Almighty, yield myself to Thee as Allwise, and turn to Thee as to supreme perfection and Goodness. I beseech Thee, most tender Father, that Thy most living fire may purify me, that Thy most clear light may illumine me, and that Thy most pure love may so avail me that, without hindrance of mortal things, I may return to Thee in Happiness and Security.

MARGARET OF NAVARRE AND JEANNE D'ALBRET
—DEFENDERS OF THE REFORMATION

◆ ◆ ◆

MARGARET OF NAVARRE (1492-1549), also of Valois, of Angoulême and of Alençon, was Queen of Navarre and sister of King Francis I of France. She gave refuge to French Reformers in her palace and became a godmother of the Reformation.

JEANNE D'ALBRET (1528-1572), daughter of Margaret and Queen of Navarre, was the mother of Henry IV, who issued the Edict of Nantes giving France religious liberty. She held services for the reformed in her palace apartment and had the Bible translated into the Béarnnois dialect.

PIONEERS OF A NEW FAITH

THE REFORMED CHURCH in France had stanch and powerful supporters in Margaret and her daughter Jeanne, queens of Navarre, a kingdom in the south of France which formerly included part of Spain.

Both women were in their own right pioneers of religious freedom in France, but a further reason they occupy an important place in church history is because one was the grandmother and the other was the mother of Henry IV of France (Henry of Navarre) who issued the famous Edict of Nantes in 1598. This decree ended the French wars of religion and established religious toleration, guaranteeing the Huguenots, or French Protestants, the basic rights of free exercise of religion, civil equality and fair administration of justice.

Although Margaret never publicly became a Protestant, she was like a godmother of the Reformers in her own kingdom of Navarre and in her brother's kingdom of France.

Margaret was first married at seventeen to Charles, Duke of Alençon. Martha Walker Freer, in her *Life of Marguerite of Navarre*, describes her as tall and slender and with "most regal grace in her deportment and gestures. Her eyes were large and of a deep violet hue. Her complexion was fair and the color of her cheeks most delicately fresh. Her hair, which was very long, was of pale gold color." Her beauty of soul as she grew older, says this biographer, gave a new radiance to her face.

Pierre de Brantôme, French chronicler of her time, comments: "At fifteen years of age, the spirit of God began to manifest itself in her eyes, face, walk, speech, and in all her actions. . . . She had a heart devoted to God and she loved mightily to compose spiritual songs." As she grew older she spent more time reading the Bible, and often commended herself to God, praying to Him to guide her.

In 1512, as she was nearing twenty, the grain of mustard seed for Reform was first planted in Margaret's heart by Jacques Lefèvre d'Étaples, called "the Pioneer Spirit of the Reformaion." Lefèvre, who had written a commentary on the Epistles of Paul, preached a return to the Christianity of Christ and the Apostles and spoke up boldy for reform in the Church five years before Luther nailed his famous theses on the door of the Castle Church at Wittenberg, Germany.

Lefèvre's impassioned plea found a ready response in Margaret, who was predisposed to champion the cause of spiritual freedom, and she translated her sympathy into action without considering the consequences to herself. As early as 1521, when the Reformers feared persecution in France, Margaret assured them: "The King and Queen are firm in their decision to make it understood that the truth of God is not heresy, and that, more than ever, they are intent upon the reformation of the Church." So close was she to the Reformers that she was suspected of heresy, but she defended herself with the courageous words: "Divine truth is not heresy."

After the death of Charles in 1525, Margaret was married to Henry d'Albret (Henry II) King of Navarre, eleven years her junior. French policy dictated the marriage. Her brother needed Henry's friendship. He could thus form an alliance with Spain and open the passes of the Pyrenees to a Spanish army, which could easily march against France. Henry II also needed the friendship of Margaret's powerful brother.

By this time Lefèvre was securely established as the queen's spiritual adviser, having fled the concerted fury of the established Church and its followers. His convictions remained unchanged, and Margaret's loyalty to the principles he taught was undimmed.

Another Reformer who owed much to the fearlessness of his sovereign was Clément Marot, French hymn writer, especially known for his translation of the Psalms, sung in the Church of France for three centuries. When he was arrested for heresy he spent his time in prison writing poems until Margaret had him freed. Had she not accomplished this, the Reformers declared they would have lost one of their most able servants.

While she worked in behalf of the Reformers wherever the opportunity offered, Margaret never came to an open break with the Papacy at Rome, largely because of the position of her Catholic brother, Francis I. When an enemy complained to him that his sister was favoring Protestantism, while his sympathies were with the Catholics, he replied: "If what you say is true I love her too well to allow her to be troubled on that account." In the presence of her enemies, he often remarked: "My sister Margaret is the only woman I ever knew who had every virtue and every grace without any admixture of vice."

Margaret's palace at Nerac became a radiating center for religion and culture. In her private apartments, in an underground hall beneath the castle terrace, Lefèvre and other Reformers preached, and she observed communion with them at a table set by her servants.

Word of these "fastings in the cellar" finally reached the ears of her husband, Henry II, and he was so angered that one day he burst in upon a service and struck his wife in the face.

This was too great an insult to be passed over lightly. Margaret reported it to her brother, who threatened war with Henry. The latter begged his wife's forgivness and promised to investigate the new doctrines for himself. From that time on, the persecuted had a friend in Henry as well as in Margaret. Leading refugee Huguenots could always find sanctuary at Nerac and often discussed passages from the Bible around the palace table.

Margaret and Henry II labored for the advancement of their little mountain kingdom, making improvements in agriculture and commerce, encouraging the manufacture of cloth, aiding learning, and opening hospitals for the poor.

She accomplished much for the people of her kingdom, but her more important place in history is not as Queen of Navarre but as the beloved and influential sister of Francis I, King of France. When he was captured at the Battle of Pavia, a defeat for which her husband was largely blamed, she prayed for his release and assured him in a letter that

the further they remove you from us, the greater becomes my firm hope of your deliverance and speedy return, for the hour when men's minds are most troubled is the hour when God achieves His masterstroke . . . and if He now gives you, on the one hand, a share in the pains which He has borne for you, and, on the other hand, the grace to bear them patiently, I entreat you, Monseigneur, to believe unfalteringly that it is only to test your love for Him and to give you leisure to think about how much He loves you . . . He has permitted this trial, after having united you to Him by tribulations to deliver you for His own glory—so that, through you, His name may be known and sanctified, not in your kingdom alone, but all Christendom.

While imprisoned in Madrid, Francis I asked that his sister be brought to him. She made her way to Spain as fast as she could, wearing black clothes, and with her head swathed in a white veil that fell from her shoulders to the ground. Not a jewel nor a ribbon did she wear.

She was eager to raise her brother's spirits, for on her arrival she found him ill and depressed and chanting Isaiah 38:1-2: "In those days was Hezekiah sick unto death. . . . Then Hezekiah turned his face toward the wall, and prayed unto the Lord."

Margaret had an altar erected in her brother's prison room, and, assembling the members of his household, lords and domestics alike, all knelt in prayer and received the communion from the hands of the Archbishop of Embrun.

The king, now sustained by a Higher Power, began to improve, and he said: "It is my God who will heal my soul and body; I pray that I may receive Him." Margaret had shared in her brother's miraculous recovery.

Literature found in Margaret of Navarre not only an inspiring patroness but also a contributor. In 1533 she published *The Mirror of the Sinful Soul,* a volume of religious poems based on David's words: "Create in me a clean heart, O Lord," in which she dwells on the infinite power of God, passionately praises disdain of earthly pleasures, and looks forward to a world regenerated through Christ.

In one poem, "The Vision," she points out that the body in itself is always dead. It is only when yoked with the soul that it may attain eternal life. She views death as the end of a dark imprisonment, when through the intercession of Christ we are enabled to exchange the shackles of the body for a spiritual body that shall not die.

Margaret's chief place in literature, however, is not as a religious poet but as compiler of the *Heptameron,* a collection of medieval society tales, supposed to have been told in seven days.

Her dying words were prophetic: "God, I am well assured, will carry forward the work He has permitted me to commence, and my place will be more than filled by my daughter, who has the energy and moral courage, in which I fear I have been deficient."

The poet Charles d'Saint-Marthe commented in his oration at her funeral that she was "sovereignly perfect in poetry and philosophy and consummate in the Holy Scriptures, to such a degree as to cause even the wisest to marvel greatly."

Jeanne, the daughter of Margaret and her second husband Henry II of Navarre, was born January 7, 1528. She inherited her mother's diplomatic ability, her love of learning, and her natural inclination toward things of the spirit. She carried on her mother's noble work, and in some respects more effectively than her mother, for Margaret was less remarkable for what she did than for what she aspired to do. However, Jeanne's influence did not go beyond her own kingdom of Navarre, for she lacked her mother's close relationship with the court of France.

In 1548, when she was twenty, she was married to Antoine, Duke of Bourbon, Count of Vendome, a weak, vacillating ruler, and a philanderer. She bore him five children, only two of whom, Henry IV and Catherine, lived to be adults.

The queen proclaimed Calvinism the religion of Navarre and became the stalwart champion of Calvin's followers, the Huguenots. When her enemies tried to keep her from attending services of a Calvinist minister, she courageously declared: "It is not my purpose to barter my immortal soul for territorial aggrandizement." When Catherine de Médicis, the queen-regent of France, advised her to yield at least outward conformity to the Catholic faith, she answered: "If I, at this very moment, held my son, and all the kingdoms of the world together, in my grasp, I would hurl them to the bottom of the sea, rather than peril the salvation of my soul."

Threatened by her enemies with the loss of her powers as queen, she replied: "I would rather be poor than cease to serve God." Further threatened with the thought that in her position toward the Reformed in the Church, she was lessening the heritage of her son Henry IV, she retorted: "Instead of lessening my son's heritage, I augment it, and increase his greatness and honor, means by which every true Christian ought to speak."

Proceeding steadily and positively in her work of reform, one of her first acts was to apply for a license to hold private services of the new Reformed faith in her palace apartment. And from her castle at Pau, she issued her edict abolishing Roman Catholic worship throughout her province of Béarn, and ordaining that all churches in areas having a majority of Protestants be delivered over to them. In places where the two religions were equally balanced, she decreed that the Church should be used jointly by both Catholics and Protestant worshipers.

Jeanne worked untiringly to spread the Gospel and foster the study of theology, making a large grant for a college of theology at Orthez. Under her auspices her household chaplains translated the New Testament into the Béarnnois dialect of the Basques of Lower Navarre. These Basque people had been Christians since the fifth century, but they had no Bible in their own difficult and unusual language. Several copies of this Basque translation of the Bible are still in existence.

Ever a faithful student of the Bible, Jeanne remembered what Calvin had written her when she became a Protestant in 1560: "Unless we betake ourselves daily to the Holy Scriptures the truth that we once knew oozes away little by little till it is all gone, except that God shall come to our aid. In His infinite wisdom He has seen fit to prevent you from descending to such a pass."

Persecution made her more steadfast in upholding the doctrines of Reform, and her palace became a school for the study of the new doctrines. She boldly announced:

The Church has not maintained her pristine innocence and vigor—her purity and holiness of doctrines and practice. The Church has exchanged the spiritual for the carnal. Her roses are become thistles. Her charity is nothing but chilling vanity. Her priests and bishops, who should be like Timothy, chaste, sober, humble, hospitable, watching night and day to cherish the holy fire which glows in the bosom of every true priest of God, have defiled themselves.

Taking her pattern from King Jehoash, eighth ruler of Judah, who reduced Baal worship and repaired the temple, one of her first acts was to destroy images in churches. In doing so, she proclaimed: "I have not undertaken to start a new religion, but only to build up the ruins of our ancient faith, in which design I feel certain of a fortunate issue."

She lived through a long period of religious wars. Catherine de Médicis, called by some "the sixteenth-century Jezebel," schemed to separate Jeanne from her husband Antoine and win him back to the Catholic faith, thus bringing the kingdom of Navarre under her sway.

Antoine spent a large part of the time in France, where he was a regent, and Jeanne was wise enough to know that Catherine de Médicis' influence might well triumph. When Jeanne visited France, Antoine treated her with contempt and tried to force her to become a Catholic. Led by Catherine de Médicis, Jeanne's enemies plotted against her life. Realizing that she was in danger, she asked to be permitted to leave France. Permission was granted, but plans already had been made to murder her on her journey back to Navarre.

With great courage and adroitness, she successfully led her little army of guards and attendants through a land of enemies, receiving Huguenot recruits as she passed. Jeanne's brother-in-law, the Prince of Condé, was the military and political leader of the Huguenot army. He guarded Vendôme when she spent the night there, thus preventing her enemies from murdering her.

Later, when her son joined her in Navarre, she threw his fortune and hers into the religious war on the side of the Huguenots. When she heard that the Prince of Condé had been murdered, she mounted her horse and rode out to her army, whose flags were draped in mourning for the brave leader. On one side of her rode her son, on the other, the son of Condé. Bringing her horse to a halt, she faced her troops:

Does the memory of Condé demand nothing but profitless tears? No, let us unite and summon back our courage to defend a course which can never perish and to avenge him who was its firm support. Does despair overwhelm you— despair, that shameful feeling of weak natures? When I, the queen, hope still, is it for you to fear? Because Condé is dead, is all therefore lost? Does our cause cease to be just and holy? No. God, who has already rescued you from perils innumerable, has raised up brothers-in-arms worthy to succeed Condé. To these leaders I add my own son. Make proof of his valor. . . . Behold also Condé's son, the worthy inheritor of Condé's virtues. Soldiers, I offer to you everything in my power to bestow—my dominions, my treasure, my life, and that which is dearer to me than all —my children. I make here a solemn oath before you all—and you know me too well to doubt my word—I swear to defend to my last sight the holy cause which now unites us, which is that of honor and truth.

A breathless silence followed. Then wild shouts went up and the army hailed her son as their leader.

The white-plumed prince gave a ringing command as he wheeled his horse to lead his troops into battle. Drooping flags were raised, despairing men were galvanized into action, and with a thunder of hoofs the army rode into battle.

The fighting was long and bloody, but young Henry led his victorious army back to the city that night.

The queen returned to her palace in triumph, but a new plot was in the making, one which led to the infamous Massacre of St. Bartholomew. Catherine de Médicis was already planning the marriage of her daughter, Margaret of Valois, to Jeanne's son, Henry of Navarre. This would unite Navarre and France and bring Navarre back to the Catholic faith.

The queen became increasingly concerned about her son's prospective marriage, and at one time she called him to her and said: "My son, if you ever had need to supplicate the Almighty, it is now in this our extremity. I, for my part, pray to Him incessantly to aid us in this negotiation, so that this marriage may not be accomplished in wrath but granted as a merciful blessing to augment His glory and our repose. . . . I pray God that for your salvation and His glory, He may give you all needful things."

Nothing could allay her apprehension, however, and she finally decided to go to Paris. She was received with a great ovation, but she was scandalized by the luxury and debauchery of the French court and decided to oppose the marriage. She wrote her son:

Your betrothed is beautiful, very circumspect and graceful, but brought up in the worst company that ever existed (for I do not see a single one who is not infected by it). . . . I would not for anything have you come here to live. This is why I desire you to marry and to withdraw yourself and your wife from this corruption which (bad as I supposed it to be) I find still worse than I thought. If you were here, you could not escape contamination without great grace from God.

Physically exhausted by sorrow, worry and excitement, she suddenly became ill in Paris. There were rumors that she had been poisoned by Catherine de Médicis. Several of the leading Huguenots, including de Coligny, took care of her.

A few hours before her death on June 4, 1572, she asked that the fourteenth, fifteenth and sixteenth chapters of the Gospel of John be read to her. Then she made her will, and asked that her son remain faithful to the Protestant religion in which she had reared him. She begged him not to be lured by voluptuousness and corruption, and to banish atheists, flatterers and libertines.

In her last prayer she implored: "O my Savior, hasten to deliver my spirit from the misery of life and from its prison in this suffering body, so that I may offend Thee no more, and enter joyfully into the glorious rest which Thou hast promised, and that my soul longs for."

The wedding of her son to the French princess, which had been planned to bring an end to the religious war between Catholics and Protestants, was a disaster for the Protestants. During the festivities in August, following Jeanne's death in June, the Massacre of St. Bartholomew's Day began in Paris, killing thousands of Huguenots. Henry was forced to accept the Catholic faith. But four years later, in 1576, Henry of Navarre escaped from Paris, retracted his statement of conversion and placed himself at the head of the Huguenots.

In 1589 he became King of France, succeeding Henry III. In order to bring peace to France, Henry, in 1593, once more declared himself a Catholic. Five years later he granted religious liberty to Protestants in the Edict of Nantes, which embodied the ideals of his mother and grandmother, both of whom were compassionate, intellectual women, spiritually alive to the religious life of their times.

Margaret, Jeanne and Henry IV form a strong trio, suggesting the New Testament threesome, Lois, Eunice and Timothy. Just as the sublime faith of the grandmother Lois and the mother Eunice prepared Timothy for his great work with Paul, so did the religious zeal of Margaret and Jeanne prepare Henry IV for his religious toleration act in favor of the Huguenots.

Unlike Timothy, however, Henry IV had many weaknesses that brought on domestic problems that stained his career. It is possible that had he remained under the influence and watchful eye of his mother during his boyhood and early manhood instead of being sent away to school and college at the insistence of his father, his character would have benefited. However, even though his personal life may not have been above reproach, in his public actions he tried to live up to the high principles instilled in him by his mother. He best expressed this attitude and his deep sense of royal responsibility in a letter written to his sister Catherine in 1599: "God created me for this kingdom and not for myself, and all my wits and my care will be employed solely for its preservation and prosperity."

KATHERINE VON BORA—
WIFE OF MARTIN LUTHER
(1499-1552)

◆ ◆ ◆

She left her convent in 1523, near the beginning of the Reformation, and two years later became the wife of Martin Luther, a former monk. She lived up to Proverbs' ideal of wife and mother.

THE MATRIARCH OF THE PROTESTANT PARSONAGE

HAD KATHERINE VON BORA been unequal to her role as wife of Martin Luther, founder of the German Reformation and father of the Lutheran Church, their marriage might have injured the Protestant cause. But she honored her position and is revered as matriarch of the Protestant parsonage.

In 1517, when Luther posted his ninety-five theses against indulgences in the Catholic Church, he called marriage a "noble and holy estate." His proposals created a furor all over Germany and brought him into prominence overnight. A new world was in the making for Katherine von Bora, who in a few years was to share this great man's life.

One of Luther's most famous lectures in his classroom at Wittenberg

University was on Galatians, in which Paul declares his religious independence from men and his dependence on God. As Luther translated the
New Testament, this Galatian epistle gave him a new sense of independence.

He called Katherine his "Galatian." She brought him a new kind of
independence. Later, however, he chided himself for giving "more credit
to Katherine than to Christ, who has done so much for me."

Their marriage in 1525 created a storm of criticism in ecclesiastical
circles all over Europe. Philip Melanchthon, Luther's collaborator in the
German Reformation, thought marriage had lowered his friend's prestige.
Erasmus, who paved the way for the Reformation by his merciless satires
on the doctrines and institutions of the Church, called this marriage nothing more than a comedy. Henry VIII of England, who had six wives himself, two of whom he beheaded, referred to Luther's marriage as a "crime."
Other leaders, however, heaped praise upon Luther and his bride and sent
them wedding gifts.

Katherine von Bora was twenty-six and Luther forty-two when they
married. She was not beautiful, to judge by her portrait painted by Lucas
Cranach, but she possessed shrewdness, good sense and kindliness. She had
wide-set, intelligent eyes, delicately molded nostrils, prominent cheekbones
and slightly reddish hair which she combed back over a high forehead.

They enjoyed twenty-one happy years together, though their home life
was somewhat strenuous. Their house became a working center for Luther's
momentous reform, which drove a wedge in Western Christendom that
cracked it asunder. Katherine moved quietly in the background amid all the
activities which were to mark her husband as one of the great men in
history.

How many these activities were! Luther lectured at the University of
Wittenberg and wrote numerous religious treatises and catechisms. A lover
of music, he also wrote hymns, including the famous "A Mighty Fortress
Is Our God." In heading the movement that eventually resulted in various
Protestant denominations, Luther also broke away from St. Jerome's Latin
Vulgate Bible and made his own German translation, which for centuries
remained the principal German version. He prepared a new church service,
periodically preached sermons to German peasants, and finally, seven years
after his marriage, completed his translation of the entire Bible into
German.

Fortunately for the Protestant faith, Katherine Luther became a sixteenth-century example of the ideal wife and mother of Proverbs 31:10-31.
Every line of this Bible portrait could be applied to her.

"The heart of her husband doth safely trust in her, so that he shall have no need of spoil." Many times Luther expressed his faith in Katherine and wrote such comments as this to friends: "I would not change my Katie for France and Venice, because God has given her to me, and she is true to me and a good mother to my children." At other times he referred to her as "my beloved Kate" and "Master Kate."

"She will do him good and not evil all the days of her life." Katherine Luther nobly fulfilled her role as wife, mother and hostess.

"She seeketh wool, and flax, and worketh willingly with her hands. . . . she bringeth her food from afar." Katherine Luther looked after the orchard which supplied her family with apples, grapes, peaches, pears, figs and nuts. She also had a fish pond which furnished trout, carp, pike and perch for the family dining table, and a barnyard with hens, ducks, pigs and cows. She sometimes did the slaughtering herself.

"She riseth also while it is yet night, and giveth meat to her household." In addition to her own children, Katherine Luther mothered the two daughters and four sons of one of Luther's sisters, a son of another sister, the son of his brother, another nephew and a great-nephew. Tutors of the Luther children and students in Wittenberg University also boarded at her house. It was not uncommon for the Luthers to sit down to a table with a long row of boarders, some of whom had nothing more than a "thank you" to give.

"She considereth a field, and buyeth it: with the fruit of her hands she planteth a vineyard." In the later years of their marriage, Katherine Luther was instrumental in getting her husband to buy from her brother her own family home at Zulsdorf, Germany. There the family spent several weeks each summer.

"She girdeth her loins with strength, and strengthenth her arms." No homemaker in Christian history ever worked harder.

"She stretcheth out her hand to the poor." Katherine Luther rejoiced when she could set up extra cots in an unused portion of her house so that she could take in more of the homeless who came to her door. Among these were monks and nuns who had left their monasteries and had no work and no place to go. When she set up a hospital in her home and took in the sick, she became a master with herbs and poultices. She brought her husband through numerous illnesses, many of which could be attributed to his rigorous monastic discipline and fastings, and to the tremendous pressure under which he later labored. Her son Paul, who became an able physician, said his mother was a good doctor herself.

"Her husband is known in the gates, when he sitteth among the elders of the land." Before his marriage Luther had not observed regular hours of eating and sleeping. His wife brought every comfort into his daily life.

"She openeth her mouth with wisdom; and in her tongue is the law of kindness." Katherine Luther demonstrated this on many occasions. During the early years of their marriage, when Luther was ill and near death, he turned to his wife and said: "My dearest Kate, if it [death] be God's will, accept it. May He care for you and Hans." Katherine's answer was: "My dear Doctor, if it is God's will I would rather have you with our Lord than here. But I am not thinking just of myself and Hans. There are so many people that need you. But don't worry about us. God will take care of us." This was typical of Katherine Luther's faith and kindly spirit.

"She looketh well to the ways of her household, and eateth not the bread of idleness." Katherine Luther was a woman of enormous energy, who turned the old Black Cloister of Wittenberg into a livable spot.

"Her children arise up, and call her blessed; her husband also, and he praiseth her." Katherine Luther was a devoted mother to her six children: Hans, Elizabeth, Magdalena, Martin, Paul and Margaretha. The second child, Elizabeth, lived less than a year, and Magdalena passed away in her father's arms when she was thirteen, shortly after he had sought to comfort his wife by reminding her: "Kathie, remember where our Magdalena came from."

Nothing showed the trust Luther had in Katherine better than the words in his will, in which he left their small estate to her and not to the children:

I desire the children to look to her for support, not she to the children, and that they may hold her in honor and be subject to her, as God has commanded. . . . For I consider that the mother will be the best guardian of her own children, and will make use of such dowry and property, not to the injury and detriment of the children, but for their use and advantage; for they are her own flesh and blood, and she has borne them under her heart.

Katherine Luther also typified the last words of Proverbs on the model wife: "But a woman that feareth the Lord, she shall be praised." Martin Luther was generally cheerful and had faith in his God, yet occasionally he became moody. At such times Katherine sought to comfort and encourage him. Once when nothing seemed to raise Luther's spirits, he decided to leave home for a few days to see if a change would not help him, but he returned grieved in spirit.

On entering the house, he found his wife seated in the middle of the room, dressed in black, with a black cloth thrown over her head, and looking quite sad. A white handkerchief she held in her hand was damp, as if moistened with tears.

When Luther urged his wife to tell him what was the matter, she replied: "Only think, my dear Doctor, the Lord in Heaven is dead; and this is the cause of my grief."

He laughed and said: "It is true, dear Kate; I am acting as if there was no God in Heaven." Luther's melancholy left him.

He called marriage a school for character, and his own character as well as Katherine's strengthened in marriage. Family relationships formed the framework for the institution of marriage set up by Luther for the clergy, and his own marriage measured up to every standard of good family life.

Katherine came of the eminent and noble family of von Bora of Meissen, Germany, and is referred to by one of Luther's modern biographers, E. G. Schwiebert, as "the aristocratic nun." The date of her birth, January 29, 1499, was recorded on a silver medal which her husband gave her to wear around her neck.

She was well prepared for her important role as the wife of one of the greatest religious leaders of all time. Her mother, Katherine von Haubitz, died shortly after her birth. After the second marriage of her father, Hans von Bora, when she was about five, she was sent to a convent where her mother's sister was abbess.

This was the rich Cistercian Cloister Marienthron, in Nimbschen, close to the border of Saxony. Most of the nuns and novitiates were of noble lineage. This vast stone cloister, in a beautiful valley of shady woods and silvery streams, was surrounded by green fields tilled under the supervision of the nuns. Here Katherine gained the knowledge of practical farming which she turned to good account as Martin Luther's wife. She learned to write well in German and to understand some Latin. She also learned the meaning of prayer in this cloister with its twelve altars.

Luther's attack on ecclesiastical authority reverberated in the monasteries and convents, and both monks and nuns began to seek freedom in the years after 1520. The revolt spread to the cloister where Katherine served and she, with eight others, one of whom was her father's sister, decided to break with their secluded life. According to Luther's new teaching, their continuance in the cloister was incompatible with the salvation of their souls. When they entreated parents and friends for help, all turned a deaf ear.

There are many conflicting reports of the details of their escape. The three thousand biographies and treatises written about Martin Luther and his work contain some contradictions, but it seems quite certain that these nuns sought the aid of Luther himself. This subjected him to great danger, for the person liberating nuns, according to canon and civil law, might expect the death penalty.

Luther, it is thought, enlisted the aid of Leonard Koppe, a merchant from the nearby town of Torgau who delivered supplies to the Nimbschen cloister. Among these supplies were barrels of herring. An arrangement was made for him to conceal the nuns in the empty barrels being returned to him.

On the night before Easter in 1523, the merchant's canvas-covered wagon drew up before the convent and loaded. Through the late hours of the night and early hours of the morning the wagon, with its cargo of nine fugitive nuns, made its way for some twenty miles away from the cloister.

They paused for Easter and Easter Monday at Torgau and attended the parish church there. This was in a "New Saxony" governed by Frederick the Wise and Duke George, who were friendly toward Luther.

The day after Easter Monday, Katherine von Bora and the eight other nuns rode openly another twenty miles from Torgau to Wittenberg, where Luther lived in the abandoned Black Cloister monastery. When the wagonload of nuns drew up to the monastery, he exclaimed: "This is not my doing; but would to God I could, in this way, give liberty to enslaved consciences and empty the cloisters of their tenants. A breach is made, however."

Luther accepted the responsibiltiy of finding homes, husbands or positions for these nuns, not an easy task in the sixteenth century.

For two years Katherine von Bora lived in Wittenberg, probably in the household of Lucas Cranach, the celebrated painter. The Cranachs became close friends of hers. (Years later Cranach painted portraits of several of the Luther children as well as of Katherine and her husband.)

In the Cranach household Katherine learned homemaking at its best and also came in contact with famous personages, among whom was the King of Denmark, who gave her a ring she later treasured highly. Students in Wittenberg, observing her many good qualities and also her excellent housekeeping, dubbed her "Catherine of Siena." This was high praise, for the twelfth-century Catherine had been a model housekeeper as well as a saintly woman. Work in the Wittenberg household prepared Katherine von Bora for the larger role she was to fill when she presided over her own big household and entertained her husband's famous friends from many parts of Europe.

All of the nuns who had escaped with Katherine soon found husbands. Luther suggested that Katherine marry Dr. Kasper Glatz, a former rector of the University of Wittenberg; but she refused to accept him because she considered him too sanctimonious. His colleagues regarded him as somewhat miserly. She was very particular in her choice of a husband.

In her embarrassment over Dr. Glatz, she turned to a Dr. Nicholas von Amsdorf, on Luther's advisory staff, who had come to call at the home where she was staying. She sent word through Amsdorf that, though she would not take Dr. Glatz, she was not unreasonable and would accept Amsdorf or Luther himself. Luther at this time had no thought of marriage since he expected to be burned at the stake as a heretic at any time.

Finally, however, he wrote friends: "While I was thinking of other things, God has suddenly brought me to marriage. . . . God likes to work miracles." Their wedding in the Black Cloister, which was to be their home, was followed two weeks later by a housewarming. At this same time, June of 1525, their marriage was publicly proclaimed in the town church.

In October, Luther confided to a friend: "My Katherine is fulfilling Genesis 1:28: "And God blessed them, and God said unto them, Be fruitful and multiply, and replenish the earth."

In late May 1526, he wrote: "There is about to be born a child of a monk and a nun." On June 8 he rejoiced: "My dear Katie brought into the world yesterday by God's grace at two o'clock a little son, Hans Luther."

Sometime after this, Luther said: "The dearest life is to live with a godly, willing, obedient wife in peace and unity. Union of the flesh does nothing. There must also be union of manners and mind." In a passage from the famous *Table Talk,* a book of Luther's conversations compiled by some of Katherine's boarders, he is reported to have said: "Were all the leaves in the woods of Torgau each given a voice, they would still be too few to sing the praises of marriage and condemn the wickedness of celibacy."

In Katherine's years of married life, she was naturally overshadowed by her famous husband, and her own spiritual life is more a matter of inference than of record. Luther offered her a reward if she would read the Bible through. He paid her the highest compliment later when he remarked: "Katie understands the Bible better than any Papist did twenty years ago." While absorbed in his many church affairs, he thanked God for his "pious and true wife on whom a husband's heart can rely."

A conscientious mother, Katherine Luther taught her children well, as is indicated in this letter which Luther wrote his son Hans when the boy was four years old:

Grace and peace in Christ, my dear little son. I am happy to see that you are studying well and saying your prayers faithfully. When I come home I will bring you a nice present. . . . I know a lovely garden where many children in gold frocks gather rosy apples under the trees, as well as pears, cherries and plums. They sing, skip and are gay. And they have fine ponies with golden bridles and silver saddles. I asked the gardener who were these children, and he said: "They are the children who like to pray and learn and be good."

This letter reveals Luther's tender love for his children and reflects the joyous home life of the family, where the mother was the heart of it all.

Dr. F. Townley Lord, in his *Great Women in Christian History*, says Katherine "is entitled to go down in history as one of the great home-makers of the world. . . . In her own career she is typical of the movement from the seclusion of the nunnery to the richer, fuller life of the home: a movement, shall we not say, which was inspired by the true spirit of the Gospel."

None of her many sorrows was greater than the loss of her husband in 1546, twenty-one years after their marriage. He had gone to his native town of Eisleben in Saxony, to settle disputes between the quarreling counts of Mansfeld. Having suffered from ill health for ten years, he was not equal to the severe winter he had to endure there.

Katherine's deep affection for her husband is expressed in this letter which she wrote to her sister soon after his death:

Who would not be sorrowful and mourn for so noble a man as my dear lord, who served not only a single land, but the whole world? If I had a principality and an empire, it would never have cost me so much pain to lose them as I have now that our dear Lord God has taken from me, and not from me only, but from the whole world, this dear and precious man.

For new strength Katherine Luther turned to Psalm 31. "In thee, O Lord, do I put my trust; . . . deliver me in thy righteousness. . . . Be thou my strong rock."

In June 1546, Charles V declared war against the Protestants and the Schmalkaldic War began. Armies moved on Wittenberg, where Katherine Luther continued to live in the Black Cloister. By the middle of winter it became dangerous for her to remain there and she and her children first fled to Magdeburg, then wandered from place to place.

When she was told that Wittenberg was again safe, she returned home joyfully with her children. A second time she was forced to flee to Magde-burg. Finally in June 1547, she went home again. She had no funds, and there were new taxes because of the war. Her gardens were ruined, her cattle gone, her barns and sheds burned. Some of Luther's friends stood by her faithfully, and she was able to borrow money to rebuild. She later earned a living by taking in student boarders.

In 1552 the bubonic plague spread over Wittenberg, and the university was moved to Torgau. Katherine decided to seek refuge in this town to which she had journeyed to safety as a nun almost thirty years earlier. En route the horses pulling the carriage in which she and her four children were riding became frightened. Anxious for her children's safety, she jumped out of the fast-moving vehicle and tried to stop the horses, but she fell into a ditch of water. This experience was too much for her gallant spirit. She soon developed bronchial trouble and for several months lay ill, comforting and sustaining herself by praying:

Lord, my Saviour, Thou standest at the door and wouldst enter in. O come, Thou beloved guest, for I desire to depart and be with Thee. Let my children be committed to Thy mercy. Lord, look down in mercy upon Thy Church. May the pure doctrine which God has sent through my husband be handed down un-adulterated to posterity. Dear Lord, I thank Thee for all the trials, through which Thou didst lead me, and by which Thou didst prepare me to behold Thy Glory. Thou hast never forsaken nor forgotten me. Thou hast evermore caused Thy face to shine upon me, when I called upon Thee. Behold, now I grasp Thy hand and say, as Jacob of old: Lord I will not let Thee go, unless Thou bless me. I will cling to Thee forevermore.

When Katherine Luther died in 1552 she was buried in the parish church at Torgau, the same church which she had reached on Easter Sunday in 1523 after her escape from the convent.

She represented the new spirit of the Reformation, and played no small role in transferring the ideal of Christian service from the cloister to the home.

TERESA OF ÁVILA—

BELOVED WOMAN OF THE CARMELITES

(1515-1582)

* * *

Her writings are among the great works of Christendom. She reformed the Carmelite Order and is revered as Spain's most beloved woman saint. She is the only woman on whom the Catholic Church conferred the title Doctor of the Church.

SHE COMBINED MYSTICAL DEVOTION WITH PRACTICAL ACHIEVEMENT

FEW WOMEN in Christian history have risen to the spiritual eminence of Teresa of Ávila, patron saint of Spain, leader of reforms within the Catholic Church and one of the most outstanding women in Spanish history. After nearly four centuries, her fame is still growing, and biographers are still writing the story of her life and work.

Like the patriarchs of old, she talked with God and God talked with her. Like Job, she had many tribulations but learned to see God's hand in all of them. Like Paul, she was a true apostle going from place to place, laboring diligently to build God's kingdom. Like Mary of Bethany, she was spiritually sensitive; like Martha, she was practical.

Teresa was born in 1515 in Ávila, an old walled city of central Spain and capital of the province bearing the same name. The city is situated on a ridge which slopes to the river Adaja and forms part of a mountain shelf of four thousand feet elevation in the very heart of Spain.

Teresa's father, Alonso Sanchez de Cepeda, a gentleman of good family, had three children by a first wife and seven sons and two daughters by a second. Teresa was a daughter of his second wife, Beatrice Ahumada. Her parents were devout people. "It helped me," she wrote, "that I never saw my mother and father respect anything but goodness." Her father read religious books, and his little Teresa soon became interested in them, especially those about the lives of the saints.

Even as a child she preferred to be alone and learned to repeat long prayers with great devotion. In her room she had a picture of Christ talking with the Woman at the Well. Remembering St. John's account (4:14-15) of this Samaritan Woman to whom Christ revealed, "Whosoever drinketh of the water that I shall give him shall never thirst," Teresa often spoke in prayer the words of the Samaritan Woman: "Give me this water and I thirst not."

Her mother, who had taught her to say her first prayers, died when Teresa was twelve, and Teresa experienced her first real loneliness. She turned from human loss to the infinite resources of God and derived great comfort from thinking of the Mother of Christ, feeling in her the maternal affection she needed.

In appearance she must have been a typical Castilian girl. She has been described as having fair, rosy skin, well-defined eyebrows, wavy brunette hair, dark eyes that laughed and danced when she smiled, pretty teeth, a small, symmetrical nose, and a vivacious manner.

In her account of her adolescent years, she confessed that at this time she read frivolous, rather than religious, books. She also began to enjoy fine clothes and perfumes and to engage in lengthy conversations with a worldly cousin. Later she was to look back upon these years as wasted ones and lament them.

Concerned that Teresa had begun to enjoy a gay life, her father placed her, when she was fifteen, in a convent to be educated. A consecrated nun instilled in her a new appreciation for virtue and she soon recovered her childlike fervor for the things of God.

Not long after entering the convent she became ill with a violent fever and was sent home to recuperate. During this period she read the Epistles of St. Jerome, which paid high tribute to Roman women who had led lives consecrated to Christ. After reading these letters, Teresa decided to give her life to the Church.

She talked with her younger brother Antonio about the impossibility of finding real or lasting happiness except in the service of God, and together they made their plans for the monastic life. In November 1533, on the same day that Antonio entered the Order of Saint Dominic, the twenty-year-old Teresa joined the Carmelites.

The sudden change in her habits of living and the food she ate brought her a profound sadness of mind and sickness of body. She became so ill that she began to doubt her ability to live the religious life. During this period of inner conflict, she began to study and practice what was called mental prayer, a form of communion with God which she was to spend almost twenty years trying to master. In the early period of her struggle, she came upon the words: "Enter into yourself." With these words she began her life as a mystic. Though she went to extremes at times, her mysticism gave her a religious height attainable in no other way.

Once again she became so seriously ill that she was sent to her sister's home to recuperate. The winter fields surrounding the house were enfolded in a silence and peace that restored Teresa. In the distance she could see pine forests silhouetted against mountains white with snow. Lifting up her heart toward the mountains, she found them bringing her nearer to God. Her thought and meditation here made her aware of how to take the initial steps in mental prayer. This practice she developed. It was to be the basis of her teaching all her life. Once she wrote:

> I used to try as much as I could to bring God present within me, and this was my manner of prayer. . . . Although we are always in His presence, it seems to me it is otherwise with those who practice mental prayer, for there they are, seeing that He observed them, while others can be in His presence for days at a time and never even remember that God sees them. . . . Mental prayer is nothing else, in my opinion, but friendly conversation, frequently conversing alone, with One Who we know loves us.

In the twenty years during which she sought to overcome self through mental prayer, she jotted down notes about it in her *Life*, still regarded as the best treatise on this type of prayer. Teresa explains that mental prayer is for anybody who loves God sincerely enough to try it. The beginner may not succeed at first, she says, but with persistence he is sure to be rewarded.

First the inner self must be stilled. Next comes concentration on spiritual meditation. The repose of the soul, as Teresa terms it, and perfect union of the soul with God are the final stages. Its four degrees may be described as tranquillity, union, ecstasy and, finally, spiritual marriage. She deals at great length with the four virtues of love, detachment, humility and obedience as the chief requirements for mental prayer.

For few saints was the ascent to God as hard as it was for Teresa. During the years spent in the study and practice of prayer, she suffered many emotional and physical conflicts. In her trials she showed an amiable sweetness and meekness of temper. Once she was so near death that her grave was dug. After she awoke from her long, deathlike trance, she reported that she had seen communities of women organized through her efforts and many souls blessed because she had found a way to God.

In later years, when she experienced extraordinary spiritual joy in communion with God, she had such mystical experiences as the elevation of her body. But like Mary, who "kept all these things, and pondered them in her heart" (Luke 2:19), Teresa also pondered her heavenly experiences in secret.

Those of her mystical experiences which were seen or felt by others soon became the subject of conversation. People who did not understand ridiculed and censured her, but she never bore them ill will. Some even reviled and shunned her, but the more she was rejected, the more earnestly she practiced the virtues of charity, patience and humility.

From her twenty-fourth to her forty-fourth year, she suffered much both in mind and body.

Finally her prayer life began to settle down solidly "like a building," she said, "that already had mortar in it." Even her ailments, such as headaches and nausea, which persisted until her last years, did not seem to matter to her any more.

When she was in her forties, she had an experience which changed her life. She went one day into the oratory, and on seeing a picture of Christ covered with wounds, she was suddenly moved. Casting herself down before the picture, she poured forth a flood of tears and earnestly besought Him to strengthen her. She felt all her scattered worldly interests leave her, and from that moment she made the sufferings of Christ the object of her prayer and His service the only goal of her life.

A new era now began for her in which she was not only aware of the presence of Christ but seemed to sense His service to humanity. She was ready now to do whatever He asked of her, most of all to serve the afflicted, the poor and needy, as He had done.

She had a burning desire to perform some great Christian work, and felt no labor would be too difficult for her, no martyrdom too hard. She longed to cry aloud, she says, and tell all God's children not to be content with small services, not to miss the tremendous things He would do for those who gave themselves entirely to Him. Her own words best express her feelings at this time:

> Thine am I, I was born for Thee,
> What wouldst Thou, Master, make of me?
>
> Give me death or give me life
> Give health or give me infirmity
> Give honor or give obloquy
> Give peace profound or daily strife,
> Weakness or strength add to my life;
> Yes, Lord, my answer still shall be
> What wilt Thou, Master, have of me?
>
> 'Tis Thou alone dost live in me.
> What wilt Thou I should do for thee?

At forty-six, Teresa entered upon the most active and useful period of her life. She became a leader of the Counter Reformation, which acknowledged many of the abuses the Protestants criticized, but attempted to bring about regeneration and reorganization within the Church itself. She wrote:

When I see the great necessities of the Church, I am so afflicted by them that it seems to me a thing of mockery to be troubled by anything else, and so I do nothing but commend them to God; for I see that one person wholly perfect, with true fervor of love for God, will be worth more than many who are lukewarm.

Her special service to the Church was the expansion and reform of the Order of the Carmelites which, according to tradition, had originated on Mount Carmel in Palestine. Her objective was to restore the austerity and the contemplative life practiced by the first Carmelites. She imposed an even stricter rule than that originally adopted. Her reformed Order, known as Barefoot Carmelites, spread over Europe, to Spanish America and to the East, especially India and Persia. She established sixteen nunneries of her Order and fourteen convents of Carmelite Friars. Prayers, silence, strict retirement and penance were the chief requirements she laid upon her monks and nuns. She followed Christ's example in working among the poor and needy. Complete poverty was an essential part of her rule.

In 1561 her sister and brother-in-law assisted her in planning and building her first home for Barefoot nuns. The next year she opened her first convent for Carmelites in Ávila. But the town rose up against Teresa, because in her new convent she had set aside the lax discipline then common among religious orders. She was not afraid of opposition, for she was confident of the rightness of her cause. She and her nuns now sought to surpass each other in humility, penance and affection for God. Their whole lives were built around prayer.

Primitive simplicity, Teresa determined, would govern their manner of life. In the convents in which she had spent her young womanhood, she had seen too much laxity and too many nuns who were materialistic. She went back to the simplicity of the early days of the Order. Her nuns' habits were of coarse brown serge, their veils had no pleats or folds, they wore their hair short, slept on straw, ate no meat and were strictly confined to their cloister. Though they became known as the Barefoot Carmelites, they were not entirely barefoot, for they wore sandals of rope. Shoes were regarded as a sign of luxury (Luke 15:22). They took literally Jesus' charge (Mark 6:8, 9) to His disciples to take "no scrip, no bread, no money" and to "be shod with sandals."

Teresa thought nothing of moving into a bare house where there were not even beds, for she heard Christ say: "Enter as you can. . . . How often I slept on the ground."

She herself set an example of austerity. Her own tiny room contained no furniture. She had no cover except a piece of sackcloth. Yet in this cheerless atmosphere she wrote at least two of her masterpieces and carried on a voluminous correspondence.

Even when her Order expanded, simplicity continued to be the rule. She still preferred small buildings, small chapels, small oratories. She never neglected necessary Christian work with the excuse that it involved too much expense. If the work needed to be done, she began it inexpensively.

In her first convent of the Barefoot Carmelites, Teresa spent the five happiest years of her life. When the general of the Carmelite Order visited Ávila, he was so much impressed with what she had accomplished that he authorized her to found other houses. Thus encouraged, and in her fifty-second year, she began her larger work.

She possessed a remarkable talent for organization and had the rare gift of being able to lead both men and women, drawing admiration from prominent men of the Church for her ability as well as her spirituality. She had a sensitive, observant mind and an adventurous spirit.

Her vigorous personality comes through in statements like these: "Rest, indeed! I need no rest; what I need is crosses"; "If Thou wilt [prove me] by means of trials, give me strength and let them come"; "Strive like strong men until you die in the attempt, for you are here for nothing else than to strive."

Though she walked with her head toward the stars, her feet were on the ground. For with all her sanctity, she possessed keen business ability. She understood human nature and could give shrewd practical directions.

She founded convents at Medina, Toledo, Valladolid and other places. Afterward she established a monastery at a poor village called Durvelo, and a second one at Pastrana. The first monk at Durvelo was St. John of the Cross, who became a great mystic, a devoted friend to Teresa, and her chief assistant in the reform of Carmelite monasteries.

In the next fifteen years she traveled throughout central Spain, going as far south as Madrid and Seville, everywhere founding convents and monasteries. Her indomitable spirit rose above the attacks of others. She suffered persecution and slander, but she was so oblivious of self that what the world said about her did not trouble her.

Her life during this period suggests Paul's words: "We are troubled on every side, yet not distressed; we are perplexed, but not in despair; persecuted, but not forsaken; cast down, but not destroyed" (II Cor. 4:8, 9). Through all of her tribulations, Teresa's spirit was daily renewed.

She often traveled over terrible roads in a rude little cart drawn by a donkey, or sometimes on muleback; she went through flood and snow, careless of icy winds or scorching suns. Once, when she became ill, the only room available was one previously used for pigs; on another night she camped in the open field.

She preferred to have the nuns who accompanied her travel in coaches so that they might pray in seclusion. They had a little bell which they rang at the proper time for silence and prayer, even as their coaches jolted and creaked with every movement of the mules.

Teresa overcame obstacles of all sorts. When she went to establish a convent in one old house, she found it falling apart. The porch was piled with refuse, the walls were crumbling, the floors were filthy, and the roof had so many holes that the stars shone through at night. But she and her nuns cleaned it thoroughly and set up an altar on the porch. They shut out the street and concealed the unsightly walls with blue damask. They had no nails with which to hang the cloth, but Teresa found nails in a decayed door in a stable. Finally a little bell was hung in the corridor, and Teresa knew that Christ had one more resting place, however humble, in an unfriendly world. This episode was typical of her pioneering spirit of determination.

In the digging of a well, she exhibited faith. Others declared it would be labor wasted but she said: "His Majesty can not fail us when we need the water." Finally from the newly dug well the water came forth in a copious stream, cold and clear.

In dealing with her nuns, she gave wise counsel, even in seemingly unimportant matters. She told them that it was foolish to complain of trifling ailments. Real illness was different. Women, she said, could pamper themselves too much. "As soon as we begin, daughters, to conquer this little carcass, it will not bother us so much. . . . Try not to fear death and loss of health. Leave all to God, and let come what may come."

Many of her words to her spiritual daughters echo the New Testament:

Let those who are now alive, who have seen these things with their own eyes, consider God's graciousness to us and the troubles and disquiet from which He has delivered us; and let those who are to come after us, who will find everything easy, for the love of our Lord, never allow any observance tending to perfection to fall into disuse. Let them never give men occasion to say of them what is said of some other order, "Their beginning was praiseworthy." We are beginning now —let us go on from good to better. Let us never happen to have them say of us, "This is nothing—these are extremes." . . . Be brave and dare with a holy boldness.

Her five major books and several smaller ones place her among the great Christian writers. Her autobiography is an important document of the Christian faith and in its frankness has been compared to the *Confessions* of St. Augustine. As a study of a Christian's ascent from conversion to death, it has been likened to Bunyan's *Pilgrim's Progress.*

Not since the records of Paul, says her recent biographer William Thomas Walsh, has a more remarkable record been written than Teresa's *The Interior Castle,* also called *The Mansions.* She is also author of *The Way of Perfection* which, like *The Interior Castle,* describes the progress of the soul toward perfect union with God.

Her *Book of Foundations* describes the founding of Carmelite convents and monasteries, and forms a supplement to her autobiography. Her fifth book is *Meditations on the Songs.* She also wrote a large number of letters and various treatises on religion, scribbled at breakneck speed. She never rewrote or reread what she wrote, but her personality communicates itself with great immediacy and urgency. The Anglican scholar, E. Allison Peers, has made the most recent English translation of her writings, *Complete Works of St. Teresa,* in three volumes, based upon the critical edition of the saint's work by the Spanish Carmelite P. Silveria de S. Teresa.

In her writing she reveals her belief that God had summoned her to greatness. "God held me by the hand," she said at one time, and at another, "I could hear His slightest whisper." In all things she tried to please God and to be obedient to Him, though she never failed to realize that she fell far short of perfection. She had such reverence for God that she often acknowledged His presence with the spoken words: "Your Majesty." She had heard Him say to her in a voice of great love: "Thou shalt now be mine, and I am thine." Teresa's deep knowledge of God's goodness and power enabled her, during the later years of her life, to let Him use her in whatever way He directed.

She never forgot to ascribe every good thing to God and to thank Him for all His works. In one of her many illnesses, she crawled on her hands and knees to the altar to offer praise to God.

She seemed always to be conscious of the grandeur and majesty of God and dreamed of new worlds to conquer and great deeds to be done for Him. But she soon learned that God is not so much concerned with the greatness of one's work as the love with which it is done. As she tried to live more fully in His presence, her life seemed to flow from God.

She realized such close spiritual companionship with Christ that she called herself Teresa of Jesus, a name more often used for her than her own family name, Teresa de Cepeda. Early in her life she had begun to think of Christ as her spiritual partner and had learned how to find union with Him. What Teresa termed her spiritual marriage with Christ occurred when she was fifty-seven. At this time she had reached such spiritual perfection, through years of communion with Him, that she wondered whether there could be any further advance in this world. But she found that there was.

Like Christ, she had been more or less silent for a long period of time, and then, after her years of preparation through prayer, she was able to help others find Him, and He came close to her in her love for humanity. Like Him, she was willing to surround herself with poor people, several of whom, like St. John of the Cross, rose to spiritual eminence.

Teresa possessed many of the qualities of true greatness. She had humility without servility. When she visited a palace she requested the most humble quarters for herself. She had courage to a remarkable degree, even the courage to appear in her patched garments before King Phillip II of Spain when she needed his counsel and help.

At sixty-four she suffered a heart attack, but continued to work. She went to Malagon, where she was opening a new house. Finding the work delayed, she gave orders vigorously like a sea captain and set herself to sweeping up debris. This was typical of her. Later she had another heart attack, but she still continued her work, founding a new house at Villaneuva de la Jara. She left there apparently in good health. As her cart rumbled through the frozen countryside, crowds gathered to see this woman who had risen to a high place but still chose to wear a patched, coarse homespun habit, a linen toque with plain veil, without folds or pleats. Her simplicity, sincerity, quiet intensity of purpose, humility and spiritual power gave radiance to her countenance.

As she journeyed on to Ávila, she and her nuns barely escaped being dumped into mud and thrown over a precipice. Later, when she encountered terrible floods on her way to Valladolid, she heard a voice say: "Indeed you can go, and do not be afraid, for I shall be with you." Unafraid, she continued on her way.

Though sick of body and heart, she continued working a little longer. When a wound opened in her throat, she carried on her business from a couch screened by a curtain. Finally, in 1582, as she lay dying at Alba, she was asked if she wished to be buried in her own convent at Avila, her birthplace. She whispered to the priest: "Must you ask that, my father? Is there anything I can call my own? Will they not give me a little earth here?"

After her death, these lines which she had written on a slip of paper were found in her Breviary:

> Be not perplexed,
> Be not afraid,
> Everything passes,
> God does not change.
> Patience wins all things.
> He who has God lacks nothing;
> God alone suffices.

CHAPTER 3

Women of a Time of Awakening

ANNE HUTCHINSON—THE FIRST WOMAN
PREACHER OF NEW ENGLAND

(1591-1643)

♦ ♦ ♦

She arrived in the Massachusetts Bay Colony in 1634. She was the mother of sixteen. Persecuted by the Puritans because she criticized the clergy, she was banished to Rhode Island. Her persecutors followed her there. At her husband's death she sought refuge in wild Indian country of New Amsterdam, where she, six of her family, and two members of her household met death at the hands of Indians.

A WOMAN MISUNDERSTOOD, MISJUDGED AND MISTREATED

ANNE MARBURY HUTCHINSON, the mother of sixteen children, was the first American woman to fight for religious liberty even though it led to her imprisonment and banishment. The first to hold religious discussions for women in her home, she is the inspiration behind the women's missionary society in America.

On August 18, 1634, she left England with her husband William Hutchinson, and her children, in search of religious liberty. During her nine-year residence in America, until her death in 1643, she suffered intolerance and religious persecution. She established three homes. The first was in Boston, but she was forced to move to a second at Portsmouth, Rhode Island, and a third near what is now Pelham, New York. Her banishment to this third wilderness, the Dutch settlement of Vredeland, resulted in her death and that of eight other members of her household in an Indian massacre.

Anne Hutchinson grew up in England and worshiped in the Established Church. Her father was a minister who received his license to preach soon after his graduation from Christ College, Cambridge. He was an independent thinker and a man who would scorn to withhold his views for the sake of expediency. Even during Anne's childhood he was haled before the ecclesiastical court, condemned for his unorthodox preaching, and cast into prison. Upon his release he was forbidden to revisit his former parish at Northampton, England, but he still refused to bridle his tongue and he was tried and convicted again. This time he was unfrocked.

As a girl Anne was caught up in the religious resurgence that followed a plague in 1603 when the people turned to the Church for consolation. She had inherited her father's deep sincerity along with his determination to follow only the spiritual path that was revealed to him. She was destined to suffer for this integrity, but she was to carve for herself a unique place in history as a prophetess, spiritual healer and unwavering and dauntless fighter for religious freedom.

In 1612 in the ancient St. Mary Woolchurch in London, Anne married William Hutchinson, a dealer in textile fabrics. They went to live in her husband's town of Alford, Lincolnshire County, England, which remained her home for the next twenty-one years. During this time she gave birth to fourteen of her children, only one of whom died in infancy, an unusual record for those times.

Long before she arrived in America, Anne broke with the Established Church. She did not confine herself to one minister but went about listening to many, always searching for the truth. Later she declared: "The Lord did discover to me all sorts of ministers and how they taught." At the same time, she studied avidly the Authorized King James Version of the Bible, published just a few months before her marriage.

She was profoundly influenced by discussions on Antinomianism, which opposed legal rules in favor of obedience to the Spirit, a doctrine preached in parts of Germany during the Reformation. Her group declared that "just because you observe the letter of the law is not proof that you are good in your heart."

Anne Hutchinson was a spiritual-minded believer, and her own blameless life testified to her sincerity of purpose. Her spiritual exaltation generated enthusiasm, and many looked upon her with admiration despite official disapproval.

She was a devoted follower of John Cotton, former vicar of St. Botolph's Church in Boston, Lincolnshire, England. She sought his counsel many times, and he respected her. Anne thought of Cotton as a faithful, sincere friend, and she and her entire family expected to sail to America with him in 1633. When she found she was with child, she decided to wait until the next summer, but her son Edward made the voyage with Cotton. Because of these close family relationships, Anne was deeply shocked and hurt when Cotton later turned against her and joined her Massachusetts accusers.

Unable to find religious tolerance in England, Anne felt confident it must exist in the New World, so she migrated to America with her husband. Her fifteenth child, born in the Massachusetts Bay Colony in March of 1636, was given the Biblical name of Zuriel (Num. 3:35) meaning "My work is God," indicative of his mother's love of the Bible.

Anne became influential in Boston, then a farming town with a population of about one thousand, and she opened her home to large classes of women. It is estimated that as many as eighty overflowed to the doorsteps of her farmhouse at the corner of Washington and School Streets, opposite the home of John Winthrop, colonial governor.

Although no description has been left of her home, one may assume it was comfortable, for both she and her husband had inherited legacies. No doubt her house had ample bedrooms to accommodate her many children. Downstairs were the parlor and a kitchen, which also served as a family living room. These rooms were probably furnished with handsome pieces she had brought from England. Here friends and neighbors gathered for her religious discussions.

Others beat a pathway to her door, and she brought physical as well as spiritual healing to many, especially sick babies. The women, faced with tribulations in the New World, found in Anne Hutchinson calm assurance. "The Spirit within," she told them, "controls the right actions of man. He who has God's grace in his heart cannot go astray."

It was common to hear her admirers remark: "Come along with me. I'll take you to a woman that preaches better Gospel than any of your black coats that have been at the university, a woman of another kind of spirit who has had many revelations of things to come."

Her growing leadership among Boston women, however, created jealousy and animosity. Some considered it disturbing to have women gathering for an exchange of religious views. This Hutchinson woman, they said, who took part in theological discussions and voiced her protests quite freely, was a contributing cause to the spread of dangerous doctrine.

She called some of the clergy "a company of legal professors, who lie poring over the law which Christ hath abolished." In December of 1636, a group of these disgruntled ministers called at her house. Among them was her English minister John Cotton, but he let the others do the talking. She held her ground with them, but her frankness in speaking out led her into serious trouble.

Her harshest enemies compared her with "that woman Jezebel, which calleth herself a prophetess, to teach and to seduce my servants" (Rev. 2:20). Her friends, however, thought of her as a Priscilla, who "expounded unto Apollos the way of God more perfectly" (Acts 18:26).

Certainly she was trying to expound the way of God more perfectly to her classes. These women, among whom she had her largest following, could not come to her defense, for they had no public vote, and Paul's counsel (I Cor. 14:34, 35) against women speaking out in the churches was narrowly interpreted and harshly applied. The ministers' explanation of the verses was a contradiction of Christ's teaching that men and women are equal before God. Anne asserted that Paul was speaking not to all women in churches but to the young women at Corinth who had worshiped in pagan temples and who had not gained sufficient experience to assume church leadership.

When Anne voiced further protests against the literalism and bigotry of the Massachusetts Puritans and the intolerance of the clergy, she added fuel to their resentment and her enemies began to unite against her in earnest. Here was a "mere woman" who believed in the direct control and guidance of the Spirit within. They justified their condemnation by saying she might lead others to consider themselves superior to laws, both moral and civil.

A synod of ministers was called at Newton, Cambridge, to discuss Anne Hutchinson's case. She was tried there in a gloomy church during the cold days of November 1637.

This lonely woman of forty-six walked valiantly down the aisle in her blue Puritan frock with white fichu and cuffs and her blue bonnet with its wide band of white. Slight in build, unusually attractive and magnetic, she calmly took her place on the stand. Intelligent, refined and keen of wit, she made an effective witness as she stood before her judges to defend the fundamental right of free worship.

Her family did not go with her to her trial. Her husband, deputy to the General Court of Massachusetts from May 1635 to September 1636, and judge of the district court, no doubt trusted in her own ability. Already disgusted with conditions in the colony, she may have induced him to stay at home. He could have had no idea of the dangers his wife faced.

During the proceedings Anne asked: "Why should I be condemned? I conceive there is a clear rule in Titus that elder women should instruct the younger [Titus 2:3, 4, 5]. When I was in old England," she continued,

"I was much troubled at the constitution of the churches there, so far troubled indeed, that I would like to have turned separatist. . . . But the Lord revealed Himself to me that I must come to New England, yet I must not fear or be discouraged. And the Lord said 'I will not make a full end of thee.' " In these words she disclosed the fact that she had received revelations from the Lord.

Her inquisitor demanded: "How did you know that it was God that did reveal these things to you and not Satan?"

She hastened to reply: "How did Abraham know that it was God that bid him offer his son? . . . I, too, knew by the voice of His own spirit to my soul."

She was placing herself too high, her enemies thought, and the court condemned her. Governor Winthrop, who made the announcement, declared: "You are now banished from out our jurisdiction as being a woman not fit for our society."

Anne persisted: "I desire to know wherefore I am banished."

The governor answered: "Say no more—the court knows wherefore, and is satisfied."

Quoting to them the sixth chapter of Daniel, she reminded her accusers: "Then said these men, we shall not find any occasion against this Daniel except we find it against him concerning the law of God." Pointing to her enemies, she declared: "It was revealed to me that they should plot against me, but the Lord bid me not fear. . . . Take heed what you go about to do unto me, for I am in the hands of the eternal Jehovah, my Saviour. The bounds of my habitation are cast in Heaven. . . . Take heed how you proceed against me, for I know that for this you go about to do to me God will ruin you and your posterity and this whole state."

This statement angered her accusers. She was declared guilty of "keeping two public lectures every week in her house and for reproaching most of the ministers, excepting Mr. Cotton, for not preaching a covenant of free grace."

Her penalty was four months' imprisonment, but since the colony did not yet have a prison, she was committed to the home of a relative of one of the ministers who had accused her. Her husband and other disillusioned residents made plans to leave Massachusetts Bay, rejoicing that they could depart from a colony so narrow in its views.

In March 1638 she was asked to appear in her own First Church of Boston, on the charge of holding unorthodox opinions. Settlers from far and near, even Governor Winthrop, crowded into the little church to watch the proceedings. But Anne's main supporters, the women she had taught, were not there, for some were already banished, some had left in disgust, others were afraid to appear. Accompanied by her son Richard and her son-in-law Thomas Savage, she proceeded down the church aisle, a picture of womanly dignity.

"Sister Hutchinson," spoke the presiding elder in reading the admonishment, "here are divers opinions laid to your charge and I must request you in the name of the church to declare whether you hold them or renounce them as they are read to you."

After he had read the long list of her alleged heresies, she argued the points, maintaining that the Bible supported her views. As more texts were quoted she became irritated and made some biting retorts which her accusers immediately characterized as too "forward," especially since she was a woman speaking to church elders.

As the evening wore on and only a fourth of the opinions had been covered, one of the elders proposed that she be admonished on the subjects so far discussed, but this required a unanimous vote.

Her pastor John Wilson spoke out boldly against her to the assembly. A censure of a member was supposed to have the unanimous support of the church. But since her admonishment was opposed by her faithful son and son-in-law, one of the elders proposed that they be eliminated from the right to vote. John Cotton rebuked them in stinging language.

Anne's son Richard became so disillusioned with the new colony that he soon sailed to England, never to return, and her son-in-law left Massachusetts Bay for Rhode Island. She, however, continued to fight her battle. When the time for the third examination came, her husband and other members of her family had already gone to Rhode Island to set up a new home to which she could turn when her trial had ended.

During her final day in the Boston church, Pastor Wilson, misinterpreting a statement she had made, sharply rebuked her: "You say you can commit no sin."

"If my heart is right I cannot sin," she calmly answered.

"Is your heart right?" he asked sneeringly.

"I am trying to make it so," gently answered Anne Hutchinson.

When a prepared confession was produced, she was directed to read it aloud. She did so in a low voice and with her head bowed. But her confession contained little more than the two facts that she had misinterpreted the Bible and had made some unkind remarks about the clergy. For these faults she asked the prayers of those assembled, admitting that "the root of all was the height and pride of my spirit."

To this one of her accusers shouted at her: "You have stepped out of your place. You have been rather a husband than a wife, a preacher than a hearer, and a magistrate than a subject." Another cried out at her: "You set yourself in the room of God above them, that you might be extolled and admired and followed after. Your iniquity hath found you out."

The elders called again for her excommunication. Her English vicar, John Cotton, transferred the task of pronouncement to Pastor Wilson. "In the name of the Lord Jesus Christ, and in the name of the church, I do cast you out," he said sternly. "I do deliver you up to Satan. I do account you from this time forth to be a Heathen and a Publican and so to be held of all the brethren and sistern. . . . I command you in the name of Christ Jesus and of this church as a Leper to withdraw yourself out of this congregation."

As she left the church, cultivated, charitable, spiritually sensitive Anne Hutchinson turned and said: "The Lord judgeth not as man judgeth. Better to be cast out of the church than to deny Christ."

Two days after being cast out of the First Church of Boston, Anne Hutchinson was directed by Governor Winthrop "to be gone within a week from Massachusetts Bay." As she left to join her husband and children in Rhode Island, she remembered God's promise: "Fear not, for I am with thee. . . ."

With child before the trial began, and now with that child growing heavier within her, she pressed on to the frontier in Rhode Island. Her last child, the sixteenth, was born on Aquidneck, not many miles from Providence, where Roger Williams was settled. The trials and anxieties of the months before had affected her health, and her baby was stillborn.

Soon she renewed her lectures and her healing ministrations, but her troubles were not over. Her Massachusetts Bay persecutors sent a delegation to Rhode Island to make inquiries and to warn the church against Anne Hutchinson. They interviewed her husband, chief magistrate of Rhode Island, and tried to influence him against his own wife, but he retorted: "I am more nearly tied to my wife than to the church. . . . She is a dear saint and a servant of God."

When Anne's Boston enemies asked permission to address her church at Portsmouth, they were refused. When they made a personal call at the Hutchinson home, saying they came from the Lord and the church, she asked: "Which Lord do you mean? There are lords many, and gods many, but I acknowledge but one Lord. . . . Your church is not the church of Christ."

Her opponents even threatened the validity of the titles of the Hutchinson property in Rhode Island and imprisoned her son Francis, who had remained a member of the Boston church. They also threatened to take her back to Boston, which would have meant prison or the lash. Her sister Katherine Scott, described as a "grave, sober and ancient woman" and the mother of many children, was later subjected to indignity by the exposure of her person in public and cruel punishment by the lash.

Anne Hutchinson became so terrorized that her family talked of leaving Rhode Island and going farther into the wilderness. As she was planning to leave, she lost her husband, her devoted companion of thirty years. His death prompted her to make an even hastier departure from Rhode Island, which had been her home for four years.

She chose the distant territory of New Amsterdam, where she would be under the protection of the Dutch, and where her persecutors from Massachusetts Bay could oppress her no longer. There were two ways of reaching this new frontier. One was to travel one hundred and thirty miles over an inland route, the other was to go by water in a crude craft. She chose the latter and in the late summer of 1642, she and her family landed at Flushing, Long Island, and chose a homesite at Vredeland near the present Pelham, New York.

This was an area where the Indians had conspired to destroy all white settlers, but Anne assumed that if her family treated the Indians well, they would be as friendly as those in the Rhode Island area. She remembered again: "The Lord bid me not fear."

On a summer evening, a year after her arrival, the Indians entered her home and killed her, six younger members of her family and two members of the household. These included her daughter Anne, about eighteen, and Anne's husband, William Collins, another daughter Katherine, fifteen, Mary, sixteen, a son Francis, about twenty-one, and another son William, twelve, as well as a house servant and farm hand.

The blackened ruin of Anne Hutchinson's home was her tomb, but her seed was not destroyed. It was all as God had said to her: "I will not make a full end of thee." Her nine-year-old Susanna, who had been captured by the Indians in the raid, remained unharmed and was released to her own people fourteen years later. Anne's son Richard was safe in England. Her son Edward had remained in the Boston home. Her daughter Bridget was married to John Sanford, who became president of Rhode Island in 1653. Her grandson Peleg Sanford led the colony of Rhode Island from 1680 to 1683.

Anne's granddaughter Susanna, the child of her son Edward, married Nathaniel Coddington, son of William Coddington, one of the founders of the colony of Rhode Island and at various times its governor. Her great-great-grandson Thomas Hutchinson was the last royal deputy-governor of Massachusetts and the author of a history of the colony. Her faithful son-in-law Thomas Savage was later commander in chief of the Massachusetts forces in King Philip's War.

In 1904, two hundred and sixty-six years after the First Church of Boston had excommunicated Anne Hutchinson for heresy, a tablet was affixed to the building, bearing the following inscription:

This tablet is placed here in honor of Anne Hutchinson, born in Lincolnshire, England, about 1592; received into membership of this church 1634; banished from Massachusetts by decree of Court 1637; killed by the Indians at Pelham, New York 1643; a breeder of heresies, of ready wit and bold spirit. She was a persuasive advocate of the right of Independent Judgment.

The principles of civil liberty and religious freedom, for which Anne Hutchinson pioneered, were written into the Constitution of the United States. The spirit of Anne Hutchinson, the first woman preacher and the first fearless defender of religious freedom in New England, survived her persecution and death.

MARGARET FELL FOX—
WIFE OF GEORGE FOX
(1614-1702)

✦ ✦ ✦

She suffered persecution for her religious beliefs. Her home, Swarthmoor Hall, was a focal point for the early work of the Quakers. She guided, befriended and inspired them during the first half-century of their history and helped them to create a closer Christian fellowship.

SHE HELPED OTHERS TO FIND GOD WITHIN THE SOUL

MARGARET FELL FOX was almost as important in the early years of the Quaker movement as its founder George Fox. She has been described as a woman with a "presence refreshing to the righteous, a voice pleasing and a prayer powerful." Will Caton, one of the early Quakers, called her "a precious jewel in the hands of the Lord." Thomas Salthouse, another early Quaker, writing Margaret for her prayers and advice when persecution fell upon Friends, said to her: "Ye are filled with a spirit of wisdom, meekness, sincerity and supplication."

An able, educated woman for her time, she brought enthusiasm and stability to the rapidly growing movement. Because she possessed a pioneering spirit, boundless energy, kindness, courage and strength, and because she inspired love in all who came into her presence, she grew influential in the Quaker movement. She preached, taught, wrote, organized women's meetings and dispensed hospitality. Cultivated, wise and strikingly handsome, she also had the poise to go before kings and the charm to obtain a hearing for her cause.

Unlike later Quakers, she loved color and chose to wear colors herself. When Friends turned to uniform blacks and browns, she reminded them that Jesus bade them consider the lilies, "how they grow in more royalty than Solomon." She reminded them too of the changing colors of the hills. "Why then must we all be in one dress and one color?" she asked. "This is silly, poor Gospel. It is more fit for us to be covered with God's Eternal Spirit and clothed with His Eternal Light, which leads us and guides us into righteousness and to live righteously and justly and holily in this present evil world."

Margaret Fell Fox taught and preached, dressed in her tight-waisted, full-skirted frocks of mellow colors, often accented with a wide white collar. But most of those to whom she ministered were not so conscious of the colors she wore as of the radiance in her face created by the Inner Light, which Friends defined as the presence of God within the soul. It was His Light shining in her which led others and guided them to live righteously and justly.

Margaret was married to Judge Thomas Fell when she was seventeen, and at this young age she became mistress of his large estate, Swarthmoor Hall, situated in Lancaster County, England, northwest of the wide sands of Morecambe Bay. They enjoyed a happy married life for twenty-six years until his death in 1658.

Judge Fell was a member of the Long Parliament and vice-chancellor of Lancaster, the duchy in northern England where he and Margaret lived. As a lawyer, he was honored for his justice, wisdom, moderation and mercy. Though he did not join the Quakers, as did his wife, he offered them the hospitality of his home, and it became for them a place of refuge and renewal, both physical and spiritual. George Fox later said of Judge Fell that "he was a mighty service for Truth." Judge Fell's prominence in Parliament and the Court gave Margaret an influence she never hesitated to use to help persecuted Quakers.

Like her husband, Margaret was a member of the English nobility. She was born in 1614 at Marsh Grange in Lancashire. Her father John Askew left a considerable estate. There is a tradition that she was a great-granddaughter of Anne Askew, who was tortured for her religious beliefs and finally burned at the stake in 1546 by order of Henry VIII.

Margaret and Judge Fell had seven daughters—Margaret, Bridget, Isabel, Sarah, Mary, Susannah and Rachel—and a son George. Her daughters, women of achievement and character, were sympathetic with their mother's Quaker beliefs. Rachel was her mother's close companion throughout her long service to the Quakers, and Sarah also rose to greatness in the movement.

George Fox, at that time a wandering preacher of twenty-eight, came to the Fell home for the first time in 1652. A vital message flowed from his central theme of a true, pure life in the light of the Spirit of God. He wanted men and women to give up all outward forms and come face to face with the Spirit of God, and worship Him in Spirit and Truth. He already had given up using complimentary titles, keeping to the plain "thee" and "thou," "for surely," he said, "the way men address God should be enough to them to address one another."

Margaret and her entire household were impressed with this tall, burly man of great strength, dressed in a rough suit of leather which he had made himself and which he wore over clean white linens. She caught the spirit of George Fox's work on his first visit. Later she said of young Fox: "He opened for us a book that we had never read in, nor indeed had ever heard that it was our duty to read in. . . . And he turned our minds toward the light of Christ as they had never been turned before."

At this time she was the mother of seven children, yet she used to travel long distances to hear "the best ministers" and kept open house for many of them. But their teaching had failed to satisfy her. Fox's unconventional ministry roused her hopes and stirred her imagination and she resolved to join his movement.

It was no light sacrifice, however, for a woman of Margaret Fell's position in the county to throw in her lot with the unpopular Quakers. It meant she must risk the loss of comfort, riches and the esteem of her neighbors. Her family could not hope to escape the fate of the humbler Friends. But she was not seeking escape into an easy way of life. She was seeking God.

At once she assumed a position of responsibility and authority in the Quaker movement, and her power for organization showed itself very early in the establishment of a Fund for the Service of Truth. This made it possible for poor traveling preachers to continue their labors. It relieved their sufferings in prison, provided them with ready cash, clothes and books, and paid their passage to distant countries. Contributions were made to Margaret Fell, who herself was the most generous giver to the Fund.

She also formed an Association of Friends who met together to seek the Inner Light, believing that His Spirit was always with them, and that, if anything was to be said, He would put it into their hearts to say it. Margaret complied wtih George Fox's idea that there be only an informal society. In this early period he had no desire to found a new Church. The Church, he said, was the whole body of Christ's faithful people everywhere. His people simply called themselves Friends, who met together to wait upon the Lord. For almost half a century the Fell home continued to be a meeting place for Friends and neighbors who, like other Fox followers, "trembled at the word of the Lord," thus becoming known as "Quakers."

Among the early Quakers who frequently visited the Fell home was William Penn, founder of Pennsylvania. His father, Admiral Sir William Penn, was a personal friend of King James II and one of the king's instructors in naval affairs. Though born to wealth and position, the younger Penn had shown that he preferred the comradeship of the persecuted to the company of the titled. The Penns and Fells brought rank, education and means to the new Quaker movement, which had begun among humble people.

For her Quaker beliefs, Margaret was willing to do as Christ bade: "Take my yoke upon you, and learn of me" (Matt. 2:29). She was sent to prison three times, always for trifling causes.

Her first arrest, which occurred some years after the death of Judge Fell, was for holding open Quaker meetings in her home. She would not call secret assemblies as other Nonconformists were doing.

When authorities forbade her to hold Quaker meetings at her own home, where they had met for many years, she had the courage to say: "While it pleases the Lord to let me have a house, I would endeavor to worship Him in it." She declared that her friends and neighbors were meeting there in obedience to Christ's command that God be worshiped in Spirit and in Truth, and that those who gathered in her house were "peaceable, quiet and a Godly, honest people."

"What law have I broken," she asked, "for worshiping God in my own house?"

In her own *Works,* mostly written while in prison, she tells of her trial. She refused to lay her hand on the Bible, as authorities commanded her to do, and she said: "I never laid my hand on the Book to swear in all my life." She reminded her persecutors that Christ had commanded His followers not to swear any oath.

When the judge warned Margaret Fell that breaking the common law might cost her her life, she courageously took her stand: "I must offer and tender my life, and all, for my testimony, if it be required of me."

Defending herself and showing great ability and considerable knowledge of the law, she denied the Crown's right to prosecute her, as she was no transgressor. "There is no law against the innocent and righteous," she declared. "You have work enough besides, if you do not meddle with the innocent, and them that fear the Lord." Accepting her persecution nobly, she said: "What I suffer is for the Lord's sake, and I am freely given up to His will, and pleasure, what He permits and suffers to be done unto me, in which doing I shall rest content whether it be mercy or cruelty."

The judge declared her outside the king's protection, an outlaw in fact, and made her forfeit all of her estate, real and personal, to the Crown. He also directed that she be imprisoned for four years.

Some years later Margaret wrote: "The great God of Heaven and Earth supported my spirit under this severe sentence." She soon realized, as she afterward recorded: "Although I am out of the king's protection, yet I am not out of the protection of the Almighty God."

With her Bible at her side, she never felt alone in prison. In fact, her long months there gave her time to pore over it and to understand even better the Inner Light which can penetrate the dark, damp walls of a jail.

Though Margaret Fell had many anxieties during this confinement, her spirit was equal to the demands made upon her. Her first year in prison was a time of the dreaded plague, and Friends died by the hundreds. One of her daughters, ill with the disease, was among the few who recovered. The Great Fire of London consumed a large part of the city at that time. Margaret often feared for her daughters as they traveled to visit her, for they had to cross Morecambe Bay, with its sands which were often treacherous in winter because of storm or sudden mist or rain, and dangerous in summer because of the shifting river channels and quicksand. She was concerned about the young, unmarried daughter she had left at home, and she longed to see her recently born grandchildren.

Margaret's greatest anxiety, however, was for her son. He was a law student in London and she worried about his companions. He had no sympathy with his mother's religious beliefs, and even co-operated with her enemies. While she was helpless in prison, her errant son tried to confiscate all the Fell property, even that belonging to his sisters, and also the property his mother had inherited from her father. Her son did not leave London, however, to take possession of Swarthmoor Hall, and his sisters stayed on during their mother's imprisonment and were there to greet her on her return.

Coming out of the cold, dreary walls of prison into the light of her own home in June, the loveliest month in the year, Margaret Fell saw God in all His goodness. Because she had suffered in a jail cell, where storm and wind and rain broke through, she could appreciate all the more the oak-paneled rooms of the home she had known so long and the warm sun playing on orchards and gardens.

Once more she fed the spiritually hungry, and also presided at the long dining table, serving her guests tasty dishes from her own recipes. Once again Friends came to enjoy Swarthmoor Hall's spacious bedrooms with their carved walnut four-poster beds and warm feather mattresses. Margaret heard again the gentle murmur of the brook through Swarthmoor's open windows.

She never indulged herself for long in physical comforts. Soon she set out to visit Quakers in jails, cheering them with her presence and comforting them in the sufferings she knew only too well. She visited remote farms and villages to preach about the Inner Light. Usually she traveled on horseback, accompanied by one or more of her daughters and several servants.

In 1669, about a year after Margaret Fell was released from prison, George Fox wrote in his journal: "I have seen from the Lord a considerable time before, that I should take Margaret Fell to be my wife." In a public meeting of Friends, Margaret Fell became the wife of George Fox, who now had a following of about one hundred thousand Quakers scattered over the British Isles. Ninety-four Friends signed their marriage certificate and William Penn sent his words of approval.

"Both Margaret and George Fox regarded their marriage as pre-eminently spiritual. It culminated years of knowledge of each other, close spiritual and mental co-operation in the work of the Church," says Isabel Ross, a descendant of Margaret Fell and author of *Margaret Fell, Mother of Quakerism.*

During their twenty-two years of marriage, Margaret and George Fox's work kept them apart for intervals that were longer than their periods together. His strong frame was already weakened by imprisonment in Nottingham (1649), Derby (1650-1651), Carlisle (1653), Laundeston (1656), Lancaster and Scarbourough (1664-1666), sometimes under almost unbearable conditions.

After their marriage he gave even more of his time to building up the Quaker community and caring for the poor. He made provisions for the accurate registration of births, deaths and marriages. Margaret became his "helpmeet" in all this activity.

In April of 1670, seven months after their marriage, Margaret was imprisoned for a second time, for refusing to swear an oath to the Commonwealth. Swearing was contrary to Quaker beliefs and she, like other Quakers, was willing to suffer any persecution for her beliefs. Her son, even more hostile toward his mother after her marriage to George Fox, again joined her enemies. But her husband assured her that if she "kept in the seed of God"—a favorite phrase of his—"she might have trials, but she would have dominion, wisdom and patience."

Margaret's son died in October, leaving to his own daughter the land that had been Margaret's separate estate before her marriage, part of which rightly belonged to her daughters. During this difficult period of Margaret's second imprisonment, George Fox, worn out by constant travel and brutal attack, suffered another illness, from which he was slow to recover.

In April 1671, Margaret Fox received her liberty by a decree of the king himself. In the same document he granted her share of Swarthmoor Hall to two of her daughters. Margaret herself had access to Swarthmoor Hall during the remaining years of her life. It also served as a haven for George Fox for two long intervals, first in 1675-1677 and again in 1678-1680. The first time he came to recuperate from a two-year imprisonment. The second time he came to arrange his papers and prepare his great *Journal*.

These were the longest periods he and his wife were together. Although they were greatly devoted to each other, their first allegiance was to God and His work. "We were both willing to live apart for some years upon God's account and in His truth's service," wrote Margaret, "and to deny ourselves of that comfort which we might have had in being together."

While George Fox traveled in the West Indies and in America and later when he journeyed to Holland and North Germany, Margaret continued her own work. The letters of love and encouragement that passed between them expressed the deepest Christian faith.

In her long ministry of spreading the Inner Light of Christ, she had the blessing of her husband, who believed in the work of women in the Church. Quakers were in agreement with Paul's words: "There is neither male nor female: for ye all are one in Christ Jesus" (Gal. 3:28). George Fox called women "helpmeets for men" and sought to use and develop their special gifts. A consistent champion of women, he said at one meeting: "Encourage all the women that are convinced, and mind virtue, and love the truth and walk in it, that they may come up into God's service, that they may be serviceable in their generation."

Inspired by her husband's attitude, Margaret wrote tracts and letters on the subject. She revealed her spiritual discernment and clear, logical mind in a tract to justify the ministry of women, written while she was imprisoned in Lancaster Hall. She pointed out the spiritual equality of man and woman and attacked those who denied the right of women to speak in churches. She reminded her readers that it was Martha to whom Jesus first declared that He was the Resurrection and the Life, and that it was to the Woman of Samaria that He declared He was the Messiah. She exhorted her readers to remember that the women of Galilee followed Him and ministered to Him, that women of Jerusalem wept for Him and that "many women were there" (Matt. 27:55) when He was nailed to the cross and laid in the tomb.

In speaking of Priscilla, a teacher of the celebrated Apollos, Margaret Fox wrote: "We do not read that Paul despised what Priscilla said, because she was a woman, as many now do."

Margaret Fox said that people were confused about Paul's remark: "Let your women keep silence in the Church." "Paul is speaking," she wrote, "to women who are still under the Law, and it is they who must be silent, for they are not ready to speak, not having yet received the Holy Spirit." She reminded her readers that Paul obviously looked forward to women receiving the Holy Spirit, for he soon gave instructions that when women "pray and prophesy they should have their heads covered." "Why should he give instruction thus," she asked, "if he did not consider it right for women to pray and prophesy as men did?" Finally she made a plea that men should not try to limit the power of God by reserving it for themselves alone.

Margaret wrote countless letters to Friends who needed her courageous support, for many in the early days were attacked by soldiers, who often beat them with swords and struck them with the butt-ends of their muskets.

She wrote letters to Charles II, in which she pleaded with him to consider the Friends' plight before it was too late and before God's punishment fell on him. In one of her visits to the king on behalf of the Friends, she was compared to Esther when she went before King Ahasuerus on behalf of her people.

One of her greatest services was her work in establishing women's meetings. In one of her letters in 1675 she expressed the longings of Quaker women that they be used for the service of God. She assisted in organizing and training them in midwifery, social welfare, widows' aid and in other helpful capacities. For more than thirty years Margaret Fox and her daughter Sarah were the guiding spirits of women's meetings.

Constantly attacked because of her views, her third and last imprisonment occurred sometime between 1680 and 1685 when a man who had been jailed for sheep-stealing, and a woman accomplice who was later hanged, made unfair charges against her. She was imprisoned for sixteen days and given a widow's fine of twenty pounds, though as George Fox's wife her fine should have been only ten shillings. Her persecutors came and took from Swarthmoor Hall two steers, a fat ox, calves and cattle valued in all at forty pounds.

Ill, weary and full of anxiety, Margaret Fox journeyed to London when she was seventy, to appeal to the king once more on behalf of Friends suffering many persecutions. Charles II, nearing the end of his life, was unfriendly to her, although twenty years before he had been kind. She said his death a short time later "confirmed by word, which God put into my heart, that I was sent to bear my last testimony to the king."

When James II became king, she begged him to check the persecutors of Friends. In the spring of 1687, he issued his Declaration of Indulgence for all Nonconformists, and signed the Toleration Act in 1689. These steps brought new freedom but fell short of complete victory.

When Margaret Fox was seventy-six, she made her ninth visit to London to be with her husband. Although ten years her junior, he was now too infirm for the long journey north to Swarthmoor. She rode again, as she always had, on horseback across the sands to Lancaster and there hired a coach to London. "The Lord's special hand was in it," she wrote, "that I should go then, for he lived but half a year after I left him; which makes me admire the wisdom and goodness of God in ordering my journey at that time."

George Fox died in London on January 13, 1691, two days after he had spoken and prayed with great power at a meeting. William Penn at once wrote to Margaret at Swarthmoor: "O he is gone and has left us in the storm that is over our heads, surely in great mercy to him, but as an evidence to us of sorrow to come. . . . A prince indeed is fallen in Israel today."

Margaret Fox, courageous in the loss of her husband, replied: "I trust in the same powerful God, that His holy arm and power will carry me through, whatever He hath yet for me to do. . . . I know His faithfulness and goodness, and I have experienced His Love."

She spent the last decade of her life, except for one more visit to London, at her home, surrounded by loving children and grandchildren. On her last trip to London, when she was eighty-three, she journeyed again by horseback and coach. Several difficulties were creating disunity among Friends, and, in trying to influence them as she believed George Fox would have done, she exhorted them to remember the simplicity of Christ's teaching and reminded them of the troublemakers in the early days of the Christian Church. "So there are now many troublemakers, as well as witnesses for the Eternal Truths," she declared.

While in London she addressed a letter to William III, the new king, in which she thanked him for his gentle government, clemency and gracious acts, and expressed the hope that Friends would be a blessing rather than a grievance. She also wrote two long letters to the Society of Friends, warning them against overemphasis on outward and unessential things.

She retained her mental vigor, her spiritual understanding and her wisdom until the end of her long life. Her last words, written to Friends with a faltering hand, were: "I give this my Testimony while I breathe upon the earth, that I shall stand for God and Truth." She died on April 23, 1702, and was buried in an unmarked grave overlooking the sands of Morecambe Bay. Her devoted daughters spoke of her care for the Church, her preaching, piety, wisdom, and her great and long suffering which she endured with so much patience.

Her life story is a vital one, for the truths that she taught are eternal. She spoke of "the Lord present and near," and she said: "He is not a God far off, but one who may be witnessed and possessed."

The Quaker movement, called one of the most radiant endeavors to turn Christianity toward the Light Within, was incalculably strengthened by George Fox's wife and "helpmeet" Margaret. She it was who helped Friends to "turn to the Light, wait in the Light, keep their minds within the Light, and walk in the Light."

MARY FISHER—

PIONEERING MISSIONARY IN NEW ENGLAND

(1623?-1698?)

✦ ✦ ✦

A Yorkshire servant girl who was persecuted for her Quaker faith in England and America, she was the first to take the message of the Inner Light to colleges in England. Later, as a Quaker missionary, she spoke to the Sultan of Turkey.

SHE WITNESSED TO HER FAITH DESPITE PERSECUTION

A FAVORITE TEXT among the early Quakers was the prophecy of Joel: "And also upon the servants and upon the handmaids in those days will I pour out my spirit" (2:29). This was fulfilled in the life of Mary Fisher, a Yorkshire servant girl. She was won over to the Quakers in about 1651 when George Fox preached to the household of Richard Tomlinson and his wife at Pontefract. The conversion of an entire household was a common event in early Quakerism.

Mary did not remain a maid for long, for like her mistress she began to preach the Quaker doctrine. Soon she was imprisoned in York Castle, on the charge of "speaking to a priest"—her own parish minister. During her imprisonment of sixteen months there were other Quakers in the group and she learned from them much more about the Quaker doctrine, a preparation that served her well for her later ministry.

When Mary Fisher was released from prison in 1653, she set forth with a woman companion, Elizabeth Williams, into the Fen region of England, where Elizabeth Hooten, the first Quaker minister, had suffered her first imprisonment for preaching the Gospel.

A violent controversy was being waged on paper between George Fox and the leading divines. Fox believed that ministers of Christ were not made merely by studying Hebrew, Greek, Latin and the Arts, but that real preparation for the ministry came from a knowledge of Christ's life and work.

Acting upon this Quaker belief, Mary Fisher, the humble servant girl, decided to take the message of the Inner Light to the students at Sidney Sussex College, where John Milton and Oliver Cromwell had studied.

A complaint was made to the Sussex mayor, William Pickery, about Mary Fisher and her woman friend, who were preaching in the college. When brought before the examiner and asked their names, they told him their names were written in the Book of Life as laborers of the Gospel (Phil. 4:3). When he demanded their husbands' names, they told him they had no husband but Jesus Christ.

Upon hearing this, the mayor grew angry and issued a warrant to the constable to whip the women at the Market-Cross till the blood ran down their bodies. The examiner then commanded them to take off their clothes, but they refused. Then he stripped them naked to the waist, put their arms into the whipping post and executed the mayor's warrant so cruelly that their flesh was miserably cut and torn.

The constancy and patience which these two women expressed under this barbarous usage was astonishing to the beholders, for they endured the cruel torture without the least change of countenance or appearance of uneasiness, and in the midst of their punishment sang and rejoiced, saying: "The Lord be blessed, the Lord be praised, who hath thus honored us, and strengthened us to suffer for His name's sake."

This account is recorded in *A Collection of the Sufferings of the People Called Quakers for the Testimony of Good Conscience, from 1650-1689*, taken from the original records by Joseph Besse.

Another early report relates that at the end of this barbarous punishment the servant girl Mary Fisher and her companion said to the executioner: "If you think you have not done enough, we are here ready to suffer more for our Saviour Christ." They realized the executioner knew not what he had done. And like the martyr Stephen, Mary Fisher and her companion knelt down and prayed: "Lord, lay not this sin to their charge" (Acts 7:60).

As Mary Fisher and her companion were led back into town, they exhorted the people to fear God, and not man. They predicted, like prophetesses of old, that this was the beginning of the sufferings of the people of God. They were then driven out of town, and no one had the courage to help them.

News of their unmerciful flogging—they were the first of the Quakers to suffer such treatment—sent a shudder throughout England. The Friends themselves published the story of their inhuman treatment in a pamphlet, *The First Persecution*.

Mary Fisher was imprisoned a second time at York for speaking to a priest in her native town. One of her fellow prisoners, Thomas Aldam, wrote: "Mary Fisher is much grown in the power since her last imprisonment."

In 1655, when the Quakers began their foreign missionary activity, Mary set out for America with another companion, Ann Austin, an older woman and the mother of five children. They stopped first at Barbados in the West Indies. Mary's letter to George Fox, written on January 30 1656, from Barbados, says:

> My dear father—let me not be forgotten of thee but let thy praise be for me that I may continue faithful to the end. If any of our Friends be free to come over they may be serviceable here as many are convinced and many desire to know the way. I rest, thy child begotten into the truth.

When Mary Fisher and Ann Austin arrived in Boston in May 1656, the authorities were prepared to go to any lengths to prevent the introduction of the Quaker doctrine into the New World. The women were kept prisoners on the ship while their trunks were searched. No less than one hundred books were found in their possession. These were burned, and the women were landed and imprisoned. They were deprived of light and books, and their window was boarded up so that nobody could see them or talk with them.

Mary Fisher and her friend might have starved in this prison had not an elderly citizen bribed the jailer to let him provide them with food. They were stripped naked while in prison and their bodies were searched for marks of witchcraft. Then they were shipped back to Barbados. Their bedding and even their Bibles had been confiscated to pay the jailer's fee, but Mary Fisher was finally able to return to her native land.

In the early summer of 1657, she left England to journey to Turkey with five other missionaries, three men and two women. She was now thirty-four, an attractive and devoted servant of her faith. After a tedious and dangerous voyage, the party of six landed on the southern coast of Greece. From here, Mary Fisher continued toward Turkey alone, setting out to walk five or six hundred miles, across the Morea Peninsula (the Peloponnesus) through Greece and Macedonia and over the mountains of Thrace toward Constantinople. She began her journey fearlessly, again depending upon the Inner Light for strength.

She was welcomed by wandering shepherds as she passed through little towns of tents pitched wherever water and pasturage were available. No doubt she was accorded the primitive Eastern hospitality.

Stranger though she was, speaking a different tongue and wearing Western clothes, she let it be known that she was traveling as the bearer of a "message to the king from the Most High God." The puzzled peasants either accepted these credentials or regarded her as a madwoman.

In the autumn of 1657, the Sultan had removed his court from Constantinople and was living in Adrianople, with his army of twenty thousand men. After weeks of lonely travel Mary Fisher made her way to the Sultan's tent raised high on a small hill. Unafraid, she appeared before this decrepit old ruler.

Mary Fisher, a former servant girl, was ushered in to the Sultan with all the honors accorded an ambassador. She was probably wearing her simple gray Quaker frock, a striking contrast to the riot of gold and scarlet of the Turkish court.

William Sewel, the Quaker historian, in his book *History of the Rise, Increase and Progress of the Christian People Called Quakers,* published in 1795, tells of Mary's interview with the Sultan:

The Sultan bade her speak the word of the Lord to them, and not to fear, for they had good hearts and could hear it. He also charged her to speak the word she had to say from the Lord, neither more nor less, for they were willing to hear it, be it what it would. Then she spoke what was upon her mind. The Turks hearkened to her. . . . Then the Sultan desired her to stay in the country, saying that they could not but respect such a one, as should take so much pains to come to them so far as from England, with a message from the Lord God. He also proffered her a guard to bring her into Constantinople. . . . But she, not accepting this offer, he told her it was dangerous traveling, especially for such a one as she; and wondered that she had passed so safe so far as she had; saying also that it was in respect to her, and kindness that he proffered it, and that he would not do anything that she should come to the least hurt in his dominions. She, having no more to say, the Turks asked her what she thought of their prophet Mahomet and she answered she knew him not, but Christ the true prophet, the Son of God, who was the Light of the World, and enlightened every man coming to the world, Him, she knew.

There were no visible results of her enterprise among the Turks, but her story and witness stirred the courage of fainthearted Christians. When she returned to London, she wrote to another Quaker in January 1658:

I bore my testimony for the Lord before the King unto whom I was sent, and he was very noble unto me . . . and he and all that were about him received ye words of truth without contradiction. . . . There is a royal seed amongst them which in time God will raise. They are more near truth than many nations. There is a love begotten in me towards them which is endless.

After twelve years of traveling, preaching and persecution, Mary met William Bayly, a master mariner and a preacher among the Quakers. He recognized in this dauntless traveler a kindred spirit and asked her to be his wife. She accepted, and enjoyed nearly forty years of life as a mother and homemaker, raising two daughters and a son. Until her death in Charleston, South Carolina, in 1698, she gave all of the time she could to the women's work among Quakers.

MME JEANNE GUYON—
FRENCH MYSTIC
(1648-1717)

• • •

Though a member of high French society, wife of a man of wealth and the mother of five children, she was imprisoned in the Bastille for her religious beliefs, but she never complained. She wrote forty books, including a twenty-volume commentary on the Bible, and made an eight-year apostolic pilgrimage through France and Switzerland.

SHE BORE MANY CROSSES WITH TRANQUILLITY

"WE MAY SEARCH many centuries before we find another woman who was such a pattern of true holiness," said John Wesley of Mme Jeanne Guyon of France. "How few such instances do we find of exalted love to God, and our neighbor; of genuine humility; of invincible meekness and unbounded resignation."

The American missionary Adoniram Judson, while in a Burmese prison, tried to console himself by imitating Mme Guyon's meek acquiescence. He used to repeat William Cowper's translation of her verses:

> No bliss I seek, but to fulfill
> In life, in death, Thy lovely will;
> No succour in my woes I want,
> Except what Thou art pleased to grant.
> Our days are numbered—let us spare
> Our anxious hearts a needless care;
> 'Tis Thine to number out our days,
> And ours to give them to Thy praise.

She was reared a Catholic and never gave up her faith, but is best known in history as one of the leading exponents of Quietism. This system of religious mysticism teaches that spiritual perfection is attained when self is lost in the contemplation of God, the eternal reality. Though the principles of Quietism were practiced by some of the early saints and are still practiced by Quakers, Molinos of Spain is regarded as the founder of Quietism while Mme Guyon represents it at its best.

She achieved a meek and quiet spirit and a triumphant faith and through more than forty years of her life sought to give herself wholly to God. God, she said, must be loved with a pure, divine love, not a corrupt, self-interested love. All of us, she believed, have personal access to God, who dwells at the "fine point" of each human spirit.

Mme Guyon learned so well to quiet her own inner self that she was able to bear her crosses with tranquillity, even when imprisoned in the Bastille for four years because of her religious beliefs. She wrote: "I being in the Bastille say to Thee, O my God, If Thou art pleased to render me a spectacle to men and angels, Thy holy will be done! . . . There is nothing for me to do but adore Thee and carry my cross."

She wrote behind the ten-foot-thick, cold, damp walls of one of the most horrible of prisons, in a tiny cell which lacked light, ventilation in the summer or heat in the winter, and had a heavily padlocked door. But in prison she, like Paul and Silas, learned to sing.

Sanctification by faith, an inward experience based upon faith alone, appears throughout her writings. She believed that what gravity is to the physical universe, faith is to the soul. A sanctified heart is a holy heart from which selfishness is excluded and which loves God with all its power of love. She could say with the apostle: "I live; yet not I, but Christ liveth in me; and the life which I now live in the flesh, I live by the faith of the Son of God, who loved me and gave himself for me" (Gal. 2:20). She knew that he to whom the grace of sanctification can be truly ascribed is one with Christ, one in His meekness, contentment, benevolence, one who in his life and actions bears the seal of divine favor. All her adult life Mme Guyon struggled to achieve a sanctifying spirituality.

She learned to be willing to do as Christ did. She went on errands of mercy, without tumult and noise; she did good to others without asking or expecting anything in return; she tried to attain His spirit in all things. "We need not wait until tomorrow," she said, "for the second coming of Christ, but we may see Him today, if we learn to still our inner selves." She labored not for Christ in the clouds, but for Christ in the affections; not for Christ seen, but for Christ felt; not for Christ outwardly represented, but for Christ inwardly realized.

She taught a religion not of ceremony but of the heart, of affections rather than of form, not of creeds but of God. Her enemies within her own Catholic Church regarded her theory of Quietism as too abstract and too remote from man's daily life, her theology as inconsistent. To her the eternal Church was the Church of "Christ's living compassion for the ever-changing multitude."

She moved in the highest circles of French society and associated with King Louis XIV, his secret wife Mme de Maintenon, Bishop Bénigne Bossuet and Archbishop François de Fénelon, one of the leading churchmen of her time and her defender until his death. Eminent though she was in society, Mme Guyon was more truly eminent in her faith in God, her alms and her good works.

Her Christian philanthropy was vast and far-reaching. She dispensed hundreds of loaves of bread and took into her home the sick and suffering. Among these was a poor soldier found dying in the road near her house in Paris. Ragged and unclean though he was, she gave him all the attention of a sister until his death fifteen days later. A woman of refined feelings, she performed services for him that were repugnant; but she had learned the meaning of Christianity, and she practiced it.

Mme Guyon not only nursed the poor but later established hospitals, one at Thonon and another at Grenoble, France. Not all of her alms were known to the public, for she employed a person to give help privately so that the source would not be known.

More important than her acts of charity were her labors to teach other souls the ways of God. For eight years she made a pilgrimage through towns of France and Switzerland, leading what she called an "apostolic life." She desired to share with others what she had found. After her conversion at the age of twenty, her religion had become not a mere round of ceremonies, not something to be sought for outside, but something possessed within the heart. As the practice of prayer became easier for her, new strength, new feelings and views began to fill her life.

In her efforts to teach others, Mme Guyon wrote forty books, all in French. Among these are her seven-hundred-page autobiography, which has passed through numerous editions. In its search for the spiritual self, it has been compared with St. Augustine's *Confessions*. She also wrote, mostly at night, in time taken from sleep, a twenty-volume commentary on the Bible. In this she emphasized that the essence of religion is interior and spiritual and founded upon simplicity, truth and justice. She is the author of *Spiritual Torrents,* teaching the way to the true silence of the soul. To her the Torrents are souls that issue from God and have no repose until they have returned and lost themselves in Him, never again to find themselves. But they lose neither their nature nor their reality, only their former condition of separation.

Her book on prayer entitled *The Method of Prayer* is based on Paul's enjoinder, "Pray without ceasing" (I Thess. 5:17). To Mme Guyon, prayer and religion were the same thing. She taught that we must learn to seek God Himself, not just His gifts, that we must become nothing in ourselves, before we can receive His fullness. "Every Christian," she wrote, "can elevate himself by meditation . . . to silence in the presence of God, in which the soul without being inactive acts no longer except by divine impulse. . . . the simplest are the best fitted for it."

She knew that inward holiness regulates the outward life. The more a soul becomes like God, the more clearly it discerns God's excellencies. If we attack our enemies, frequently we shall be wounded, if not totally defeated, but if we cast ourselves into the simple presence of God, we shall find an inner strength. She appealed to pastors and teachers to begin not with external matters but with principles which strengthen and renew the heart, and lead the soul to God. *The Method of Prayer* became popular among the devout, but it was condemned by Catholic churchmen, who found her ideas in sharp contrast to those taught by the Church at that time.

Many of Mme Guyon's works are still available, and countless books have been written about her. Some denounce her character and charge her with heresy, calling her a dangerous prophetess who did not conform to the true pattern of holiness. Others call her a deluded, neurotic woman. But many who have studied her books and the record of her life find in Mme Guyon the qualities of a saint and mystic, one who knew the true secret of life and found the way to an inner peace. Among her admirers are T. C. Upham, whose *The Life of Madame Guyon* is the standard work on her life; T. T. Allen, who translated her autobiography into English; and Michael de la Bedoyere, author of a story of her life entitled *The Archbishop and the Lady*. The latter declares that "spiritually, she was the mother of a new people of God, a creator of new life, not a sharer of life with anyone less than the Divine. . . . In the roll of woman heroes she ought to have a much higher place."

Mme Guyon was born at Montargis in a moist and wooded section of France south of Fontainebleau. Her maiden name was Jeanne Marie Bouvier de la Motte. Though her mother and father were both religious, it was her father and his daughter by a former marriage who drew the little Jeanne closer to the things of God.

When she was only two and a half years old she attended the Ursuline Seminary in Montargis. At four she was placed with the Benedictines, where she was surrounded by examples of goodness. Young though she was, she learned to love God. At ten she went to a Dominican convent, where a Bible had been left in her room. She spent days reading it, committing many parts to memory. Through this study she learned to look to God alone for direction and at an early age she determined to make every sacrifice for God.

As a young girl she not only dispensed alms but read devotional books and inscribed the name of Christ in large characters upon a piece of paper which she attached to her person, so as to be continually reminded of Him. She vowed to aim at perfection and to do the will of God in everything. She wanted to become a nun, but her plans were opposed by her father, who believed she might be religious without secluding herself from the world.

When she was fifteen, her family moved from Montargis to Paris. In her autobiography she says that at this time her vanity increased. Her face has been described as of Grecian mold, her eyes brilliant, her forehead high and her manners refined. She is said to have been tall, with a distinguished bearing, and to have had remarkable powers of conversation. Appearing in society wearing a smooth satin gown of a delicate pastel color, with low-cut neck, sleeves puffed and gracefully billowing skirt, she must have been particularly lovely.

Soon after she entered Parisian society, she met her future husband, Jacques Guyon, a man of wealth and noble position, but twenty-two years her senior. His father, in the reign of Henry IV and under the auspices of the distinguished minister, the Duke of Sully, had completed the Canal of Briare, connecting the Loire with the Seine. He was a man of great wealth and prominence.

No sooner had the sixteen-year-old bride entered the home of her husband and his mother than she realized it was a house of discord. If she expressed an opinion, her mother-in-law accused her of starting a dispute, compelled her to perform humiliating tasks and gave even the servants precedence over her. A troublemaker, the mother-in-law carried tales to her son about his young wife. He was sick most of the time and cared for by a nurse who dominated him. The nurse found it more to her advantage to sympathize with the mother-in-law than with the young wife. When the latter visited her own family, on her return she heard only bitter speeches about them from her mother-in-law.

The young wife soon saw that as God had made Joseph a slave in Egypt, so He had placed her in this home, "for God meant it unto good" (Gen. 50:20). Tribulation was necessary, she believed, to bring her to fullness of the inward life. Beholding the hand of God in all she suffered, she wrote in her autobiography: "Thou hast ordered these things, O my God, for my salvation. In goodness Thou hast afflicted me."

Tribulation and a desire to serve God more fully changed Mme Guyon.

She gave up some of her personal vanities and read only devout books, one of which was the *Imitation of Christ* by Thomas à Kempis. People began to notice in her countenance a growing spiritual sensitivity.

At the age of twenty, she renounced dancing, plays and parties, and wondered how she could have enjoyed them. As she dispensed alms, she began to say: "O my Divine Love, it is Thy substance—I am only the steward of it. I ought to distribute it according to Thy Will."

About this time, the second of her three sons was born. She was also the mother of two daughters. Her first son, she relates in her autobiography, born at the time of her greatest trials with her mother-in-law, became a son of sorrow.

New tribulations continued to come her way. When she was a young mother she contracted smallpox and her whole body became covered with sores. But while she was thus afflicted she sought peace within. She confided to God: "Thou didst smite me without but did not cease to bless me within." Though left with pockmarks all over her once beautiful face, Mme Guyon could still say: "In augmenting my exterior crosses, Thou didst not cease to increase my inward graces and happiness."

Her eldest son, who was especially dear to her, was also stricken with smallpox, and did not survive. She wrote: "The Lord giveth and the Lord taketh away. Blessed be His name." In all her sorrows Mme Guyon never charged God falsely.

She turned now more than ever to helping the sick and needy. She made ointments. She dressed wounds. She paid the funeral expenses of paupers. So strong became her desire for communion with God that she arose at four o'clock each morning to pray.

When she was twenty-eight, her husband, sick most of their twelve years together, became more seriously ill than ever before. Admitting that she had probably done things displeasing to him, she knelt at his bedside during his last illness and assured him that she had never intentionally wronged him. His final words to her were: "It is I who have done wrong rather than yourself. It is I who beg your pardon. I did not deserve you."

Mme Guyon was left with three children, two sons and an infant daughter born a few months before her husband's death. She had already lost two of her children, her eldest son and her eldest daughter. Having inherited a large estate from her husband, she was always provided for and also had an abundance to share with others.

She began to wonder if it were wise to continue living in the same house with her mother-in-law. On Christmas following her husband's death, she said to her mother-in-law: "My mother, on this day was the King of Peace born. He came into the world to bring peace to us. I beg peace of you in His name." Her mother-in-law, unmoved by her entreaty, later gave notice that the two of them "could no longer live together."

With her three surviving children and her little daughter's nurse, Mme Guyon left home, knowing that God had used her mother-in-law's jealousy and fierce temper to humble and purify her own spirit.

Through more than forty years of widowhood, Mme Guyon's spirit was humbled again and again. She began to perform duties submissively, in thankfulness and silence. In her tribulations, she wrote:

> There are but two principles of moral life in the universe, one which makes ourselves, or the most limited private good, the center; the other, which makes God, who may be called the universal good, the center. When self dies in the soul, God lives; when self is annihilated, God is enthroned.

Though she turned more and more to things of the Spirit, she was the head of a family and could not disregard its claims. For five years she attended to the needs of her children, their education, and her own business affairs. During this period she refused offers of marriage.

At the end of her first five years of widowhood she began to feel a call to the "apostolic life," and wished to devote herself to teaching and service to others. She asked herself if she could now leave her children in better hands, God's hands. Carefully she chose a religious school in which she placed her two sons. She decided it was best to take her five-year-old daughter and the child's nurse with her, as well as two maidservants. Later, for protection, her party was joined by her spiritual director, Father Francis Lacombe, who earlier had helped her to find a deeper experience of God.

In her thirty-fourth year she began her journeys as an apostle for inner religion. Though she departed with some misgivings for Geneva, where she was to teach and work for five years, she was strengthened when she opened her Bible and read: "When thou passest through the waters, I will be with thee; and through the rivers, they shall not overflow thee; when thou walkest through the fire, thou shalt not be burned; neither shall the flame kindle upon thee" (Isa. 43:2). During her eight-year pilgrimage, she thought of the world as her country and mankind as her brethren. Her work took her to many places in France and Switzerland.

Her chief mission was to teach that holiness is based on faith. She felt that she had been sent to teach a weary world effective methods of prayer. On her first journey by boat down the Seine, she discovered that she was literally covered with crosses made of leaves and twigs her little daughter had gathered on the riverbanks. The child did not know what she had done but her mother felt immediately that this was God's way of telling her she had many crosses to bear. But her spirit was like Paul's when he went up from Jerusalem for the last time. She remembered that he had said: "And now, behold, I go bound in the spirit unto Jerusalem, not knowing the things that shall befall me there; save that the Holy Ghost witnesseth in every city, saying that bonds and afflictions abide me" (Acts 20:22, 23).

Wanderings, persecution, imprisonment and exile lay ahead of her, but she was not afraid. She traveled by carriage, mule and post-wagon, sometimes along the edge of steep and terrible cliffs or over high mountain passes. Unafraid, she wrote:

How wonderful, O my God, at this, as at many other times, has been Thy protection over me. How many perils have I passed through. How often hast Thou checked the foot of the mule, already slipping over the precipice. How often have I been exposed to be thrown headlong from frightful heights into hideous torrents, which, though rolling in chasms far below our shrinking sight, forced us to hear them by their horrible noise. Thou, O God, didst guard me in such imminent dangers.

Once she was in a storm at sea, but again she was not afraid. She wrote: "If it be the Lord's pleasure to plunge me in waves, it shall be mine to perish in them." When the money that she carried ran short, she did not forget that her store in Providence could never be exhausted.

A brutal muleteer once tried to lead her party to a dangerous inn, but again she realized God's protection and the muleteer was thwarted in his plans. In such dangers, her strength seemed to increase. Her carriage was once stopped by four well-armed robbers who opened her litter. They saw not a frightened but a courageous, smiling woman in a stiff black dress. Her hood, fastened under her dimpled chin, enclosed a face with twinkling eyes. In a moment the robbers had disappeared and she thanked God for His protection. To Geneva, Lyons, Annecy, Gex, Thonon, up Mont Cenis, to Turin, Grenoble, Marseilles and Genoa she journeyed, devoting herself to the spiritual good of others.

Church leaders became jealous of her increasing popularity with the masses in France and Switzerland. They called her a heretic when they found some of her teachings at variance with Church doctrine. Soon she suffered heavier persecutions. Her books were burned publicly, although they had passed the censors earlier. Her mail was intercepted. The little garden near her cottage was torn up. The windows in her house were broken. Her servants were taken from her. New insinuations were made against her character. Finally she was arrested and spent seven years in prison because of her religious beliefs.

She was in and out of prison about seven years of her life. Her final years of imprisonment were the most difficult. On the last day of December

1695 she was sent to Vincennes. On August 28, 1696, she was sent to Vaugirard, a village near Paris, where her place of confinement seems to have been connected with a monastery. In September 1698 she was transferred to the Bastille for four years. For the last two years she could receive no visitors, hold no conversations, and write no letters.

Her only resource was prayer. Mme Guyon never lost her faith in God. She was fully convinced that in God's time and way, innocence and truth would prevail.

A maidservant, whom she had led to a knowledge of Christ, remained with her in prison and died in the Bastille. She believed that God had given her mistress remarkable powers and had called her to a great work. "The more I love God, the more closely I find myself bound to her," the maid asserted. When others slandered Mme Guyon, this servant, faithful for twelve years, remained her witness. Had the servant consented to say an unfavorable word against her mistress, persecutors undoubtedly would have set her free as a reward.

Insinuations were made against Mme Guyon's character because her spiritual adviser, Father Lacombe, traveled in her party, which also consisted of her daughter, the child's nurse, and the servants.

Father Lacombe was later cast into prison and finally transferred to a hospital for the insane. Here he who had been Mme Guyon's stanch defender before his mental illness, was made to sign a paper falsely confessing misconduct with his patroness at the time he was a member of her party.

It is to her credit that when he had left, many years earlier, Mme Guyon had said: "Perhaps I may never see him again, but I shall ever be glad to do him justice."

Archbishop Fénelon, one of the most celebrated churchmen of Jeanne's time, was her firm friend for twenty-five years. When her enemies employed all possible means to destroy her character, Fénelon might have curried favor with Louis XIV had he denounced her, but he remained loyal. "It would be infamous weakness in me," he declared, "to speak doubtfully in relation to her character, in order to free myself from oppression." Their friendship is immortalized in one hundred of their letters which have been called "one of the most precious documents for the study of mystic thought transmitted to us from the past."

Fénelon regarded Mme Guyon as one of the great mystics of the Church. He spoke of her as a rare soul called to a high destiny. Her ideas stimulated him to climb the ladder to greatness. She was tireless in her effort to make him realize the importance of his own mission. His celebrated *Maxim of the Saints* explains the experiences of the inward life and the doctrine of Pure Love. Fénelon's work is, in part, an exposition of Mme Guyon's views as he understood them, and as she had personally explained them to him. These maxims are so similar to her thoughts that she often seems to be speaking through him.

"The holy soul is a soul with God," he writes, "moving as God moves; doing as God does; looking as God looks. Though Christ suffered much in His physical system, in His inner and high nature, He was peaceful and happy."

Obviously Mme Guyon achieved this kind of happiness or she could not have sung in her prison cell in the Bastille, where she remained for four years. While in prison she wrote "The Christian Life," a hymn which appears in *The Methodist Hymnal* and many other collections today. Translated by William Cowper, it has been set to the music of a Gregorian chant. Her words follow:

> My Lord, how full of sweet content,
> I pass my years of banishment!
> Where'er I dwell, I dwell with Thee,
> In heaven, in earth, or on the sea.
>
> To me remains nor place nor time:
> My country is in every clime:
> I can be calm and free from care
> On any shore, since God is there.
>
> While place we seek, or place we shun,
> The soul finds happiness in none!
> But with a God to guide our way,
> 'Tis equal joy, to go or stay.
>
> Could I be cast where Thou art not,
> That were indeed a dreadful lot:
> But regions none remote I call
> Secure of finding God in all.

When she became ill in prison, and Louis XIV could no longer conscientiously condemn her, he signed her release for six months in January 1702. After seven years in Vincennes, Vaugirard and the Bastille, her children hardly recognized their mother, so ill was she from privations which she had suffered.

Only two of her children survived her. Her daughter, who had married first the Marquis de Vaux and after his death the Duc de Sully, lived in Paris. Her son Armand Jacques Guyon lived at Blois, a city one hundred miles southwest of Paris. To this place Mme Guyon was banished after her release. Louis XIV renewed her release for another six months and then indefinitely, but she was never again a completely free woman. She could not change her home without the king's permission and one word from him could have sent her back to prison.

Though she lived almost fifteen years longer, she suffered many infirmities. Amid them all she glorified God by her patience in suffering, saying: "My life is consecrated to God, to suffer for Him, as well as to enjoy Him." And she still declared: "All that I know is that God is infinitely holy, righteous and happy; that all goodness is in Him."

So well had she overcome self that she said she had no purpose or desire to be remembered. She had only one objective and that was to remain established in the great and Divine Center. "Let God glorify Himself," she wrote, "either by establishing my reputation among men, or by destroying it. . . . If it is God's will that I should suffer rebuke, misrepresentation and calumny, let me not desire the removal of the yoke which His hand has imposed upon me, until He Himself shall desire it." She left her vindication to God, and she knew she would find Him faithful.

Mme Guyon's death occurred on June 9, 1717, at the age of sixty-nine. She was buried at Blois, in the Church of the Cordeliers. A monument with a Latin inscription was erected to her memory.

She closes her autobiography:

He who speaks only of the All-ness of God and the nothingness of the Creature is in truth and the truth is in him. For if we drive out of ourselves what has been usurped and we believe to be ours, then truth will necessarily live in us. My children, take this lesson from your mother; it will afford you life. But though you hear it through her, do not take it as though it came from her or belonged to her; but take it from God as His truth. Amen.

In her last will and testament, Mme Guyon proclaimed in part:

It is to Thee, O Lord God, that I owe all things; and it is to thee, that I now surrender up all that I am. Do with me, O my God, whatsoever Thou pleasest. To Thee, in an act of irrevocable donation, I give up both my body and my soul, to be disposed of according to Thy will. Thou seest my nakedness and misery without Thee. Thou knowest that there is nothing in heaven, or in earth, that I desire but Thee alone. Within Thy hands, O God, I leave my soul, not relying for my salvation on any good that is in me, but solely on Thy mercies, and the merits and sufferings of my Lord Jesus Christ.

SUSANNA WESLEY—

MOTHER OF JOHN AND CHARLES WESLEY

(1669-1742)

◆ ◆ ◆

She was the youngest of twenty-five children and the mother of nineteen. Her son John, her fifteenth child and the founder of Methodism, was born at Epworth rectory. Her son Charles, her eighteenth child, a hymn writer, was also born there. She endured hardships but never swerved in faith.

SHE TAUGHT HER CHILDREN TO ENDURE HARDSHIP

SUSANNA WESLEY'S HOME at Epworth was an almost perfect Christian household, and there, in her Church of the Household, she planted the first seed of Methodism and kept it alive by her vigilant nurture. Her son John, founder of the Methodist movement, never forgot the Sunday evening services his mother conducted in their home in the Church of England rectory at Epworth, about a hundred and fifty miles north of London. At first, she held the services in her ample kitchen, but later they grew in size and spread through her whole house and to the barn.

John Wesley felt that if his mother could win souls, other women could also engage in this labor of love. Women became invaluable helpers in the Methodist movement owing to his encouragement. The English author Isaac Taylor says:

Susannah Wesley was the mother of Methodism in a religious and moral sense; for her courage, her submissiveness to authority, the high tone of her mind, its independence and its self-control, the warmth of her devotional feelings, and the practical direction given to them, came up and were visibly repeated in the character and conduct of her son.

Few mothers in history have possessed the spiritual sensitivity, the stamina and the wisdom of Susanna Wesley. She was John's ideal, and he hoped he might find a wife like her, but he failed. At forty-eight he married a widow, Mary Vazeille, but she harassed him with unfounded suspicions and annoyances, and finally deserted him, taking some of his journals and papers which she never returned. John Wesley used to say he believed the Lord had a purpose in his marriage, for if his wife had been a better help-mate he might have been unfaithful in the work to which God had called him.

John was Susanna's fifteenth child and Charles her eighteenth. At Oxford Charles was a member of the so-called Holy Club, which met to read the New Testament in Greek. John joined the little band and became its leader. Devout young men, they visited the poor and sick, prisoners and debtors, and went without all luxuries and many necessities so that they might help others. Living according to the method taught to John and Charles by their devout mother, the young men were nicknamed "Methodists."

The training Susanna Wesley gave her children is indicated by this letter she wrote her eldest son Samuel, who also became a preacher:

Consider well what a separation from the world, what purity, what devotion, what exemplary virtue, are required in those who are to guide others to glory. . . . I would advise you to arrange your affairs by a certain method, by which means you will learn to improve every precious moment. . . . Begin and end the day with Him who is the Alpha and Omega, and if you really experience what it is to love God, you will redeem all the time you can for His more immediate service.

Endeavor to act upon principle and do not live like the rest of mankind, who pass through the world like straws upon a river, which are carried which way the stream or wind drive them. . . . Get as deep an impression on your mind as is possible of the constant presence of the great and holy God. He is about our beds and about our paths and spies out all our ways. Whenever you are tempted to the commission of any sin, or the omission of any duty, pause and say to yourself "What am I about to do? God sees me."

She practiced what she preached to her sons. Though she gave birth to nineteen children in the years between 1690 and 1709, and was a naturally frail woman and busy with many family cares, she set aside two hours of each day for private devotion. She made this decision when she already had nine children. No matter what intervened, at the stroke of the clock she retired to spiritual communion. In her biography *Susanna Wesley, The Mother of Methodism,* Mabel Brailsford comments on this:

When we ask ourselves how twenty-four hours could hold all normal activities, which she, a frail young woman of thirty, was able to crowd into them, the answer may be found in these two hours of daily retirement, when she drew from God, in the quietness of her own room, peace and patience and an indefatigable courage.

Susanna Wesley's trials could have overwhelmed her. Only nine of her nineteen children lived to be adults. Samuel, her first-born, did not speak until he was five. She called him during those years "son of my extremest sorrow," and she prayed for him night and day. One day when he was nearly six, he disappeared for several hours. When his mother began to call for him, quite suddenly in a perfectly articulate voice, he answered: "Mother, here I am!"

Another child smothered in its sleep and was brought to the mother, without any warning, as a little corpse. Her twins died, as did her first daughter Susanna. Between 1697 and 1701, five of her babies passed away. A daughter was deformed for life, owing to the carelessness of a maid. Some of her children had smallpox.

Other difficulties beset her. Debts mounted and the family's credit was exhausted. Susanna's husband, never a practical man, could not make ends meet for his family, and had it not been for the management of his wife, they would often have had no bread. Though her family was never without food, it was frequently so hard to get bread that she once confessed to a friend: "I had so much care to get it before it was eaten, and to pay for it after, it has often made it very unpleasant to me. And I think to have bread on such terms is the next degree of wretchedness to having none at all."

Regarded from a purely material point of view, Susanna Wesley's story is one of uncommon misery, hardship and failure. Spiritually, however, it is a life of true riches, glory and victory, for she never lost her high ideals nor her sublime faith. During a severe trial, she went to her room and wrote:

> Though man is born to trouble, yet I believe there is scarce a man to be found upon earth but, take the whole course of his life, hath more mercies than afflictions, and much more pleasure than pain. All my sufferings, by the admirable management of Omnipotent Goodness, have concurred to promote my spiritual and eternal good. . . . Glory be to Thee, O Lord!

In her "Household School," for six hours a day through twenty years, she taught her children so thoroughly that they became unusually cultured. There was not one of them in whom she did not instill a passion for learning and righteousness.

When her husband, in exasperation, asked her: "Why do you sit there teaching that dull child that lesson over the twentieth time?" she replied calmly: "Had I satisfied myself by mentioning the matter only nineteen times, I should have lost all labor. You see it was the twentieth time that crowned the whole."

When her son John became a noted man, he begged her to write down some details of the education of her children, to which she reluctantly consented. She confessed: "No one can, without renouncing the world in the most literal sense, observe my method. There are few, if any, who would devote about twenty years of the prime of life in hopes to save the souls of their children."

She began to train her children by a rather strict method of living as soon as they were born. From their birth she also began to train their wills, making them realize they must obey their parents. They were even taught to cry softly, to eat and drink whatever was given to them. Drinking or eating between meals was never allowed, unless they were sick. At six, as soon as family prayers were over, they had their supper. At eight they were put to bed and told to go to sleep. "No such thing was allowed in our house," this mother reports, "as sitting by a child till it fell asleep." The loud noise children generally make was seldom heard in the Wesley house. Laughter and play, on the other hand, were common sounds.

The spiritual welfare of her children mattered most to Susanna. She gave them an appreciation of the things of the spirit, and this teaching she carried on into their more mature years. Even when she was an old woman, her son John still came to his devout mother for counsel. Not to Methodists alone but to the whole world Susanna Wesley gave a new freedom of faith, a new spark of vital religion and a new intimacy with God.

It is no wonder that this mother who so often prayed, "Grant me grace, O Lord, to be wholly a Christian," should produce a great Christian like John Wesley. "Help me, Lord," she prayed, "to remember that religion is not to be confined to the church or closet, nor exercised only in prayer and meditation, but that everywhere I am in Thy Presence."

All her life Susanna Wesley was surrounded by those who prayed and preached. She was the twenty-fifth child of Dr. Samuel Annesley, a famous Nonconformist pastor, by his second wife, the daughter of a member of Parliament. Susanna's father was a Doctor of Divinity of Oxford University and in 1648 was chosen to preach the Fast sermon for the House of Commons. At his parish at St. Giles, Cripplegate, he preached to one of the largest congregations in London.

Susanna, born January 20, 1669, was always accomplished beyond her years and, instead of playing with dolls or practicing the harpsichord, she spent much of her girlhood considering religious matters, such as the merits of the controversy between the Church of England and Nonconformists.

She was a very beautiful girl in a family of beautiful women, but her beauty never overshadowed her disciplined mind nor her pious spirit. She had a patrician nose, well-defined eyebrows, dark hair, a soft mouth and gleaming eyes. When she was married she must have been lovely in her dress with softly draped neckline, tight waist and full skirt, and with her hair arranged to frame her noble countenance. Of Dr. Annesley's family of handsome daughters, Susanna was considered the loveliest and his favorite. Although she was the youngest of his twenty-five children, he left her in his will what he most valued, his manuscripts and family papers.

Her husband Samuel, whom she married in 1689, was the son of a Nonconformist minister, Rev. John Wesley, for whom her famous son was named. Both Susanna Wesley and her husband left the Nonconformists and returned to the Church of England, where he first became a curate in London. His income was sixty pounds a year, less than three hundred dollars.

She and her husband did not remain long in London after their marriage, for he accepted another position as curate at South Ormsby, a parish of thirty-six houses and two hundred and six persons. The rectory was a mud hut. Eight years later she and her husband moved to Epworth, a parish in the eastern part of England, about a hundred and fifty miles north of London. Here Susanna spent the next forty years of her life until her husband's death.

At Epworth she fought disease, fires and countless other problems, especially after her husband was imprisoned for inability to pay accumulated debts.

During this period she had to shoulder the entire responsibility for the dairy herd, the pigs and hens, in addition to her regular household duties and the teaching and religious training of her children.

While her husband was still in prison, one of his enemies killed all the cows, depriving Susanna of her main means of support. Even in this predicament her chief concern was for her husband, who she feared might not have enough food in jail. Casting about in her mind for some way to help him, she thought of her wedding ring, the only piece of jewelry she owned. She sent it off to him at once, thinking it might buy him a few necessities, but Samuel returned it.

When Samuel rejoined his family, Susanna's problems mounted. Somehow, from their meager income, money must be found to pay his expenses when he had to go up to London for church convocations. For seven successive years he made the journey from Epworth to London.

Each of these years Susanna was looking forward to the birth of another baby, but throughout all the trials of her faith she never lost heart. She just prayed more fervently and found new strength in her Bible.

Her love for the Bible is shown by the names she gave seven of her children: Samuel, John, Martha, Mary, Mehetabel, Jedidah and Kezia. The latter, named for Job's second daughter, was born in 1709 when the family was undergoing trials like Job's. Their three-storied, seven-room house made of timber and plaster with a thatched roof, burned to the ground only a few weeks before Kezia's birth. It was the second time the house had caught fire, but now nothing was left of it. With it went the family's clothes, the furniture and the library purchased at great sacrifice. Only two bits of charred paper from the library escaped the flames. One was a copy of "Behold the Saviour of Mankind," the only hymn written by Susanna's husband. It is now in *The Methodist Hymnal*. The other was a fragment of his beloved Polyglot Bible with only this sentence legible: "Sell all thou hast. Take up thy cross, and follow me."

Before the blaze made headway, all of the family had escaped except six-year-old John. Finding it impossible to reach John, the father knelt down and commended his child's soul to God. The boy then made his way to the window and was rescued a moment before the burning roof fell into the room. The family and neighbors knelt together in prayer, thanking God that all eight children had been saved.

As was her custom, Susanna Wesley bore this tragedy with courage. Her husband wrote: "All this, thank God, does not sink my wife's spirits." She saw God's hand in the experience, particularly in John's miraculous escape.

"I do intend to be more particularly careful of the soul of this child, that Thou hast so mercifully provided for, than ever I have been," she wrote, "that I may endeavor to instill into his mind the principles of Thy true religion and virtue." From this time on she tried harder than ever to train her son John for some great purpose.

Amid her duties she found time to write three religious textbooks for her children: *A Manual of Natural Theory, An Exposition of the Leading Truths of the Gospel* (a scholarly commentary on the Apostles' Creed), and finally a practical exposition of the Ten Commandments. In addition she wrote a sixty-page manuscript entitled "Religious Conference between Mother and Emilia." Emilia was one of her daughters who, while running the household during her mother's illness, once wrote: "Then I learned what it was to seek money for bread, seldom having any without such hardship."

Susanna Wesley understood better than her husband the needs and dreams of their children, for she had both sensitive perception and womanly intuition.

For instance, when John began to think of becoming a clergyman, he wrote to his father, who counseled him to wait. It was his mother who sent him a letter of encouragement: "I was much pleased with your letter to your father about taking holy orders," she said, "and liked the proposal well. I approve your decision and think the sooner you are a deacon the better."

Samuel soon came round to his wife's point of view. She was the stronger personality, but she was also a loyal wife who never lost sight of her husband's good points nor blamed him for his bad management of family affairs and mounting debts.

A woman of great intellectual ability as well as clear judgment, Susanna took pleasure in advising her son regarding his reading for the ministry. She recommended the *Imitation of Christ* by Thomas à Kempis and *Rule for Holy Living* by Jeremy Taylor. After reading the latter, John Wesley wrote his mother: "I resolved to dedicate all my life to God—all my thoughts and words and actions."

These encouraging experiences with John helped Susanna Wesley during a time of increasing anxiety about some of her other children. Several of her daughters, tired of the family struggle with poverty, made unfortunate marriages. Hetty, after early difficulties with an irresponsible suitor, married an uncongenial and illiterate journeyman plumber. Martha married a curate who led a most unworthy life. Mary, the daughter who had been crippled in her childhood through the carelessness of a maid, died in childbirth a year after her marriage. Kezia died at thirty-two.

During many of their troubles, Susanna's husband buried himself in a dissertation on the Book of Job, only five hundred copies of which were printed.

Finally, in 1735, the debt-burdened, disappointed Samuel Wesley passed away as his son John was praying at his bedside.

Shortly after her husband's death, Susanna Wesley left Epworth Rectory, where she had suffered and toiled, and went to live with her daughter Emilia.

In October of 1735, at the invitation of General James Oglethorpe, founder of the Georgia colony, John and Charles Wesley went to Georgia as missionaries to the Indians and settlers. Susanna bade her sons good-by, and as she did so, John expressed concern at leaving his aging mother. But she replied: "Had I twenty sons, I should rejoice that they were all so employed, though I should never see them more."

The mission they established later became a refuge of English debtors and other unfortunate individuals. John Wesley's little group met every Wednesday evening in Savannah. Years later, in 1781, he wrote: "I cannot but observe that these were the first rudiments of the Methodist societies." It was not until a few months after he returned from Georgia, however, that the first Methodist meeting was held in London, on May 13, 1738.

On John's return to England he resumed his preaching throughout England. Several years later, Susanna Wesley had the great joy of hearing her son John preach, night after night under the open sky, to a congregation which covered all the hillside at Epworth. He remembered his mother's

Epworth meetings when he had heard her preach on Sunday nights to two hundred neighbors who had crowded the parsonage. He remembered, too, the words of his father: "The inward witness, son, the inward witness."

At thirty-six John made a home for his mother in London in a room over an old foundry at Moorfields that had been fitted up as a church and dwelling. These must have been happy days for his seventy-year-old mother, who discussed theological questions with him. She approved his field preaching and often accompanied him, sometimes standing by his side amid an audience of twenty thousand people.

In addition to his preaching John was also building chapels, going among the poor, never weary, never despondent, never fretting. Charles, too, was becoming well known, not only as a preacher but especially for hymns that were sung at the first Methodist meetings, among which were the now-famous "Jesus, Lover of my Soul" and "Love Divine, all Love Excelling." He wrote more than three thousand hymns in all.

At the time when the Methodists had achieved real strength, Susanna's life drew near an end. While preaching in Bristol one Sunday in July 1742, John Wesley learned that his mother was ill and returned in haste. The following Friday she awakened from sleep to cry: "My dear Savior, art Thou come to help me at my last extremity?"

Later that day, while her children stood about her bed, she said: "Children, as soon as I am released, sing a psalm of praise to God." She died on the premises of the foundry, where the first Methodist chapel was opened. She was buried in Bunhill Fields cemetery, opposite which, thirty-five years later, her son John built his famous Chapel in the City Road. John said of her funeral: "It was one of the most solemn assemblies I ever saw, or expect to see, on this side of eternity."

A simple stone first marked her grave. Another stone was added in 1828, and in 1870 an obelisk of Sicilian marble was erected to her memory.

The following prayer, one of her most meaningful, rings down the centuries:

I praise Thee, O God, for illuminating my mind and for enabling me to prove demonstratively that Thy wisdom is as infinite as Thy power. Help me to use these discoveries to praise and love and obey, and may I be exceedingly careful that my affections keep pace with my knowledge.

As I am more rationally persuaded that Thou art infinitely wise, so may I learn by this knowledge to practice a more hearty and universal subjection to Thee, more cheerfully to bow before the order of Thy providence, to submit my reason so far to my faith as not to doubt those points of faith which are mysterious to me through the weakness of my understanding.

May I adore the mystery I cannot comprehend. Help me to be not too curious in prying into those secret things that are known only to Thee, O God, nor too rash in censuring what I do not understand. May I not perplex myself about those methods of providence that seem to me involved and intricate, but resolve them into Thine infinite wisdom, who knowest the spirits of all flesh and dost best understand how to govern those souls Thou hast created.

We are of yesterday and know nothing. But Thy boundless mind comprehends, at one view, all things, past, present, and future, and as Thou dost see all things, Thou dost best understand what is good and proper for each individual and for me, with relation to both worlds. So deal with me, O my God. Amen.

LADY HUNTINGDON—
EIGHTEENTH-CENTURY REVIVALIST
(1707-1791)

♦ ♦ ♦

Founder of the evangelical branch known as Lady Huntingdon's Connexion, she inspired early Methodist leaders John and Charles Wesley and George Whitefield. She sponsored about sixty chapels in the British Isles, financed a seminary for ministers and aided in the establishment of missions in Georgia.

A SERVANT OF THE CHURCH

LIKE PHEBE OF PAUL'S TIME, Selina, Countess of Huntingdon, was "a servant of the church and a succourer of many" (Rom. 16:1-2). Like Priscilla, she also had a church in her house, often referred to as a Bethel by clergymen and laymen alike.

When rigid formality chilled the Church in eighteenth-century England, she became one of its most enthusiastic lay workers, seeking most of all to bring a new spiritual vision to the people in her own upper classes. "What shall I render unto the Lord?" she asked. Often she likened herself to a ship before the wind, carried on by an impulse she could not resist or describe.

Her income, large though it was, did not suffice for her enormous expenditures during almost half a century, but God met her needs in various ways. Wealthy friends gave her lavish donations, and she made heroic sacrifices herself, first selling her jewels in order to build another chapel, and finally moving to living quarters so humble that a visitor later expressed amazement that so distinguished a person should live in such plain surroundings.

When the Church of England, to which she was so long loyally attached, refused to open its churches to Methodist clergymen and revivalists, she became their liberal patroness, and she was the virtual foundress of the Calvinistic Methodists, a group sometimes referred to as Lady Huntingdon's Connexion.

Her objective was to spiritualize the Church. She had no idea of creating a dissenting body, but when she saw Methodists being hooted at, stoned and thrown into pits and ponds, she vigorously defended their cause. Her support of those who preached the simple Gospel astonished her friends. Some ridiculed her as a fanatic and exclaimed, as Festus did to Paul: "Thou art beside thyself" (Acts 26:24). Not at all dismayed, Lady Huntingdon assumed the ever-increasing burden of her Connexion. She carried on faithfully into her eighties, often using her administrative ability, tenacity and vision, and doing the work of a bishop. Her chief method of supporting Methodist clergymen was to appoint them as her chaplains.

In his biography of her, *The Coronet and the Cross,* Alfred H. New tells an anecdote concerning a call on George III and Charlotte Sophia at their palace at Kew. Lady Huntingdon had come to see them on a church matter, but she stayed to converse on many topics. The king said to her:

"I have been told so many odd stories of your Ladyship, that I am free to confess I felt a great degree of curiosity to see if you were at all like other women. I am happy to have the opportunity of assuring your Ladyship of the very good opinion I have of you, and how very highly I estimate your character, your zeal and abilities, which cannot be consecrated to a more noble purpose."

The king then referred to the ministers of her branch of Methodism, who, he understood, were eloquent preachers. He repeated a conversation he had had with a learned prelate who had complained of some of her Ladyship's students and ministers, asking: "What shall we do with them?"

His majesty told her he had replied: "Make bishops of them."

The prelate had responded: "That might be done, but please your majesty, we cannot make a bishop of Lady Huntingdon."

The king said he had remarked: "It would be a lucky circumstance if you could, for she puts you all to shame. . . . I wish we had a Lady Huntingdon in every diocese of England."

Selina Hastings, the second of three daughters of Washington Shirley, second Earl of Ferrers, was born at Stanton Harold in Leicestershire, England, in 1707, during Queen Anne's reign. Her mother was Mary Levinge, daughter of Sir Richard Levinge, solicitor-general for Ireland and Speaker of the House of Commons. When Selina was nine, she had a deep religious experience at the funeral of a playmate, and afterward made it a habit to pray and read the Bible. A few years later, when she entered fully into English society, her prayer was that she might marry into a serious family.

In 1728 she became the bride of Theophilus, ninth Earl of Huntingdon, a man of high character, intelligence, good disposition and wealth. They had four sons and three daughters. Selina was an affectionate and tender wife and mother.

In the early years of her marriage, when she lived in the ancient mansion of her husband's family, Donnington Hall, in Donnington Park, Leicestershire, social activities occupied a great deal of her time. In 1739, when the then Prince of Wales, later George IV, celebrated his birthday with an elaborate ball, she attended, wearing a handsome gown of white satin embroidered with chenille and gold ornaments, designed with a split underbodice of black velvet encrusted in patterns of large stone vases, flowers and gold shells. She was a lady of breeding, born to command, and she must have made a striking picture with her large, expressive eyes, pretty mouth and noble forehead.

At the age of thirty-one, Lady Huntingdon was stricken with a serious illness, during which she became a close friend of her husband's sister, Lady Margaret Hastings, who was the wife of a Methodist minister, Benjamin Ingham. Both Lady Margaret and her sister Lady Elizabeth had been among the first ladies of the English aristocracy to become interested in Methodism.

It is possible that her intimate association with her sister-in-law and their many talks during her convalescence may have led to Lady Huntingdon's decision to "become a new creature" and dedicate the rest of her life to God.

As soon as she was well enough, she joined the Methodists and began to attend their services. Her husband accompanied her and gave her his full support even though certain members of the nobility were critical of her for sponsoring this new teaching and urged him to forbid her to have anything to do with it.

All of Lady Huntingdon's friends were amazed at the change in her as she withdrew more and more from the social scene and devoted all her energies to furthering the cause which had claimed her interest.

When John and Charles Wesley preached in her neighborhood, she sent word to them that she was with them in heart, and she bade them God-speed. Afterward John Wesley was a frequent guest at Donnington Hall.

Three years after her recovery, in 1741, Lady Huntingdon wrote:

My whole heart has not one single grain of thirst after approbation. God fills every void in my life. I have not one wish, one will, one desire, but in Him. He hath set my feet in a large room. All God's children seem as so many machines appointed for uses with which I have nothing to do. I have wondered and stood amazed that God should make conquest of all within me by love. Others may be conquered by lesser gifts and graces, but what must that evil heart be that nothing but the love of God can conquer? I am brought to less than nothing, broken to pieces like the potter's vessel. I long to leap into the flames to get rid of my sinful flesh, that every atom of these ashes might be separate, that neither time, place, nor person should stay God's spirit.

Later sorrows brought her closer to the Church. In 1743 she lost two sons, one aged eleven, the other thirteen, in an epidemic of smallpox. "May He increase my faith," she prayed, "animate my heart with zeal for His glory, enlarge my sphere, and make me more faithful in the sphere in which I serve." In 1761 she lost her beloved namesake at the age of twenty-six, and her last son died two years before her own death. Only one of her seven children survived her.

Her husband died in 1746, leaving her a wealthy widow of thirty-nine. She determined now to serve the Church more faithfully with both her time and her money. Every year after this her labors increased and her self-denying efforts multiplied.

Drawing closer to the Methodists, she asked: "If God came near to Abraham and Moses, why should He not come near to these new servants? Why should not the same light that shone on Mount Sinai, the Mount of Transfiguration and upon Saul on his way to Damascus manifest itself in England today?" She also extended a helping hand to the new Methodist apostles.

When George Whitefield, the famous Methodist preacher, returned to England in 1748, after a second missionary trip to America, his former congregation at the London Tabernacle had dispersed. His funds were so low that he had to sell his household furniture in order to pay debts on the orphange "Bethesda," which he had established on five hundred acres of land ten miles from Savannah, Georgia. Lady Huntingdon invited him to preach at her house in Chelsea and at her other homes in London, Brighton and Bath. Remembering that Paul preached privately to those of special distinction, Whitefield rejoiced that he could combine sermons in Lady Huntingdon's home with his public work.

Among the notable men who came to her home to hear Whitefield were

David Hume, the Scottish philosopher and historian, Horace Walpole, the author, Lord Bolingbroke and Lord Chesterfield. Bishops of the Church of England came incognito and sat in a curtained recess dubbed "Nicodemus' Corner." Women of high position flocked to hear the new minister too, and soon other mansions of the rich resounded with the new interpretation of the Gospel of Christ.

Whitefield said to Lady Huntingdon: "A leader is wanting. This honor has been put on your ladyship by the great Head of the Church." One of the Congregationalist leaders, Dr. Philip Doddridge, said of her: "I think I never saw so much of the image of God in a woman upon the earth."

She was a friend to all of the early Methodist leaders. When Doddridge became so ill that he could not preach, she raised the money to send him and his wife to Portugal, where he died a short time later.

In this pioneering period of Methodism, leaders were benefited by Lady Huntingdon's apostolic zeal. John Wesley, born into the Church of England, had first brought Methodists together into societies in 1738, but they now became divided.

In 1741 Whitefield separated from Wesley on doctrinal points. One of Lady Huntingdon's great services was to bring John and Charles Wesley and Whitefield back together again, through tactful letters to each, recommending their co-operation.

Soon afterward Whitefield preached in Wesley's chapel. Wesley read the prayer, assisted by Whitefield, and twelve hundred persons received the Lord's Supper from their hands at the conclusion of the ceremony. "Thanks be to God," said Lady Huntingdon, "for the love and unanimity displayed. May the God of peace and harmony unite us all in the bond of affection."

To Charles Wesley, also one of her chaplains, she wrote: "What blessed effects does the love of God produce in the hearts of those who abide in Him."

Later, Lady Huntingdon, Whitefield and the two Wesleys cemented their Christian harmony by what Charles Wesley called a "Quadruple Alliance." They agreed to meet as often as convenient and co-operate in their common work. Calvinistic evangelists also came to her house for counsel. So fervent was the spirit of her own group and the Wesley group that it was difficult to distinguish between them.

Her missionary enthusiasm and liberality took her on many religious missions in the British Isles. In 1748 she went to Wales, accompanied by her two daughters and a number of clergymen. For fifteen days her picturesque cavalcade of carriages, drawn by prancing horses, wended its way through the large towns and remote villages of Wales. Her evangelists preached as Jesus had, with a mountain for a pulpit, and the heavens for a sounding board. They spoke not on obscure points of morality nor on theological controversy but on the stirring and simple truths of the Gospel. Thousands were awakened to a new understanding of Christ's Gospel, and church life was quickened throughout Great Britain.

The fact that Lady Huntingdon accompanied her evangelists on tours seems to have been purely an act of courtesy and Christian fellowship, and John Wesley expressed thankfulness to God for "her gracious presence, which attended such a tour from the beginning."

Urging followers of her Connexion that "the more apostolic we are the better," she never failed to lead the way herself. Frequently she retired into her room to pray. Before the opening of a chapel at Brighton—one of about sixty she established—like Jacob of old, she wished to wrestle with God for His blessing on this sanctuary reared to His name.

Providing places of worship as fast as they were needed, especially in Wales, she found her labors becoming heavier and heavier. She had to follow up the work of her missionaries, trustees and committees, inspect their chapels, regulate salaries, direct funds, counsel, control and encourage, all of which she did with marvelous tenacity of purpose.

In early 1768 six students in Edmund Hall, Oxford, were expelled from the university for holding Methodist meetings. The first to show concern, Lady Huntingdon inquired: "Why not start a seminary for these and other such young men?"

She consulted John Wesley about her plans, telling him that they must first select spiritual-minded young men and then prepare and sustain them for the ministry. She proposed to give them a free education during the three-year term, and supply them with food, lodging and a new suit of clothes annually. Then they were permitted to minister to the Protestant faith of their choice.

When her seminary was opened in August 1768 at Trevecca House, a massive old twelfth-century mansion near Talgarth in South Wales, Whitefield preached the sermon. In a few years Trevecca was turning out young ministers imbued with the spirit of their founder.

It is doubtful if any woman in Christian history ever gave such valuable guidance for ministerial students as this:

Two points I must lay down as the most indispensable qualifications for a minister of the everlasting Gospel. The first is the invariable conviction that the Church of Christ can have no establishment on earth, but that which came down from Heaven on the Day of Pentecost. This is the true Church of Christ under all denominations on earth. It cannot continue to exist without faith, which is the gift of God. Ordinances must be administered by faith and received by faith. . . . The more scriptural and simple your sermons and to the heart, the better. Apply to facts, with the knowledge of evils in your heart. That is the truth our Lord must bless. He can witness to nothing else, as He essentially and emphatically is truth itself. . . . I write thus, hoping and believing that you have counted the cost, and that you truly mean to devote yourself unreservedly to the Lord Jesus Christ.

In 1777 Lady Huntingdon opened her chapel at Tunbridge Wells, England, in a large building called the Pantheon, which had been erected originally for purposes of entertainment. Knowing that the people in the area were poor, she asked that no collection be made, and that first winter she financed the young minister who preached there.

Her burdens continued to mount. Whitefield, who had died at Newburyport, Massachusetts, in 1770, bequeathed to her the orphanage "Bethesda." She accepted the responsibility, appointed a superintendent, and bought up claims of heirs at law to Whitefield's other property in America.

Shortly thereafter she called upon ministers and students in her Connexion to meet at her ministerial school at Trevecca, where, after a careful examination of the volunteers, Lady Huntingdon chose a missionary band which in six weeks was on its way to Savannah to preach the Gospel in the American colonies.

To meet the spiritual needs of the New World during the next few years, ministerial reinforcements were supplied from Trevecca. Four years after Lady Huntingdon's missionaries reached America, the Revolutionary War began.

At the end of the war her property was appropriated by the states. She corresponded with George Washington in an effort to carry on her work, but her property rights had been irrevocably lost.

Ahead of her time in her thinking, Lady Huntingdon at first thought it would be possible to infuse the new teaching into the Church of England, for which she had a strong attachment. However, in 1779 she was forced to admit defeat. In order to protect her chapels from suppression or appropriation by the Established Church, she had to avail herself of the Toleration Act, which enabled all religious societies not subject to the established ecclesiastical power to control their own chapels. Lady Huntingdon's Connexion now took its place among the dissenting churches.

In her last days she was grateful that her Christian faith had carried her through many family sorrows. When her cousin murdered his steward, without a moment's hesitation she undertook the disturbing duty of taking his children to see him in prison as he awaited execution.

Lady Huntingdon did not outwardly condemn or shun the society of her aunt, Lady Frances Shirley, whose way of life did not meet the standards of Christian morality. She later had the joy of seeing Lady Shirley become a Calvinistic Methodist, and her aunt left almost all of her fortune to Lady Huntingdon.

Although she had much grief, she rejoiced in a life of achievement. One hundred thousand persons were privileged to hear the Gospel in chapels which she had founded. Her seminary at Trevecca trained new evangelical ministers who preached throughout Great Britain.

Her body grew weaker, but her spirit remained indomitable. Her serenity, a reflection of her Christian faith, never failed. To friends who inquired how she was, she replied: "I am well. All is well, well forever. I see, wherever I turn my eyes, whether I live or die, nothing but victory. . . . I am as conscious of the presence of God as I am of the presence of those I have with me."

Almost to the last, Lady Huntingdon controlled her Connexion with her customary wisdom. When she knew death was near, she asked that an association be formed to carry on her work. She died in June 1791 at Spafields, next door to the chapel she had erected.

She had outlived all of the early Methodist leaders. Her last will read: "The grand view and desire of my life has been the good of all mankind." The residue of her fortune went for the support of her chapels.

SECTION II

SPIRITUAL BIOGRAPHIES
OF CHRISTIAN WOMEN FROM THE
EIGHTEENTH TO THE TWENTIETH CENTURY

◆ ◆ ◆

CHAPTER 4

Women Who Pioneered

"MOTHER ANN" LEE—
FOUNDER OF THE AMERICAN SHAKERS
(1736-1784)

♦ ♦ ♦

She joined the Shaking Quakers in England in 1758 and established the first Shaker colony in the United States. When she made a two-year journey (1781-1783) among the Shaker colonies of New England, she suffered persecution.

THE FIRST WOMAN TO FOUND A RELIGIOUS SOCIETY
IN AMERICA

IN 1776, about the same time the American colonists declared their independence, Ann Lee and her small band of followers established the first Shaker colony in a district known by the Indian name of Niskeyuna (now Watervliet), about eight miles northwest of Albany, New York.

Like other ascetic groups, including the self-denying Essenes of Christ's time, Ann Lee's Shakers were known for their strict moral discipline, the purity of their lives and their testimony against sins. They wore simple dress, were charitable to the poor, and sought the blessing of Divine Providence in all their labors. A convert was required to pay all his debts, discharge his legal obligations and make restitution for all the wrongs he had committed against his fellow creatures.

In their ownership of communal property, the Shakers became the largest, most permanent and, in many respects, the most significant of American religious communities. At the heart of their community life was a love of God and the practice of godlike qualities in their daily lives.

Joseph Meacham, a former Baptist lay preacher from Enfield, Connecticut, "Mother Ann's" first convert in America, advocated the establishment of an order of trades. Although the Shaker economy was based on agriculture and stock raising, it soon branched into related activities.

By 1790, six years after Ann Lee's death, Shakers had started a garden-seed industry which continued to expand until the Civil War cut off its Southern markets. They were the first group in America to collect, raise and package such products as medicinal herbs, roots, barks and vegetable extracts for the pharmaceutical market. About the same time, they introduced broomcorn and began a broom industry which became the mainstay of some communities. They also developed a fine strain of sheep from whose wool was produced the flannel for Shaker cloaks.

They pioneered in such trades as tanning and shoemaking, weaving, shingle- and brick-making, fruit and vegetable canning, beekeeping and the manufacture of buttons and buckles. In 1789 they started a chair business that developed nationally in the last quarter of the nineteenth century. They also excelled in machine design. Sister Sarah Babbitt of Harvard, Massachusetts, is credited with designing the circular saw and conceiving the idea of cutting nails from a single sheet of metal.

Strong in their conviction that the Church must come to terms with its worldly environment, they were the first to establish trades within its confines. The Shaker Covenant of 1795 read: "We believe we were debtors to God in relation to each other, and all men, to improve our time and talent in this life, in that manner in which we might be useful."

This establishment of trades within the Church seemed to stem from the hard, honest work of Ann's father John Lee, a blacksmith from a pathetically impoverished area of Manchester, England. There she was born in 1736, the second of eight children. She had no schooling and during her childhood was employed in a textile factory, first as a cutter of velvet and a helper in preparing cotton for the looms, and later as a cutter of hatters' fur. She also worked as a cook in an infirmary in Manchester. In these humble occupations, she became known for her faithfulness, neatness, prudence and economy.

She has been described as a handsome woman with a fair complexion, blue eyes and light chestnut hair. Her glance was keen and penetrating, and her manner inspired confidence and respect. A serene radiance illuminated her face when she talked of God, and many called her beautiful.

In 1758, when she was twenty-two, she joined a society of religious dissenters led by Jane and James Wardley, Quaker tailors living in a bleak little town, Bolton-on-the-Moors, twelve miles northeast of Manchester. Ten years earlier, the Wardleys had come under the influence of the French Prophets, a Calvinist sect, who, after the revocation of the Edict of Nantes in 1685, sought religious freedom in England. Like many other sects and like the primitive Church itself, their worship was exuberant and included singing, dancing, shaking and shouting, speaking with strange tongues, and prophesying.

Most of the members, like Ann, were laboring people who worked hard all day and held worship services in the evening. Some of the group were derisively called "Shaking Quakers" or "Shakers," because of their shaking during services. Actually, they regarded this practice as a form of dancing based upon Old Testament customs. They cited the story of the Israelites' escape from the Egyptians at the Sea of Reeds. Then Moses' sister Miriam "took a timbrel in her hand; and all the women went out after her with timbrels and with dances" (Exod. 15:20). They also quoted the Biblical passage telling that David "leaped and danced before the Ark of the Lord" (II Sam. 6:16). And they reminded themselves of the Psalmist's words: "Let them praise his name in the dance" (Psalm 149:3).

The Shakers believed that Christ's Second Coming was near and that this time He would appear in the person of a woman. Because Ann Lee claimed to have had a vision in which Jesus Christ revealed to her divine manifestations of truth, the Wardleys and others were convinced that she was the one for whom they had been waiting. It was in this way that Shakerism was born.

Among the manifestations that came to Ann were what she called "the mystery of iniquity," as practiced in the lusts of the flesh. Sex uncontrolled, she said, was the root of all human misery and suffering. She never condemned the marriage institution, but considered it less perfect than celibacy. She taught that from the beginning of God's Creation the means of physical birth was designed to be merely temporary, a stepping-stone to a superior order. After having served its purpose in producing and continuing the race, the material life of sex must be supplanted by the life of the soul. In the most pointed manner she testified that no soul could follow Christ in spiritual regeneration while living in the works of natural regeneration.

From this time on Ann Lee was regarded by the Shakers as their spiritual mother. It is to her credit that she never claimed this honor for herself, nor did she assume that she was worthy of it.

Long before she came to America, "Mother Ann" found solace from her earthly woes in her beliefs. She experienced injustices in her working conditions and much sorrow in her marriage and in motherhood. At her father's insistence and despite her pleadings, in 1762 she had been married to Abraham Standerin (also Stanley, or Standley), a blacksmith like her father and described as a kind, vigorous fellow but unsuited to Ann's temperament.

They had four children, all of whom died in infancy. Deliveries were difficult, and Ann suffered much in body and soul. Following the death of her last child, she turned more zealously than ever to the Shaking Quakers for comfort.

She was willing to suffer anything for her faith and was cruelly abused and several times imprisoned in both England and America. Once she was dragged out of a meeting by a mob, cast into a Manchester prison, and put in a cell so small that she could not stand upright. For fourteen days she was without food, until a Shaker boy, James Whittaker—so the story goes —secretly brought a bowl of nourishing fluids to the keyhole of her prison cell. Every twenty-four hours she sucked the liquid mixture through a short tube. When she was released from prison, her enemies were astonished to see her walk out looking as well as when she had entered.

Another time when she was stoned she declared: "I felt myself surrounded by the presence of God, and my soul was filled with love. I knew they could not kill me, for my work was not done; therefore I felt joyful and comfortable, while my enemies felt confusion and distress."

In 1774, after it was revealed to "Mother Ann" in a vision that God had a chosen people in America, she made her plans to leave England. Among the seven who journeyed with her were her husband, and also her brother William Lee, who later became head of the movement.

They embarked from Liverpool on the *Mariah,* commanded by a Captain Smith of New York. Before they set sail, they praised the Lord in songs and dances which so enraged the captain that he threatened to throw them overboard.

After they were far out at sea, the vessel sprang a leak, and water flowed in so rapidly that the captain warned that all might perish before morning. But "Mother Ann" assured him that he must "be of good cheer. Not a hair of our heads shall perish. We shall arrive safely in America." Then she encouraged the sailors, and she and her companions assisted at the pumps. The vessel kept afloat so miraculously that the captain gave her little group liberty to worship as they chose.

The party landed in New York August 6, 1774. Because all were poor, they separated to seek employment. Ann and her husband found work in New York City, she as a domestic servant in a Queen Street house, and he as a blacksmith.

The Revolutionary War, declared soon after their arrival, brought new problems. Like the Quakers, this sect took no part in war, and Ann was sent to prison for speaking out against it. Later she was jailed in Poughkeepsie, New York, and the authorities planned to banish her to the British Isles. After being confined six months for her religious faith, she was released, without trial, by order of Governor Clinton.

After the Revolutionary War, Ann went to Albany, brought her followers together and established the first American Shaker colony at Niskeyuna. Situated deep in the woods, it was an ideal place to withdraw from the world. By this time Ann was not living with her husband, though she spoke of him with respect, saying: "The man I married was very kind; he would have been willing to pass through a flaming fire for my sake." Her devotion to her work became a barrier separating them.

In a few years the colony at Niskeyuna built simple but comfortable dwellings and barns. Members raised good crops and engaged in their own arts and crafts. Although she had said that new converts would surely come in, a long period passed before the colony grew in numbers.

In 1779, when a religious revival occurred in Lebanon Valley, New York, some thirty miles from the colony, many of those attending the revival began to visit the Shakers. Some leaders of the revival finally joined the colony and turned over considerable property to it. Believers began to come in from Connecticut, Massachusetts, New Hampshire and Maine, and some went home and formed colonies of their own.

Violent persecutions followed. "Mother Ann's" greatest trial came in 1781, when she and her brother William Lee and Elder James Whittaker made their famous visitation to the little groups in Massachusetts and Connecticut, and were accused of being dangerous radicals or spies. They were savagely abused, and she was subjected to the greatest torment of all. But she courageously continued her work, and eight closely federated communities resulted from her mission in New England.

All she had undergone no doubt hastened Ann's early death in 1784, at the age of forty-eight. Her ten years in America had been difficult, but her mission had been accomplished. Shakerism was well established in the eastern United States, and later spread to Kentucky, Indiana and Ohio.

With the passing of almost two centuries since Ann Lee's death, she and her Shakers are honored for having made a unique contribution to American life. They set new standards in agriculture. Their ritual dances and spiritual songs enriched American folk traditions. Their skills in handwork opened up new industries. Samples of their arts, crafts and products are now displayed in twelve major galleries in the Shaker Museum at Old Chatham, New York, founded in 1950. Five additional buildings are devoted to blacksmithing, weaving and cobbling. There is also a small Shaker library covering a wide range of Shaker writings.

After the peak of Shaker influence was reached before the Civil War, their numbers diminished. Though there are now very few Shakers, they have left a vivid record. "Mother Ann" Lee's story is a dramatic chapter in the religious history of the United States.

ELIZABETH FRY—
LEADER OF PRISON REFORM
(1780-1845)

● ● ●

She accomplished greater prison reforms than any other woman in history. Kings asked for her counsel and her influence spread throughout the British Isles and Europe. She performed many other Christian services in her native London, where she raised her eleven children.

"I WAS IN PRISON, AND YE CAME UNTO ME"

"SHE FOUND IN THE SILENCE that mysterious power which loves the unlovely into lovableness." Thus does Evelyn Underhill in *Mystics of the Church* describe Elizabeth Fry, Quaker minister. History refers to her as "The Angel of the Prisons."

In 1813 Elizabeth went to the governor of Newgate Prison in London and asked: "Sir, if thee kindly allows me to pray with the women, I will go inside." Permission was granted and when the prison door closed behind her, she felt she had entered a den of wild beasts. This was virtually true. Three hundred women with their numerous children were crowded into four small rooms, without beds or bedding or extra clothing, without classification or employment. There was only one male attendant and his son to look after them. In these crowded quarters the women lived, cooked, washed and slept. The odors were foul and the language obscene. At the window gratings they begged of passers-by and used their shillings to buy liquor in the taproom, the only recreation provided for them. The closeness of the rooms, the wickedness, the nearly naked condition of many of the women—all this was too horrible to describe, and Elizabeth Fry was appalled.

She had to bear with the most hardened creatures and help them know that she had come not in a spirit of judgment but of mercy, not to condemn but to comfort and relieve. She began to see in them a few remaining sparks of nearly extinguished spiritual fire which might yet be "fanned into a flame."

With the wife of a London clergyman and ten Quaker women, in 1816 she formed an Association for the Improvement of the Female Prisoner in Newgate. Its object was to provide, besides clothing and employment, instruction in the Bible and other subjects and to train the women in habits of order, sobriety and industry.

The success of Elizabeth Fry's committee was so dramatic that city authorities adopted the rules it formulated. This was the beginning of what are now regarded as the first principles of prison management: separation of the sexes, classification of criminals, female supervision for the women, useful employment, and adequate provision for religious and secular training.

Elizabeth Fry was a tall woman and the Quaker costume of plain brown dress with a full skirt, tight-fitting waist and snowy white fichu became her well, as did the Quaker bonnet which framed her serene countenance as she entered the forbidding doors of Newgate Prison on her errands of mercy.

Inside, she would remove her bonnet, take a low seat facing the prisoners and open her Bible. To the women crowded around within those dank, damp walls she must have seemed a heavenly vision. As they listened to her sweet voice reading the age-old promises, at least some of them must have found new hope. She liked first to turn to the verses in Isaiah 53:6, 7:

All we like sheep have gone astray: we have turned everyone to his own way; and the Lord hath laid on him the iniquity of us all.
He was oppressed, and he was afflicted, yet he opened not his mouth. . . .

Then she would read part of Psalm 24:3, 4:

Who shall ascend into the hill of the Lord? or who shall stand in his holy place?
He hath clean hands, and a pure heart; who hath not lifted up his soul unto vanity, nor sworn deceitfully.

Elizabeth also found appropriate for her hearers Psalm 27, in which the Psalmist sustains his faith by the power of God, and Psalm 69, in which he prays in affliction and praises God.

Finally she turned to Matthew 7, where Christ ends his Sermon on the

Mount, and to Christ's Parable of the Vineyard, Matthew 20:1-16. When she finished reading, the women prisoners began to understand that courage, holiness, justice and strength are from God.

One of her first practical measures was to open a classroom for the children of inmates in one of the prison cells. She described that first classroom this way: "The railing was crowded with half-naked women, struggling together for front places with violence and begging in loud voices for money." The school was far more successful than Elizabeth Fry thought it could be, for young mothers as well as their children clamored to learn.

One of her next steps was to supply women prisoners with material for handwork. Some said that women so long accustomed to vice and violence could not be induced to work, but Elizabeth inspired them with a desire to create.

Later she invited prison authorities to her home to discuss the hiring of a matron to supervise the women prisoners, the first such matron in Newgate's history.

Both inside and outside prison, Mrs. Fry prayed:

O Lord, may I be directed what to do and what to leave undone; and then may I humbly trust that a blessing will be with me in my various engagements. . . . Enable me, O Lord, to feel tenderly and charitably toward all my beloved fellow mortals. Help me to have no soreness or improper feelings toward any. Let me think no evil, bear all things, hope all things, endure all things. Let me walk in all humility and Godly fear before all men, and in Thy sight.   Amen.

She succeeded because she knew how to apply Christianity to her problems, and because she was willing to labor on with patient, indomitable perseverance month after month and year after year. The authorities cooperated with her more and more as they saw the transformation she brought about. It became uncommon now to see half-naked, half-drunk women cursing, and singing licentious songs. The women's prison began to take on the appearance of a well-regulated family.

Six years after Elizabeth Fry started her prison reform, the great Virginia congressman, John Randolph, came from America to visit London. He reported to a friend:

I saw the greatest curiosity in London—aye, and in England, too, sire—compared with which Westminster Abbey, the Tower, Somerset House, the British Museum, Nay, Parliament itself, sink into utter insignificance. I have seen, sir, Elizabeth Fry, in Newgate, and I have witnessed there, sir, miraculous effects of true Christianity upon the most depraved of human beings—bad women, sir, who are worse, if possible, than the Devil himself. And yet the wretched outcasts have been tamed and subdued by the Christian eloquence of Mrs. Fry. Nothing but religion can effect this miracle, sir.

Her reform extended far beyond Newgate. She and her committee visited every convict ship as it left the Thames River, and read and prayed with the women prisoners before they set forth on their long voyage to the penal settlement in Australia. She saw that they were provided with materials for work during their restless days at sea; and hoped that the sale of their finished articles might keep them from starvation when they reached the settlement.

Knowing that conditions in Australia were horrible, she asked: "What happens to women convicts who are transported to Australia?" An Anglican minister in Australia replied that many of the women on their arrival were driven to vice to obtain either food or lodging. Elizabeth Fry presented this report to the proper authorities in England and suggested: "Cannot the men convicts build barracks for the women? Surely delay is impossible." At her instigation, homes to receive women prisoners were opened at Parramatta and at Hobart. Finally, in 1836, a member of her Newgate committee visited Australia to investigate the conditions among women convicts there.

Elizabeth Fry made many journeys in the British Isles and on the Continent in the interest of better prison conditions. In 1818 she went to Scotland and the north of England, and the next year published notes on her tour. The value of her work was recognized by the House of Commons, and this recognition led to an extensive correspondence with persons interested in prison reform in Italy, Denmark and Russia. In 1827 she visited houses for the insane and the hospitalized in Ireland. She went to France in 1838 to confer with leading prison officials and examine houses of detention in Paris, Rouen, Caen and other places. The next year she obtained an official permit to visit any prison in France.

Before returning to England she inspected jails in Geneva, Zurich, Stuttgart and Frankfort on the Main. In the summer of 1840 she traveled to prisons in Belgium, Holland and Prussia and the next year to Copenhagen, Denmark.

Elizabeth Fry's concern for the needy and the suffering knew no bounds. In 1819, within six hours after she had learned a man had frozen to death in the streets of London, she and her committee set to work to prepare a shelter for the homeless in London at night, so that such a tragedy might not occur again. Warm bedding, as well as soup and bread, were provided for those needing shelter from the cold. She and her committee found jobs for the unemployed and organized classes for destitute children. They also opened a shelter for homeless children in London. She organized libraries for coast guardsmen in more than five hundred stations around Britain. She also established the Nursing Sisters of Devonshire Square, a pioneer English institution for the training of nurses.

As her philanthropies increased, her problems often seemed too heavy for one woman to bear. But true Quaker that she was, she would go into the silence and pray: "Lord, be pleased to help and strengthen me in all this . . . in all my perplexities make a way where I see no way."

The miracle of her life was that she could accomplish all these things and yet succeed so admirably as a wife and mother. One of her biographers, Janet Whitney, in her book *Elizabeth Fry, Quaker Heroine,* declares:

> She is the most outstanding example in history of a woman other than royal who accepted marriage and many times motherhood, and still maintained an active public life. But she is also an example of the difficulty of the double feat. The wide opportunities that were opening out before her required time, attention and vigor. But her life had to swing, like a pendulum, constantly and daily, from the large to the small.

Elizabeth Fry's Christian concerns dated back to her childhood. As a little girl she wrote in her diary: "I love to pour wine and oil into the wounds of the afflicted."

When she was seventeen she added:

> I do not know if I shall not soon be rather religious, because I have thought lately what a support it is through life. I think anybody who has real faith can never be unhappy. . . . What is best of all, it draws virtue.

A few months later she said: "A thought passed my mind, that if I have some religion, I should be superior to what I am."

Born in May 1780 in Norwich, England, a hundred and fifteen miles northeast of London, she was the fourth of twelve children and one of seven daughters of Catherine and John Gurney, devout Quakers. Her father, an English banker and wool stapler, belonged to a famous family that traced its lineage back to the Norman Conquest. Their home, Earlham Hall, was a stately mansion, built of mellow red brick, and it had large, irregular rooms and passages, cupboards and nooks. Elizabeth spent a happy childhood, playing on Earlham's sunny lawns, amid its apricot and lime trees, by the banks of a nearby brook, and along the carriage road that led from her house to the Quaker meetinghouse.

At eighteen she experienced a great spiritual illumination during a sermon by the American Quaker, William Savery. At that time he prophesied that she would have a high calling.

Later, when she entered London society, she found that it did not interest her. Returning home to Earlham Hall, she met a "plain friend," Deborah Darby. Following a memorable evening with Deborah, Elizabeth wrote in her diary:

After we had spent a pleasant evening, my heart began to feel itself silenced before God and without looking at others, I felt myself under the shadow of the wing of God. . . . After the meeting my heart felt really light and as I walked home by starlight, I looked through nature up to nature's God. . . . I know not what the mountain is I have to climb. I am to be a Quaker.

From that time on she tried to develop the inner, not the outer self, and as Paul said of Jesus, she now "went about doing good." (Acts 10:38).

In 1800 Elizabeth married Joseph Fry, member of a prominent and wealthy Quaker family and a merchant in tea, coffee, spices and other East Indian products. As a young matron, her lovely house in Mildred's Court, London, became a meeting place for members of the sect. It was not unusual for her to entertain from thirty to sixty at a meal. In later years, however, when she became absorbed in prison reform, she gave up entertaining.

Her philanthropy began in a small way when she was a young mother in London. She would gather her skirts around her and make her way through children, pigs and poultry, by narrow passages and up broken staircases, until she found those who needed her care. She vaccinated some, induced others to send their children to school, persuaded the slovenly and unkempt to adopt more orderly habits, and introduced all to the Bible. On the shelves in her home she kept an abundant supply of garments for those in need and an ample stock of medicines for the sick. Wherever she called, her presence expressed benevolence, harmony and love.

She began her prison reform in 1813 when she had already given birth to eight children, but her most active public work did not start until 1816. Of her eleven children, seven bore Biblical names, and David, the last, was born nine years after his mother's first visit to Newgate Prison.

In all her undertakings, Elizabeth Fry had the co-operation of her husband Joseph. Her Christian concerns became his, and often Joseph Fry went with his wife on her errands of mercy. She had his blessing even when she went into the Quaker ministry ten years after her marriage. This was in keeping with the Quaker tradition for women, and Joseph Fry was a liberal husband. Her eminent contemporary Mary Somerville said of Elizabeth Fry's ministry: "Her voice was fine, her delivery admirable and her prayer sublime."

In addition to her first home in Mildred's Court in London, Elizabeth presided over another beautiful place, Plashet, and a smaller one on Upton Lane. In the last house she realized to the full the roles of wife, mother, grandmother, minister and friend to countless people.

Although she had elegant houses, beautiful gardens, plenty of servants and other luxuries during the early years of her marriage, later her husband's business failed and she had to live in a smaller home in Upton Lane. She accepted her material losses with serene composure, declaring that her faith and love were as strong in adversity as in prosperity. When she parted with her beloved home, Plashet, she said: "I see that I have many blessings left and do earnestly desire to estimate them as I should."

Later she learned that her loss of a big house was for the best, for after this she was called to other countries to assist in prison reform. She gave many kings and princes her wise counsel. One of her most quoted statements was made to the king of France, to whom she said: "When thee builds a prison thee had better build with the thought ever in mind that thee and thy children may occupy the cells."

When Frederick William IV, King of Prussia, came to England for the christening of the infant Prince of Wales, the king asked to visit Newgate Prison with Elizabeth Fry. In his presence, she read to the prisoners the twelfth chapter of Romans, dealing with the surrendered life, the various duties of the Church and the Christian spirit. Her voice rose to a crescendo as she read: "So we, being many, are one body in Christ, and every one members one of another" (Rom. 12:5). When she knelt, the king followed her example and listened attentively to her beautiful, extemporaneous prayer.

The scene was a moving one—the monarch of a great nation, dignitaries of England and common prisoners all praying to their common Creator. When they rose, the king offered his arm to Mrs. Fry and they walked out together. Later, he visited her at her London residence, where she presented to him her six daughters, her daughters-in-law, her five sons, twenty-five grandchildren, and other members of her family.

Her most active years were now ending. She had often worked beyond her strength, but when she bore the burden of almost overpowering opposition to prison improvement, she could say: "I feel the rock always underneath me."

In one of her last talks to her children, she warned them against undue love of riches, against too many indulgences and luxuries, and against extravagance, vanity and immodesty in dress. Above all she counseled: "I fear whether there is not a danger of quenching or grieving the Holy Spirit of God by too much attention to outward rather than the inward teaching of the Holy Spirit."

She worked until a few months before her death on October 12, 1845. Among her last words as she lay dying were: "I can say one thing—since my heart was touched at seventeen years old I believe I never have awakened from sleep, in sickness or in health, by day or by night, without my first waking thought being how best I might serve my Lord."

Elizabeth Fry's death caused widespread sorrow in London and elsewhere. Many riding in carriages and thousands on foot joined her funeral procession, to honor this woman to whom Christ's words applied: "I was in prison, and ye came unto me" (Matt. 25:36).

ANN JUDSON—FIRST AMERICAN
WOMAN MISSIONARY TO THE FAR EAST
(1789-1826)

◆ ◆ ◆

First wife of Adoniram Judson, she suffered with him in his pioneering experiences in Burma and saved his life during the 1817-1818 war between the English and Burmese. She assisted him in his translation of the Bible into Burmese and wrote a history of the Burma Mission.

"IN DANGER HE CAN INSPIRE ME WITH FORTITUDE"

ANN HASSELTINE JUDSON and her husband Adoniram Judson were the first Americans to establish a mission in the Far East. Her willingness to suffer, combined with her rare intelligence, strength of mind, patience and practical common sense give her an honored place among women in the American missionary field. Her journals and letters and her record of the Burma mission all bear witness to the fact that she walked closely with God.

She was born in Bradford, Massachusetts, in 1789. Like the saints of old, she spent a great part of her time reading religious books and praying, even as a young girl. Impressed by the New England religious revival of 1806, she resolved to devote her life to religion and prayed: "Direct me in Thy service, and I ask no more. I would not choose my position of work, or place of labor. Only let me know Thy will, and I will readily comply."

She studied at Bradford Academy and, with characteristic New England energy, began teaching when she was eighteen. When she was twenty-one she met Adoniram Judson, a Congregational minister and a graduate of Andover Theological School, at a meeting of the first American Board of Commissioners for Foreign Missions held in the home of her father, Deacon John Hasseltine.

Adoniram soon proposed marriage to Ann, and she pondered this step which would take her as a missionary into a foreign land. In her journal she wrote:

> I am a creature of God, and He has an undoubted right to do with me as seemeth good in His sight. I rejoice that I am in His hand—that He is everywhere present and can protect me in one place as well as in another. . . . When I am called to face danger, to pass through scenes of terror and distress, He can inspire me with fortitude, and enable me to trust in Him. . . . Whether I spend my days in India or America, I desire to spend them in the service of God, and be prepared to spend an eternity in His presence. . . . I am quite willing to give up temporal comforts and live a life of hardship and trial, if it be the will of God. . . . "Behold the handmaid of the Lord; be it unto me according to thy word" (Luke 1:38).

Soon after, Adoniram wrote to Ann's father and mother, John and Rebecca Hasseltine:

> I have now to ask whether you can consent to part with your daughter early next spring to see her no more in this world. Whether you can consent to her departure for a heathen land, and her subjection to the hardships and sufferings of a missionary life. Whether you can consent to her exposure to the dangers of the ocean, to the fatal influence of the southern climate of India; to every kind of want and distress, to degradation, insult, persecution, and perhaps a violent death. Can you consent to all this for the sake of Him who died for her and for you?

This turned out to be a prophetic letter, for Ann Judson was to suffer most of the things Adoniram mentioned. On the New Year's Day before their marriage the twenty-four-year-old Adoniram wrote to Ann:

> It is with the utmost sincerity, and with my whole heart, that I wish you, my love, a happy new year. May it be a year in which your walk will be close with God, your frame calm and serene; and the road that leads you to the Lamb marked with purer light. May it be a year in which you will have more largely the spirit of Christ. . . . May this be the year in which you change your name, in which you will take final leave of your relatives and native land, in which you will cross the wide ocean, and dwell on the other side of the world, among a heathen people.

Ann (sometimes called Nancy) Hasseltine and Adoniram Judson were married in Bradford on February 5, 1812, and left the next day for India. As their brig, the *Caravan*, sailed across strange seas, Ann wrote in her journal: "I never had a greater sense of our obligation to live devoted to God." At a shipboard service the sermon was on "Lukewarmness in

Religion," and she wrote: "I felt that a great part of it was applicable to myself. When I consider the indifference with which I have regarded and treated so great a being as God, I am confounded."

During the four-month voyage, Ann and Adoniram read *Lives of the Martyrs and Saints,* as well as several books on baptism. On their arrival in Calcutta, June 18, they made the momentous decision to join the Baptist Church. They were baptized by immersion in a Calcutta chapel and wrote home about their change in conviction: "We are both confirmed Baptists, not because we wished to be, but because truth compelled us to be."

Their sudden change in church membership caused criticism at home, but good came from it. Baptist churches in America, awakened to their duty to carry on foreign mission work, formed the Baptist General Convention in Philadelphia in 1814 and appointed the Judsons as Baptist missionaries with freedom to select their own field of labor.

Shortly after their arrival in India, they found that the East India Company distrusted missionaries and they were ordered to return to America.

After several weary months of indecision they decided to try to set up a mission in Rangoon, then ruled by a despot who opposed all forms of missionary teaching. Ann wrote in her journal:

I acknowledge the kind hand of the heavenly Father. In changing my name, He has allowed me to take the name of one who loves the cause of Christ, and makes the promotion of it the business of my life. One who is, in every respect, the most calculated to make me happy and useful, of all the persons I have ever seen.

Ann's first house in Rangoon was built of teakwood on two acres of ground, and had orchards and gardens. She soon adopted the Burmese costume with its light tunic of bright-colored gauze and a skirt of bright silk, slit at the ankle. This dress made her appear taller than she actually was. A lovely brunette with olive skin, finely molded features, deep-set eyes and a winning manner, she made a pretty picture.

She began to study Burmese, but soon discovered it would be difficult to preach Christianity in a language lacking the words God, Heaven and Eternity.

In January 1815, while with child, she was stricken with fever. Embarking for Madras, a seaport on the Bay of Bengal, she hoped to profit by a change of climate; in six months she returned home, well. In September she gave birth to a son, Roger Williams, the first child born of white parents in Burma. She had neither a doctor nor a nurse in attendance at the child's birth, only her husband.

Eight months after his birth, her first child died of jungle fever, and was buried in a little enclosure in the mission garden. Ann wrote at this time: "God is the same when He afflicts as when He is merciful, just as worthy of our entire trust and confidence."

Ann now began to help Adoniram translate the Scriptures into Burmese. First she translated the Book of Jonah, which especially appealed to the Burmese mind. She also opened a school for Burmese girls. In 1816 the first printing press and type were brought into Burma to produce the tracts for the Judsons to use in their teaching.

In 1822 Ann became so weak from a tropical illness that she had to return to America to regain her strength. She found it took greater courage to leave her husband in Burma than it had to leave her home ten years earlier. "Rangoon has been the theater in which so much of the faithfulness, power and mercy of God has been exhibited," she wrote as her boat sailed westward.

En route to America she visited England and Scotland, and met William Wilberforce, philanthropist and advocate of the abolition of the slave trade, as well as other well-known people who asked her many questions about the Burmese mission.

Taking leave of her British friends in August 1822, she sailed to America, recording in her journal: "The same kind and glorious Being, who has directed my steps and at times granted me His Presence, is still, I trust, with me."

A yellow fever epidemic was raging in Massachusetts when she reached America in September 1822, so she did not go to her home in Bradford, but first visited in Philadelphia, and later in Baltimore, where she spent the winter.

Ill and under many demands from friends, she did not get enough rest. She spent much time preparing her account of the *American Baptist Mission to the Burman Empire,* the main source of information about the Judsons' work, published in March 1823.

After visiting her family in Bradford, she set sail for Burma in the late summer of 1823. When Adoniram met her at the dock in Rangoon, he rejoiced that she was well and strong once more. During the two and a half years she had been away, Adoniram had finished his translation of the New Testament into Burmese, and had written a summary of the Old Testament in twelve sections. His translation of the entire Bible into Burmese required twenty-four years.

During their first nine years in Burma, Ann and Adoniram Judson had made only eighteen native converts, but they were not disheartened. They now went up the Irrawaddy River to Ava, the capital of Burma, hoping to establish a mission there. The small boat in which they were traveling was like an oven when the thermometer rose to 108 degrees in the shade, but had to serve as their home until a crude board house could be built.

When they arrived in February, war was already threatening between the Burmese and the English, and by June they were surrounded by the noise and confusion of battles. For the next two years, they experienced sufferings and dangers which have had few parallels in missionary annals.

Soon after war was declared, Adoniram was seized by a posse of men, thrown to the ground and bound with a whipcord. In spite of Ann's entreaties and offers of money, she saw him dragged off to the courthouse and was later informed that he had been thrown into the death prison. A guard of ten ruffians was posted before the Judson house. Her servants were placed in stocks. With four of her Burmese schoolgirls, she was a virtual prisoner in the inner room of her own house.

During the next seven months, while she was awaiting the birth of her second child, Ann was beset by tribulations, but she asked God for strength. Despite the close watch on her home, she managed to slip out or send Burmese friends to her husband and his English companions with supplies of food and clothing.

She spent hours each day before government authorities pleading for her husband's life. After nightfall she went to the prison to take him food. Once, with some buffalo meat she had obtained, she made him a mincemeat pie according to her New England recipe.

She had promptly destroyed all letters and records of the Burma mission lest they be used to convict her husband of spying. She concealed his New Testament translation in a pillow so hard and uncomfortable and ordinary in appearance that no one would be tempted to confiscate the translation. She managed to hide her personal notes to her husband in the spout of a teapot.

In a long letter to her husband's brother she told how she was often threatened when she was alone at night. She said she did not think of her dangers but only of the suffering Adoniram endured as he lay on the bare prison floor, with his feet in chains.

The only period when she did not visit him daily was after the birth of their daughter, Maria Elizabeth Butterworth Judson. When the puny, sick baby was twenty-one days old, Ann carried her to the prison door for her father to see. She found her husband with about a hundred other prisoners shut up in one room where no air could enter except through cracks in the boards. From incessant perspiration and lack of food he looked closer to death than life. Afterward he was stricken with tropical fever, and it seemed as if his death were near.

Obtaining permission from the authorities to put him in a small bamboo hut in the governor's enclosure, opposite the prison gate, and to give him medicines, she left her own house to watch over him. The hut was so small that they could not stand upright, but it was a palace in comparison to his former crowded prison quarters.

While he was recovering, Adoniram was removed secretly to another prison. Not knowing where they had taken him, Ann snatched up her three-month-old daughter and with two adopted Burmese children set out to find him. She made part of the trip by covered boat, part in an open cart, jolting through heat and dust, her baby in her arms.

At the end of a long, difficult journey to Amarapura, Ann learned that only two hours before her arrival Adoniram had been sent on to Oung-pen-la. Exhausted as she was, she followed on foot. She found him imprisoned in an old building without a roof, chained to other prisoners, and almost dead with fatigue, the soles of his feet nothing but raw flesh after his eight-mile walk over burning sand and gravel.

Since she was without food or shelter for herself and the children, Ann had no course but to accept the jailer's invitation to share his two-room hut which already housed him and his family.

For the next six months she and her baby and the two Burmese children slept on mats spread on the floor in a filthy room half filled with grain, and without so much as a chair to sit on. But Ann was scarcely aware of her own privations; her thoughts were filled with the plight of her husband. She was assisted at this time by a Bengalese cook who had previously helped her at Ava.

During the first week in the jailer's room at Oung-pen-la, one of the Burmese children who had been helping her care for little Maria came down with smallpox. When Ann walked to the prison now, she carried Maria in her arms, but it was not long before the second Burmese child, the baby and finally Ann herself developed the disease.

When she and the children had recovered after many months and Adoniram's health was finally restored, she was stricken with one of the tropical diseases almost always fatal to foreigners. She became so weak that she could hardly walk, but she set out for Ava, to procure medicine and food. The last four miles she traveled in a cart through mud so deep that the oxen could barely move.

Ann returned to Oung-pen-la with her strength exhausted. She managed to crawl in on the mat floor of the wretched bamboo hut she had left, and there she collapsed and lay ill for two months.

She was so emaciated that her former Bengalese cook, who had aided her through many trials, burst into tears when he saw her. Later she reported that she and her husband would have died had it not been for his faithful care. He tended them both, carrying food to the prison as Ann had done, and often depriving himself that they might have enough.

The loss of her sick mother's milk caused little Maria to suffer more than any of them and her cries were heart-rending. By sending presents to the jailer, Ann obtained permission for Adoniram to leave prison long enough to take their starving baby around the village to beg a little nourishment for her from nursing mothers.

After this illness Ann herself was never well. Toward the end of the war, she contracted spotted fever and could not move. During this time her husband was placed in another obscure prison where she could not find him. Even the food she sent by a bearer was returned. Of this period she wrote:

> If I ever felt the value and efficacy of prayer, I did at this time. I could not rise from my couch. I could make no efforts to secure my husband. I could only plead with that great and powerful Being who has said, "Call upon me in the day of trouble and I will hear, and thou shalt glorify me." God made me at this time feel so powerfully this promise, that I became quite composed, feeling assured that my prayers would be answered.

When the war ended and the Judsons were once more under the protection of the British, a Calcutta paper reported that it was owing to the "repeated eloquence, and forcible appeals of Mrs. Judson, that the untutored Burman was finally made willing to secure the welfare and happiness of his country, by a sincere peace."

On February 21, 1826, the Judsons joyfully left the scene of their sufferings in Oung-pen-la and returned to Rangoon. Soon they went to Amherst, in lower Burma, to set up another mission there.

Not long after their arrival, Adoniram was called back to Ava, to help as a translator in the peace negotiations. He went largely with the hope of obtaining religious toleration in Burma and he and Ann parted with cheerful hearts. They had been saved in so many trials and misfortunes that a separation of a few months seem trivial. But within three months Ann was stricken with a violent fever, and died October 24, 1826, at the age of thirty-seven. She was buried at Amherst under a hópia (hope) tree while their Burmese converts wept over her grave.

Weeks later, at Ava, Adoniram received the news of Ann's death and wrote to her mother at Bradford: "I commend myself and motherless child to your sympathy and prayers." Three months later he returned to Amherst to his little Maria. Always a sick child, on April 24, 1827, she died at the age of two years and three months. Her father buried her under the hópia tree beside the new grave of her mother. This time he wrote to Ann's mother:

We made the child's last bed in the small enclosure that surrounded her mother's lonely grave. Together they rest in hope, under the hope tree, which stands at the head of the graves; and together, I trust, their spirits are rejoicing after a short separation of precisely six months. And I am left alone in the wide world. My own dear family I have buried; one in Rangoon, and two in Amherst.

Although Ann Judson did not live to see the realization of all her dreams, her husband's translation of the Bible into Burmese became the foundation stone of Christianity in Burma. Before his death, the Christian movement in Burma had sixty-three churches under the leadership of one hundred and sixty-three missionaries, native ministers and assistants.

Seven and a half years after Ann's death, the lonely Adoniram Judson married Sarah Hall Boardman, widow of another missionary in Burma. After her death, he married Emily Chubbock. But it was Ann Judson who had been the real pioneer with him for Christian faith. Like Sarah, wife of Abraham, she had forsaken home and country for all the vicissitudes of life in a strange land in order to be near her husband. The first American woman to go with her husband as a foreign missionary, her faith sustained her through all the sufferings.

EMILY H. TUBMAN—

AN EXAMPLE OF CHRISTIAN STEWARDSHIP

(1794-1885)

♦ ♦ ♦

Church schools were supported, ministers educated, evangelism aided, churches built and New Testament Christianity extended by her efforts and gifts. Twenty-seven years before Lincoln's Emancipation Proclamation, she freed her slaves.

"IT IS MORE BLESSED TO GIVE THAN TO RECEIVE"

FROM HER LARGE FORTUNE, Emily H. Tubman gave lavishly to the church and the charities which uphold the Christian way of life. She looked upon her money as a sacred trust, and found in her stewardship of it the truth of Christ's utterance: "It is more blessed to give than to receive."

Born during George Washington's first term as president, she lived under twenty-two presidents. When she died at the age of ninety-one, Grover Cleveland was serving his first term. During the last five decades of her life, she gave thousands of dollars to the Christian Churches (Disciples of Christ) and at her death she left another fortune to their expanding programs.

Her generosity enabled Alexander Campbell, one of the founders of the Christian Churches (Disciples of Christ), and other pioneers to evangelize and build up the church rapidly during the years immediately preceding and following the Civil War.

Joseph Richard Bennett, in his 1958 thesis for the Christian Theological Seminary (formerly the School of Religion at Butler University), *A Study of the Life and Contributions of Emily H. Tubman*, points out:

> In recent years, many historians of the Disciples have written varied accounts of the pioneer fathers of the Restoration Movement in America. A disturbing factor is that the majority of these accounts have overlooked entirely the life and works of Mrs. Emily H. Tubman, as documented sources and references were not readily available. It is to be noted, however, that the name of Mrs. Tubman should be associated with those of Alexander Campbell, Isaac Errett, and James S. Lamar. She, too, helped to forge and shape the Brotherhood of Disciples into the far-reaching Christian force which it is today. . . . It is necessary that credit be given not only to the men of the Restoration Movement, but also to the Christian pioneer, Mrs. Emily Tubman, whose stewardship helped to preserve the movement.

> Disciples of today are challenged to study the Christian character of Mrs. Tubman which exemplifies intelligent faith and unyielding convictions. She was convinced that the Church of Jesus Christ should be simple in its message, organization, and practice. She was convinced that it should be patterned after examples of the Church which are recorded in the New Testament, free from human dogma and tradition.

In her long lifetime, Emily Tubman witnessed the development of the United States into a great nation. She was born March 21, 1794, in Ashland, Hanover County, Virginia, about twenty-five miles north of Richmond, the daughter of Ann Chiles and Edmund Pendleton Thomas. Her father went to the blue-grass basin of Kentucky soon after that state was admitted to the Union.

As the state's first land registrar, he acquired more than seventeen thousand acres of land in payment for his services. Death came to him early, when Emily was nine years old, and he left four other children. Emily's legal guardian was Henry Clay, the famous orator and statesman.

Little is known about Emily's early education, but her brother Landon A. Thomas was graduated from Yale in 1822, and practiced law. In later years she too studied law in order to equip herself to administer her husband's estate.

In 1818 she traveled from Frankfort, Kentucky, to Augusta, Georgia, with her mother's cousins Colonel and Mrs. Nicholas Ware and their niece Mary Ariuton Ware. The journey was made on horseback, and Emily's clothes for the trip were carried in her saddlebags.

During her stay in Augusta she met Richard C. Tubman, an Englishman who had made a large fortune as a Southern planter and exporter of cotton, indigo and tobacco. They were married the same year in the elegant Telfair Street home of Colonel Ware, a member of the Georgia state senate. Colonel Ware bought wedding gowns in New York for both Emily and his niece Mary, who was married about the same time.

Soon after the wedding the Tubmans traveled by carriage with a retinue of servants to visit Emily's mother in Frankfort, but they returned to Augusta to live, for Mr. Tubman's business interests were there. He was a generous husband and showered many luxuries on his beautiful wife. Tall, straight, dignified, with brown eyes full of love and understanding, Emily was a distinguished-looking woman and a welcome addition to Augusta society.

In 1825 when the Marquis de Lafayette, French statesman, officer and friend of Washington, visited Augusta in his tour of the United States, young Mrs. Tubman was in charge of arrangements for the banquet at the Planter's Hotel. She also had the honor of leading the minuet with the illustrious general.

Despite her social graces and charm as a hostess, Emily was an earnest student of things spiritual, and a dutiful wife. Each Sunday she went with her husband to St. Paul's Episcopal Church in Augusta, where he was a vestryman, even though she did not become a member. In her study of the Bible she had come to the conclusion that immersion as practiced by Christ and the Apostles was the proper form of baptism, so in October 1828 she was baptized in the Kentucky River in Frankfort.

On her return to Georgia she took her certificate of baptism, but she never joined either the Baptist or the Episcopal Church.

After her baptism, she became a friend and admirer of Alexander Campbell, and followed his teachings in The *Millennial Harbinger,* a periodical to which the Tubmans subscribed from its beginning in 1830.

Emily's husband, ill the last years of his life, died in her arms as they were journeying by carriage from Georgia to Kentucky in 1836. In his will he declared that it was his desire to have his widow apply to the legislature of Georgia ("if they in their wisdom should deem it expedient or politic") to pass a law enabling her to emancipate all his Negroes, with the exception of a few household servants. The laws of Georgia against the liberation of slaves were very strict. The time was twenty-seven years before Lincoln's preliminary Emancipation Proclamation of 1862. It was no easy task that lay ahead for Emily Tubman, and she was to meet and overcome many obstacles before her goal was achieved.

A short time after her husband's death, she and Captain and Mrs. Edward Campfield began to meet together on Sunday mornings to read the Scriptures, sing hymns and observe the Lord's Supper. The next year Emily and four others organized the First Christian Church in Augusta. It was there she began to think of the large fortune she had inherited from her husband as a sacred trust for the furtherance of religion.

She had become a large stockholder in the newly organized Georgia Railroad, which grew into one of the major systems of the South. Because it was needed by the Union forces for transportation, it was not ruined by the Civil War. Many of her land, bank and bond investments survived the critical postwar years. She may also have had investments in England, where her husband exported the products he raised in the South.

One of her first gifts was eight thousand dollars to erect a brick church building on Reynolds Street, records J. Edward Moseley in his book *Disciples of Christ in Georgia*. The small congregation that used this church was poor, and Emily was happy to provide them a place in which to worship. When the church was rebuilt in 1876, her gift to it was more than a hundred thousand dollars. This church building, known as First Christian, is still in use.

As Emily began to search for a place where her slaves could go if they were freed, she became acquainted with the work being done by the United States government to establish Liberia, on the west coast of Africa. In 1844, eight years after her husband's death, she called her slaves together and gave each his choice of remaining with her or being given his freedom. Sixty-nine chose freedom and asked to be sent to Liberia.

Mrs. Tubman chartered a ship from Baltimore, and her former slaves landed at Harper, the leading city of Cape Palmas, Liberia. She also contributed generously to a fund which provided homes and supplies for Negroes arriving in Liberia from the United States.

In helping her slaves to go to Liberia, she was obeying the recommendations of her own Christian Church, which as early as 1827 had approved the Colonization Society's objective "to colonize and free people of color in a fertile part of Africa, where they may enjoy full liberty and become messengers of the gospel."

Emily Tubman's name and influence still live in the Republic of Liberia.

One community there is named Tubmantown. William Vaccanarat Shadrach Tubman, elected the eighteenth President of the Republic of Liberia in 1943 and re-elected in 1951, is the grandson of William Shadrach and Sylvia Ann Elizabeth Tubman, two of the sixty-nine Negroes Emily Tubman sent to Liberia in 1844.

President Tubman's wartime and postwar administration has been called the most progressive period in Liberia's history. Richard P. Hunt, writing in *The New York Times* in December of 1957, stated that signs of material progress and hope of reform in Liberia stem "from the personality and policies of William V. S. Tubman, now in his fourteenth year as President and virtually a one-man government of the 110-year old Negro Republic. Most of the advances appearing today are credited to the programs he has launched since 1944."

To the seventy-five of her slaves who did not go to Liberia Mrs. Tubman gave land, clothing and regular provisions until they were able to support themselves. She was among those Southerners who realized that legal freedom was not the only need of the Negroes, and that until they understood the significance and responsibilities of their freedom they would need help. She also concerned herself with their spiritual well-being. At her death she left a two-story stone house on Greene Street in Augusta to Gus Dorsey, her butler and carriage driver, and his wife Rebecca, her cook.

The Bible, both during and after the Civil War, was Emily's comfort and example. When General William Sherman of the Union Army was marching on Georgia, threatening to "smash things to the Sea," she knew he might reach Augusta, where Confederate ammunition was produced. In this hour of her spiritual need, she turned to her Bible. In one of her letters written at this time, she said:

> The Book of books not only comforts us here under the various trials and bereavements of life, but by diligent study of its divine teachings, educates and prepares us for the enjoyment of the highest and more holy society of heaven.

Realizing that the love of Christ's Gospel and the light of His life were destined to make human emancipation world-wide and human brotherhood as universal as His own presence, she followed the Bible in regard to the slavery question. Her guide was Paul's statement: "There is neither bond nor free . . . for ye are all one in Christ Jesus" (Gal. 3:28).

Emily had great compassion for the sufferings of the Confederate soldiers and their families. When she saw many soldiers crowded into the makeshift hospital in St. Patrick's Roman Catholic Church, in Augusta, she bought an ice machine, described as an ammonia absorption system, the first to be operated in America. Joseph Richard Bennett, in his thesis, points out that "it seems quite probable that Mrs. Tubman's ice machine marked the beginning of a new industry for the South, which was greatly needed during the struggling years of the Reconstruction Era."

After the war was over, she and other stockholders of the Georgia Railroad agreed to provide free transportation to weary Confederate soldiers who had no money for their fare back to their homes. She also fed and clothed the families of many Confederate soldiers who died in the war.

Because she gave cheerfully and unostentatiously, she was much beloved. Her Frankfort pastor described her as one who was "simple in her tastes and manners, natural in her speech and behavior, sincere and genuine in all things." He added that "one could approach her as easily as a child its mother. Free of haughtiness and affectation, those who knew her best loved her most, and all who sought her friendship were sure to obtain it."

Remembering that the Christians of Paul's time did not look upon their possessions as their own but shared them with others, Emily too shared what she had with the poor and needy—all of whom found in her a friend.

She gave funds to rebuild Hunter Street Church in Atlanta, and another church in Athens, Georgia. She supported the work of the early pioneers of the Disciples of Christ and gave large or small gifts for the construction or furnishing of practically every one of the church buildings erected by this religious body in Georgia.

To encourage manufacturing and help to provide desperately needed jobs in the South during the Reconstruction period, she helped to establish the John P. King Manufacturing Company, a textile plant in Georgia. Her great-nephew Landon Thomas is president of this firm in Augusta, the city which was her home for more than sixty years.

She spent her summers in Frankfort, her girlhood home. In 1870 the Ann Street Church of Frankfort burned down. Though the struggling congregation could not raise funds for rebuilding, and were without a leader, they met occasionally in the courthouse. Learning of this, Mrs. Tubman bought land to increase the size of the old church lot to a hundred square feet. Then she built a new church of Romanesque architecture. Her gifts to this church, where her brother was a trustee, are recorded as early as 1852.

In 1882 Emily Tubman provided the building and endowed the minister's salary for another church in Augusta (known today as Central Christian Church), and she finally extended her help to other denominations as well.

Her gifts to church colleges were many. In 1857 she endowed the Tubman Chair of Modern Languages at Bethany College in West Virginia. Later she gave one-fifteenth of the endowment for Bethany's Chair of Sacred History. She also contributed generously to other colleges of the Christian Church, including Hiram College at Hiram, Ohio, Transylvania College at Lexington, Kentucky, and Northwest Christian University (now Butler University) at Indianapolis.

When people thanked her for her generosity, she often replied: "I am a steward of the Lord, and only hold this money in trust, and my supreme joy is to dispense it to advance His Kingdom or to relieve human suffering."

While on a preaching mission in Augusta in November 1871, Isaac Errett visited her in her home. She was seventy-seven years old at this time, and he wrote of the "constant flow of conversation on spiritual themes" that went on around her. He also stated:

It is beautiful to look on such a life, rising so sweetly and grandly above the ordinary plane of selfishness on which the world, and too largely the Church, moves; and it is blessed beyond expression to look on the freshness, heartiness and gladness, unwithered by age, with which a life is invested and crowned that has thus devoted itself.

A charming hostess, she entertained both in her spacious house in Augusta and in her Frankfort summer home. On a visit to Kentucky in 1844, her former guardian, Henry Clay, came to pay his respects to her. The *Frankfort Commonwealth* of that year reported that Mrs. Tubman, "the favorite of every circle in which she is known," entertained Clay "with much courteous hospitality at her home during his late southern trip." After his death in 1852, she contributed generously to the Henry Clay Monument in the Lexington Cemetery.

On three different occasions she was hostess to Alexander Campbell as he traveled through Georgia founding his Christian Churches. He first visited her when he toured the South in 1838-1839. He came next in 1845, and again in 1857. J. Edward Moseley relates that when Campbell went to Europe in 1847, Mrs. Tubman sent him three hundred dollars for the poor of Britain and Ireland. She had first met Alexander Campbell shortly after her baptism in 1828. Like him, she believed that the restoration of the Apostolic faith was the only hope for the ultimate triumph of Christ's religion. Because of her broad views on the Church, on slavery and on giving, she was a disciple after Campbell's own heart.

When Emily Tubman died June 9, 1885, her minister J. S. Lamar declared in his funeral address: "If I were called upon to characterize

Mrs. Tubman's life in one sentence, I should say that, like Stephen, she was full of faith and good works." She was buried in her family cemetery at Frankfort on a low-lying hill overlooking the winding Kentucky River, almost within sight of the grave of Daniel Boone, who had guided the pioneers into Kentucky.

In a memorial book issued at her death, Georgie Darsie observed: "May her great life be like the seed that fell on good ground, which after its own kind, brought forth thirty, sixty and a hundred fold."

A marble tablet in the First Christian Church at Augusta bears her name and the Latin inscription: *Si Monumentum Requiris Circumspice* (If you seek her monument, look around).

MARY SMITH MOFFAT AND
MARY MOFFAT LIVINGSTONE—
MISSIONARY MOTHER AND DAUGHTER

◆ ◆ ◆

Mary Smith Moffat (1795-1870), the wife of Robert Moffat, helped him establish a missionary station at Kuruman, Africa, where they served forty years. She was the mother of ten children, the eldest of whom became the wife of David Livingstone.

Mary Moffat Livingstone (1820-1862) braved lions, storms and other dangers with her distinguished husband in Central Africa. He called her the "main spoke in my wheel." She had a home with him only four years during their twenty years of marriage.

EACH SHARED HER HUSBAND'S SENSE OF DIVINE MISSION

MARY SMITH MOFFAT and her daughter Mary Moffat Livingstone, the most eminent mother-and-daughter pair in missionary history, helped to spread Christianity in Africa. With her husband Robert Moffat, Mary spent forty years there. Their daughter Mary married David Livingstone and shared many of his missionary burdens.

The mother, Mary Moffat, was born in New Windsor, England, the eldest daughter of James Smith, a Scotsman, and Mary Gray Smith of

England. She was educated at a Moravian School in England, which fostered in her a desire for Christian service. Her letters, compiled by her son John S. Moffat, in *The Lives and Letters of Robert and Mary Moffat*, give information about her life and reveal her innermost thoughts.

About the time of her engagement to Robert Moffat, Mary wrote to his parents to console them in their unhappiness at their son's desire to be a missionary: "Surely you would be willing to be deprived of an earthly comfort, to have more of the consolations of the spirit of God."

Soon after this the twenty-four-year-old Mary left her girlhood home in Dukinfield and journeyed to London by coach. From there she sailed to Cape Town, South Africa, where she and Robert Moffat were married on December 27, 1819. "Surely it ought to afford consolation that I am now united to one who counts not his life dear to himself," she wrote her brother.

Mary Moffat, the bride, set out with her husband on her first missionary journey traveling six hundred miles by ox-drawn wagon from Cape Town to their final destination, Kuruman, in the interior of Cape Province.

At first they passed through fertile valleys with awe-inspiring mountains in the background, but the way soon led into the dreary parched region of the Karroo Desert. They measured the journey from water hole to water hole, where they could quench their thirst and that of their oxen.

Mary Moffat undertook many such journeys during her forty years in Africa, as did her daughter. Often these trips were made in a train of heavily loaded wagons, jolting over unmarked paths and leaving little trace behind them. They traveled eight or twelve hours a day at a pace of about three and a half miles an hour. Occasionally, a forest was found too dense, or a quagmire too deep, and they would have to turn back and find a new path. They would detour past new channels cut by the heavy summer rains, and often cross raging rivers, taking most of the day to get their wagons up and down the steep banks and across the expanse of sand. There were huge anthills to be avoided and stones or stumps hidden in the grass which might damage the wheels and axles of the heavy wagons. The long-suffering oxen sometimes became infected with lung sickness, a disease which ravaged South Africa, or they became disabled by sore feet caused by daily plodding through torrential rains.

At night the oxen would be unyoked, and if the camp was in a forest, all hands would make a corral of mimosa bushes to enclose the party as well as the oxen which otherwise might be seized by bushmen or attacked by wild animals. A fire would be started, the kettle put on and supper prepared. Then they would have a worship service around the fire. The only sounds that could be heard during the night were the dismal howl of a prowling hyena or the yelping of the jackals. Mary Moffat grew in courage and was not alarmed by these sounds, nor was she too frightened at the appearance of a snake or a large scorpion around the dying campfire.

Both mother and daughter learned to make a home in a mud hut, and rear their children in the jungle, miles from civilization. Both tried to teach savage black children the Christian Gospel. Both saw their husbands penetrate farther into the interior and never knew whether they would see them again. The courage of the mother, Mary Moffat, was passed on to the daughter, Mary Livingstone.

Mary Moffat's first kitchen was separate from the house, and the only place for the smoke to go out was through the door. She washed in the cold water of the river, beat her clothes clean on a stone, and made her own soap from sheep's fat. She smoked and salted her meat to keep the moths out. She ground her wheat herself and baked in a brick oven, always keeping a lump of leaven for the next baking. She prepared her own curd from the milk of six or seven lean African cows, which gave no more milk than one fat cow. She cleaned her floors with cow dung mixed with water and learned to appreciate it, because, as she wrote her family back in England, "it lays the dust better than anything, and kills the fleas which would otherwise breed abundantly."

Despite the hardships and drudgery of her life, Mary Moffat helped her husband build at Kuruman what was later described by their son-in-law David Livingstone as an "oasis in the desert." Their church, he said, was one of the largest he had seen at any mission station, and their gardens "excellent."

Mungo Murray, a traveler who reached Kuruman early in June 1845, twenty-five years after Mary and Robert Moffat set up a home there, wrote:

We stayed a short time at the station of that grand old patriarch of missionaries, Mr. Moffat, where we received all the kindly hospitality, attention and advice possible from him and Mrs. Moffat—verily the two best friends travelers ever came across. I shall never forget their affectionate courtesy, their beautifully ordered household, and their earnest desire to help us on in every way.

With the passing of time, Mary Moffat's home and landscape acquired real beauty. After a much-needed rain, for example, she rejoiced:

The willow tree is majestic; the syringas have been one sheet of blooms, and the perfume delicious, and now the orange trees are sending forth their still more grateful scent. The pomegranate hedge, with its numerous scarlet flowers, exceeds everything. The grass is again growing, and all nature looks gay at Kuruman.

Early in the spring of 1820, Mary had become severely ill, but a few weeks later she was restored to perfect health and gave birth to a lovely daughter. "Surely this is the Lord's doing and is wonderful in our eyes," Robert Moffat said. This daughter, Mary (later Mrs. Livingstone), was born at the Moffats' first home at Griqua Town on April 12, 1820.

In these early years Mary Moffat shared her husband's hardships and heartaches. When a severe drought set in, the natives would blame it on these "new white strangers." When they tried to teach the native children, the parents protested, saying they did not want their children to become "Dutchmen," their name for all strangers. Language differences, too, hindered them in their work at Kuruman.

On one occasion Mary wrote home: "Could we but see the smallest fruit, we could rejoice midst the privations and toils which we bear; but as it is, our hands do often hang down." The natives grew careless and seldom entered the church, but "our consolation," she said "is derived from the promises of the immutable Jehovah. We walk by faith and not by sight."

As time went on, she saw the importance of their pioneering work and wrote to her family in England: "The longer we live in this land, the more convinced we are of the necessity of missionaries being here, being fully persuaded that it is only the gospel of peace which can raise the degenerate sons of Adam."

Busy as she was with mission duties, Mary Moffat was even busier as a homemaker and mother. She bore ten children, several of whom she lost. She also made a place for three homeless native children. Robert Moffat had come upon a party of bushmen who were digging a grave large enough for a dead mother and her two live children. Tribal custom demanded this sacrifice of the children. After begging for them, he brought the two back to Mary, who welcomed them.

Three years later she took another native child they had heard crying among the stones on the side of a hill not far from the house. The night before, it had been buried alive next to its dead mother and covered with stones. Its nose was bleeding, its eyes bleared from lying in the cold all night and its entire body bruised by the stones. When Mary Moffat made a place in her home for the child, fed it with a spoon and bathed it, the natives were astonished that this white woman should love so poor an object. She named the baby Sarah Roby and had her baptized, "feeling I had a command from God Himself," she said, "to nurse the child for Him."

There were times in these first years of missionary effort when Mary's husband was discouraged and prone to cry out with the prophet: "Is this the right path?" But she remained strong in faith and would console him, saying: "We may not live to see it, but the awakening will come as surely as the sun will rise tomorrow."

Even when there seemed to be no possibility of spreading the faith, she wrote a friend: "Send us a communion service: we shall want it some day." When the communion plate arrived from England three years later, the situation seemed even more hopeless, for the natives were fighting, but Mary Moffat and her husband held on, and she sustained him when the going seemed hardest.

Suddenly in 1828 there appeared to be a great awakening among the natives. It came, as such things do, without any human or visible cause. Heathen songs and dancing ceased and the meetinghouse was crowded before the service began. The songs of Zion and the outpouring of prayers were to be heard everywhere. The moral condition of the people improved. They exchanged their dirty clothes for clean ones. The station enjoyed prosperity in temporal matters. Robert now had more time for his translation of the Gospel of Luke and other Scriptures into Sechwana, the language of the natives. Mary wrote back to England: "Our gracious God has been very condescending to spare the lives of His unworthy servants to witness some fruits of missionary labor." Her little daughter Mary, now eight years old, began to notice the work of her parents.

The next year Mary and Robert Moffat, with their two daughters Mary and Agnes, journeyed by ox wagon to the Wesleyan School near Grahamstown. Leaving his family there, Robert rode four hundred miles further to Cape Town, taking his Sechawan translation of parts of the Bible in his saddlebag. His wife, going by sea, joined him there later. He arrived at the Cape only to discover that no printing firm would publish the Bible in an African language translation. Undefeated, he and a companion set the type and afterward, upon obtaining a printing press, were enabled to issue it themselves.

Two years later, Mary Moffat again set out from Kuruman to visit her two daughters at Grahamstown and to enter a third child in the school. This time she took along an extra wagon, so that she might bring back a large quantity of printing materials. Her escorts through the wilderness were five Bechwanas, once unsafe companions but now loyal and responsible since the Moffats had brought them Christianity and taught them the ways of civilized people.

In 1835, when Mary gave birth to a second son, her fifth child, it seemed that she would never be strong again. But as she looked out from her windows toward the new stone church, her strength was renewed.

The years from 1837 to 1839 brought tranquil prosperity to the mission.

The community of believers grew larger, and as they advanced in spiritual life, their outward demeanor and manner of living improved also.

In 1839 Mary and Robert Moffat journeyed to England, their first trip since their marriage twenty years earlier. Three days after they put out to sea, Mary gave birth to another child. While she convalesced, her six-year-old died and was buried at sea. Another child became desperately ill but finally recovered.

During her stay in England, she gave birth to another child, but her husband scarcely saw it in its first months, as he was in his native Scotland on speaking engagements. At this time he translated the Psalms and the Scripture lessons, and wrote his *Missionary Labors and Scenes in Southern Africa.*

While in England, Mary Moffat often thought of Kuruman and yearned, she said, "to get home to see again where we so long toiled and suffered, to see our beloved companions in the toils and sufferings, and to behold our swarthy brethren and sisters again."

When they finally returned to Africa, they stopped at a post one hundred and fifty miles from their mission. Here they were met by the thirty-one-year-old David Livingstone, who a short time before had been mauled by a lion, which had been raiding his cattle pen. David was a young doctor with a medical degree from the Faculty of Physicians and Surgeons in Glasgow. In London he had heard Robert Moffat speak of his experiences as a missionary in Africa, and had been inspired to become a missionary himself.

Since he was without medical assistance or a place to live, he journeyed on to Kuruman with the Moffats. There he became attracted by their twenty-three-year-old daughter Mary, who no doubt nursed him while he was still a semi-invalid.

After nearly four years of African life as a bachelor, David longed for a home and a wife like the sturdy, refined and tactful Mary, in her neat Victorian muslin frocks. He proposed to her under an almond tree at Kuruman, and when she accepted him he returned to his station at Mabotsa, two hundred and twenty miles farther north, to prepare a home for her.

His deeply religious feeling in regard to his marriage is apparent from his first letter to her:

And now, my dearest, farewell. Let your affection be towards Him much more than towards me: and kept by His mighty power and grace, I hope I shall never give you cause to regret that you have given me a part. Whatever friendship we feel towards each other, let us always look at Jesus as our common friend and guide, and may He shield you with His everlasting arms from every evil.

The home David prepared for Mary was fifty-two by twenty feet in dimension and had thick walls. He started with stone and had to finish with mud when a falling stone nearly broke the arm that had been mauled by the lion. Snakes were also common at Mabotsa. In making the door, he happened to leave a small hole at the corner. Early one morning, when called to the door, he stepped on a snake, but was not bitten.

David and Mary were married in January 1845 in the mission church that still stands in Kuruman. Her father recorded the marriage in the church minutes in his own handwriting.

After Mary had established a well-ordered home for David at Mabotsa, he wrote to his mother in Scotland: "Only yesterday I said to my wife, when I thought of the nice clean bed I enjoy now, 'You put me in mind of my mother; she was always particular about our beds and linen. I have had rough times before.' "

Mary Livingstone taught an infants' school, just as her mother had done at Kuruman. She managed their household on her husband's salary of one hundred pounds a year (then about five hundred dollars). When they married he had already spent a part of this to maintain native teachers, and to equip his medicine chest. Mary was to learn that comforts and personal happiness must be sacrificed.

Disappointed at the results of his work at Mabotsa, two years later David decided to take his family forty miles northward to Chonuane, the center of the Bakwain tribe. Mary, who was expecting her second child, joined him later, holding her sick firstborn Robert in her arms as she journeyed by ox wagon to Chonuane. When she saw that she must cross a flooded river, she burst into tears. She had already crossed eastward through the villages of a strange tribe and was now heading to an even denser district among warring tribes. Though her courage faltered, she finally went forward valiantly.

Soon after she reached Chonuane, the corn bin became empty and she and David and the children had to go to her parents' mission station, almost three hundred miles away, for a fresh supply. An old woman who had seen Mary, the bride, depart about two years before, exclaimed: "Bless me. How lean she is! Has he starved her? Is there no food in the country to which he has been?" This was more than Livingstone could bear. He knew how Mary had suffered, but these comments from those who had seen her as a bride made him concerned about the sacrifices she was making. However, she was to learn that her husband gave his heart to his work.

Not even Chonuane was her home for long. Leaving her and their two little children there in August 1847, David went on to Kolobeng, to explore the possibilities of establishing a third home, the last real home Mary was to have in her nearly twenty years of marriage. While she remained at Chonuane, he commented: "Mary feels her situation among the ruins a little dreary and no wonder, for she writes me that the lions are resuming possession and walk around our house at night."

Her new home at Kolobeng, meaning "haunt of the wild boar," seemed to have been the haunt of everything wild—hyenas, buffaloes, zebras and elephants. When she and the children joined David there, they lived in a drafty, dusty, fly-infested hut of poles and reeds while he built another house. He fell from the roof of this house, cut himself severely with an ax and had other injuries that befall amateur builders. Their work at Kolobeng, however, bore richer fruit than at either Mabotsa or Chonuane. David decribed their life there thus:

The daily routine—up with the sun, family worship, breakfast, school, then manual work as required—ploughing, sowing, smything and every other sort. Mary busy all the morning with culinary and other work; a rest of two hours after dinner; then she goes to the infant school with an attendance of from 60 to 80.

Like her mother, Mary made her own candles and her soap from the ashes of the plant Salsola. She churned her butter in a jar, ground her meal, baked her bread in ant-mud covered with hot ashes, and ground her bran three times. When there was no meat, she learned to roast locusts, and to broil frogs and caterpillars.

In April of 1849, when Mary's third child, Thomas Steele, was born, David was already planning another exploration six hundred miles into unknown country. By August 1, he arrived in sight of what he described as "an unbounded sheet of water." This was Lake Ngami, which was about twenty miles long and ten miles wide at that time.

Returning a short time later, he made a second trip to the lake, taking Mary and the children with him. Trees were felled to make way for their wagons. The tsetse fly on the banks of a river compelled them to cross in another direction. This time they went sixty miles out of their way so that David might minister to a party of English hunters, ill with malaria.

An unfinished sketch by a young artist, Alfred Rider, who went to the lake immediately after its discovery, shows Mary and her family in mid-Victorian dress. She was the first white woman the natives had ever seen and her presence filled them with awe and respect.

At Kolobeng she gave birth to her fourth child, Elizabeth, who soon died from a sickness raging among the Bakwains. Weakened by the trip to the lake and suffering from an infection probably caused by some insect, Mary became temporarily paralyzed.

A few months later David, who put his missionary service above comfort, home, family and everything else, set out on another exploration. Writing to a friend, he said: "My wife, poor soul, I pity her, proposed to let me go for a year while she remains at Kolobeng." If her paralysis had improved, he would have taken her to the Cape for treatment, but she was not able to travel that far, and so he took her to her mother's home at Kuruman, where she was able to rest, and recuperated temporarily.

The Moffats and Livingstones had a disagreement over this third journey north. Mary Moffat thought her daughter had already suffered enough, and spoke to David of the death of his last child and of Mary's paralyzed condition. In the name of everything that was "just, kind and even decent," she besought him to abandon the idea of such a trip. She told David that if his arrangements were not in accordance with God's plan, he might be prevented from carrying out his own plans. George Seaver, in *David Livingstone, His Life and Letters,* takes the view that Livingstone's aim as an active missionary was incompatible with his duties as a father and husband and one or the other had to be sacrificed.

David lived by the gospel: "He that loveth son or daughter more than me is not worthy of me" (Matt. 10:37), and he wrote in his journal: "God had an only Son, and He was a missionary and a physician. A poor, poor imitation of Him I am, or wish to be." David had one goal now, and that was to open a passage to the sea on either the eastern or western coast of Africa.

He turned once more toward the Zambesi, again taking his wife and children with him. He hoped to open this great river and western Africa for European colonization. Mary was once more with child, her fifth. In a letter to a friend, David poured out his fears:

It is a venture to take wife and children into a country where fever—African fever—prevails. But who that believes in Jesus would refuse to make a venture for such a Captain? A parent's heart alone can feel as I do when I look at my little ones and ask, shall I return with this or that one alive? However, we are His and wish to have no interests apart from those of His kingdom and glory. May He bless us and make us blessings even unto death.

Through heavy sand and thick bush, Mary and the children pressed on with him, over a course so winding that they could scarcely see the front oxen. Livingstone, telling of this, writes:

The supply of water in the wagons had been wasted by one of our servants, and by the afternoon only a small portion remained for the children. The idea of their perishing before our eyes was terrible. It would almost have been a relief to me to have been reproached with being the entire cause of the catastrophe, but not one syllable of upbraiding was uttered by their mother, though the tearful eye told of the agony within. In the afternoon, to our inexpressible relief, some of our men returned with a supply of that fluid of which we had never before felt the true value.

The Livingstones soon came to the borders of a marsh where the Mababe River terminates. They knew they were within the lands of the Makololos, a region infested with mosquitoes. Mary's presence again probably made for kinder relations, for Chief Sebituane of the Makololos asked to be introduced to her.

David was determined to explore further, from the Zambesi to the Cape. "Providence seems to call me to regions beyond." Leaving Mary and the children at Chobe camp, he proceeded northeastward by horseback through dense jungles. His horses swam most of the swamps, as he pushed forward. But he rejoined Mary without undue delay.

She had now given birth to a son, William Oswell, named for one of David's explorer companions. At this child's birth, Mary was again afflicted with partial paralysis. Now David knew that he must rush her to the Cape. Before he left he wrote to his directors in the London Missionary Society, stating:

Nothing but a strong conviction that the step will tend to the Glory of Christ would make me orphanize my children. Even now my bowels yearn over them—they will forget me. But I hope when the day of trial comes I shall not be found a more sorry soldier than those who served an earthly sovereign. . . . I am so sure that it is the will of our Lord I should go, I will go—no matter who opposes.

After six months of wearisome travel from Chobe camp, Mary and David and the four children reached Cape Town in March of 1852. From there she and the children sailed for England in April. It was a sad parting for them all, and David poured out his heart in these words:

My dearest Mary—How I miss you now, and the dear children. My heart yearns incessantly over you. How many thoughts of the past crowd into my mind. I feel as if I would treat you all more tenderly and lovingly than ever. . . . I never show my feelings; but I can say truly, my dearest, that I loved you when I married you, and the longer I lived with you, I loved you the better.

She and the children were separated from him for about four years. Not only were they "homeless and friendless," says George Seaver, "but were often living on the edge of poverty in cheap lodgings: at first in Hamilton where the older Livingstones resided but proved unhelpful; afterwards in Manchester, Kendal, Epsom, but nowhere with any settled abode or peace of mind." Early in 1854, with recovered health, Mary Livingstone begged, "almost in desperation, a passage to the Cape, but was either dissuaded by the Directors or changed her mind, which proved to be fortunate."

Livingstone, unaware of her adversities, faced many himself as he forged his way through the jungle, first to Loanda. "I shall open a path into the interior, or perish," he asserted. Traveling on to Linyanti, he declared: "I will place no value on anything I have or may possess, except in relation to the kingdom of Christ." Advancing to Quiliman, he said: "I view the end of the geographical feat as the beginning of the missionary enterprise."

Before beginning this journey, he went back to their house at Kolobeng and found the Boers had taken away sofa, table, bed, all the crockery, Mary's desk, smashed the wooden chairs, taken away the iron ones, torn out the leaves of all books and scattered them in front of the house, smashed the bottles containing the medicines, broken the windows, taken away the bellows, anvil, all the tools—in fact, everything worth taking, even coffee, tea and sugar.

In his four-year epochal journey, Livingstone made such important discoveries that the map of Central Africa had to be redrawn. When he finally arrived in England on December 9, 1856, Mary forgot her months of deep and terrible anxiety and her many sacrifices.

The honors that awaited him in the British Isles showed her that their sacrifices had not been in vain. He was now a man of great renown. Her father wrote to him: "The honors awaiting you would be enough to make a score of light heads dizzy, but I have no fear of their affecting your upper story."

For the next six months he was praised everywhere. The Colonial Secretary, R. W. Rawson, said: "I am convinced that Livingstone's name will live amongst the first heroes and the first benefactors of our race." He had indeed opened Africa to European civilization. The Bishop of Cape Town commended him for bringing the spirit of Christ into pagan regions. His old tutor lauded him for his contribution to zoology and paleontology. Others exalted him for his services to geography, geology, climatology and astronomy. They spoke of him as "one of the moral giants of the race."

The Royal Society elected him a fellow. He was invited to visit the queen. Charles Dickens, reading of his accomplishments, eulogized him thus: "I used to think I possessed the moral virtues of courage, patience, resolution and self-control. . . . I find that these turn out to be nothing but plated goods . . . my self-esteem oozed out of me."

With Mary beside him, Livingstone enjoyed eighteen months of acclaim. Reserved and quiet in society, neither she nor David cared for grandeur. He realized better than anyone that hard work brought the greatest happiness. In responding to praise, he once remarked: "In Africa I have had hard work. I find that all eminent men work hard. Eminent geologists, mineralogists, men of science in every department, if they attain eminence, work hard, and that both early and late."

He began to plan another African exploration on which Mary would accompany him. Applause was loud when this was announced at a dinner in his honor. He rose to reply, and concluded with praise of his wife, saying: "She had always been the main spoke in my wheel." He was glad indeed, he said, to be accompanied on this new trip by his guardian angel.

Mary's plans, however, were changed. Within a month of the time she was to sail with her husband and children for Africa, she found she was again with child. She became ill at sea, and David wrote to his daughter Agnes:

> Mama was so ill all the way from Sierra Leone that I was obliged to land her at the Cape, but no sooner did I go ashore to book a room for her at the hotel than I heard that Grandpa and Grandma Moffat were there, waiting for us. . . . Now Mama is to go up to Kuruman with them, remain there for sometime and then join me by going up through Kolobeng towards the Makololo country. . . . I parted with Mama on the 1st day of May and sailed out of Simon's Bay while Mama waved her handkerchief as long as she could see me waving my cap.

To a friend, Livingstone wrote: "It was a bitter parting with my wife, like tearing the heart out of one."

As soon as possible after the birth of her sixth child and second daughter, Mary left Kuruman for Scotland, to be near her other children, but she longed to be reunited with her husband. During this time she suffered such spiritual darkness that she has been referred to as a "dejected Christian." In her nearly twenty years of marriage, she had lived with her husband in a home of their own for only four.

Finally she sailed to meet David on the Zambesi delta. There were six months of heartbreaking frustrations during the off-loading and temporary disposal of vast quantities of cargo. Livingstone was desperately anxious to get his wife out of the fever-ridden delta and up to higher ground, but she was stricken with a sudden illness. Her husband never left her, and sat by the side of her rude bed, which was formed of boxes but covered with a soft mattress.

After six days she sank into a coma. Livingstone had faced many difficulties and braved many dangers, but he wept like a child. He knelt down and prayed as best he could. In less than an hour she was gone. The next day he buried her beneath a large baobab tree in the grounds where she had walked with him only a few days before.

He wrote in his journal:

It is the first heavy stroke I have suffered, and quite takes away my strength. . . . I loved her when I married her, and the longer I lived with her I loved her the more. . . . Oh my Mary, my Mary! how often we have longed for a quiet home, since you and I were cast adrift at Kolobeng; surely the removal by a kind Father who knoweth our frame means that He rewarded you by taking you to a better home, the eternal one in the heavens.

Among the many comforting letters he received was one from Mary's mother, Mary Moffat, in which she said:

I do thank you for the detail you have given me of the circumstances of the last days and hours of our lamented and beloved Mary, our first-born, over whom our fond hearts first beat with parental affection!

This brave mother lost her missionary son Robert four months after she lost her daughter Mary Livingstone. She also lost another daughter, Elizabeth, who had married the missionary Rogers Price. But her other children carried on in the missionary field. Ann served with her husband Jean Fredoux, the French missionary. And her son John became his father's assistant and finally took over the Kuruman post.

After forty years of sacrificial service, Mary and Robert Moffat were ready to lay down the burden of their work at Kuruman. On a Sunday in May 1870 Robert Moffat preached his last sermon. As she walked out from the service in her prim little bonnet and full-skirted, tight-waisted Victorian dress Mary Moffat carried her seventy-five years with graceful poise. She entered the ox wagon which was to take them to the coast, while throngs of native friends clasped her hands in a last good-by.

Shortly after her arrival in England, she died. Her husband exclaimed sadly: "For fifty-three years I have had her to pray for me!" He lived twelve years longer, never forgetting how Mary had watched over his health and comfort with a care which grew more constant through the years. He thanked God for such a wife, and her children thanked God for such a mother.

MATERIAL ON PAGES 198 THROUGH 203 DE-
LETED SINCE PERSONALITY NOT SUITABLE
FOR THIS COMPILATION

NARCISSA WHITMAN—
MISSIONARY TO THE INDIANS
(1808-1847)

♦ ♦ ♦

The first mission home in the Pacific Northwest was established by her. She taught Indian children at her missionary outpost at Waiilatpu. After the death of her only child, she mothered homeless frontier children. She was the only woman killed in the massacre by non-Christian Cayuse Indians.

SHE REJOICED IN CHRISTIAN SERVICE ON THE FRONTIER

NARCISSA WHITMAN SYMBOLIZES the pioneer missionary woman on the American frontier at her very best. As she helped to build a Christian community among the Indians of the Northwest, she experienced all the anxieties, disappointments, hardships and heartaches of primitive Christians; and yet like them, she rejoiced "in making these sacrifices for Christ."

She and her husband Marcus, a missionary-physician, crossed the Rocky Mountains and Columbia River into Old Oregon to establish the Presbyterian Mission there in 1836. With them were a single man, William Henry Gray, and another missionary couple, Rev. Henry Harmon Spalding and his wife Eliza. They have been called "the apostles paving the way for the American occupation of the Pacific Northwest" with its millions of acres of fertile soil and its illimitable forests.

In writing to her family about this epochal expedition, Narcissa commented: "Was there ever journey like this performed, where the sustaining hand of God has been so manifest every morning? Surely the children of Israel could not have been more sensible of the pillar of fire by night than we have been of the hand that has led us safely on."

Narcissa's letters and diary, the best sources of information about her life, are quoted in *Marcus Whitman, M. D., Pioneer and Martyr*, by Dr. Clifford Drury, and in *Marcus Whitman, Crusader*, by Archer Butler Hulbert and Dorothy Printup Hulbert.

These books give an account of Narcissa's missionary experiences, as she and her husband followed the Oregon Trail and set up their mission at Waiilatpu, the Indian name for "the place of the rye grass." This was about twenty-five miles from Fort Walla Walla, now covered by waters of the Columbia River, and about seven miles from the present Walla Walla, Washington, the site of another old fort. The latter city is now the home of Whitman College, founded in the Whitmans' memory in 1859 and a depository for many of their records, including Narcissa's diary and letters.

Narcissa Whitman rode over South Pass, on the Continental Divide, on July 4, 1836, seven years before the first great Oregon immigration of 1843. She was the first American white woman to stand on the crest of the Blue Mountains and view the fertile valley of the Columbia River. The forest in the Blue Mountains is now called the Whitman National Forest. She was the wife of one of the first graduate doctors to practice west of the Rockies, as well as one of the first great missionary-farmers of the Northwest. With him she established one of the first mission homes in the Pacific Northwest.

Narcissa was her husband's helpmate as he taught the Indians the arts of civilization, erected mills, plowed fields and sowed and harvested crops. She often rode beside him on horseback, carrying his medicines and surgical instruments in two saddlebags. She stood by his side as he ministered to both the physical and spiritual needs of the Indians.

One Indian, speaking admiringly of her, said she had hair "like the gold of the sunset." She was a little above medium height, had blue eyes and well-formed features and would have graced any formal social affair of her time. A New York girlhood companion described her voice as being "sweet and musical as a chime of bells." Narcissa later said: "I was not aware that singing was a qualification of such importance to a missionary."

B. F. Nichols, who spent the winter at the Whitmans' station in 1844-1845, paid Mrs. Whitman this compliment:

She seemed endowed with a peculiar magnetism when you were in her presence so that you could not help thinking yourself in the presence of a being much higher than the ordinary run of humanity. I have heard her pray, and she could offer up the finest petition to the Throne of Grace of any person I ever heard in my life. She was always gentle and kind to the Indians, as she was to every one else. She took an interest in every one at the mission, especially the children. Every one loved her, because to see her was to love her.

Narcissa could trace her ancestry to Pilgrims. Her father, Judge Stephen Prentiss, had a sawmill and flour mill in Prattsburg, New York, and helped build the First Presbyterian Church there in 1832. Her mother Clarissa, who took the lead in family religious matters, had joined the Prattsburg Presbyterian Church the year before Narcissa's birth.

The third of nine children, Narcissa was born March 14, 1808, and had the distinction of being the first white baby baptized at Prattsburg. Her birthplace there has been restored in recent years and a highway connecting Prattsburg with Naples is called the Narcissa Whitman Highway.

When she was eleven years old, she made her confession of faith with fifty-nine others who came into the church after a religious revival in 1818-1819. The minister took for his text Isaiah 53:11: "He shall see of the travail of his soul, and shall be satisfied." This seemed to point toward her career. She knew she wanted to spend her life in building the church.

She was educated in Emma Willard's "Female Seminary" at Troy, New York, and at the Benjamin Franklin Academy at Prattsburg. She and her sister afterward conducted a kindergarten.

Her husband had a religious awakening in Plainfield, Massachusetts, not far from his birthplace of Rushville, about the same time that she did. Both heard Rev. Samuel Parker as he went through western New York raising funds for the support of missions among the Indians. As the American Board of Commissioners for Foreign Missions would not accept single women as missionaries among the Indians, and single men needed helpmates, Rev. Samuel Parker suggested marriage to Marcus. When his appointment as a missionary came in January 1835, he went to Narcissa, and successfully proposed marriage. She then applied to the board and was also accepted.

With the Rev. Mr. Parker, Marcus made an exploratory trip as far west as Wyoming to determine if missionary work was feasible there and if the hazards would be too great for Narcissa. Certain that it was safe for her to accompany him, he returned to Angelica, New York, where the family now lived. There the marriage was solemnized on February 18, 1836, in the church where she sang in the choir and taught a girls' class.

She wore a dress of black bombazine, which set off her golden hair to advantage. In her trousseau were several alpaca prints in bright colors which she knew would appeal to the Indians' love for color. All of her trousseau frocks were made with pleated pointed waists, mutton-leg sleeves and fancy neckerchief collars.

The day after the wedding Narcissa left with Marcus for Ithaca, New York, then proceeded to Ohio and Pennsylvania, part of the way by sleigh. Going down the Ohio and up the Mississippi and Missouri rivers by boat, they finally came to Liberty Landing. By May 14 they had reached the Otoe Mission, a few miles from what is now Omaha, Nebraska. Here they joined the American Fur Company caravan and began their trek over old buffalo paths that ran between rivers and mountains. Old Oregon was still about nineteen hundred miles away.

Their caravan has been described as a moving village, with its wagons, various kinds of seeds, a large supply of clothing, four hundred animals and some seventy men, and the two women riding sidesaddle. As it moved only about fifteen or twenty miles a day across the wilderness, Narcissa was reminded of the Children of Israel as they journeyed from Egypt to Palestine. Pestilences followed them, as they had the Children of Israel. In the swamps they were overtaken by mosquitoes; along the Columbia River, by fleas.

The Indians often stared at Narcissa and Eliza Spalding, the first white women they had ever seen. The mountaineers, also attracted by the novelty of such visitors from the outside world, often joined in the religious services along the trail. So keen was the interest of these trappers in the Bible that Narcissa observed: "If we had packed one or two animals with nothing but Bibles they all would have been sold or given away."

In her diary she gives minute details of how their party cooked, ate and slept, and of scenery they passed along the way. Through every experience, no matter how trying, she expressed her belief in the Providence of God and His kind protection. She kept her trusting faith as they passed across "streams full of falls," over steep mountain paths so narrow as scarcely to afford room for the animal to place its foot, and through areas inhabited by warlike Indian tribes. Amid such dangers, she later wrote her family, she was "in a peaceful state of mind," and if she had "ten thousand lives" she would "give all for God," and longed "to be more like Him, to possess more of His meek spirit."

Sometimes the axletree of the wagon broke or the wagon stuck in the creek. A great wonder it was, she further observed, that it "was not turning somersaults continually." Occasionally she and Eliza rode atop their luggage as their springless conveyance creaked and rumbled over the rough trails. Finally it was converted into a two-wheeled cart and taken as far as Fort Boise, the first wheeled vehicle to go that far west.

"Long for rest but must not murmur," Narcissa wrote. She also recorded how she pitied the poor Indian women who continually traveled in this manner. Sometimes the party trekked through long stretches of prairie, rocky and sandy, without water for man or beast. The only shade they could find would be a lone, scraggly tree. Finally they came into the mountains where the trails were like winding stairs, and in some places so steep that the horses were as frightened as the travelers.

Though often weak, restless and scarcely able to sit sidesaddle on her horse, Narcisssa wrote her mother: "But I have been diverted by the scenery and carried out of myself by conversation about home and friends. Let me tell you how I am sustained by the Lord in all this journey." Again, in her weariness, when she dreaded the long day's ride ahead, she told them she remembered Christ's comforting words: "Lo, I am with you alway, even unto the end of the world" (Matt. 28:20).

When they had nothing but buffalo meat to eat and only dried buffalo dung to cook with, she did not complain. She rejoiced later, however, when they had good salmon boiled in hot springs, also wild duck, fresh-water clams and wild gooseberries.

On July 4 they reached the South Pass of the Rocky Mountains and crossed the Continental Divide. Just out of Fort Walla Walla on the Columbia, the party separated briefly, the Whitmans going ahead and reaching Fort Walla Walla on September 1, 1836. "The whole company galloped almost all the way to the Fort," Narcissa wrote. On their arrival, they were treated to fresh salmon, potatoes, tea, bread and butter. For another meal they had pork, turnips, cabbage and tea. Narcissa wrote this glad message to her family:

Here we are all at Walla Walla, through the mercy of a kind Providence, in health, and all our lives preserved. What cause for gratitude and praise to God! Surely my heart is ready to leap for joy at the thought of being so near the long desired work of teaching the benighted ones the knowledge of the Saviour, and having completed this journey under such favorable circumstances.

Finally on that first Sabbath she wrote:

This has been a day of mutual thanksgiving with us all. This first Sabbath in September, a Sabbath of Rest, first completing a long journey, first in the vicinity of our future labors. All of us here before God. It is not enough to us alone to be thankful. Will not my beloved friends at home unite with us in gratitude and praise to God for His great mercy? It is in answer to your prayers that we are here, and are permitted to see this day under such circumstances.

While the Indians were away on their summer hunt, the Whitmans and Spaldings went to Fort Vancouver, described by Narcissa as "the New York of the Pacific."

"What a delightful place this is," she wrote. "Here we find fruit of every description, apples, peaches, grapes, pears, plums and fig trees in abundance; also cucumbers, melons, beans, peas, beets, cabbage, tomatoes and every kind of vegetable." She tells also of coming upon strawberry patches and grapevines. God, in His goodness, was providing for her bountifully.

She and Eliza Spalding remained at Fort Vancouver for a few weeks while their husbands prepared homes for them. Marcus chose Waiilatpu;

Spalding journeyed about one hundred and twenty-five miles farther northeast to Lapwai. Their other nearest neighbors were the missionaries in the Methodist Mission in the Willamette Valley, three hundred and fifty miles away. It had been established two years earlier by Rev. Jason Lee and Rev. Daniel Lee, but no women came there until 1837, and then not across the Oregon Trail but by way of Cape Horn.

Narcissa's first home at Waiilatpu measured thirty-six feet long by thirty feet wide, and was one and a half stories high. The front main section was constructed of blocks similar to adobe, made of dirt dug from the cellar. Attached to the full length of one side was a twelve-by-thirty-six-foot lean-to kitchen of split logs set in grooved posts. The original earthen-block foundation was discovered recently during excavations on the site.

Narcissa first turned her kitchen into a classroom. She drew the Indian children to her like a magnet when she rang her hand bell and promised to serve them from large pitchers of milk. They began to respond to the thoughtfulness of this pretty woman who had come across the continent to minister to them. But they were not as thoughtful of her. They brought so many fleas in with them that she could use her kitchen as a classroom for only a little while.

On her twenty-ninth birthday, Narcissa gave birth to a daughter Alice Clarissa, named for the child's two grandmothers. She rocked and sang to her little daughter and her wilderness home was filled with a new joyousness.

High water in the cellar of their first house eroded the earthen-block foundation and threatened to cause its collapse. In 1840 Marcus built for Narcissa a Mission House on safer, higher ground. It was a large building, in the shape of a "T," one hundred and eight feet long. Weary travelers had a pleasant surprise when they came upon this house with its smooth whitewashed walls, green doors, slate-colored woodwork and yellow floor. Religious, educational, medical and other community activities were conducted here and it served as a refuge later for the overflow of new settlers. However, there was also an Emigrant House completed in 1841, constructed and painted in a similar manner to the Mission House.

About the time the Mission House was finished, Narcissa assisted in the organization of the Presbyterian Church, the first Protestant church west of the Rockies. When the first seven members, including themselves, the Spaldings, a Hawaiian couple and a mountain settler, observed their first Lord's Supper together, Narcissa wrote home about the inspiring event.

The next fall the board sent reinforcements for the Oregon Mission, among whom were Mr. and Mrs. Cushing Eells. Mrs. Eells has described the Whitmans' house as being constructed of the roughest kind of new lumber, sparsely furnished with hand-made furniture: "The bedsteads are boards nailed to the side of the house, sink fashion, then some blankets and husks make the bed; but it is good compared with traveling accommodations."

Narcisssa made her own soap and candles, washed, ironed, cooked, sewed, taught in church, and copied a seventy-two-page book in the language of the Nez Percé Indians. It was printed on a press that arrived from the Sandwich Islands in 1838.

She also aided her husband in Indian camp meetings. Of one open-air service held in January of 1839, she wrote in her diary that, after her husband's sermon, "an Indian wife who confessed her sins became so repentant that her tears fell to the ground so copiously that I was reminded of the Sinful Woman who washed her Saviour's feet with her tears."

With thankful hearts, Narcissa and Marcus witnessed these first fruits of their labors. Their home life, too, was happy. Their little daughter had begun to imitate and talk with the Indians, who loved her very much. That spring Narcissa wrote this happy message to her parents: "My Clarissa is my own little companion from day to day, and dear daughter." She requested that the child's name be written in the family Bible, and beside that her birth date, and the place of her birth, the Oregon Territory.

On Sunday, June 23, 1839, after worship services, Dr. Whitman took his little daughter into the garden and cut her a stalk of rhubarb. A while later, running to her mother, the child said: "Mama, dinner is almost ready; let Alice get the water." Narcissa soon noticed that two cups were missing from the table. A hired helper came to report he had found two cups by the banks of the river that flowed near the house. Narcissa hurried outside, Marcus following her. When they reached the river, a frantic search was begun. Finally an old Indian went down in the water among the roots of the tree where the cups had been found. Here he came upon the body of the Whitmans' beautiful little daughter.

Narcissa's profoundly Christian character is revealed in every note of the sad event. "Lord it is right; it is right," she prayed. "She is not mine but Thine; she has only been lent to me for a little season, and now, dearest Saviour, Thou hast the best right to her; Thy will be done, not mine."

The child was buried north of the Mission. Spalding preached the service from II Kings 4:26, quoting the words of Elisha to the Shunammite: " 'Is it well with thee? is it well with thy husband? is it well with thy child?' And she answered, 'It is well.' "

In a letter to her parents, Narcissa calmly confided to them: "Although her grave is in sight every time I step out of the door, my thoughts seldom wander there to find her. I look above with unspeakable delight—and contemplate her as enjoying the full delight of that bright world where her joys are perfect."

The Indians had loved "The Little White Cayuse," as they called her. And with Alice buried at Waiilatpu, Narcissa wrote, "we are bound with its destiny."

She managed to "mother" numerous children. The first was a little half-Indian girl who was brought to her covered with lice, dirty, half-starved and poorly clad. More than a year later, the child had blossomed under her care, and to a certain degree she satisfied the Whitmans' aching hearts. Before long Narcissa made room for another half-Indian girl and then a little boy. He, too, was brought to her nearly naked, half-starved and covered with dirt and lice, and some Indian boys had shaved a finger-wide strip from one ear to the other, and from his forehead to his neck, crossing at right angles. One of his feet had been badly burned.

The biggest increase in her family came in the fall of 1844 when the seven Sager children were left with her. Both parents had died on the trail to Oregon. Her new orphans included a baby of five months, a little lame girl and five others.

In 1840-1841 there were no less than seven missionary families at Waiilatpu. "We feel that we need much patience and wisdom to get along with so many, and much strength," she wrote her family. And she prayed for a "meek, lowly and quiet spirit." Before word could be sent that missionary differences had been adjusted, a large party of settlers arrived with the message that Waiilatpu must be closed. Marcus proposed to go east, to plead their case to the board, and on October 2, 1842, was on his way.

With a heavy but brave heart, Narcissa bade him good-by as he mounted his horse and started out on his long journey across the continent with A. L. Lovejoy, a New England lawyer. She asked God's protection for her beloved husband and strength for herself to carry on in his absence.

It is comforting to turn the pages of Narcissa's diary and to see with what confidence she expressed the belief that an Almighty arm was guiding her husband safely through all perils. He needed her prayers. This was one of the most difficult rides in American history. Rumors of unfriendly Indian tribes made it necessary for Marcus and his companion to detour southwest. They nearly lost their lives while fording the Colorado River. Their food gave out in the mountainous country near Taos, New Mexico, and they had to eat their pack mules and dog, until they were rescued by a party of hunters.

In her cabin alone, with her half-Indian children, Narcissa had her own trials. By this time the Indians were becoming antagonistic, jealous of the white man's flocks and fields of waving grain. "Were it not for sustaining grace I should sink under it; but the favors of the Lord are many and great," she wrote in a letter to her family.

One night, shortly after her husband's departure, she was wakened by an intruder trying to enter her sleeping quarters. She slammed the door and refastened the latch, but the intruder raised it a second time, and her strength was not equal to his. All the time she cried out for John, a trusted employee of the Hudson's Bay Company. The intruder, finally becoming alarmed, ran away.

The next day a wagon was sent, and Narcissa and the children journeyed to Fort Walla Walla for safety. A few weeks later she went to the Methodist Station at The Dalles, the first mission to be established by the Methodists on the south bank of the Columbia River.

Soon after her departure, the mission gristmill was burned by the Indians, and the stored grain and threshing mill were all destroyed.

Marcus made a perilous journey back East to Washington and New York. His return trip was made by wagon train, with one thousand immigrants, the largest migration to Oregon up to that time. This set the precedent for the subsequent history of the Oregon Trail and made the Northwest and its resources more secure for the United States. Homeseekers literally poured into the Mission, some half-starved and some sick.

The reunited Whitman family went back to Waiilatpu in early November 1843. "Here we are, one family alone, a center post, about which multitudes will or must gather this winter," she wrote her family in 1844. "And these we must feed and warm to the extent of our powers. Blessed be God that He has given us so abundantly of the fruit of the earth that we may impart to those who are thus famishing."

The immigration of 1845 was three times greater than the one the year before. In 1846 Marcus and Narcissa were responsible for the welfare of sixty-nine men, women and children inside their crowded mission walls. Fifty were immigrants. The other nineteen were members of their family, which now included school children entrusted to their care. The winter of 1847 was very severe and resulted in the loss of many of the Indians' horses, again causing discontent. A virulent form of measles and dysentery had been brought in by the immigrants and Dr. Whitman ministered to whites and Indians alike. The Indians took hot steam baths and then jumped into the cold river, a treatment that probably killed many who might otherwise have survived, but they blamed Dr. Whitman, calling him a sorcerer.

On the afternoon of November 29, 1847, an Indian came to the side door asking for Dr. Whitman. Marcus took his medicine case and entered the kitchen, where two Indians waited. One, drawing a tomahawk from under his blanket, struck Dr. Whitman on the back of his head. The first blow stunned him. He lived for a short while after the attack.

Hearing the tumult in the kitchen, Narcissa rushed in. She drew her husband to a couch and was trying to revive him when she was shot in the breast. She fell without a groan, recovering enough to kneel at the couch where her husband lay. She prayed, "Lord save these little ones," but several of her adopted children died in the massacre.

The last words of the talented, gifted, devoted Narcissa Whitman were: "Tell my sister that I died at my post."

Narcissa and her husband and other victims of the massacre are buried side by side at the foot of a one-hundred-foot hill at the top of which stands a shaft of Vermont marble. From this hilltop, on a clear day, can be seen the hills bordering the Columbia River to the west. The Oregon state line is less than a mile to the south of the monument. Walla Walla and College Place, Washington, are visible to the east, and the Blue Mountains lie in the background. Many of the wild plants that grew on the hill when Narcissa climbed it to watch for her husband to come home from trips still grow here. In an address in 1950, Dr. Chester C. Maxey, president of Whitman College, summed up their lives in these words:

There has been no other couple like the Whitmans in American history—no wooing more strange, no wedding more extraordinary, no marriage more proof against stress and storm, no union of purpose and effort more perfect, no failure more pathetic, no ending more terrible, and no immortality more sublime than theirs. Forces they did not control or understand brought their lives together in a noble enterprise that failed; forces they did not control or understand brought their lives to a dire and agonizing close. Yet so greatly did they live, so magnificently did they labor and serve, that forces they set in motion will forever enrich the civilization they helped to plant on the western slopes of the Continental Divide.

FLORENCE NIGHTINGALE—
MINISTERING ANGEL IN THE CRIMEAN WAR
(1820-1910)
♦ ♦ ♦

The inspiration for embarking upon her nursing career came from the Protestant Deaconesses at Kaiserwerth on the Rhine. She contrasted their happy lives with the empty ones of some of her friends.

SHE GAVE UP A LIFE OF EASE TO MINISTER TO OTHERS

FLORENCE NIGHTINGALE, heroine of modern nursing, declared that "Christ is the author of our profession." She regarded nursing as an art requiring even more unswerving devotion and energetic preparation than that of sculpturing or painting. "What is the having to do with dead canvas or cold marble," she asked, "compared with having to do with the living body, the temple of God's spirit?"

Like Joan of Arc, she heard a voice outside herself when she was seventeen. She was sure that God had called her to His service, and she was filled with confidence and faith, relates Cecil Woodham-Smith, in her biography entitled *Florence Nightingale*. Florence felt that God spoke to her directly four times after this, and she gave the exact dates later in her life. By the time she was twenty-four, she knew that her destiny was to serve the sick and dying.

Born in Florence, Italy, May 15, 1820, she was named for her lovely home city on the Arno. Her father, William Edward Shore, a banker, took the name Nightingale when he fell heir to the estates of Peter Nightingale. He and his daughter had deep sympathy for each other, and he taught her Greek, Latin, German, French, Italian, history and philosophy. He even taught her to read the Bible from the Greek text.

On her mother's side, Florence was descended from altruistic people. Her great-grandfather, Samuel Smith, a London merchant, was admired for his humanitarian principles. Sympathizing with American colonists in their fight for freedom, he relinquished his title to a large part of the city of Savannah, Georgia. Her grandfather, William Smith, a wealthy art connoisseur, sat in the House of Commons for forty-six years, fighting for the weak and oppressed.

Florence's mother did not inherit the qualities of her father or grandfather. Material things came first in her life. She loved travel, elegant parties and big houses. She was the mistress of two mansions, Embley Park in Hampshire and Lea Hurst in Derbyshire. She lived a busy social life and was waited upon by maids, footmen, valets and coachmen. When she launched her two daughters in society, she added six bedrooms to Lea Hurst and made it the center of her entertaining because her Embley Park house had only fifteen bedrooms.

Florence was completely unlike her mother and her frivolous, spoiled sister Parthenope. She turned down several good offers of marriage, one with Richard Monckton Milnes, a Cambridge graduate and heir to a large estate. He later became a Conservative member of Parliament, a patron of letters, a poet and an intimate of Tennyson and Thackeray.

After his marriage he continued to have high regard for Florence, and he made a speech when leading London citizens gathered November 29, 1885 "to give expression to a general feeling that the services of Miss Nightingale in the Hospitals of the East demand the grateful recognition of the British people."

Florence loved with a deep devotion her father's sister, Aunt Mai. Better than any member of the family, she understood Florence's desire for the things of the spirit and she became her niece's spiritual mother. Early in her girlhood, Florence wrote: "I craved for some regular occupation, for something worth doing, instead of frittering time away on useless trifles." When she wished to train for nursing, her parents behaved as if she had wished to be a kitchenmaid, but her Aunt Mai understood.

Before Florence could be worthy enough for God to reveal her path of service, she knew she must conquer her temptation to shine in society which occasionally conflicted with her desire to devote her life to others. Graceful and blessed with a delicate complexion and lovely thick chestnut hair, she was a beautiful dancer and an excellent mimic. She loved pretty clothes and sometimes the glitter and gold of society seemed tempting.

In 1842, when she was twenty-two, England was in what has been called "the hungry forties." She and her friends had an abundance of good things to eat, but many people were starving. That year she wrote: "My mind is absorbed with the idea of the sufferings of man, it besets me behind and before . . . all that the poets sing of the glories of the world seem to me untrue. All the people I see are eaten up with care or poverty or disease." She began to believe, even though her family was horrified at the idea, that her destiny lay among the miserable of the world.

When Julia Ward Howe, author of "The Battle Hymn of the Republic," visited the Nightingale home in England, Florence asked her: "Dr. Howe, do you think it would be unsuitable and unbecoming for a young English-woman to devote herself to works of charity in hospitals and elsewhere as Catholic sisters do?" Dr. Howe answered: "Go forward . . . live up to your inspiration and you will find there is never anything unbecoming or unladylike in doing your duty for the good of others."

When Dr. Elizabeth Blackwell, the first woman doctor in America, was their guest and went on a walk with Florence in the garden, the girl looked up at her family's handsome home and asked: "Do you know what I always think of when I look at that row of windows?" And then she ad-mitted to Dr. Blackwell that if she had her way she would place beds there and organize a hospital.

Florence Nightingale deliberately detached herself from marriage and even friendships. On a trip to Egypt, she wrote in Cairo: "O God, Thou puttest into my heart this great desire to devote myself to the sick and sorrowful. I offer it to Thee." As she journeyed on to Greece, she stopped one day at the Pass of Thermopylae; while looking at a rainbow in the sky, she prayed: "Give me my work to do."

A few weeks later, at the Institute of Protestant Deaconesses at Kaiser-werth on the Rhine, she contrasted the lives of the Kaiserwerth deaconesses, who were mostly peasant women, with the lives of some of the people she knew at home who were "going mad for want of something to do." Flo-rence enjoyed the religious atmosphere at Kaiserwerth and the Spartan life lived by the nurses, who looked upon their work as service for God. From there she wrote: "Now I know what it is to live and to love life. . . . I wish for no other earth, no other world than this."

Her family met her in Cologne, and when they learned what she pro-posed to do, they treated her as if she had committed a crime. Begging for their understanding, she said: "Give me time, give me faith. Trust me, help me. Say to me: 'Follow the dictates of that spirit within thee.' My beloved people, I cannot bear to grieve you. Give me your blessing!"

Back in London, she took a position in the Institution for the Care of Sick Gentlewomen in Distressed Circumstances. When the committee wanted to confine this charity to Church of England patients, she fought to change the rules so that Catholics, Jews and Protestants could be ad-mitted.

In the summer of 1854 she superintended the nursing of cholera patients in London. But her greatest opportunity for service came when war broke out in the Crimea. She went to superintend a corps of volunteer nurses. A hospital was established at Scutari, and in two days she had six hundred soldiers under her care. In three weeks the number had reached three thousand.

A born general as well as a nurse, Florence Nightingale immediately tackled horrible neglect and mismanagement. Directing calmly but firmly, she brought order out of chaos. Her endurance seemed superhuman when she stood for twenty hours at a time. The correspondent and commissioner of the London *Times* reported: "When all the medical officers have retired for the night and silence and darkness have settled down upon those miles of prostrate sick, she may be observed alone, with a little lamp in her hand, making her solitary rounds."

The soldiers looked upon her as a ministering angel and many would kiss her shadow as it fell across them. One soldier said: "Before she came there was much cussin' and swearin', but after that it was holy as a church." She was welcomed by neither the military nor the medical officers, and had to fight her way through much red tape. Soon English sentiment in her favor was so strong that all hospitals in the area were placed under her supervision.

She contracted hospital fever and after two years of toil returned to England. Queen Victoria summoned her to Balmoral Castle and gave her a red enamel cross emblazoned with diamonds. Grateful people of England subscribed two hundred and fifty thousand dollars as a testimonial, and she used it to found the Nightingale Home for Nurses at St. Thomas's Hospital.

After the Crimean War she led a quieter life, for her health had been affected, but she continued to work for army sanitary reform and for army hospitals. She also promoted rural hygiene and worked for other improvements, in addition to writing *Notes on Nursing*, one of the classic guides to the profession.

Florence Nightingale lived to be ninety but became blind in her last years and suffered periods of loss of memory. Though many in England wanted her to be buried among the honored dead in Westminster Abbey, her wish for a simple burial was carried out. She was buried in the family grave at East Wellow and her tombstone bears only the inscription: "F. N. Born 1820. Died 1910."

CHAPTER 5

Women Who Built

CATHERINE BOOTH—

"MOTHER" OF THE SALVATION ARMY

(1829-1890)

* * *

The Salvation Army was founded by her husband, William Booth, with her constant help. She shared his aspirations and herself became a famous preacher. She not only mothered this institution but was the mother of eight children, who formed an army of Christian workers.

SHE WAS FILLED WITH THE TRUE SPIRIT OF CHRIST

LIKE SARAH, mother of Isaac, Catherine Mumford Booth once heard a voice say: "I will make thee Mother of Nations." As the mother of eight children whom she sent forth to serve the afflicted, the downtrodden and the forgotten, and as "Mother" of the Salvation Army, she holds an honored place among the great women of the Christian faith.

She saw the Salvation Army, whose "purpose was to carry salvation through the land, and whose commander-in-chief was God," develop from its tiny nucleus, the humble Christian Mission in London's East End, into one of the largest Christian forces in the world. Today it numbers some four million in uniform doing work in eighty-six countries and territories, and speaking a hundred and three languages.

Catherine Booth was quite literally the mother of this Army, nurturing it in its infancy and seeing it through almost three pioneering decades.

[218]

Afflicted from childhood with curvature of the spine and later with symptoms of tuberculosis and angina pectoris, she was never strong, but she persevered against these and other immense odds. Although she said, "I can scarcely remember a day of my life which has been free from pain," scores of times she arose from her sickbed to face eager, waiting crowds. She became one of the most famous women preachers of her country.

Born at Ashbourne in Derbyshire, she was the daughter of an itinerant Methodist preacher, John Mumford. Her mother, Sarah Milward Mumford, left the Church of England to become a Methodist. Before Catherine reached her teens she had read the Bible through several times and learned to pray unceasingly. At sixteen she passed through a religious experience of which she said: "I was so happy that I felt as if I was walking on air." Her subsequent career demonstrates that the foundations of her faith were laid in her youth.

Her courage was great at all times. Even when her father, a former temperance advocate, took to heavy drink, she was thankful for the joys she could still experience. "Help me to be more fully decided in all things," she prayed, "and not to confer with flesh and blood, but to be bold to take up and firm to sustain the consecrated cross."

In June of 1855 she was married to William Booth, whose family, once wealthy, was now poor. In the first fortnight of their marriage, they went out together, as did the Apostles, to teach, to preach and to pray among the poor and lowly. She rejoiced that she had married a minister, because, as she said, she could occupy "the highest sphere of Christian usefulness." Her husband rejoiced that he had obtained favor of the Lord in finding such a wife.

A few months after their marriage, she wrote to William:

I believe that if God spares you and you are faithful to His trust, your usefulness will be untold, and beyond our present capacity to estimate. God seems to be preparing you in your own soul for greater things yet.

In later years, she helped him lay the foundation for a structure which rose far above their early expectations. Her assistance doubled his power for good, for where he was creative and had a particular talent for organization, she was critical and analytical. The happy combination of these faculties largely constituted their effectiveness as a couple. She would run to him from the nursery or from the kitchen to pass her opinion upon an article, an appeal, a dispatch or some new development of the work. She was often at his side, helping him in the pulpit, on the street and in the hovels of the poor.

In one of the letters written shortly before their marriage, she said:

> Don't let controversy hurt your soul. Live near to God by prayer. Oh, I do feel the importance of spiritual things, and am in a measure living by faith in the Son of God! Just fall down at His feet and open your very soul before Him, and throw yourself right into His arms.

Together William and Catherine set down some important rules for marriage. The first was not to have secrets that affected their mutual relationship or the interest of their family. The next was not to have two separate purses. Another was not to argue in the presence of the children. God blessed their marriage, which was guided by such intelligent principles, all the days of their lives.

Though William Booth was born to the Church of England, he was a minister in the Methodist New Connexion at the time of their marriage. In their fifth year together, as he was closing his service, Catherine walked to the pulpit, asking that she might say a word. So fervent was her address that soon she was invited to speak from many pulpits. Her first sermon subject was "Be filled with the Spirit."

She regarded woman's active participation vital to the triumphant march of Christianity and it became an essential doctrine in the Booth creed that in Jesus Christ there was neither male nor female. The Gospel, they said, like nature, placed both sexes on a footing of complete mental and spiritual equality.

She preached and worked to deepen the dedication and extend the usefulness of women. "It will be a happy day for England," she once observed, "when Christian ladies transfer their attention from poodles and terriers to destitute and starving children." She reminded women that living for pleasure and filling their days with eating, drinking, dressing, riding and sight-seeing, left no time to serve God. They were too occupied with self, she said, to develop spiritual resources.

Fighting to awaken the Church, she understood why Paul spent much of his life visiting and writing to the churches. She took up her cross, was transformed by it, and like Paul gloried in the new life that unfolded for her. Believing that religion meant doing the will of God, she implored:

> What can we do to wake the Church up? Too often those who have its destinies in the palm of their hands are chiefly chosen from those who are mere encyclopedias of the past rather than from those who are distinguished by their possession of Divine Power. For leadership of the Church something more is required.

She had formed these views about the time her husband broke with the Methodist New Connexion in 1861 and began his career as an independent revivalist. For both of them his decision meant an itinerant life with no settled home, a difficult course to choose in face of the needs of their growing family.

When William came home and announced, "Kate, I have found my destiny," she realized that the question of their daily livelihood would present a serious problem, for their work would be among the poverty-stricken residents of London's East End. How would they live? They did not know, but her response to his decision was unwavering. "We have trusted the Lord once for our support," she said confidently, "and we can trust Him again." She helped her husband bear in mind that all things are possible to God, even amid apparent impossibilities. Thus began the Booth's first Christian Mission, the seed which grew into the Salvation Army and spread a transforming faith around the world.

Her early experience enabled her, as a team-worker with her husband, to forge the Salvation Army into a militant and triumphant Christian force. The Salvation Army prayers later came to be called "knee drills," and Bible reading, "taking one's rations." This military vocabulary was introduced into other phases of the work. Mission houses were "citadels" and "forts," every revival was heralded as a "battle," every convert a "prisoner of war."

During this early period, Catherine saw the Salvation Army increase in wisdom and stature. As the work expanded and numbers grew, meetings were held wherever room was available. One of the first halls was a stable which the group cleaned and whitewashed. Later a Sunday service was held in a saloon vacated during the early morning hours, while other meetings took place in an old warehouse.

Catherine herself designed the Salvation Army women's uniform—a plain tunic and blouse, and a Puritan bonnet resembling those the Quakers had worn and called "The Hallelujah Bonnet." After designing it, she observed:

> It seemed clear to me from the teaching of the Bible that Christ's people should be separate from the world in everything which denoted character and that they should not only be separate but appear so. Otherwise what benefit would their separation confer upon others? As I advanced in religious experience I became more and more convinced that my appearance ought to be such as to show everybody with whom I came in contact that I have renounced the pomp and vanities of the world, and that I belonged to Christ.

This unifom, which her daughters and daughters-in-law were also to wear, took her like a true Christian Crusader across many religious frontiers, to work among many faiths, in churches, in chapels, theaters, tents, and in the open air.

It was no easy task for Catherine Booth to rear her family as they went from place to place in their self-sacrificing service. She who was so home-loving had to spend her time traveling much of her life. But she never neglected her children's Christian welfare. She counseled them, watched with wisdom over their spiritual development, education and courtships, and taught them that it is not so much what one does as how much one loves, for love, she said, is the fulfilling of the law. She was like Susanna Wesley, who had taught her children to live by a definite method, saying that Christian service demands not only training for work, but training for sacrifice and consecration.

Like Hannah, mother of Samuel, she dedicated each of her eight children from infancy to service for God. Not all of them remained with the Salvation Army but all received their training there and committed themselves to the cause of the Gospel. Her children and their families form an impressive list of leaders in Christian work.

Her eldest son, William Bramwell, succeeded his father as second general of the Salvation Army and was largely responsible for the development of the Army. Her second son, Ballington, was founder and chief general of the Volunteers of America. Her eldest daughter, Catherine, married Arthur Sidney Clibborn, a Salvationist colonel, who adopted the name Booth-Clibborn. Her next daughter, Emma, married Frederick St. George De Latour Tucker, a former judge in India, who adopted the name Booth-Tucker and compiled the two-volume life of his mother-in-law, *Memoirs of Catherine Booth* (1895). Her next son, Herbert Henry (or Howard), pioneered the movement in Canada. Her sixth child, Marian Billups Booth, was a staff captain in the Salvation Army, but owing to physical weakness could not face arduous service. However, her next daughter, Evangeline, born on Christmas Day in 1865, the year the Salvation Army was founded, served as the first and only woman general of the International Salvation Army (1934-1939). The last daughter, Lucy Milward, married Emmanuel Daniel Hellberg, a Swedish Salvationist, who changed his name to Booth-Hellberg.

The wives of two of her sons also devoted their lives to the cause of Christ. Her eldest son, William Bramwell, married a South Wales girl, Florence Eleanor Soper (1861-1957), who was leader for many years of the Salvation Army's work among women and whose seven children also served in its ranks. Ballington married Maude Charlesworth (1865-1948), who succeeded her husband as president of the Volunteers of America. She was also one of the founders of the Parent-Teacher Association.

No family in recent Christian history has served so diligently the poor and the outcast, the prisoner and the hoodlum, bringing to them the healing ministry of Christ. They went forth to many nations of the world —Catherine to France, Emma to Ireland and Switzerland, Bramwell to Sweden, Ballington to the United States. After Catherine's death in 1890 her children carried the work into even more distant corners of the globe.

Seeing her children grow into their larger responsibilities, she declared, as had Mary, mother of Jesus: " 'My soul doth magnify the Lord,' for His grace and truth shown to my children. He hath given me the desire of my heart." Her home was truly a Bethel, and there she trained her family of warriors for Christ.

She was a woman of intense humanity and practical sympathy. One of her first home calls was made upon a woman standing on a doorstep with a jug in her hand. Catherine Booth afterward reported: "My divine teacher declared, 'Speak to that woman.' Satan suggested, 'Perhaps she is intoxicated.' " Catherine overcame her hesitancy and offered her help. She discovered that the woman's husband was a drunkard. Expressing her sorrow, Catherine asked if she could come inside, but the woman answered: "You could do nothing with him now." Catherine replied: "I do not mind his being drunk, if you will let me come in. I am not afraid."

The woman led her to a man sitting in a chair with a jug by his side. Drinking had reduced him to the level of a beast though he had once been responsible and intelligent. Walking forward in God's strength, Catherine talked to the man, read to him the story of the Prodigal Son and prayed with him. His response to her witness encouraged her belief in the importance of personal contact. From that time on she devoted two evenings a week to systematic house-to-house visitation.

Once she went to a place where she found a poor woman and her new twins lying on a heap of rags. By her side was a crust of bread and a small lump of lard. Catherine bathed the twins in a broken dish and afterward related that "the gratitude of those large eyes that gazed upon me from that wan and shrunken face, can never fade from my memory."

Later she watched her own children set out on difficult missions, taking the message of Christianity among the poor and the outcasts of London, into places where brickbats were sometimes hurled at them, into prisons and saloons. Even her beloved Evangeline set forth, humbly clad, to sing in London streets and to collect pennies to buy coal for the poor. If Catherine Booth had fears for her children, she never expressed them. She helped her children realize that God walked beside them. Her notes of love and comfort to them are numerous. Once when Evangeline was low-spirited Catherine wrote her:

I can better counsel you—not to give way to lowness while you are young. . . . Rise up on the strength of God and resolve to conquer. My love for you makes me desire your highest good. How can love desire less? Anything that desires less is selfishness, not love. You may have others who will be more demonstrative but never who will love you more unselfishly than your mother or who will be willing to do or bear more for your good.

Catherine taught her family to prize the contribution women could make to Christian progress. As her boys went forth to serve, she tried to impress them with the fact that their sisters were as intelligent and capable as they were. She often reminded them that "Jesus Christ's principle was to put woman on the same platform as man, although I am sorry to say His apostles did not always act up to it."

To one of her children she once declared: "We are made for larger ends than earth can compass. Oh let us be true to our exalted destiny."

In their self-abnegation, Catherine and William Booth created a monument to the spirit of Christ and against the spirit of Mammon. Like members of the early Christian community at Jerusalem, they never accepted profits for themselves from such things as books, hymns or magazines, but placed them in the treasury for the common good. They not only refused money for themselves but taught their children not to worship wealth.

Catherine had other revolutionary ideas about money and service. To a woman who was spending endless hours on an elaborate piece of embroidery for a church bazaar, she said:

Why don't you give the money, and use your time for something better? . . . Don't sit at home making other people's finery. Visit the sick and seek to save the lost instead. It makes me burn with shame to think how money is raised for so-called religious purposes by entertainments, bazaars, etc., at which there is frequently gambling to raise money for Jesus Christ, whom they say they love more than fathers, mothers, husbands, wives, houses, or anything else on earth.

Talking against fashionable believers, she observed in a letter:

There are thousands talking about His second coming who will neither see nor receive Him in the person of His humble and persecuted followers. No. They are looking for Him in the clouds! What a sensation there would be if He were to come again in a carpenter's coat. How many would recognize Him then, I wonder? I am afraid it would be the old story, "Crucify Him!" . . . Oh for grace always to see Him where He is to be seen, for verily, flesh and blood doth not reveal this unto us! Well, bless the Lord, I keep seeing Him risen again in the forms of drunkards and ruffians of all descriptions.

Realizing the pitiable and helpless position of young girls caught in prostitution, she helped to establish London's first Rescue Home, placing it under the supervision of her daughter-in-law Mrs. Ballington Booth. Out of the efforts of the Ballington Booths grew the Volunteers of America. Catherine Booth appealed in a letter to Queen Victoria for the protection of young girls under sixteen, saying that crimes against them were undermining the social fabric and "would bring down the judgments of God upon our nation." She also protested to Prime Minister Gladstone that the House of Commons was too much absorbed with matters relating to property and taxes to find time to concern itself about the destruction of England's womanhood.

After years of fighting in the Army she had helped to found, she had learned to be a "good soldier" in regard to personal suffering. It was discovered in 1888 that she had cancer and had only two years to live, but she received the news with the calmness of a true Christian. She had only one anxiety—that she would not be able to nurse her husband in his last hours.

"There have been few persons in the history of mankind who met affliction with so much fortitude, who repined so little under acute pain," St. John Ervine says about Catherine in his biography of William Booth. In her last illness, she continued to send messages to her "soldiers." To a group of them facing difficulties, she wrote:

As I lie here on the brink of the Eternal World I want to tell you that you need have no fear for the integrity of those who have the direction of this great movement. God is with them. I would gladly have stayed here a little longer to have pushed forward the war, and to have taken part in the special effort for a hundred thousand souls just inaugurated by the General, but I shall hear of their ingathering as surely, and rejoice in it as fully, in the country whither I am going. Goodbye. I will meet you in the morning.

Fifty thousand gathered on the Salvation Army's twenty-fifth anniversary to hear her last message. Though she knew her days were numbered, her words pointed toward the future: "Love one another. Help your comrades in dark hours. I am dying under the Army flag; it is yours to live and fight under. God is my salvation and refuge in storm."

On October 4, 1890, this frail but valiant servant of Christ passed on. She lay in state in London's Congress Hall, wearing her bonnet, tunic and blouse, with her Bible in her hands and her flag by her side. For five days, fifty thousand persons filed past. Among these were five thousand women officers of the Army and a thousand other women workers.

At the end of her funeral service, her husband arose and spoke of her as the "flower in his garden for years, his shadow from the burning sun." He described her as a "servant who had served him without fee or reward, who had administered, for love, to his health and comfort," as a friend "who had understood the rise and fall of his feelings, the bent of his thoughts, and the purpose of his existence." He praised her also as the mother of his children, "who had cradled and nursed and trained them for the service of the living God," as a wife "who for years had never given him real cause for grief, who had stood by his side, ever willing to interpose herself between him and the enemy, and ever strongest when the battle was fiercest." He concluded by saying that his heart was full of gratitude because God had lent to him such a treasure for so long a season, one who was a real warrior for Christ.

Catherine Booth's example is still a power for good, for love, for inspiration. Her books, including *Female Ministry, Aggressive Christianity, Life and Death, Popular Christianity, Papers on Godliness* and *Practical Religion,* are still being read. She is remembered for her work in defining the position of women in the Salvation Army and for using their neglected talents. She had extraordinary ability to transform vague religious beliefs into living reality. She stands out as one of the most vital and courageous Christian workers of all time.

LUCY WEBB HAYES

—FAITHFUL FIRST LADY

(1831-1889)

✦ ✦ ✦

As the wife of President Rutherford B. Hayes, she was a great influence for good. She brought to the White House an appreciation for the highest standards of a Christian home.

"EXALT THE HOME AND YOU LIFT UP THE NATION"

LUCY WEBB HAYES, wife of Rutherford B. Hayes, nineteenth President of the United States (1877-1881), was perhaps the most religious-minded First Lady to occupy the White House. Her home was openly Christian, and she brought to the Capital the hallowed American custom of daily family prayers.

President and Mrs. Hayes could see no reason to abandon the habit of a lifetime when they moved to the White House, and they served no wine or alcoholic beverages. Convinced that their example of abstinence was right, they knew it would have a wide influence in society.

"It is true I shall violate a precedent," declared Mrs. Hayes, "but I shall not violate the Constitution, which is all that, through my husband, I have taken the oath to obey. As for my countrymen, they are accustomed to independent action." Because of her stand, she was dubbed "Lemonade Lucy," and the Hayes administration was known as the "cold water regime."

She later explained to a friend: "I had three sons just coming to manhood and starting out in society, and I did not feel as if I could be the first to put the wine cup to their lips." The oldest son, Webb Cook Hayes, who had just graduated from Cornell University, was serving as his father's secretary. Another son, Birchard, was in Harvard Law School, while a third, Rutherford, was a student at Cornell. The two younger children, Fanny and Scott, lived in the White House. Three sons had died in their childhood.

Frances E. Willard, president of the Woman's Christian Temperance Union, paid this tribute to Mrs. Hayes: "Total abstinence has never had such a standard-bearer as this noble woman, and centuries from now, her steadfast adherence to the truest Christian hospitality will be told as a memorial to her."

Lucy Webb Hayes looks down on White House visitors today from a handsome portrait painted by Daniel Huntingdon and presented to the White House by the Woman's Christian Temperance Union. The maroon velvet dress in which she is shown is typical of her White House wardrobe. It is simply designed, made from rich material, and does not have a low neckline—a style she never wore. She wears no jewelry and her hair is arranged plainly at the back and held in place by a comb. She was a woman of medium height and full figure, and she had a singularly gentle and winning face and a tender light in her eyes. Serene and poised, she had a sunny disposition that always looked on the bright side of things.

She brought to the Capital much experience as a hostess, for she had twice been First Lady of Ohio, first from 1868 to 1872 and again from 1876 until the following year, when her husband left the Governor's Mansion to become President.

Sunday evenings at the White House, while she presided, had a character all their own. Hymnbooks were distributed and hymns were sung. She had a warm contralto voice and sang with a joy that brought spirit into the service. After her guests left, many said that these evenings gave them the feeling that there were great things in life to interest the human spirit and to demand its allegiance.

Lucy Webb was graduated with first honors from the Wesleyan Female Seminary in Cincinnati in 1852. She holds the distinction of being the first college-educated First Lady of the United States. Her marriage took place in December of 1852. She and her husband were strong supporters of the Methodist Church in their home town, Fremont, Ohio. When the denomination built a new church there, they bore one-fourth of the expense of construction. When this structure was burned some years later, they contributed a similar proportion to the cost of its restoration. They did not limit their interest to the Methodist communion in Fremont, however, but gave assistance and encouragement to other churches, Catholic as well as Protestant.

Lucy was reared in a family that did its duty in "behalf of the weak, the ignorant, the needy." After the death of her father, Dr. James Webb, in Chillicothe, Ohio, she and her mother and the other children freed the family slaves and continued to take an interest in their welfare, repeatedly giving them assistance.

During the Civil War, while her husband served with the Union forces, she spent two winters with him in camp in Virginia, helping to nurse him back to health. Throughout the war she worked in other hospitals and camps. Soldiers of her husband's regiment (including Major William McKinley, who later became President), admired her greatly. On their twenty-fifth wedding anniversary, celebrated while she was First Lady, Major McKinley and others of the regiment gave her a large silver platter bearing an affectionate inscription.

During their residence in Washington, President and Mrs. Hayes attended the Foundry Methodist Episcopal Church. When the Woman's Home Missionary Society of the Methodist Episcopal Church was organized in 1880, Mrs. Hayes became its first president, a position she held for nine years. The Lucy Webb Hayes Training School for Deaconesses in Washington was named in honor of her.

During her presidency of the organization, she expressed her firm convictions in a statement in Syracuse, New York:

The cornerstone to practical religion is the Golden Rule. . . . If by reason of our neglect of home work the stream of unchristian tendencies from abroad and the flood of indifference and vice in our own country, shall overwhelm our cherished institutions, all missionary work at home and abroad will suffer alike by the common calamity.

With America and American homes what they should be, we need not greatly fear the evils that threaten us from other lands. We can easily shun or safely meet them, if our duty is faithfully done in behalf of the weak, the ignorant, and the needy of our own country. If our institutions, social and political, are imperiled today, it is largely because the wealthy and fortunate, engrossed as they are in the midst of our vast material progress and prosperity, are not sufficiently mindful of what was taught by the words and life of the Founder of our blessed religion: "Whatsoever ye would that men should do to you, do ye even so to them."

She added that "America is the cradle of the future for all the world. Elevate woman, and you lift up the home; exalt the home and you lift up the nation."

Eight years after leaving the White House, Lucy Webb Hayes died suddenly on June 25, 1889, at "Spiegel Grove," her home in Fremont, Ohio. Her husband survived her by less than four years.

The poet John Greenleaf Whittier said of her:

> Her presence lends its warmth and health to all who come before it;
> If woman lost us Eden, then such as she alone restore it.

NETTIE FOWLER McCORMICK
—AN INTERNATIONAL CHRISTIAN

(1835-1923)

* * *

Christian institutions all over the world benefited from her generosity. She was called "Mother" of McCormick Theological Seminary. Her Chicago brownstone house was called "a Christian half-way house between the Orient and the West."

WITH OUTSTRETCHED HAND SHE HARVESTED CHRISTIANS

NETTIE FOWLER McCORMICK, deeply religious by nature, training and practice, became one of the most generous Christian philanthropists of her time. "She declined a life of ease and social pleasure for one of stewardship and service," says Stella Virginia Roderick in her biography *Nettie Fowler McCormick.*

A Methodist by birth but a Presbyterian from her girlhood to the end of her long life, she did much for Presbyterians all over the world. She was, however, first and foremost a Christian, and her work extended to many denominations and causes. Her deep concern for the needs of the Church in America did not blind her to the world-wide mission of Christianity.

Nettie Fowler came from a religious family. Her Methodist grandmother, Nancy Fish Spicer, once wrote as a New Year's resolution: "I will by the assistance of God try to seek Him with all my heart." Her Mother,

Clarissa Spicer Fowler, was deeply devout, as was her father, Melzar Fowler, who died when Nettie was a young girl.

She was born at Brownville, New York, near the St. Lawrence River, February 8, 1835, and went to Utica in her girlhood, where she joined the Presbyterian Church and took part in a Sunday-school class. At this time she wrote: "Great reason have I to praise the Lord that such an institution was formed." Nettie sang in the choir and played the church melodeon. She was educated at Genesee Wesleyan Seminary at Lima, New York, a Methodist institution.

When she was twenty-two she visited Chicago, where she met her husband, Cyrus H. McCormick, twenty-six years her senior. He invented and developed the grain reaper now manufactured by the International Harvester Company. They were married January 26, 1859, and enjoyed nearly twenty-six happy years together. In later years she called his letters "the most precious material thing I possess."

At his death in 1884 Cyrus left her a large estate, which she regarded as a sacred trust to be used for good causes. She was a woman who "wove life with three threads, business, family, philanthrophy," and she never "neglected one for the other." She was a devoted mother to her six children. Her youngest daughter developed a mental illness which brought constant care and grief to her. She paid loving tribute to this daughter, however, by naming Virginia Hall at Tusculum College in Tennessee for her and also the Virginia McCormick Library at the Seminary in Chicago.

Nettie McCormick has been called the "Mother" of the McCormick Theological Seminary in Chicago, to which her family gave more than four million dollars. The seminary occupied a leading place in her heart, for she felt that no effort was so important as that invested in the training of young men to preach the Gospel of Christ. The library was entirely her gift, as was the gymnasium erected after her death. Fowler Hall, which she and her sons built, bears her own family name. In addition to buildings and furnishings, she provided large sums for repairs, refurnishing, special pledges, the establishment of fellowships and scholarships, and books. In 1905 she and her sons set up an endowment to pay the president's salary.

A great part of her work as a Christian philanthropist centered on the world's youth. She made it possible for John R. Mott of the Student Volunteer Movement and later chairman of the World's Student Christian Federation "to go to the ends of the earth" in behalf of youth programs. In paying tribute to her, he said: "As a giver she showed statesmanship, strategy. . . . There was spaciousness and scope in her conceptions." With her help he formed the World's Student Christian Federation at the ancient Swedish royal castle of Vadstena, the same castle where Bridget of Sweden, almost six centuries earlier, had founded her Order of the Brigittines.

Mrs. McCormick was a personal friend of many religious leaders of her time—Dwight L. Moody, the evangelist; Sir Wilfred Grenfell, missionary to Labrador; and George Livingstone Robinson, who studied the sanctuary at the ancient Arabian rock city of Petra.

Her husband's first gift to Tusculum College marked the beginning of her own interest in Southern Mountain Schools. She tried to improve the daily lives of the people by offering them domestic science and manual training. She also helped to establish Sunday schools and churches. The practice cottage used for training in domestic science was one of her innovations adopted by the Presbyterians from Puerto Rico to Alaska.

Her children called her three-story brownstone house on Rush Street in Chicago, a short block from the roar of North Michigan Avenue, "a Christian half-way house between the Orient and the West." Built in 1870, it remained her home for nearly forty years and became a center of international Christianity. Religious and philanthropic meetings were held in her home and there was always a coming and going of missionaries. "The greatest gift of all," she asserted, "comes from self-sacrifice and devotion of the missionaries themselves."

She filled special requests in various parts of the world, such as an improved water supply, a moving-picture film, and a motorcycle. Her larger expenditures were, for example, twenty-five thousand dollars for the first college building on the new Alborz College campus in Teheran, twenty-five thousand dollars to a hospital in Siam, two thousand dollars for the first women's hospital in Persia, twenty-five thousand dollars for theological education in Korea.

She aided a language school at Nanking, a pioneer undertaking of newly arrived missionaries. In India she gave agricultural machinery and land to an experiment in creative application of the Gospel by way of the plow. In 1896 she herself went to inspect, at Asyût in central Egypt, a school which had been started in 1865 in a slightly remodeled donkey stable. To this she gave additional funds which enlarged its facilities.

About 1870 she worked zealously for the Woman's Board of the Presbyterian Mission of the Northwest. She was its second treasurer, for thirty-four years its vice president, and finally honorary vice president. She edited *The Interior*, a religious paper in which she became interested before her husband's death.

In her late sixties Mrs. McCormick became deaf, but she did not regard it as a bitter affliction, for she said it gave her time to think, and saved her from hearing "mean things." A woman with a confident trust in divine Providence, she wrote a sick relative: "We plan—and God steps in with another plan for us and He is all-wise and the most loving friend we have always helping us."

Described as a strikingly handsome, tall, graceful woman, she had clear-cut, well-balanced features, luminous brown eyes and slightly curling dark brown hair that became gray. Her spiritual awareness gave her face a sweet radiance. Nettie Fowler McCormick died at her "House-in-the-Woods" in Lake Forest, Illinois, July 5, 1922, at the age of eighty-seven.

AMANDA SMITH—

NEGRO WOMAN EVANGELIST

(1837-1915)

● ● ●

Born a slave, one of a family of thirteen children, she received international acclaim as a missionary evangelist, preaching in England, India, Africa and other parts of the world. She was a Christian of the highest type and was called "God's image carved in ebony."

"WITHOUT HOLINESS, NO MAN SHALL SEE THE LORD"

AMANDA SMITH'S story is one of spiritual triumph. She rose from the humblest beginnings to world-wide leadership in the Christian cause. Despite her own want and suffering she thought first of the needs of others. She was not embittered by the prejudice she encountered. The secret of her courage and achievement lay in her complete reliance on God.

In her autobiography, which she calls *The Lord's Dealings with Mrs. Amanda Smith*, she relates how her father, Samuel Berry, toiled all day making brooms and husk mats to pay his master for freedom for himself, his wife and his five children, one of whom was Amanda. During the harvest season, after working for his master all day, "he would walk three and four miles, and work in the fields till one and two o'clock in the morning, then go home and lie down and sleep for an hour or two, then be up and at it again." She adds that "he was a strong man, with an excellent constitution, and God wonderfully helped him in his struggle" to free his family from slavery. His final success is recorded in freedom papers on file in the Baltimore Courthouse. Eight of Amanda's younger brothers and sisters were born in liberty.

Amanda was born January 23, 1837, in Long Green, Maryland, where her father was a slave of Darby Insor. Her mother, Miriam Mathews, was a slave of Dr. Shadrach Green, also of Long Green, Maryland. Among Amanda's earliest recollections was the kind face and gentle voice of her grandmother who, she said, "was mighty in prayer." Her mother and father often remarked that it was chiefly to her grandmother's prayers they owed their freedom. Amanda's mother prayed, as a child, to be good like her mother, and she did inherit her spirit. She became an earnest Christian of steadfast faith and strong moral courage. She could make a little go a long way and she washed and ironed beautifully. "A better cook never lifted a pot," said her daughter.

Although Amanda had only about three and a half months of schooling, received a few weeks at a time in the summers, she learned to read and express herself well, both on the platform and in print. She taught herself to read by cutting out large letters from newspapers, laying them on the window sill and getting her mother to make them into words. But she had a natural gift for expression and the simple words of her autobiography are charged with spiritual power. She published her autobiography, the main source of information about her life, in Chicago in 1893, several years after returning from an evangelistic tour that took her nearly halfway around the world. The book symbolizes her motto: "Without holiness no man shall see the Lord."

When she was about thirteen she went to work in Strausburg, sometimes called Shrewsbury, near York, Pennsylvania, as a servant for a widow with five children. While she was there a revival broke out in the Methodist Episcopal Church, and Amanda was deeply impressed. She tells how during one of the meetings a young woman, whom she describes as "a power for good everywhere she went," came to her, a "poor colored servant girl sitting away back by the door. With entreaties and tears she asked me to go forward. I was the only colored girl there, but I went. She knelt beside me with her arms around me and prayed for me. Oh, how she prayed!" When Amanda went home that night, she resolved she would "be the Lord's and live for Him."

She took advantage of every uplifting influence and grew spiritually, all the while working hard and well as a servant. She gained a reputation for her Maryland biscuits and fried chicken. Though she earned but a pittance, she undertook to buy back the freedom of her sister Frances, who, though born free, had accidentally allowed her papers to be destroyed, and had been sold at auction. Although she borrowed forty dollars from her mistress, Amanda needed additional funds to purchase her sister's liberty. One day she found three hundred dollars and returned it to the man who had lost it. As a reward he gave her the fifty dollars she lacked. Immediately, she knelt and thanked the Lord for this blessing.

When her first husband, Calvin M. Devine, went South with the Federal Army and never returned, she supported herself and their daughter Mazie. Her second husband, James Smith, was a minister who lacked stability of character. Immediately after their marriage, she went alone to old Bethel Church, in Philadelphia, and sat down to listen proudly for her husband's name to be read in the long list of ministerial appointments. But she listened in vain.

Disappointed, she went home, and there James confessed: "My dear, I was afraid to tell you before I married you that I was leaving the ministry. I was afraid you would not marry me." Her disappointment was great, for she had married him thinking that through his ministry she herself might have a greater opportunity for Christian service. All through her trials with him in the years that followed, she prayed for the Lord's sustaining grace. A major source of suffering were the deaths of several of her children, but her faith brought her through these experiences: "My mother heart was sad, but nevertheless the Lord stood by me."

A turning point in Amanda's life came in 1855 in the old Green Street Methodist Episcopal Church in New York, during Rev. John S. Inskip's sermon from the text: "That ye put on the new man, which after God is created in righteousness and true holiness" (Eph. 4:24). She listened attentively as he spoke: "Now this blessing of purity like pardon is received by faith, and if by faith, why not now?" He continued to illustrate: "How long is a dark room dark when you take a lighted lamp into it?" Speaking of God's power, he said: "If God, in the twinkling of an eye, can change these vile bodies of ours and make them look like His own most glorious body, how long will it take God to sanctify a soul?"

Amanda said later: "As quick as the spark from smitten steel, I felt the touch of God from the crown of my head to the soles of my feet." There and then she made a full and unconditional surrender to God. But as a Negro woman, she was afraid to go forward and make a public confession before so many white people. "The Devil was trying to argue me out of accepting God," she observed. She prayed for strength to witness, but could not do so. She knew, however, that her soul had been sanctified, even though she had not gone up with the others to the front of the church. How did she know this? As she left the service, she said she felt "the touch of which I cannot describe. It seemed to press me gently on the top of my head, and I felt something part and roll down and cover me like a great cloak! It was done in a moment, and O what a mighty peace and power took possession of me!" It was not long after this experience that Amanda began her evangelistic work in earnest.

She realized God had set her on fire, when He had sanctified her soul. She was no longer afraid of anyone, "not even white people." She understood better the meaning of "there is neither Jew nor Greek, there is neither bond nor free, there is neither male nor female: for ye are all one in Christ Jesus" (Gal. 3:28).

Amanda saw that "when people get sanctified, everything gets better around them." But "not having proper teaching, like Israel of old, I wandered in the wilderness of doubts and fears, ups and downs, for twelve years." All the while she thirsted for God and sought to find Him. But her way was not easy. "The Lord knew that I must be disciplined for service. He began by degrees to let me down. The Devil turned his hose on me, for it was as though a man was washing a sidewalk or carriage. He seemed to come at me in various ways, in such power, that I settled down in God.

"Why does God permit these fierce temptations?" she inquires. And she answers: "It is, I believe, first to develop the strength and muscles of your own soul and so prepare you for greater service, and second, to bring you into sympathy with others, who are often sorely tempted after they are sanctified, so that you too can help them."

Her richest blessings and her most stirring revelations of God came during her most menial tasks over the wash tub and ironing table, while making the bed and sweeping the house and washing dishes. She learned that rather than trying to escape her many trials, she should ask God for strength to endure them. She discovered that she could not drive God, for He could not be driven. When she was inclined to worry about a loved one, she found it best to let go of that loved one and take hold of God.

Amanda's hardships were many. She had to take in so many washings in order to earn a living for herself and her family that many times she stood at her wash tub from six in the morning until six the next morning, and afterward would work for hours at her ironing table. She would become so sleepy she could hardly stand on her feet. She would lean her head on the window ledge and sleep a little until the first deep need had passed, then could continue until daylight with perfect ease. She had to use the greatest economy and learned exactly how much ironing she could do with a ten-cent pail of coal.

She depended on God to supply her simplest needs. When the soles of her only shoes were so broken that they did not keep her feet dry, she prayed for shoes and heard a voice say: "If thou canst believe; all things are possible to him that believeth." She answered: " 'Lord, the shoes are mine' and I put them on as really as ever I put on a pair of shoes in my life. O, how real it was! I claimed them by faith. When I got up I walked about and felt I really had the very shoes I had asked for, on my feet." Three days later, while she was at church, a two-dollar bill and three one-dollar bills were placed in her hand by a stranger. She heard a voice say: "You know you prayed about your shoes." Filled with gratitude, she observed in her autobiography: "It was the Lord's doing, and it was marvelous."

Never did she forget to thank Him for the simplest blessings. All through her life she constantly knelt in prayer, sometimes beside an old trunk or chair, or under an apple tree or by a big log. Wherever she was, she went the "knee route." She prayed that she might not become a fanatic. She prayed to understand the Trinity. She prayed when she had much to suffer from her own people, because, as she said, "human nature is the same in black and white folk." She prayed when she had only thirteen cents. She prayed when she did not have enough to eat, discovering that "a good deal of praying fills you up pretty well when you cannot get anything else." She prayed when a cold wind buffeted her and swept her into a ditch. She asked God to still the wind, and it stopped. She said that if you have no trials and hardships, there will not be anything to pray for.

In every experience Amanda sought a closer relationship to God. Through a misunderstanding, she lost one of her best friends and was hurt because the friend had grown cold and distant toward her. Suddenly she realized that she had let herself get out of God's hands into the friend's hands, and that it was time for her to turn closer to God. Once when she stood up before women of rank and wealth to sing with her beautiful voice, she suddenly realized that she was only a washwoman and she was afraid to sing. Then she remembered: "I belong to Royalty, and am well acquainted with the King of kings and am better known and better understood among the great family above than I am on earth." And she praised God in full, rich tones that rang to the church rafters.

New opportunities unfolded for her quite miraculously. She began to evangelize through the eastern states and finally as far south and west as Knoxville, Tennessee, and Austin, Texas. She once arrived in Austin at ten o'clock at night and had to wait in the railway station until morning because she was black, and a woman alone who did not know where to go. But she accepted her lot uncomplainingly, thanking God that He had said to her: "Didn't I tell you I would go before you?"

When she went to Knoxville to the first Negro church assembly below the Mason-Dixon line, she suddenly remembered she was in the land where hostility might break into open violence. Though she was in considerable danger, she was not afraid. Kneeling, she prayed: "Lord, if being a martyr for Thee would glorify Thee, all right; just to go down there and be butchered by wicked men for their own gratification, without any reference to Thy glory, I'm not willing. And now, Lord, help me. If Thou dost want me to do this, even then, give me the grace and enable me to do it." When she heard a voice say to her, "My grace is sufficient for thee," she got up and went out unafraid.

Everywhere Amanda traveled on her evangelizing missions, she wore a plain poke bonnet and a Quaker wrapper, usually of brown or black, and carried in one hand her carpetbag with her few belongings. She went forth boldly, for she knew she had received her ordination from God to preach and to change hearts. Often she went among women who would not listen to a person of her low estate, but she remained sure that God had called her.

Wherever she spoke, she saw the spirit of the Lord fall upon her listeners, "just like you would sprinkle hot coals on them," she relates. Finally when the opportunity came for her to go to England, she reasoned with herself: "Go to England, Amanda Smith, the colored washwoman, go to England. No, I am not going to pray a bit; I have to ask the Lord for so many things that I really need, that I am not going to ask Him for what I don't need—to go to England. It does well enough for swell people to go, not for me."

As if from a distance she heard the words: "You are afraid to trust the Lord and go to England, you are afraid of the ocean." And she said: "My, it took my breath, but I said, 'Lord, that is the truth, the real truth.' "

In a moment, in panorama form, God's goodness seemed to pass before me, and His faithfulness in leading me and providing for me in every way, and answering my prayer a thousand times, and now to think I should be afraid to trust Him and go to England. Oh, such a sense of shame filled me. I prostrated myself on the floor. I felt I could never look up again in His dear face and pray. I never can describe the awful sense of shame that seemed to fill me, and I cried out, "Lord, forgive me, for Jesus' sake, and give me another chance, and I will go to England."

With restored confidence, Amanda Smith did go to England in 1876, the way being provided by friends who saw that her spiritual life was deepening and that she could give others a greater understanding and fuller experience of God and what He can do. During her journey she learned more fully the meaning of Philippians 4:19: "My God shall supply all your need according to His riches in glory by Christ Jesus."

She was alone when she sailed, and "yet not alone, for the Lord bade me go, and promised to go with me." So generous had been the gifts of friends that she had a first-class passage on the steamer. Since there were no ministers aboard, the captain asked her to conduct the service. "The Lord helped me to speak, sing and pray," she reports. At the close of the meeting, passengers who had hardly glanced at her before now crowded about her. As her ship sailed across the Atlantic, she spent much time communing with God and seeing Him "in the depths of the waters around me and the vaster depths of the ether above."

Landing at Liverpool, she proceeded to Keswick to a great "holiness convention." In England she found her race did not matter, for she was welcomed everywhere solely as an inspiring Christian worker. Spending a year and eight months there, she participated in evangelistic services in Liverpool, Birkenhead, Leeds, Manchester, Newcastle-on-Tyne, Cambridge, Plymouth, London and many other places. Then proceeding to Scotland, she spoke at Perth, Aberdeen, Glasgow, Edinburgh and elsewhere.

Afterward, as she said, "the Lord marvelously opened the way for me to visit India." She never took any salary for her work but went on her missions entirely on faith. When she was ready to embark for India she received a marvelous demonstration of God's goodness. She was given by supporters every cent needed for her expenses, along with a complete new outfit of clothes for the journey and twenty-five dollars for extras. She also received enough to provide winter clothing and three months' board in advance for her daughter Mazie, who was in school in America. Until this time she had supported her daughter entirely by washing and ironing until, as she said, "the Lord thrust me out into this work."

En route from London to Bombay, Amanda briefly visited Egypt. From there she went on to India, where she spent nineteen months evangelizing in Bombay, Bareilly, Lucknow, Allahabad and Agra. She never ceased to be impressed with an awesome sense of the grandeur of her work and the sublimity of the cause in which she was engaged.

In July 1881 she returned briefly to London for the Ecumenical Conference sponsored by World-Wide Methodists at the City Road Chapel, the site where Methodism was born.

After sixty days in England, she set out for Liberia, arriving there in January 1882. Her first stop was Monrovia, and she wrote later: "The Lord was with me then, as He had been at other times and in all other lands." From Monrovia she went to Cape Palmas. There she again was blessed, and "many hearts were made whole" through her ministry. She went on to Tubman Town, three miles inland, expecting to spend only the Sabbath, but she remained four weeks, preaching and converting. While there she organized women's band meetings, young men's praying bands,

Gospel temperance societies, and children's meetings for the promotion of holiness, as she had in so many other places. She spoke in simple chapels and rude huts, stirring many with her message.

Rejoicing in all the Lord's blessings to her, she never forgot that He had brought her from an attic room in New York, when her shoes had worn through and there was only ten cents in her purse. Suddenly in Liberia, far from home, her gifts stopped. Weeks went by, steamers came and went, letters came, but she received no money. "Then God seemed to say to me, 'You are not trusting in Me; you are trusting in America; you are looking to America for help more than to Me.' I saw it in a moment. 'Lord forgive me,' I said, 'and help me to give up every hope in America and trust in Thee, the living God!' " Once again she found her needs met by help in Liberia and renewed contributions from home.

She found the way to help others too. In Africa she adopted a native boy and girl and took them to England to be educated, although the girl could not adjust to the change in climate and had to return to Africa.

Returning to Liverpool for the last time in 1890, she visited friends there before going back to America, which she had left fourteen years before. Her daughter's family met her in New York and accompanied her to Chicago.

Until 1914 she conducted the Amanda Smith Orphans' Home for colored children in Harvey, Illinois, a suburb of Chicago. She financed the first payment toward the building from sales of her book and from her evangelistic work. She died on February 24, 1915.

In summing up her life, Rev. Marshall W. Taylor, in his booklet, *The Life, Travels, Labors and Helpers of Mrs. Amanda Smith,* declares that "as an enlightened, thoroughly consecrated Christian evangelist, among Negro women, Mrs. Amanda Smith takes the first place in American history." He adds: "She is a Christian of the highest type . . . and as a simple, confiding child of God has no superior among women of any race —and may we modestly say it?—nor among women of any time."

Rev. J. Krehbiel, a minister who knew her well, refers to her as "God's image carved in ebony." And Bishop J. M. Thoburn of India, in his preface to her autobiography, declares that relatively few Amanda Smiths "would suffice to revolutionize an empire."

LOTTIE MOON—
PIONEER OF THE MISSION FUND
(1840-1912)

• • •

Her name is honored as the founder of the Lottie Moon Christmas Offering, which has brought more than fifty million dollars into a Mission Fund that represents a never-ending chain of good will around the world.

BEARER OF LIGHT TO THE WOMEN OF NORTH CHINA

FOR FORTY YEARS Lottie Moon dedicated her life to Christian service among the women of North China. The gifted, well-educated, attractive daughter of an old Virginia family, she could have chosen a comfortable life in her plantation home. Instead, she chose privation, hardship and sacrifice among people who worshiped the mud idols of their ancestors. It was to these people, especially to the women, that she sought to make Christ real. She believed that if she could bring light to the homemakers, they would be a means of transforming North China.

A woman who possessed the stanch faith of her Quaker ancestors, she went forth as had the Apostles to preach the good news of Christ. One of her forebears, Robert Barclay, Scottish theologian and preacher, had pioneered with such Quakers as George Fox and William Penn.

Her mother was Anna Maria Barclay, whose family emigrated to Philadelphia before the American Revolution. Her father was Edward Harris Moon, whose fine old plantation home "Viewmont" in Albermarle County, Virginia, overlooked the Blue Ridge Mountains. Not far away were the homes of three Presidents, "Monticello" of Thomas Jefferson, "Montpelier" of James Madison and "Ashlawn" of James Monroe. "Viewmont" was probably the oldest of them all, having been built between 1744 and 1751 by the colonial architect, Joshua Fry.

Lottie was born there December 12, 1840, and christened Charlotte Diggs Moon. The name was later shortened to Lottie. Her middle name derived from a member of her family, Sir Dudley Diggs, colonial governor of Virginia.

Her mother, a stanch Southern Baptist, was a positive force for good in her community, as a neighbor, church woman and a model Christian mother. She used to read aloud to her children from the good books in "Viewmont's" library. Lottie responded especially to *The Lives of the Three Mrs. Judsons,* which awoke in her a desire to become a missionary.

Since there was no church near their home, Mrs. Moon held services each Sunday morning in her parlor for neighbors, servants and her children. When there was no minister, she led the services herself. For ten years, she carried on this American version of a "Church of the Household," like Marcella's in ancient Rome. When the First Baptist Church was founded in Scottsville, Lottie Moon's father left his Presbyterian Church to join the Baptists with his wife.

Lottie received her early schooling from a governess at home. In 1854 she was sent to the Albermarle Female Institute in Virginia, and later entered Hollins College, where she achieved the highest grades in her class. She was one of the first Southern women to receive a Master's Degree, awarded to her in 1861 by Hollins.

After graduation she went back to "Viewmont" to help her mother during the Civil War. She directed Negro workers to the river bottoms to store food and supplies and went herself to bury the family silver and jewels in the orchard. She also assisted her sister Orianna in hospital work.

Many members of Lottie Moon's family took active part in events of their time. Two cousins, using the disguise of French washerwomen, were spies on the Southern side. A brother, Dr. Thomas Moon, and his family were on board a boat going down the Mississippi, when yellow fever broke out. Sending his loved ones to safety, he remained aboard to serve the stricken passengers, finally dying of the fever himself.

The older sister, Orianna, was one of the South's first women physicians. After studying in Paris, she went to Jerusalem to work among children suffering from the eye disease so prevalent there. She became a member of the American Christian Mission, and was baptized in the River Jordan. During the Civil War, Orianna came home and converted the buildings of the University of Virginia into hospital units. Later she and her husband John Andrews established a hospital in Scottsville, Virginia. Of her four other sisters, Anna Marie was noteworthy as the mother of twelve sons, and Edmonia as a missionary to the Far East—going out before Lottie did.

When the war ended, Lottie wanted to make a contribution to the changing South. She first tutored in Alabama. Then she taught in a school for girls in Danville, Kentucky, and later she and a friend established a small school in Cartersville, Georgia.

A new world began to emerge for Lottie when her sister Edmonia sailed for China in 1872. In her letters home she stressed the need for more workers there. In the spring of 1873 when Lottie heard a sermon on the text, "Lift up your eyes, and look on the fields; for they are white already to harvest," she made up her mind to go to China as a missionary. Her school patrons remarked: "Such a waste of fine young womanhood. How much more we need her here!" But these remarks did not influence Lottie.

Lottie was thirty-three when she set out for her new mission field in September of 1873. In a bad storm at sea she seemed closer than ever to God, and wrote home of the experience:

As I watched the mad waste of waters, howling as if eager to engulf us, I think I should scarcely have been surprised to see a Divine Form walking upon them, so sweetly I heard in my inmost soul the consoling words, "It is I, be not afraid."

After arriving safely in North China, she seemed to become more aware of the real presence of God. As she faced the daily problems of making Him more real to Chinese pagans, she realized that God had entrusted her with a work for which no sacrifice on her part would be too great. She gave up the idea of marriage with a young professor she had met in college; God had first claim on her life.

Her primary task was to master the language, history and literature of China. Soon she was going from village to village playing many roles: counselor, guide, comforter and minister to Chinese women. She spoke Chinese and wore Chinese dress. Lottie and her sister Edmonia set up housekeeping in Tengchow in a three-hundred-year-old house that soon became known as "The Home of the Crossroads." In front of her study window she planted Virginia crape myrtle, and in front of her parlor window pomegranate trees, like those at "Viewmont." The sparse furniture in the house was entirely Chinese, but her kitchen was more like one in Virginia. There she kept a jar filled with cookies, made from an old Virginia recipe, a delight to Chinese children. In this house missionaries found what they found nowhere else—the latest magazines and books from America and England, and gracious Virginia hospitality.

Lottie was happy here with her sister, but this happiness was short-lived for Edmonia became ill and was advised to return to America. Lottie accompanied her home in 1876, but by Christmas Eve, 1877, Lottie was back in Tengchow at "The Home of the Crossroads."

In 1883, Lottie decided to broaden her service and go into the villages to teach women and children. Finally, in 1885, nearly forty-five years old, she journeyed to Pingtu, an area where no woman missionary had ever gone. Travel between Tengchow and Pingtu was difficult and the journey of one hundred and fifteen miles in a *shentza,* or mule litter, required seven days. Three nights she spent in vermin-infested inns, where accommodations for man and beast were so close that she slept to the accompaniment of the champing and neighing of mules.

When she arrived in Pingtu, she rented from an opium eater a little house at the west corner of the city wall, where the people passed in great crowds. Missionaries journeying through the province found sanctuary here. At infrequent intervals she went back to "The Home of the Crossroads" at Tengchow, but she knew that there was greater need for her work in the more isolated area of Pingtu. For a long time she carried on in her evangelization there almost singlehanded. To her little flock at the farthest outpost she became comforter, helper, even pastor. It was a happy moment for her when, in 1889, the Baptist Church was organized.

A pretty woman, with lovely soft features, kind eyes, and dark hair that she wore high-swept, she began to look Chinese as she went into the villages, for she dressed in a plain Chinese coat and gown and wore embroidered satin shoes with soles made from fragments of garments too worn to be patched. Later she estimated that her shoes for three-fourths of the year cost less than eighty cents, and her winter boots a little more than a dollar. She slept on a brick bed and ate food bought in the village market and cooked in Chinese kettles.

She often traveled around the countryside in her *shentza,* and she sometimes entered areas where the people were so unfriendly that her carriers took the precaution of muffling the bells on their mules with straw. Usually she passed through these places after dusk to insure her safety. But she went fearlessly, often saying to herself, as her courageous Quaker ancestors might have said: "What is there for me to fear if God be with me?"

At first people spoke of her as "The Old Devil Woman," but she soon won her way into their hearts and they began to call her "The Heavenly Book Visitor" or "The Foreign Lady with the Big Love Heart."

"Never angry, never impatient, never resentful, she patiently wore away the prejudices and hatred by her gentle, gracious presence and her blameless life," says her biographer, Una Roberts Lawrence, in her book *Lottie Moon.*

"She had all the firmness of a man, and yet a more gentle and womanly woman it would be hard to find," wrote Anna Seward Pruitt in her book *Up from Zero.* Mrs. Pruitt was a Presbyterian, who worked with Lottie in North China.

Her greatest admirers, no doubt, were among the native people themselves. From Sah Ling Village in the Pingtu area two men walked the many miles to Tengchow to find the teacher who knew the "Words of Life."

Pastor Li of Sah Ling Village later described her:

If she had not faith she could not have gone ten thousand miles from the United States to Tengchow. If she had not zeal, she, a lone woman, would have not gone the one hundred and fifteen miles from Tengchow to the black heathenism of Pingtu. Believing the Master surely would protect her, she discounted the discouraging arguments of other missionaries, considered her own life of no importance, hearing only the Master's command. Thus God's grace came upon Sah Ling Village.

She persevered through revolutions, smallpox and plague. During the plague, people died on their own thresholds. Travelers apparently in good health died by the roadside. Poor Chinese dreaded the ruthless destruction of clothes and bedding during the plague more than they did the plague, for they lived in such extreme poverty that even the meagerest clothing and bedding was as treasured as life itself.

To these people Lottie Moon brought light, hope, strength and a knowledge of Christ and His wonder-working power. With funds always too small, she did much with a little. In the late 1870's, for example, when she opened her first school in Tengchow, she paid fifty cents a year for room rent, but when she returned to Tengchow she could not find a larger one for five dollars a year. Believing that "if the Lord gives the enlargement He will surely not withhold the funds," she worked on. When the church board did not send enough, she quietly supplied schoolbooks, catechisms, hymnbooks, and even food and clothing out of her own earnings, which were never more than fifty dollars a month.

In the *Foreign Mission Journal* she read of the missionary movement among Baptist women of the South. When her own burdens seemed heavy she wrote challenging letters home. Once she said:

It is odd that the million Baptists in the South can furnish only three men for all China. Odd that five hundred Baptist preachers in the state of Virginia alone must rely on a Presbyterian minister to fill a Baptist pulpit. I wonder how these things look in Heaven. They certainly look very queer in China.

After calling for aid that was slow to come, she pushed on, often wearied in body and disheartened in spirit. She discovered a village in the far interior where there lived a few Nestorian Christians, descendants of those who had been converted to Christianity during the period between the seventh and tenth centuries. In succeeding centuries their beliefs had become mingled with Mohammedanism and Buddhism, but Lottie discovered that some remnants of Christianity still remained and she helped these Nestorians find a deeper Christian faith.

In 1888 she made this plea to the women of the Southern Baptist Church: "Will you not, in appreciation of what Christmas means to you, share in the work in this area?" That year three thousand dollars were given in response to her call. She had hoped to raise enough to send one woman into the mission field, but the sum given made it possible to send three.

When missionaries reached Pingtu and had been trained for the work there, she journey back by *shentza* to "The Home of the Crossroads" at Tengchow. Her pioneer work at the Pingtu mission, where she had remained from 1885-1894, was finished.

New hardships awaited her at Tengchow, but she did not complain when she had to build up her work there all over again. The Boxer uprising, aimed at driving all foreigners out of China, began in 1900. At the repeated demands of the United States consul that she leave China, and upon learning that a Chinese evangelist in Pingtu had been beaten to death, Lottie went for a while to Japan where she taught. She hoped her going might lessen the Boxer attacks upon her Chinese Christians, many of whom had become stanch believers. Before one massacre, a Chinese Christian minister had preached to his Chinese congregation from the text, "Though he slay me, yet will I trust in Him" (Job 13:15), and his people had faced death fearlessly. It was a bitter trial to her to seek a safety that was not open to these Christians.

After the Boxer uprising Lottie returned once more to Tengchow, determined to work even more diligently among Chinese boys and girls as well as among women. She not only taught them but ministered to many of their needs. The Russo-Japanese War of 1904-1905 raised living expenses and there were epidemics, but she persevered, teaching Chinese children for longer hours and working harder with the mothers. The North China Woman's Missionary Union was organized in her own living room in Tengchow. This was a happy milestone in her life. She took her last furlough when she was sixty-four years old, but returned to China in a few months, for China was now her home.

Revolution broke out in China in 1911 and the American consul advised all missionaries to go to Chefoo, but she stayed on at Tengchow. Once she came home to find a great hole in the corner of her bedroom where a cannon ball had passed right over her bed. Death was in the air, but she was not afraid. By her bed lay her open Bible and in the margin she had written: "Words do fail to express my love for this Holy Book, my gratitude to its author, for His Love and Goodness. How shall I thank Him for it."

War, epidemics and poverty were the lot of her Chinese Christians. She sent all her savings to her Chinese friends in Pingtu. Her own account book shows that she gave her last dollar to the Famine Relief Fund. She was now in her early seventies, and she remembered that in an earlier famine many people of seventy were placed in caves to die. She was ready to die, in order that some of her younger Christians might live.

She made many pleas to women in America for more funds. A few pennies a day, she told them, would save a life until the next harvest. The more she thought of her starving friends, the less she ate herself, until finally she ate no food at all.

Frail and undernourished, she was ordered by her doctor to start home in December 1912 with a missionary nurse, Cynthia Miller, whose furlough was due.

They sailed from Shanghai for San Francisco, but four days later, on Christmas Eve, as their ship rode in brilliant sunshine in the harbor of Kobe, Japan, Lottie Moon died. Her ashes were sent to Crowe, Virginia, where her grave bears this simple inscription: "Faithful Unto Death."

Ten years earlier she had said: "I would that I had a thousand lives that I might give them to the women of China." She gave her one life and its influence was multiplied a thousandfold.

That Christmas of 1912 was the beginning of Lottie Moon's immortality in more ways than one. The Christmas offering she started in 1888 in the Woman's Missionary Union of Southern Baptists has grown from the three thousand dollars given that first year to the millions now contributed annually. In the first seventy-five-year period, more than fifty million dollars were raised in her name.

Beginning first with those small gifts of a handful of women in the Southern Baptist Woman's Missionary Union, the Lottie Moon Christmas Offering has built churches, hospitals and homes for missionaries. It has financed building sites, publishing plants, tracts and magazines, and it has paid the salaries of Baptist missionaries in many parts of the world. It represents a never-ending outpouring of good will to people everywhere and it helps to carry out Christ's Great Commission: "Go ye, therefore, and teach all nations" (Matt. 28:19).

MARY SLESSOR—

"WHITE MA" OF CALABAR

(1848-1915)

* * *

She was a Scottish factory girl who served as missionary in Calabar for thirty-eight years. She developed people's industrial capacities, built churches, schools, helped to bring law and order, raised the status of African women, educated many to a Christian way of life.

SHE CHRISTIANIZED THE WILDEST SAVAGES

THE CHRISTIAN INFLUENCE of Mary Mitchell Slessor extended over a two-thousand-mile area in West Africa, and thousands of natives called her "White Ma." For thirty-eight years, from 1876 until her death in 1915, she served the Calabar Mission Field, an area of Nigeria that included Duke Town, Old Town, Creek Town and Okoyong, and farther into the interior along Enyong Creek.

Her first stations, Duke Town and Old Town, known earlier as the Ivory Coast, Gold Coast and Slave Coast, were flanked by a gray level of mangrove trees; naked savages lived in the bush beyond. Into this wild country, Mary Slessor, Scots Presbyterian missionary, went alone at twenty-eight to serve with distinction and honor.

Born in Gilcomston, a suburb of Aberdeen, in 1848, she received her missionary enthusiasm from her mother, a woman solicitous of the religious well-being of her children and long interested, through her Presbyterian Church, in foreign mission work. From her mother, too, Mary Slessor inherited her soft voice and loving heart, and in her later life she said: "I owe a great debt to my sainted mother."

Her father Robert Slessor was a shoemaker, but heavy drinking caused him to give up his work, and the family had to move from Gilcomston to Dundee, Scotland. Here her mother was compelled to work in factories in order to maintain the home; and at eleven years of age Mary, too, was sent out to work, first learning weaving under her mother's supervision.

Many were Mary Slessor's heartaches in childhood. Often, for example, she and her mother sat sewing or knitting in silence through long hours, waiting for the sound of the uncertain footsteps of her drunken father. They knew that when he appeared he would throw into the fire his supper they had stinted themselves to provide. A few times Mary was forced into the streets by her drunken father, where she wandered in darkness, alone, sobbing out her misery.

She was gentle, sensitive and loving and these childhood experiences deepened her sympathy for others, made her the fierce champion of little children, and the friend of the weak and oppressed. It prepared her also for the task of combating the trade in liquor on the African West Coast and for dealing with the drunken tribes amongst whom she went to live.

Mary began her missionary service with no training except this background of self-denial, heartaches and hardships. By surrender, dedication and unwearied devotion she became one of the most heroic characters of her age. Her love for Christ made her what she was, "A Christian miracle, one for ordinary people to emulate," says W. P. Livingstone, who has helped to memorialize her name with his excellent biography *Mary Slessor of Calabar, Pioneer Missionary.*

Her only schooling after she began working as a weaver in the factory, was the reading she did to and from work. For fourteen years, as she toiled in the factory for ten hours a day, she was the main support of her family. Her only outside interest was the church, and she gave it her faithful service. Much of her reading was in the Bible, and her style of writing in later years showed this influence.

The story of Calabar, where the Presbyterian Church conducted mission work, impressed itself upon her imagination when as a child she learned of the struggle in West Africa between light and darkness. While much of Calabar was beautiful, it also was one of the unhealthiest places in the world. Disease and sudden death befell Europeans who ventured there. The natives too were among the most primitive of any in Africa. For four hundred years, Europeans had never penetrated more than a few miles inland as they traded in gold, ivory and slaves. All beyond that was a mystery of rivers and alligators, of swamps and snakes, of forests and wild beasts, of mud huts and savage natives.

Jungles and poisonous swamps, hemmed in by the pathless sea, and isolation and loneliness—all awaited Mary Slessor, but she went forth bravely to face them, knowing that Christ would have her choose the hardest places. Why should she, who had learned to feel so close to Him, be afraid of this station in far-off Africa?

The death of David Livingstone in 1873 was followed by a wave of missionary enthusiasm. In 1875 Mary Slessor offered her services to the Foreign Mission Board and was accepted at an annual salary of sixty pounds.

Setting sail for Calabar in August 1876, Mary remembered John 6:24: "When the people therefore saw that Jesus was not there, neither his disciples, they also took shipping and came to Capernaum, seeking for Jesus." Capernaum was the site of Jesus' Galilean ministry, and Calabar was to be the site of Mary Slessor's African ministry. She would teach wild savages that Christ is the bread of life and that those who come to Him will never hunger and those who believe in Him will never thirst.

All too soon she was to learn that this lighthouse of the spirit she wished to create in Calabar must be built little by little, with infinite toil and patience. "Christ was never in a hurry," she wrote. "There was no rushing forward, no anticipating, no fretting over what might be. Each day's duties were done as every day brought them, and the rest was left with God." Thus Mary Slessor pressed forward, unafraid, against appalling obstacles.

She entered her first mud hut thatched with palm leaf in Duke Town, a village that was slovenly, sordid and broiling in the hot rays of the African sun. Witchcraft was practiced and secret societies ruled the people. Although many were mentally retarded and drank heavily, she had to see them as human beings made in God's image.

Her service ranged from preaching to patching. She taught women to sew, starch and iron. She nursed the sick and gave them medicine. She set up churches and schools, and taught in both. She ministered to the sick where the only bed was a bundle of filthy rags.

Mary made one of her first visits to a family which sat around their dead child in filth, squalor and drunkenness and read to them the story of Jesus' raising of Lazarus. Then she spoke to the family about life and death and the Beyond. From this hut, she went to an area where men sold rum. When she denounced them they asked her: "Why does white man bring us rum if it is not good for us? If God's man brings rum, then is it not all right to have it?" These were among the difficult questions that she had to answer daily.

To her own hut a man brought his wife who grieved that all five of her children had died. Mary Slessor spoke of the Resurrection to this couple, while a crowd gathered to listen. Believing that twins born in a family forebode evil in that family, it was the custom among the natives to abandon all twins to wild beasts. Mary tried to make them see that twins were God's children too. To prove that they did not bring evil, she took several sets of twins into her own home, caring for them as a mother. She finally mothered so many homeless ones that her home buzzed with native children of all ages.

Mary Slessor encountered many dangers in Calabar. One day she noticed a tornado moving toward her mud hut, but she kept indoors, sewing and praying. The wind was furious, lifting fences, canoes, trees and buildings, and the roof of her own hut. Lightning, rain and thunder followed, and she was finally beaten to the ground by the violence of the rain. But she arose, collected the children, and said: "Come, let us sing." As their song gradually mingled with the lightning and torrential rains, their terror was subdued. Afterward she became dangerously ill, but with her recovery came also her determination to fight even more vigorously to overcome all obstacles.

What was Mary Slessor's secret? She expressed it best in later years in her testimony, *Our Faithful God: Answers to Prayer*, in which she said:

My life is one long daily, hourly, record of answered prayer. For physical health, for mental overstrain, for guidance given marvellously, for errors and dangers averted, for enmity to the Gospel subdued, for food provided at the exact hour needed, for everything that goes to make up life and my poor service, I can testify with a full and often wonder-stricken awe that I believe God answers prayer. I can give no other testimony. I am sitting alone here on a log among a company of natives. My children, whose very lives are a testimony that God answers prayer, are working round me. Natives are crowding past on the bush road to attend palavers, and I am at perfect peace, far from my own countrymen and conditions, because I know God answers prayer. Food is scarce just now. We live from hand to mouth. We have not more than will be our breakfast today, but I know we shall be fed, for God answers prayer.

She declared that prayer was "hedged round by conditions, that everything depended upon the nature of the contact between heaven and earth," and she likened the process to a wireless message, saying: "We can only obtain God's best by fitness of receiving power. Without receivers fitted and kept in order the air may tingle and thrill with the message, but it will not reach our spirit and consciousness." She knew equally well that all prayer was not worthy of being answered. To one who said he had prayed without avail, she wrote: "You thought God was to hear and answer you by making everything straight and pleasant—not so are nations or churches or men and women born; not so is character made. God is answering your prayer in His way."

Her religion was a religion of the heart, and her communion with her Father was natural, childlike. She spoke to Him as a child to her father when she needed help and strength, or when her heart was filled with joy and gratitude, at any time, in any place. When a woman in Scotland asked her how she attained to such intimacy with God, she replied: "Ah, woman, when I am out there in the bush I have often no other one to speak to but my Father, and I just talk to Him."

She did more than talk. She practiced this oneness, even in moments of deepest trial and sorrow. The night she had word that her mother had died in Scotland, she set forth, feeling God's presence all about her, to conduct her regular prayer meeting in the bush. Living among a people who carried a constant burden of sorrow and spiritual darkness, she managed somehow to carry light wherever she went, even into this darkest bush country, where the hungry came to her to be fed, and the sick to be healed. Even the bush king came for counsel regarding his problems with the British government.

After spending twelve years at Duke Town, Old Town and Creek Town, Mary Slessor in 1886 went into the district of Okoyong to stay thirteen years, saying as she went: "I am going to a new tribe up-country, a fierce, cruel people, and everyone tells me that they will kill me, but I don't fear any hurt—only to combat their savage customs will require courage and firmness on my part." This shy, solitary woman went forward to Okoyong, her Puritan simplicity and childlike faith overcoming her inner fears. She knew that liquor, guns and chains were practically the only articles of commerce that entered this more remote and primitive area of Calabar. Gin or rum was in every home. It was given to every baby. All work was paid for in guns or rum. Fines were paid and debts were redeemed with rum. Everyone drank it—many drank it all the time. Quarrels resulted, then guns came into play. After that there were padlocks and chains.

As her canoe, paddled by natives, glided down Old Calabar River, she reflected: "Who am I, a weak woman, to face wild savages alone?" But she knew she was not alone. God was with her. And so she pushed on to face another angry mob, to face violence and murder, harems, sorcery, war and runaway slaves in a forest dark and mysterious.

During days and nights when she knew there was not a sober man or woman within miles of her, she did not cower with fear but continued to fight the evil of drink with energy and skill, exercising an imperious power over savage people. From her humble home, without windows or floors, closets or decent furniture, Mary Slessor ruled these people with all the power and dignity of a queen. With love and wisdom and prayer she won over the cruelest savages of the bush country, until they came to revere her. Immensely practical as well as deeply devout, she opened up trade for them with other peoples, and for once they experienced prosperity. She built schools and taught their children. She opened churches ("kirks") and preached in them. She tenderly dressed their most loathesome sores. A sufferer herself from chronic malarial infection and a martyr to pain, her days were filled with unremitting toil for the natives, who saw and felt her Christian spirit.

In 1891, when Mary went home to Scotland on furlough, she took with her a Negro girl, Jean, whom she looked upon as her own daughter. In later years Jean was to become an effective servant of God, a student of the Bible and a helper in carrying on Mary Slessor's work. Mary took Jean to Scotland a second time, as well as three other black children or "bairns" as she called them, first outfitting them in new clothes.

For Mary Slessor, furloughs in Scotland became farther apart, and finally Calabar was the only home she knew. Giving up every personal pleasure, she accepted all the consequences that the renunciation of self involved. Each time she pushed farther into the interior of Calabar, she forded more swamps, climbed taller hills, and faced wilder peoples. In order to cover more territory, she finally learned to ride her bicycle on the paths in the bush. Her clothes were simple and she went barefooted and bareheaded. She learned to live with most of her clothes always in boxes. Her bed was without springs and she had the most primitive cooking facilities. Her labors were never-ending; she often arose at night after a short rest, lighted a candle and answered a batch of correspondence.

At Okoyong she assumed new duties. The government invested her with the powers of a magistrate, and she presided over the native court. She accepted no salary, although her missionary salary was always less than five hundred dollars a year.

"What is money to God?" she asked. "The difficult thing is to make men and women. Money lies all about us in the world and He can turn it on to our path as easily as He sends a shower of rain." He did turn it on to Mary Slessor's path. Never was she in real need for funds for the extension of her work, for buildings, furniture, teachers' wages, medicine and many other necessities. She managed to keep her needs simple, and somehow they were met by friends, known and unknown, at home and abroad, who were interested in her brave and lonely struggle. When her purse was empty, gifts flowed in.

"God is superbly kind in the matter of money," she said, "I do not know how to thank Him." On one occasion, when she was a little anxious, she cried: "Shame on you, Mary Slessor, after all you know of Him." She reminded herself: "It isn't Mary Slessor doing anything. It is God." Then her needs were met and her problems answered. Although she remained poor in the things of the world, she was so rich in the things of the spirit that her little mud "kirks" grew and her schools flourished. She had constant contact with the unseen, and this was the source of continuing power.

In 1902 Mary moved on farther inland, along Enyong Creek. Here she worked until 1910, and from 1910 to 1915 she pressed on into the higher reaches of the Enyong Creek. Wherever she went, there were countless tasks to perform all over again: building, cementing, painting, varnishing, teaching, preaching, healing. But she seemed to grow more wonderful, the older and frailer she became. Her greatness was never in her surroundings, for she paid little attention to these, but in the hidden life which she caught glimpses of now and then.

Gentle-looking, below the average in height, Mary had short lank brown hair, a winning smile, and skin that in the hot African sun had become like yellow parchment. She was described by a newspaper writer, who once came to Africa to see her, as being dressed "in a skimpy tweed skirt, a cheap nun's veiling blouse and a forlorn broken picture hat of faded green chiffon with a knot of bright red ribbon." Her hands were hard and rough and often bled from too much heavy outdoor work. The skin of her palms was gone and her nails were worn to the quick. But in describing the pitifully clad Mary Slessor, the reporter wrote: "She conquered me if she did not convert me."

Her resourcefulness and sense of humor took her over many rough places. She had no alarm clock, for she seldom needed one. One day, however, an important mission awaited her. In order to rise very early, she tied a cock to her bedpost, and it crowed lustily early the next morning. Once during an illness, her doctor who had come from another station, sent over a fowl. "I'm no meat-eater, doctor," she rejoined. "Why did you send that fowl?"

"Because it could not come itself," was all the satisfaction she got. And she laughed with her doctor.

Though ill more often than she was well, Mary Slessor lived to the age of sixty-six and was active till the last. "It is a dark and difficult land, and I am old and weak—but happy," she said. Her bright and eager spirit rose about the frailties of her body, for she could see her work of thirty-eight years bearing a rich harvest.

What was the harvest of her last years? African babies in Calabar grew to manhood and womanhood and carried on the many tasks she had started. She established a home for girls, where they were taught to make baskets, weave coconut fiber, and do cane and bamboo work. She founded a rest home, where women of the mission could recuperate. She raised the status of Calabar women and secured their rights. She preached the Gospel and made thousands know how Christ can transform lives.

Her well-marked Bible bore testimony to the thoroughness of her teaching. Almost every page had a mass of notes bearing such statements as these: "God is never behind time. . . . We must see and know Christ before we can teach. . . . Unspiritual man cannot stand success. . . . An arm of flesh never brings power. . . . Half of the world's sorrows comes from the unwisdom of parents. . . . It is worthwhile to die, if thereby a soul can be born again. . . ."

Mary Slessor died of the swamp fever that had plagued her for many years. Her Negro girls—Janie, Annie, Maggie, Alice and Whitie—were all with her when she breathed her last in her roughly built, reddish-brown hut in Calabar. Her long life of toil was over. She had opened a door in a savage land, making it easier for others who followed her. Never a mere name on a list of those who served, she was a warm, living, inspiring human presence, like many others who extend Christianity farther and farther into lands where it is not known.

CHAPTER 6

Women Who Advanced

ROSE HAWTHORNE LATHROP
(MOTHER ALPHONSA)—FOUNDER OF THE
SERVANTS OF RELIEF FOR INCURABLE CANCER
(1851-1926)

+ + +

Daughter of Nathaniel Hawthorne, she devoted the last thirty years of her life to founding homes for destitute, incurable cancer patients. She started in a three-room New York flat. Her Order now has homes in many areas of the United States.

"BLESSED IS HE THAT
CONSIDERETH THE NEEDY AND THE POOR"

ONCE WHEN ROSE HAWTHORNE LATHROP was asked what she was trying to do for the sick poor, especially those afflicted with cancer, she replied:

To make impossible the homeless conditions of incurable cancer patients; to make impossible their semi-neglect in homes that are unfit for them; to take the neediest class we know—both in poverty and suffering—and put them in such a condition that if our Lord knocked at the door I should not be ashamed to show what I have done. This is a great hope and may never be fulfilled by me.

Her dream was partially realized within her own lifetime, and since her death in 1926 it has been further fulfilled. Today her spirit is manifest in the homes she founded for the sick. She said: "We must make our guests glad they crossed the threshold that is to be their last boundary, make them as comfortable and happy as if their own people had kept them and put them into the best bedroom. We must love them."

Rose Hawthorne inherited her compassion from her father, Nathaniel Hawthorne, the New England author. From her mother, Sophia Peabody Hawthorne, who was ill most of her life and knew the silent mystery of pain, Rose inherited her belief in the providence of God. She called her mother "the angel of my life."

Louise Hall Tharp has revealed the greatness of Rose's mother and aunts in *The Peabody Sisters of Salem*. Rose herself has been immortalized in two biographies, *Mother Alphonsa* by James J. Walsh, and *A Fire Was Lighted* by Theodore Maynard. The latter title is taken from Rose's stirring statement: "A Fire was then lighted in my heart, where it still burns. . . . I set my whole being to bring consolation to the cancerous poor."

Reared amid the best in New England culture and opportunity, Rose had a very happy childhood. Julian Hawthorne called his sister Rose "beautiful, gifted, impetuous, imperious, and fastidious." A poet of her time has described her as a girl with gold hair and coloring that reminded one of "a peach blossom in the sun." Literary visitors to the family called her "The Rose of all the Hawthornes."

When her father's college friend Franklin Pierce, the newly elected President of the United States, appointed him consul at Liverpool (1853-1857), Rose traveled abroad with her family. In later years, she again lived abroad with her husband, George Parsons Lathrop, journalist and author. When they returned, they bought Hawthorne's home, "Wayside," at Concord, Massachusetts, and lived there until after the death of their five-year-old only child, Francis Parsons, who succumbed to diphtheria in 1881. The boy was buried beside his famous grandfather Nathaniel Hawthorne, in Sleepy Hollow Cemetery.

Although brought up in the Unitarian faith of her parents, Rose and her husband became Catholic converts in 1891. They were comparatively happy together until he began to drink. She left him in 1894, when he became so violent that it was unsafe to live with him. He died four years later.

Rose wrote for leading magazines and assisted in the publication of her father's works, which appeared in twenty-two volumes. Her *Memories of Hawthorne,* published first in the *Atlantic Monthly,* was issued in book form in 1897. Although she had moved in literary and social circles, she decided, after losing her only child and her husband turned to drinking, to seek happiness not for herself but for others.

First she worked in a public hospital in New York. When her friend, the poet Emma Lazarus (best known for her sonnet engraved on the pedestal of the Statue of Liberty), died of cancer, and when she saw a stricken seamstress use up her lifetime savings on treatments and then have to go to the poorhouse, Rose turned her attention to cancer patients. She was about forty-five when she relinquished all her material attachments, her family ties and friends, her writing, her social life, and devoted herself to the destitute suffering from cancer.

After a period of training at the New York Cancer Hospital, she rented a tiny flat at Number One Scammel Street, New York City, in 1896, saying: "I wish to be of the poor as well as among them." Her first patient was a pathetic old lady she had met during her training. As they ate their frugal meal at an open hearth, the little old lady told Irish fairy tales which made them forget pain and poverty.

A few months later, Rose Hawthorne Lathrop rented a tenement on Water Street, New York City, where seven patients could be accommodated. Here she was joined by a friend Alice Huber, who helped her build up her institution. They supplied patients with food, medicine, fuel, rent—whatever was necessary.

Both women were deeply religious and wished to bring their work into closer relation with the Church. On September 14, 1899, they became Dominican Tertiaries, were given the Dominican Habit, and founded the Congregation of St. Rose of Lima, which came to be known as the Servants of Relief for Incurable Cancer.

Appealing for help in the daily press, Mrs. Lathrop declared: "I should like to feel that the hearts of those who help the poor are warmed toward them because they are Christ's poor, and their value to the race would be lost if they were not supported for the love of God." She wrote later: "If there are any lovely flowers left in the gardens of our lives, let us gather them as a gift to Jesus Christ although He does not beg for them." Some of those who came to her found the home so different from their former surroundings that they were heard to exclaim: "This is heaven." The most heart-rending cases found in her a friend who understood and served them gladly.

Fearful for the safety of her sick people, she planned to obtain a fireproof dwelling for them. In what she described as "the calm, laborious way in which a bird builds its nest," she began to beg for further funds to expand her work. "It is not on record that the bird stops before the nest is built unless it dies in the attempt," she asserted later. Her words were prophetic, for she did not give up until July 9, 1926, when she died in her sleep, in her seventy-fifth year.

Rose Hawthorne Lathrop's work continued to expand after her death.

One of the hospitals she established in 1901 at Sherman Park (now Hawthorne), New York, is a flourishing institution and the headquarters of the work. In May 1957 the St. Rose Home at Jackson Street and East River Drive, New York was officially opened. It is a modern six-story brick building with one hundred beds. Five other homes include: Our Lady of Good Counsel Home in St. Paul, Minnesota, Holy Family Home in Cleveland, Sacred Heart Home in Philadelphia, Rose Hawthorne Lathrop Home in Fall River, Massachusetts, and Our Lady of Perpetual Help Home in Atlanta, Georgia.

Incurable cancer patients of all faiths are cared for in these homes. In the Atlanta home, established in 1939, one hundred and twelve patients were cared for during the first year. Of these, one hundred and five were Protestants, six Catholics and one Hebrew.

The editor of a leading newspaper wrote of the work begun by Rose Hawthorne Lathrop: "Many patients, afraid when they arrive, attain a serenity which is touching and astounding. All of them moved inexorably toward the last day or night, the last minute of life, with a calm and even cheerful resignation, which is an answer to many questions."

PANDITA RAMABAI—FOUNDER OF
A MISSION, TRANSLATOR OF THE BIBLE
(1858-1922)

• • •

The mission which she established in India still thrives. Its first support came from America. She translated the Bible into Marathi and sent women to distribute Bibles throughout western India.

GOD SHALL SUPPLY THE INCREASE

PANDITA RAMABAI, the founder of Mukti Mission at Kedgaon, Poona District, India, is revered by many as India's greatest woman of the last century. Her interdenominational mission, which stands open day and night for women and children needing help, has been called one of the finest examples of Christianity in action. Although she died in 1922, Mukti Mission is no ghost of yesterday but a place pulsating with life. Here, in a very real sense, she continues to live.

The Bible that she spent fifteen years translating into Marathi was revised in 1958, the centenary of her birth; the women at Mukti helped to revise, set in type, print and bind the new edition. In the history of the Church there has probably never been another Bible that is entirely the work of women, and Pandita seems to be the only woman who has translated the entire Scripture into another language.

The greatest monument to the life and faith of Pandita Ramabai is Mukti and its ongoing ministry to the needy. It is fitting to approach the career and character of this devoted Christian leader by describing the institution she founded.

The mission is a beehive of activity. Eight hundred people live and work within the strong walls that surround Mukti. Among them, in addition to the teaching and administrative staffs, are unwanted babies, the blind, child boarders, unmarried mothers, the crippled, the sick—all to whom Christ, in His infinite compassion, extends His invitation: "Come unto me." The children are fed, clothed and educated. The blind are trained to be self-sufficient. Those with broken and spoiled lives are rehabilitated. All dwell in Mukti's House of Mercy and learn that in Christ there is forgiveness, cleansing and the possibility of all things being made new.

More than one hundred and eighty acres of farming land, irrigated from wells Pandita ordered to be dug, contribute toward the supply of grains and vegetables. Healthy herds of cows, goats and buffaloes provide abundant milk. By bullock tonga, by car and by foot, Mukti missionaries, Bible women, nurses and teachers go into the surrounding villages with the good news of the Christian Gospel.

In the room Pandita Ramabai used one can still see her low table and chairs, suggesting her short stature. The bed and its covers show her simplicity of life. Her open Bible with pages worn and marked, and the long prayer lists containing hundreds of names of those for whom she prayed individually, reveal the secret of her greatness. She was both a woman of prayer and a devoted student of the Bible.

In 1899 she built the large cross-shaped Mukti church, a sturdy structure with a seating capacity of two thousand. On Sundays, people of all ages still throng the road leading to it. On the roadside, a chapel lifts its cross heavenward as a testimony to all who pass that here Christ offers salvation to the needy.

In addition to the massive structures built in her day, all of which speak of her vision, her largeness of heart and greatness of faith, there are now new red brick buildings. Among the latter are a fifty-bed hospital with its laboratory, and a dispensary open to the needy villagers. Abundant clear water, once carried by the women from building to building, now flows through pipes to all the areas. Electric lights illuminate every corner of the mission, from the barns to the recesses of the large stone church.

Since the days when its founder built Mukti Mission it has been a beacon lighting the way to God. It is financed, as it was then, largely on faith. It now has representatives in various parts of the world—America, Australia, Tasmania, Scotland, Canada, England, New Zealand, West Australia and Ireland—and is a member of the Interdenominational Foreign Mission Association.

There is seldom enough in its bank accounts for more than one month's expenses, but in the many decades of Mukti's history, money has not failed and Mukti has no debts. Offerings come not only from all over the world but from the people at Mukti who, out of the little they receive, give back to the institution. Young people at the mission dedicate their lives to God; old people give generously of their life savings. On Christmas Sunday the people at Mukti pour forth their gifts for the manger-born Savior. Village boys come carrying roosters, working girls bring several months' wages, women contribute grain saved by going without bread for some days. Young girls give their blouse materials received a few days before for Christmas. Little children carry their candy and their new hair ribbons. These are Pandita's true memorial.

God led Pandita—scholar, saint and servant of God—in her great work from obscurity to renown, from poverty to influence. Her mother, Lakshimabai, and her father, Ananta Shatri Dongree, traveled on foot as religious pilgrims thousands of miles through India, from the snows of the north to the hot jungles of the south, visiting the temples and sacred places and reading the *puranas,* the sacred words of the Hindus.

Pandita's father, a Brahmin priest, scholar and reformer, was a forty-four-year-old widower when he married her mother, the nine-year-old daughter of a Brahmin pilgrim, and took his child-bride to his home in Mangalore, nine hundred miles away. In his youth he had received instruction from a tutor who was also teaching a princess. Through a curtain he had heard the princess repeating the words of the *puranas.* Never forgetting this voice of an educated woman, he decided to educate his wife. But his mother was so much opposed to this that he took his wife and went into the forest of Gungamul, a remote plateau in southern India. Here he built a house and continued to educate his wife, and here Pandita was born in April 1858.

Each morning at daybreak, her mother wakened Pandita with sweet words and caresses. When her father found how brilliant his little daughter was, he, too, joined in her education. By the time she was twelve, she had committed to memory eighteen thousand Sanskrit verses with all their rich stores of knowledge and wisdom. She had also learned Marathi, into which she later translated the Bible, and acquired a knowledge of Kanarese, Hindustani and Bengalese, and four other languages.

Poverty overtook her family when she was a child. Her father, a landholder and honored pandit who had acquired wealth by his learning, gave up jewels and other valuables and sold his ancestral land to pay family debts.

The family then set forth on a pilgrimage, visiting shrines, temples and sacred rivers. They were welcomed by the priests when they had gold to give, but during the terrible famine of 1876-1877, when their money was gone, the priests greeted them with cold and empty words. Again and again they were sent on their way hungrier than ever. Pandita, witnessing the suffering among child widows and women, heard her first call to service.

Her own family's suffering increased. She saw her father grow old, infirm and blind. She tenderly records:

Though his blind eyes could see me no longer, he held me tightly in his arms, and stroking my head and cheeks, told me, in a few words broken by emotion, to remember how he loved me, how he had taught me to do right, and never to depart from the way of righteousness. . . . "Remember, my child, you are my youngest, my most beloved child. I have given you into the hand of our God; you are His, and to Him alone you must belong and serve Him all your life."

Her beloved father died of starvation; then her mother and finally her elder sister. Only her brother was left. With him she wandered more than four thousand miles on a religious pilgrimage through India, often living on grain soaked in water and seasoned with a little salt. She relates of this journey:

We had no blankets or thick garments to cover ourselves; and, when traveling, we had to walk barefoot, without umbrellas, and, to rest in the night, either under the trees on the roadside or the arches of bridges, or lie down on the ground in the open air. Once on the banks of the Jhelum, a river in the Punjab, we were obliged to rest at night in the open air, and tried to keep off the intense cold by digging two grave-like pits, and putting ourselves into them and covering our bodies—except our heads—with dry sand of the river bank. Sometimes the demands of hunger were so great that we would satisfy our empty stomachs by eating a handful of wild berries.

During these wanderings, Pandita's faith in her father's idols was shaken. As he had traveled the dusty roads of India seeking spiritual peace, she too sought a way of life that would satisfy her soul. At a young people's meeting in Calcutta, she was introduced to Christ, who knew no caste, who gave neither man nor woman dominion over the other, and who loved all, Jew and Gentile alike. In India, at that time, women ranked no higher than pigs; but in Christ she found a reason for the education of women.

When she came before a college of learned men (pandits) in Calcutta, they found her learning was equivalent to theirs and gave her the name of Pandita, meaning "Learned." This name stuck with her and set her apart as one who demonstrated the ability of the women of India to learn and lead.

She became a familiar figure, wearing her simple colored sari and native shawl, as she went about India lecturing. She had soft, grayish-blue eyes full of light, a straight nose, mobile lips, wavy black hair and perfect white teeth. Innately gentle and modest, she was admired wherever she went.

Pandita determined to devote her life to raising the standards of women. "Child widows have no place in the abode of the gods," she declared, "and no hope of getting liberation, except perchance that they might be born among the higher class after having gone through millions of reincarnations." She had seen women turned out of their homes, and often sacrificed on the funeral pyre with their dead husbands. She saw that Christianity offered the answer to their plight, and she determined to help them.

Pandita's brother worked faithfully beside her in her first struggle, but he was weakened by years of privation and died in Calcutta at the age of twenty-one. His chief concern, as he lay dying, was for his unprotected sister. "God will take care of me," she told him confidently, as she sought to comfort him in his last hours. "Then all will be well," he calmly replied.

Six months after her brother's death, she married his friend, Bipin Bihari Medhavi, a graduate of Calcutta University and a practicing lawyer. They went to Silchar, in the Assam district, where he practiced law. Here, her Christian experience was enriched by the visit of a Baptist missionary. She found a copy of the Gospel of Luke in her husband's library, and a Sanskrit Bible also came into her hands. God was preparing her.

On February 4, 1882, nineteen months after her marriage, her husband died of cholera, leaving her with a little daughter Manorama, meaning "Heart's Joy." She now became one of India's more than twenty-three million widows, and felt their plight even deeper, especially that of the child widows. "This great grief," wrote Pandita, "drew me nearer to God."

Traveling with her baby, she went to the Poona District, where she lectured on the sacred literature of India. This led to the founding of a club for Indian women. It had a twofold purpose: to free women from child marriage, and to release them from the bondage of ignorance.

In 1883, when Pandita addressed the Education Committee of India, she declared:

In ninety-nine cases out of a hundred the educated men of this country are opposed to female education. If they observe the slightest fault they magnify the grain of mustard seed into a mountain and try to ruin the character of the woman. Often, the poor woman not being very courageous or well informed, is completely broken down in her character. . . . It is evident that women, being one-half of the people of this country, are oppressed and cruelly treated by the other half.

About this time she felt a restless desire to go to England. "The voice came to me as to Abraham," she said. "Throwing myself on God's protection, I went forth as Abraham, not knowing whither I went." To help finance the trip, she wrote the first of her many publications in English, *Morals for Women*. She set forth for England in 1883.

On her arrival in England, she and her little daughter were kindly received by the Church of England Sisterhood at Wantage. In the rescue work for unwed mothers there, she saw the difference between Christianity and Hinduism and expressed it in the comment:

While the old Hindu Scriptures had given us some beautiful precepts of loving, the new dispensation of Christ has given us grace to carry these principles into practice, and that makes all the difference in the world. The precepts are like an engine on a track, beautiful and with great possibilities. Christ and His Gospel are the steam, the motor power that can make the engine move.

Soon after her arrival, Pandita was baptized in the Church of England. She spent a year in Wantage before being appointed professor of Sanskrit in Cheltenham Ladies' College. Here she studied mathematics, natural science and English literature.

About a year and a half later she was invited to America by a friend, Anandibai Joshi, the first woman from India to receive the degree of Doctor of Medicine from the Women's Medical College in Philadelphia. With her little daughter, Pandita went to the United States intending to stay only a few weeks, but she remained three years to study kindergarten methods in Philadelphia. During this visit she also wrote her famous book, *The High Caste Hindu Woman*, which revealed the plight of India's women for the first time. Dr. Rachel Bodley, dean of the Women's Medical College in Philadelphia and her friend and counselor, wrote in the preface: "The silence of a thousand years has been broken." Dr. Bodley was one of the first to support Pandita's appeal for aid to found her educational home for child widows of India.

Pandita's book, published in America in 1887, opened the hearts of America's cultured, earnest women. In Boston that year, after she had spoken to an overflow crowd, the Ramabai Association was formed to provide education for child widows of India. The board of trustees was composed of Episcopalians, Unitarians, Congregationalists, Baptists and Methodists. Among the supporters were such distinguished Americans as Phillips Brooks, Edward Everett Hale and Lyman Abbott. They promised to support Pandita's school for ten years and after that to transfer the ownership into her hands.

In May 1888, Pandita said good-by to her Boston friends and sailed from San Francisco for Bombay, carrying an unfinished manuscript of her life and travels in America. After its publication in Bombay in 1889, this work received acclaim as a Marathi literary classic, showing what women could do when liberated from superstition and bondage.

She said that on her arrival in Bombay, "I fell on my knees, committed myself to the care of a loving Heavenly Father. Six weeks later when she opened the Widows' Home in Bombay, she called it "Abode of Wisdom" and said:

The home with all its privileges has been instituted for the benefit of friendless women. I wish them to see the contrast in all things where love rules. I wish them to become acquainted with as many good people as possible, to learn what the outside world is about from pictures and books and to enjoy the wonderful work of God as they walk in the garden, study with the microscope and view the heavens from the little veranda on the roof.

After 1891, Pandita seemed to realize more fully that she was God's handmaid, like the great women of the Bible. The old self was dead. Her real conversion had come, and she declared: "I found it a great blessing to realize the personal presence of the Holy Spirit in me."

Among those she cared for was the daughter of a temple harlot in Bombay. When she learned that unfortunate widows were often obliged to become temple prostitutes, she disguised herself as a religious beggar and, going from place to place, discovered the true facts for herself. Later she related:

Hundreds, I might say thousands, of widows, young and old, come to these places every year and fall into the snares of the priests. When the poor women get a little older and are not pleasing to these horrid men, they are turned out of the house to care for themselves the best they can. . . . Oh, the sin and misery and heartless cruelty of men to women which I saw there on every side is beyond description.

Returning to her own mission, she strengthened herself with Joshua's words: "As for me and my house, we will serve the Lord" (Josh. 24:15), and lived by that vow to the end of her life.

Pandita saw how great the need was and began to plan for expansion of her work. She purchased the land for Mukti Mission, planted it with fruit trees, vegetables and grain, and dug deep wells. To pay for the land, she tried to raise money on her own life insurance. This was not successful, but God did not fail her. From the biographies of Christians, she learned that "the Lord is our inexhaustible treasure." One day she received a cablegram from several American friends, who, hearing of her need, had sent her the necessary money.

Faced with the almost insurmountable tasks connected with the housing and feeding of the two hundred and twenty-five girls who soon came under her care, Pandita was inspired by Jeremiah 32:27: "Behold I am the Lord, the God of all flesh: is there anything too hard for me?"

Mukti Mission had already opened when, in 1896, a terrible famine began, in which between ten and fourteen million people of the Central Provinces of India perished. As the clamor for food increased, Pandita traveled to famine-ridden sections, gathered up six hundred young widows and children, brought them back to Mukti, and housed them in temporary grass huts. Her deep wells yielded copious amounts of water. Her fruit trees bore plentifully. Vegetables, grains and other foodstuffs were produced in abundance on her land. Because of this, she made a second trip into famine regions and returned with several hundred additional girls and women. Now she needed more workers, buildings, foods and equipment, and also an evangelistic program.

A period of great revival began at Mukti during the overcrowded days of famine. A large group of girls gathered each day for prayer in Pandita Ramabai's room. Hundreds were converted and Pandita took groups of girls to the nearby Bheema River to be baptized. During the revival, many confessed to stealing, lying, quarreling, fighting, and others renounced their former idolatry.

It was after a revival meeting that Pandita formally dedicated her mission to the work of the Lord, naming it Mukti, meaning "Salvation."

Afraid of the future no longer, she declared: "I believe if we had not a single cent in hand God would shower from heaven the funds we need. . . . We are not to take thought for the morrow. We are only to do His work faithfully."

Pandita was always expanding her work. She bought from a liquor dealer the twenty-two acres on the opposite side of the road. On this land today stands the House of Mercy, a home for unmarried mothers, ill-treated widows and incorrigible girls.

She also established a roadside bazaar to sell materials made by her people. She trained them in various vocations and needlecrafts, and among her most successful projects was a weaving school. She set up a black-smith shop, tinshop, tannery, and shoemaking and carpentry shops. Having learned printing in England, she began a bookbindery where paper cutting, folding, ruling and binding were done. She taught her girls and women to set type, and it was here that the thousands of copies of the Bible she translated into Marathi were printed and bound.

A born executive, as well as a scholar, evangelist and reformer, Pandita worked out her needs in various ways. She organized classes for lower caste children and paid each a penny a day to attend. Her girls, whom she had so recently taught to read and write, were now put to work teaching others. One of the smaller girls rescued in the famine took charge of the blind girls. Others were appointed as matrons over family groups. She built new structures every year—dormitories, storehouses, a bakery, a hospital, offices, guest rooms and the church building of dark gray stone, roofed with Mangalore tile and floored with teakwood.

Once, when more than seventeen hundred famine waifs were in need of new clothing, a large supply of garments arrived in response to her prayers. She piled them in the center of the church, and as the children crowded the great enclosure during the distribution of the clothing, she spoke from Psalm 34:10: "The young lions do lack and suffer hunger; but they that seek the Lord shall not want any good thing."

When the building of the church was finished, she had the following lines inscribed on the foundation stone:

Praise the Lord. Not by might, nor by power, but by my spirit, saith Jehovah of Hosts. That Rock was Christ. Upon this rock I will build my church; and the gates of hell shall not prevail against it. Jesus Christ Himself being the chief cornerstone, in whom all the building fitly framed together groweth unto an holy temple in the Lord. That our sons may be as plants grown up in their youth; that our daughters may be as cornerstones, polished after the similitude of a palace. Sept. 20, 1899.

Famine struck again in 1900 and before long thirteen hundred and fifty women and children had poured into Mukti. Conditions were so severe that the wells began to run low, and the fruit trees to wither. When the grass died, the cattle did not give sufficient milk for the babies. Nearly two hundred starving people appeared at her gates in one day. She had neither food nor work for them, but she invited them into her barn to pray. In one voice they asked for rain and food, after she had assured them that God could feed hundreds as easily as He could provide for two or twenty. Henceforth Mukti became known as a veritable house of prayer. With the small funds available to her she immediately made jobs for the starving and put them to work on a new schoolhouse. All told, she sustained nineteen hundred people during the most critical days of the famine.

The refugees were miserably dirty and diseased. They suffered from sores on their heads and mouths and other ailments caused by starvation. Many were mere skeletons, clamoring for food. Several rebellious girls tried to burn down the premises. Fearing the bubonic plague, which had been raging in Bombay, Pandita hired a dozen tents for the diseased refugees and moved them into the open country, twenty miles away.

On another occasion, former Brahmin friends threatened to destroy her place, but God gave Pandita a promise: "No weapon that is formed against thee shall prosper" (Isa. 54:17). Sometimes the treasury was empty. Storms came and fire broke out, but she knew that God answers prayers in famine, fire and storm.

In her last fifteen years Pandita began the immense task of translating the Bible into Marathi, using words the least educated laborer could understand. First she had to master Greek and Hebrew. She had to fit this work in amid her many other duties: appointing workers to their posts, seeing visitors, superintending buildings and supplies, and preparing dainties in her kitchen. She was growing too deaf to hear the words spoken in church services, but she used to come into the church and take her place near one of the doors. Her manuscripts were always with her. She provided many books and pamphlets from her own print shop. She printed more than one hundred thousand copies of the Gospels alone, and her own Gospel bands distributed them.

She saw Mukti grow into a large and permanent institution and dreamed of the day when her beloved and capable daughter would carry on her work. Two years before her own death, however, her daughter died. Sorrow over this loss did not cause her to abandon her work, nor did it obscure her vision. In her sixties, wearing a white robe, she was a figure of serenity and strength. She remembered the prophetess Anna in Luke, who served in the temple until she was eighty-four.

In her last months, Pandita corrected the final proofs for her translation of the Bible. She spent long hours proofreading, in addition to her work for her eight or nine hundred people at Mukti. She had nearly completed the proofreading, and the first pages of the fifty thousand copies of the Bible were already being printed by her girls, when she became ill and knew her time was drawing very near. She prayed to God for ten more days in which to complete the proofreading. In just ten days, on April 5, 1922, when the last proof was read, she fell asleep, never to wake again.

Hundreds whose lives she had saved streamed into the compound, in a strange mingling of castes. They folded their hands in reverence before the silent form of this noble Christian woman whose work marks a milestone in India's spiritual history.

HELEN BARRETT MONTGOMERY—
TRANSLATOR OF THE NEW TESTAMENT
(1861-1934)

◆ ◆ ◆

The only woman to translate the Greek New Testament into English, she was also the first woman to serve as president of the Northern Baptist Convention. She was president for ten years of the Women's American Baptist Foreign Mission Society, an author of religious books and a licensed Baptist minister.

HER CHURCH WAS ONE OF HER REASONS FOR EXISTENCE

HELEN BARRETT MONTGOMERY has been called "a woman of ten talents, who used them all." She gave so liberally of her money and herself to her church that she might be called one of the ideal churchwomen of her century.

Her most lasting contribution to the Church at large is her translation of the Greek New Testament into English. She is the only woman ever to make and publish such a translation. First issued in 1924 as the Centenary Translation, it marked the completion of the first hundred years of the American Baptist Publication Society. It was dedicated "to the supreme task of circulating the Scriptures," one of the stated goals of the Society. Her translation has since gone into fifteen printings.

In her introduction, Mrs. Montgomery explains that her aim is to offer a translation in the language of everyday life, but at the same time one that does not depart too much from the translations already familiar and beloved. Her translation does introduce some innovations. She begins each New Testament book with a brief summary, including the date it was written, authorship, aim, and characteristics. Furthermore, she provides paragraph headings to help the reader find a desired passage and remember events as they are recorded. For example, Hebrews 11:1-12 she entitles "The Heroes of Faith," and she outlines the different kinds of faith these heroes represent: Abel—the Sacrifice of Faith; Enoch—the Walk of Faith; Noah—the Work of Faith; Abraham—the Obedience of Faith; and Sarah—the Hope of Faith. Other paragraph headings in this chapter include "The Vision of Faith" and "The Journey of Faith"—giving the reader a clearer interpretation of what faith really is.

Her translation is clear, polished and stirring. For example, she translates Hebrews 11:11-12 as follows:

By faith even Sarah herself received power to conceive seed, although she was past the age for child-bearing, because she counted Him faithful who had promised; and thus there sprang from one man, and him practically dead, a nation like the stars in the heavens in multitude, or grains of sand upon the seashore, innumerable.

She has used every aid of typography to indicate dialogue, quotations and other elements of the narrative. The book was designed to be easily carried in the pocket or in a handbag, in order "to stimulate the daily reading of the Gospels," as she explains.

In the introduction she says that the translation represents "many years of happy work." She offers it, she says, in "deep humility but in the ardent hope that it may bring to some a fresh sense of the actuality and power of the wonderful records of the One Perfect Life which has ever been lived." Finally she adds that she offers this work of love, as she calls it, "in devotion to Him who is Saviour and Master."

Mrs. Montgomery was well prepared from her youth for a life of Christian service and scholarship. Her family had strong religious ties. Her grandparents, Amos and Maria Barrett, settlers of Kingsville, Ohio, were devout church people. Every night, she relates, her grandfather Barrett lined his eight children up for instruction in the Bible and family prayers. No matter how busy "Grandmother Barrett was, she used to retreat to a small house outside for her daily season of prayer. I used to steal after her," Helen writes, "and stand outside the closed door where I could listen to her dear voice as she prayed for each of her family in turn."

In her memoirs, Mrs. Montgomery relates that she loved her mother, of course, but that she "adored" her father, Adoniram Judson Barrett, who bequeathed to his children a passion for education. She confesses that her father always seemed to her like God, and obedience to him became the basis of her submission to the will of God.

From her father she inherited her love for scholarly pursuits. He believed so strongly in education that he was willing to make great personal sacrifice for it. He had worked his way through the University of Rochester, sleeping in an attic, eating the coarsest fare, and denying himself every pleasure. Afterward he became a professor of Latin and Greek and principal of a fine old academy at Lowville, New York.

Helen grew up in Bostwick Hall on the academy grounds. In the yard of her stately home were lilacs, snowballs, peonies, yellow lilies, and roses in red, white and yellow profusion. Amid such pleasant surroundings, Helen passed a happy childhood. During this time her father continued his studies at Rochester Theological Seminary.

It was her father who set the pattern for her education. Early in high school she studied Latin, and in college she studied Greek. Later she said: "I think the Greek is very beautiful, not a letter or a sound but it means something, not an accent but comes for some reason." Her desire to translate the Greek text of the New Testament is evidence of her ability as a Greek scholar.

Her father was also the major influence in her church life. He became pastor of the Lake Avenue Baptist Church in Rochester, New York, after his graduation from the seminary in 1876. Helen joined this church when she was fifteen and remained a stanch member until her death fifty-eight years later. "This church became one of my reasons for existence," she later wrote in her memoirs.

Several years after joining the church, she entered Wellesley College and majored in education. Alice E. Freeman, the president, gave her a letter of recommendation, in which she said in part: "Helen Barrett's reputation for blameless character and fine scholarship and Christian womanliness is so long and well established here that I recommend her without reserve, confident of her success as a teacher." She received a Bachelor of Arts degree in 1884. After graduation, she taught a year in the Rochester High School and later was co-principal of the Wellesley Preparatory School at Philadelphia. But her academic achievements had not ended. In later years she not only received a Master's Degree from Brown

University but was awarded three honorary doctorates—from Wellesley, Denison University and Franklin College.

In Philadelphia she met William A. Montgomery, a widower seven years her senior, and they became engaged. Writing her sister about her engagement, she said:

> I am growing more and more anxious that my life may be given without reserve to God's service. As Will said, if we start out with the purpose of always doing the very highest thing we know, we must have a great deal of courage and honest conviction, for it would often be a hard thing to choose. Before he went away he knelt down with me and together we consecrated our lives to God's work in the world, promising to make this work our first thought and asking for His strength to keep us unspotted from the world. Life seemed so grand and beautiful as we rose from our knees.

In 1887 she and William Montgomery were married. She rejoiced:

> How wonderfully good God has been to me. First, He put my passionate, wayward little feet into the dearest home where wise and tender hands slowly guided me into a happy life. . . . Then He gave me the very best educational advantages, letting me come into contact with great men and women.

When she sent her sister a gift of twenty-five dollars soon after her marriage, Helen wrote:

> Wasn't it lovely of Will to think of it? After all, little sister, it is the only way to keep money, or land, or talent, or happiness—give it away. If only every one had studied the divine arithmetic, what a world it would be.

Helen and William Montgomery used this divine arithmetic in their church-giving. For several years their own financial situation became difficult, for his capital was tied up in an investment, and they were forced to give up domestic help, sell their grand piano and their house and move into smaller quarters.

During this period, however, they gave to their church the same amount that they had previously given when business was good. The year their income was greatly reduced William Montgomery returned their joint pledge card with their customary amount, saying: "Pastor, I may have to cut this, I expect I will. But you may be sure that if I cut my pledge, it will be the last thing that I cut, not the first." He never cut it.

The next year he increased their contributions to the church, for at last he was beginning to realize returns on his investment in a self-starter for automobiles. Among his employees was its young inventor, who had no means to finance his invention. At apparently a great risk, Mr. Montgomery had used his savings to back the young man. The automobile starter business developed until it was furnishing starters for many of the early automobile companies.

The Montgomerys not only gave money liberally to their church, but they also gave their own time and energy. For more than forty years William conducted a men's Bible class. For forty-four years she was the teacher of the Barrett Bible Class and often had as many as two hundred women a Sunday. She knew and loved her Bible well, and was able to inspire her listeners with the same love and knowledge of it.

Her church work offered other challenges. In 1892, five years after her marriage, she was licensed to preach, and she frequently served as substitute pastor in her church, occupying her father's pulpit. Her husband took great pride in her on these as well as on many other public occasions. He made her more effective in this form of public service by balancing her enthusiasm with his judgment.

Albert W. Beaven, pastor of the Lake Avenue Baptist Church from 1909 to 1929, observed: "It would be impossible to understand Mrs. Montgomery without being introduced to her husband. She was able to do what she did only because he was one hundred per cent a partner with her in the enterprises in which she gave her brilliant mind. He rejoiced in her ability, gloried in the opportunities which came to her, happily supported her in every possible way, and cheered her on in every struggle. Together they were a host, who through their home life, in their church, and in all good community enterprises, continually made an impact upon the city for the things that were wholesome and which undergirded the work of the kingdom of God."

Even when they enjoyed great prosperity, the Montgomerys gave liberally to good causes instead of spending money on themselves. For years they had no automobile. Every time money was set aside to buy one, they found another cause to help. Not until his physical weakness led his physicians to recommend the convenience of a car did they actually purchase one.

Mrs. Montgomery has been described as a tall woman always perfectly at ease. She possessed contagious enthusiasm. She believed that she should present to her audiences just as attractive an appearance as possible, and she dressed quite charmingly. One writer records the striking impression she made on an occasion when she wore a small toque, or cap, resting against her dark hair, which never turned gray even when she was in her seventies. At the side of the toque swept a flame-colored feather.

Beginning in 1904, Mrs. Montgomery spoke at many schools of missions, and accepted other speaking engagements across the continent. Finally she took a world tour, speaking in many foreign countries on her favorite theme, mission work.

She was the author of the following study books on foreign missions: *Christus Redemptor*, a study of the Islam World; *Western Women in Eastern Lands*, which gave the suggestion for the Women's Missionary Jubilee in 1910 and 1911; *The King's Highway*, written after her return from a world tour of mission fields; *The Bible and Missions*, called by some experts the best mission study book of its time; *Prayer and Missions*, and *From Jerusalem to Jerusalem*. These books sold more than half a million copies and did much to educate women and girls in the highest missionary ideals.

Mrs. Montgomery had the gifts and capacity to fill positions of high trust and wide prominence. In 1914 she was elected president of the Women's American Baptist Foreign Mission Society and served in this office for ten years. She believed strongly in youth, saying that "to conserve the young life of our church for the service of the Master is one of the great unfulfilled tasks of our denomination." During her term of office the world-wide Guild of Northern Baptist Young Women was formed.

In 1910, while making plans for the Mission Jubilee, she was elected president of the Northern Baptist Convention, the first woman to hold such a position in a large church body. Immediately after her election, she was plunged into a campaign to collect an enormous sum for a denominational program.

When the Baptist World Alliance held its 1923 Congress in Stockholm, she was among the contingent of delegates who transformed the *S. S. America* into a "Ship of Fellowship," and filled it with gifts for peoples in other lands. In the great hall at Stockholm, she spoke on another favorite theme, "New Opportunities for Baptist Women."

In her campaigns and travels Mrs. Montgomery was closely associated with Mrs. Henry W. Peabody, with whom she made a trip around the world after attending the International Council of Churches in Holland. Accompanying them on this journey were their daughters, who did much while in the Orient to promote interest in mission schools.

After the trip, which took them not merely around the world but into the very heart and life of Oriental people, funds were started to found the Seven Colleges for Women of Asia, with the motto, "Lighted to Lighten." With the little Indian lamp as a symbol, the women of America in the next few years made possible the building of colleges in Japan, China and India.

A favorite and essential part of Helen Montgomery's work was providing Christian literature for women and children in non-Christian lands.

Her legacy of twenty-five thousand dollars contributed toward this aim is an example of the wise stewardship which she carried on after her husband's death in 1930.

It was at Mr. Montgomery's passing that her own health began to fail. She told one of her friends that she had a queer feeling when she had so much to say to Will and realized that he was there no longer with her. But her faith, friends noticed, burned like a lamp in a dark room, despite her loneliness, sorrow and diminishing strength.

She died on October 18, 1934, and in her will bequeathed four hundred and fifty-five thousand dollars to more than eighty selected churches, colleges, hospitals, missions and other philanthropies. This was in addition to the large gifts she and her husband gave during their lifetime.

In summing up her life, Mrs. Peabody, her friend of many years, said: "She was international long before most American women awoke to that relation, and realized that the only successful internationalists to date are Foreign Missions." She also cited the fact that she was a scholar who always retained her firm faith in the supernatural, inspired word of God.

An article entitled "A Noble Christian Woman Passes," appearing in *The Christian Century* of November 7, 1934, said in part:

> With her passing there closed one of the most interesting as well as one of the most influential careers in recent American church annals. Interesting, because it developed organically out of her loyalty to and labor for a single local congregation. The basic religious interest of her life never left that one congregation.

The article further pointed out how she had risen to the presidency of the national and international organizations, received honorary degrees, toured the world, written successful books, and attained national recognition as a scholar in her translation of the New Testament. The article asks the question: "May it not have been because she never lost this implication in the affairs of her local congregation that she was able to render such magnificent service on a national and international scale?"

MRS. CHARLES JONES SOONG—
CHINA'S GREAT CHRISTIAN MOTHER
(1869?-1931)

● ● ●

She helped to transform China through her children, one of whom is Mme Chiang Kai-shek. Her Christian ancestry dates from the Jesuits who came to China in 1601. Her husband was trained as a Methodist minister. She sent her six children to Christian schools.

SHE PRAYED THROUGH EVERY PROBLEM

CHRISTIANITY WAS a living reality for Mrs. Charles Jones Soong. Her life was a witness to its power and to the fact that its seed, once deeply planted, does not die, and knows no East or West, no race or color.

She gave China four of its most distinguished public servants. Her eldest daughter, Eling, married H. H. Kung, descendant of Confucius and government minister of finance. Her middle daughter, Chingling, married Sun Yat-sen, father of the Republic of China and revered as its George Washington. Her youngest daughter, Mayling, married Chiang Kai-shek, Chinese general and statesman. Her son, T. V. Soong, became both finance and foreign minister and a statesman in international finance. He married Anna Chang, who was educated in a Christian mission school. Inspired by their mother's noble Christian ideals, the Soong children worked for the betterment of the Chinese people, especially in educational and social matters.

She was a direct descendant of the illustrious prime minister of the Ming Dynasty, Wen Ting-Kung (Hsu Kwang-ki), who was converted to Christianity in 1601 by the Jesuit missionary Matthew Ricci. His daughter Candida—as she was called by Europeans—built churches and hospitals in seventeenth-century China. Mrs. Soong's mother broke with the Catholic traditions of her family and became a Protestant like her husband, Yuin San, who had been converted by the London Missionary Society at Shanghai.

As a young woman, Ni Kwei-tseng, as she was then named, showed her superior qualities. She was devout and well educated. She was different from other Chinese girls of her day in that she had "big feet" by Chinese standards: when she was only four and became ill, her Christian parents had her feet loosened from their painful bindings, and never bound them again.

Her husband, Charles Jones Soong, was an American-educated Methodist minister when she married him. He had left China as a lad of nine, sailing to America to live with an uncle in Boston. He later went to Wilmington, North Carolina, where he was baptized at the Fifth Street Methodist Church. As a young man, Soong had enlisted in the service now known as the American Coast Guard. The story is told that one of his captains was named Charles Jones and was so kind to him that the young Chinese boy chose to take the captain's name.

Afterward Soong was graduated in theology from Vanderbilt University and visited the Wilmington congregation, who regarded him as their son in the Gospel. He was ordained there in 1885 and soon set sail for China with his Bible, a gift from the Wilmington congregation.

When the China Mission Conference was organized, Soong was one of its original members and was appointed to a circuit in the Soochow district, where he began to preach the Gospel to his own people.

The next year, 1886, he took as his bride the seventeen-year-old Ni Kwei-tseng. They were married by a Southern Methodist missionary. He relinquished his post as an itinerant missionary in 1890, for he could not support his wife and children on his monthly pay of fifteen dollars. He wrote to his American friends: "This does not mean the giving up of preaching Christ and Him crucified." Soong continued to take an active part in the life of his church.

His first job after leaving the ministry was as an agent for a Bible society. Afterwards he founded a printing house of his own, published Bibles in Chinese and distributed them through the missions of China, thus carrying the Gospel to more Chinese than his voice could reach. He later imported foreign machinery.

Meanwhile, Mother Soong reared their six children, training them to be cultured, good, self-reliant and useful. For the love and inspiration she gave her children, she has been compared to Susanna Wesley, mother of Methodism.

She sent her daughters to the McTyeire School in Shanghai, a Methodist institution named for the bishop who sent Soong as a missionary to his native China. Mayling (later Mme Chiang), who took her mother's religious precepts seriously even as a child, went to McTyeire when she was only five. Her son, known as T. V. though he was named Paul at his birth, was sent to St. John's Episcopal School in Shanghai. Mother Soong rejoiced that her children "grew in wisdom and stature" and were nurtured in the love of God.

Later, Mother Soong sent her daughters to a Methodist college, Wesleyan, in Macon, Georgia. Mayling was sent to Wellesley College in Massachusetts, and later, as China's First Lady, became one of its most distinguished alumnae. When an honorary Doctor of Laws was presented to her in 1942, she was referred to as "one who has not asked to be ministered unto but to minister to the needs and dreams of her nation."

Mother Soong was widely known in her area as the lady who, like Dorcas, gave much to the needy. Poor mothers came to her with their sick babies, and often they went away restored by her gifts and prayers and Bible stories.

Christianity brought her into a world where East and West met. Her house in Shanghai was truly Sino-American, combining features from both worlds. Its green and yellow bathtubs had dragons on them, its beds had comfortable American mattresses, and it had other American refinements, such as gas radiators, upholstered chairs and sofas. Its dozen rooms looked out upon a stream and an enclosed courtyard.

Her family gathered regularly for Bible reading, prayer and hymn singing. Mother Soong carried all her hopes and problems to God in prayer. Often she would begin her prayers at dawn and spend hours in her third-floor prayer room. Mme Chiang said that she had confidence, no matter what she did or did not do, that her mother would pray her through. "And I must say," continued Mme Chiang, "that whenever mother prayed and trusted God for her decisions, the undertaking invariably turned out well." Her children learned not to disturb her when she prayed, even when she spent hours on her knees. As Mme Chiang explained it, "Asking God was not a matter of spending five minutes to ask Him to bless . . . and grant her request. It meant waiting upon God until she felt His leading."

Chiang Kai-shek had a profound respect for his mother-in-law, and her example was largely responsible for his becoming converted. She was at first opposed to her daughter's marriage to him, for he was not a Christian. But she told him that if he would become a Christian, she might change her mind.

"A real Christian," Chiang told her, "is one who has a personal experience of God." Feeling that he had no such experience, he would not profess conversion as a part of a matrimonial bargain. Mother Soong agreed with him and admired his honesty. He did resolve, however, that he would pray and read the Bible with an open mind.

Although Chiang had not yet changed his faith, plans finally were made for the marriage. Mother Soong insisted upon a Christian wedding to precede the elaborate Chinese ceremony. The service took place December 1, 1927, in the small Shanghai house she occupied after her husband's death. Dr. David Yui, national secretary of the YMCA in China, officiated. Z. T. Kaung, minister of the Young J. Allen Memorial Church in Shanghai, kneeled with Mother Soong, Mayling and Chiang, asking for God's blessing and guidance for the couple.

After his marriage Chiang faithfully read the Bible his mother-in-law gave him, and when his wife prayed, he knelt beside her. Once he asked his wife: "What exactly is a Christian?" She replied: "My mother is the finished product. I am a Christian in the making."

On one crucial occasion, when he and his army were trapped near Kaifeng by enemy soldiers, Chiang promised, like Jephtha of old, that if he were delivered from the enemy, he too would make a vow to God. His vow was that he would become a baptized Christian. When he and his men were freed from the trap, he returned to the room in Mother Soong's house where he had been married. Here he was baptized on October 23, 1930, the year before his mother-in-law's death.

Mother Soong's spiritual example followed Chiang in Sian when he and his army were again trapped in 1936 by enemy soldiers. All avenues of escape were closed, and Chiang was virtually imprisoned. He called for a Bible and his eyes lighted on the words of Jeremiah 31:22: "For the Lord hath created a new thing, in the earth, A woman shall compass a man." That very day his wife arrived although he had implored her not to risk the danger.

For two days Mme Chiang and her brother, T. V. Soong, talked with the two generals whose armies had trapped her husband. On Christmas Day the doors swung open, and her husband was set free.

Mother Soong's Christianity appeared in the lives of her other children. When Mme Sun's husband died she selected Christian hymns for the funeral, and asked that they be sung by a vested choir. During the period of Japanese invasion and occupation from 1937 to 1945, Mme Sun also went forth to gather "guerrilla babies"—children in the isolated mountain region of Northwest China, whose fathers were in guerrilla bands or the regular army and whose mothers were in war work. She established a dozen or more schools for these nearly abandoned youngsters. She also induced three friends to join her in giving eighty thousand dollars to equip a hospital, and organized a drive to finance a smaller one.

Mother Soong would have rejoiced in these Christian acts which she did not live to see. By 1930 she was ill with cancer, the same disease that had taken her husband earlier. Her children sought her prayers to the last. The year of her death, when the Chinese were fighting the Japanese, Mme Chiang asked her mother why she did not pray for the annihilation of the Japanese. Her mother gravely replied: "When you pray, or expect me to pray, don't insult God's intelligence by asking Him to do something which would be unworthy even of you, a mortal."

Her death in 1931 left a spiritual vacuum in her children's lives. They were now forced to develop greater inner strength themselves and to rely on their own prayers.

Mme Chiang's famous *Confession of Faith,* later to be distributed throughout China, seemed to echo the spirit of her noble mother. It says in part:

I used to pray that God would do this or that. Now I pray that God will make His will known to me. . . . When one prays he goes to a source of strength greater than his own. I wait to feel His leading, and His guidance and balance. . . . I am quite often bewildered because my mind is only finite. I question and doubt my own judgments. Then I seek guidance, and when I am sure, I go ahead, leaving the results with Him.

I do not think it is possible to make this understandable to one who has not tried it. What I do want to make clear is that whether we get guidance or not, it's there. It's like tuning in on the radio. There's music in the air, whether we tune in or not. By learning to tune in, one can understand. How is it done? By practicing the presence of God—by daily communion with Him.

TERESA OF LISIEUX—
GUIDE OF THE LITTLE WAY

(1873-1897)

* * *

In her short life of twenty-four years, she gave to the world a new concept of Christian spirituality. Her autobiography ranks with the world's spiritual classics.

SHE GAVE THE WORLD AN IMAGE OF SPIRITUAL CHILDHOOD

TERESA OF LISIEUX, in her freshness, humility, simplicity and gentleness, appeals to ordinary people of all ages. "In my little way," she stated, "everything is most ordinary; everything I do must be within the reach of other little souls also." As she so well expressed it: "I must stay little. . . . I can only offer very little things to God."

Pope Pius X called her the "greatest saint of modern times." Pope Pius XII referred to her as "a new light to guide us along what she called 'an entirely new way' to heaven, but which is rather a recall to the one way, the way of the Gospels."

Her autobiography, *The Story of a Soul,* printed first in 1897 in an edition of two thousand, ranks with the Church's spiritual classics. Its circulation has run into the millions, and it has been translated into most languages. Her fame is due in large part to this autobiography, first circulated by her prioress to all Carmelite houses, and immediately recommended for its prophetic healing quality. In it she calls herself "The Little Flower," a name by which she has come to be widely known. She says:

If a little flower could talk, it seems to me it would say what God has done for it quite simply and without concealment. It would try to be humble by saying it was unattractive and without scent, when all the time it knew it was quite the opposite.

She goes on to say that she can prove her love "only by scattering flowers," that is to say, by never letting slip a single little sacrifice, a single glance, a single word; by making profit of the very smallest actions, by doing them all for love. She declares that she will sing, "even when gathering roses in the midst of thorns, and the longer and sharper the thorns may be, the sweeter shall be my song!" She weaves "The Little Flower" imagery in and out of her story.

She confided that early in childhood she often fell asleep during the meditation but was not appalled by this memory, because she bore in mind that "little children are just as pleasing to their parents asleep as awake."

Her life and writings are an example of Jesus' words: "Except ye be converted, and become as little children, ye shall not enter into the kingdom of heaven" (Matt. 18:10). She has come to be known as Teresa of the Child Jesus in order to distinguish her from the Spanish saint Teresa of Ávila (Teresa of Jesus), for whom she was named. Both were Carmelites who had a capacity for intense religious experience and led radiant lives.

Born January 2, 1873, in Alençon, France, Teresa was the youngest daughter of Azelia Marie Guerin, a lacemaker, and Louis Martin, a watchmaker. They had nine children, but only five of them lived to maturity. Her mother died when she was four years old, and a few months later the family moved to the little town of Lisieux in Normandy, where her mother's people lived.

Nature exercised a powerful influence on "The Little Flower's" life and she rejoiced in the Normandy meadows and woodlands, gardens and fruit trees. Although surrounded by love, she felt spiritually alone as a child. But she found enjoyment in the murmur of the wind, the rumble of thunder and flashes of lightning, the lovely blue sky over the countryside, and huge daisies taller than she was, "glistening like jewels after a shower of light." Looking only for the beautiful, her thoughts are a testimonial to Paul's counsel: "Whatsoever things are lovely . . . think on these things" (Phil. 4:8).

In October 1881 she began school as a weekly boarder under the Benedictine sisters. At the age of fifteen, she entered the Carmelite Convent. Her life as a nun is beautifully portrayed in her autobiography—a delightfully honest and inspiring account of the ascent of a soul.

She confesses that she is sorry for people who lose their souls, for it is "so easy to miss your way when the paths of the world seem so attractive." She tells of growing so much in love of God that "sometimes my soul experienced real transports of love." While her soul grew strong, she learned the emptiness of things that pass, and began to realize that real nobility lies within, and not in name or position.

"Why not reserve such boundless aspirations to great souls," she asked, "who can wing their way to the stars? I am no eagle, only a little fledgling which has lost its down, yet the eagle's heart is mine, and the eagle's eyes, and despite my utter littleness I dare to gaze upon the Son of Love, burning to take my flight to Him. I long to fly and imitate the eagles, but all I can do is flutter my small wings. I am not strong enough to fly."

Her experience confirmed her belief that joy does not reside in outer things but in the very depths of the soul; that one can build a beautiful soul in the gloom of a dungeon as well as in the palace of a king. She lived so close to God that she wondered why she did not dream about Him, for she thought about Him and spoke to Him all day. Her dreams were usually about "forests, flowers, streams and the sea." Everything she saw led her toward God.

There are few people, she said, "who do not make their own limited understanding the measure of God's power." She knew that God perfects all human virtues, that "a heart given to God loses none of its natural tenderness; on the contrary, the more such tenderness increases, the more pure and divine it becomes." The thought of God's majesty and greatness helped her to put her own small troubles in their place. She loved Him alone and would not permit herself to be taken up with trivialities after she caught a glimpse of what "He has reserved for those He loves." Finally she attributed all that was good in her to the goodness of God.

Looking upon Jesus as her spiritual confessor, she declares:

Jesus does it all, and I do nothing, I hold, and know from experience that the kingdom of Heaven is within us. Our Lord needs neither books nor teachers in order to guide our souls. He, the teacher of teachers, gives His guidance noiselessly. I have never heard Him speak, and yet I know that He is within me. At every moment He instructs me and guides me. And whenever I am in need of it He enlightens me afresh.

In her writings, Teresa speaks to Jesus as she would to a person standing beside her. Actually He does seem to stand beside her as she quietly asserts:

I know that the saints have done foolish things as well as wonderful ones, and my foolishness lies in hoping that Your Love accepts me as a victim. . . . If only, my Jesus, I could tell all *little souls* about your ineffable Condescension . . . I implore You, cast Your eyes upon a multitude of little souls; choose out in this world, I beg of You, a legion of little victims worthy of Your Love.

The *Imitation of Christ* by Thomas à Kempis was her guide in youth, but she turned more to the Bible as she grew older, declaring that her head sometimes split when she read learned books, but that all seemed luminous when she opened the Bible. "A single word opens up infinite horizons to my soul, perfection seems easy," she said in a letter. "I see that it is enough to realize one's nothingness, and give oneself wholly, like a child, into the arms of the good God. Leaving to great souls, great minds, the fine books I cannot understand, I rejoice to be little because only children, and those who are like them, will be admitted to the heavenly banquet."

She tried to follow her faith in daily life by taking definite practical steps. Her mortifications consisted in checking her self-will, keeping back an impatient word, and doing little things for those around her without their knowing. The only nobility which counts, she said, consists in being willing to be ignored and despised. In a spirit of true humility, she confessed that although she wanted to be one of the saints she was "no more like them than a grain of sand trodden beneath the feet of a passerby is like a mountain with its summit lost in the clouds."

She never dwelt on her own crosses although they were many: her serious childhood illness, the death of her mother and of her dearly beloved father who had suffered two strokes and finally a mental breakdown, her many spiritual agonies, and her own slow death from tuberculosis. In her last years, she could take so little a part in convent life that she was ignored at times, but she knew that this helped her to lose her consciousness of self and to enter into an awareness of God.

Teresa of Lisieux was convinced at a very early age that she, "The Little Flower," would be gathered in the springtime of her life, and in fact she did die at the age of twenty-four. One of her final sentences was: "After my death I shall let fall a rain of roses." In this remark, says Walter Nigg in his *Great Saints*, "Teresa answered the question of life hereafter in the manner of a Saint; and she set the problems of death in the light of Christianity, according to which life arises from death. Teresa hoped to radiate strength, and thus give proof of the transcendental reality of the dead." Hans Urs von Balthasar says of her in his *Theresa of Lisieux—The Story of a Mission:* "She does not produce light, she reflects it"—and she has continued to reflect it for millions of people in over a half-century since her death.

WOMEN HYMN WRITERS—
THEY SANG TO THE WORLD

✦ ✦ ✦

Christina Rossetti (1830–1894)
Charlotte Elliott (1789–1871)
Harriet Beecher Stowe (1811–1896)
Julia Ward Howe (1819–1910)
Anne Steele (1716–1778)
Elizabeth Prentiss (1818–1878)

Selena, Countess of Huntingdon
(1707–1791)
Fanny J. Crosby (1820–1915)
Frances Ridley Havergal (1836–1879)
Jemima Luke (1813–1906)
Annie S. Hawks (1835–1918)
Sarah Flower Adams (1805–1849)

THEIR SONGS INSPIRE EACH WORSHIPING GENERATION

WOMEN HAVE WRITTEN the lyrics to some of the Church's most stirring hymns. A brief list reveals the debt all Christians owe to these gifted and devout women. Sarah Flower Adams wrote "Nearer, My God, to Thee"; Annie S. Hawks, "I Need Thee Every Hour"; and Jemima Luke, "I Think When I Read That Sweet Story of Old." Fannie J. Crosby created "Jesus, Keep Me Near the Cross," "Blessed Assurance," "Rescue the Perishing" and countless others. Frances Ridley Havergal wrote "I Gave My Life for Thee" and "Take My Life, and Let It Be"; Julia Ward Howe, "Battle Hymn of the Republic"; and Harriet Beecher Stowe, "Still, Still with Thee." Songs like these appear in many hymnals and are sung wherever Christians gather.

The writers of modern hymns join the hosts of other women who have sung unto the Lord. The first was Miriam, sister of Moses, who, after the crossing of the Red Sea, sang with the women of Israel the oldest national anthem, "Sing Ye to the Lord, for He Hath Triumphed Gloriously" (Exod. 15:21). Deborah's victory for the Israelites was celebrated in the "Ode of Deborah" in Judges 5, one of the first martial songs in history. Like the singers of earlier times, Christian women of the last two centuries have sung of their joys and sorrows, their aspirations and triumphs, their love and faith.

CHRISTINA ROSSETTI, one of the greatest English women poets, wrote "God the Father Gives Us Grace." She was the daughter of a Catholic father, Gabriel Rossetti, Italian poet and political refugee from Naples, and of an English Protestant mother, Francesca Rossetti. Her brother was Dante Gabriel Rossetti, the English poet and painter. A devout person, she poured forth her prayers and ecstasies in her prose as well as in her poetry. This appears in her book *Called to be Saints:*

How beautiful are the arms, which have embraced Christ—the eyes which have gazed upon Christ, the lips which have spoken with Christ, the feet which have followed Christ. How beautiful are the hands which have worked the works of Christ, the feet which are treading in His footsteps have gone about doing good, the lips which have spread abroad His Name, the lives which have been counted for Him.

She prayed both in her room and at a nearby church, waiting for the rare moments of rapture when God spoke to her. She retained an inner strength through her years of physical suffering which gave her power as a writer and as a person.

In spite of physical weakness and much suffering, CHARLOTTE ELLIOT's hymns show gentleness, patience and spiritual strength. Of her many hymns, "Just As I Am, without One Plea" is sung most often, but "O Holy Saviour! Friend Unseen," "My God, Is Any Hour So Sweet" and "My God and Father, While I Stray" are also well known.

For twenty-five years she edited *Christian Remembrance Pocket-Book* and revised a hymnbook for invalids, in which were included about one hundred of her own hymns. When her great age and poor health made it impossible for her to attend church, she said to her sister:

My Bible is my Church. It is always open, and there is my High Priest ever waiting to receive me. There I have my confessional, my thanksgiving, my psalm of praise, a field of promises and a congregation of whom the world is not worthy— prophets and apostles, and martyrs and confessors—in short, all I can want, there I find.

As she neared her eighty-first year, she wrote:

I feel that so great an age as mine requires three things—great faith, great patience and peace. Come what may during the year upon which we have entered, I firmly believe that goodness and mercy, like two guardian angels, will follow us during every day, in every hour, in every varying circumstance through which we have come to pass.

HARRIET BEECHER STOWE, whose *Uncle Tom's Cabin* is said to have influenced the course of the Civil War, wrote "Still, Still with Thee" not long after her little son Charles died of cholera. She said of his passing:

There were circumstances about his death of such peculiar bitterness, of what seemed almost cruel suffering, that I felt that I could never be consoled for it, unless this crushing of my own heart might enable me to work out some great good to others.

Finally, her sense of closeness to God led her to compose the well-loved "Still, Still with Thee." Her religious background fitted her for hymn writing, for her father, Lyman Beecher, was president of Lane Seminary in Cincinatti; her husband, Rev. Calvin E. Stowe, was professor of Biblical literature there; and her brother, Henry Ward Beecher, was the well-known Congregational preacher and reformer.

JULIA WARD HOWE's "Battle Hymn of the Republic" was sung during the Civil War by Union soldiers camped at night, or on the move or marching to battle. Mrs. Howe, who preached occasionally in Unitarian pulpits and was widely known as an author and lecturer, wrote the "Battle Hymn" in the dark on a scrap of paper. The war and its mighty issues were her chief concern and everything she saw connected itself in some way with the struggle. Breathing the spirit of the time, a spirit of hope, resolve and aspiration, she wrote the hymn beginning, "Mine eyes have seen the glory of the coming of the Lord! He is trampling out the vintage where the grapes of wrath are stored."

Like Harriet Beecher Stowe, many women hymn writers were closely connected with the church as choir singers, pianists and organists or as daughters, wives or sisters of ministers. ANNE STEELE was the daughter of William Steele, a timber merchant who served as pastor of the Baptist Church at Broughton, in Hampshire, England. She is the foremost of Baptist hymn writers, judging by the number of her verses in Baptist hymnals of the last century and a half, and the frequency with which they have been sung. Injured in childhood, she became an invalid, almost always in pain and often confined to her room. But she bore her suffering with resignation and wrote the triumphant "He Lives, the Great Redeemer Lives."

ELIZABETH PRENTISS wrote the well-known "More Love to Thee, O Christ," as well as other hymns and poems. She was the daughter of a Presbyterian minister, Edward Payson. Her husband, George Lewis Prentiss, was first a Presbyterian pastor, later one of the organizers of the Church of the Covenant, and afterward professor of pastoral theology at Union Theological Seminary in New York (1871-1897). She was the mother of six children and an ideal pastor's wife, for she thought of her role as one of service:

> You can't think how sweet it is to be a pastor's wife; to feel the right to sympathize with those who mourn, to fly to them at once, and join them in their prayers and tears. It would be pleasant to spend one's whole lifetime among sufferers, and to keep testifying to them what Christ can and will become to them, if they will only let Him.

Although she wrote books for children and also novels, she loved hymns so well that she said she had to pray herself out of loving them more than the Bible. Her husband paid glowing tribute to her in his book *The Life and Letters of Elizabeth Prentiss*.

In the eighteenth century, SELENA, COUNTESS OF HUNTINGDON, compiled *A Select Collection of Hymns* for her sixty or more English chapels. Her Connexion, which later became a part of Wesley's Methodists, never printed the names of the authors of these hymns, so it is impossible to know whether she composed any of the hymns or merely assembled them. Many editions of this hymnbook were published for her various chapels in London, Bristol, Sussex, Edinburgh, Lincolnshire and elsewhere.

FANNY CROSBY wrote the astonishing number of more than eight thousand religious poems, many of which have been set to music and distributed by the millions in English-speaking countries. Among her best-known hymns are: "Jesus, Keep Me Near the Cross," "Draw Me Nearer," "Blessed Assurance," "Rescue the Perishing," "I Am Thine, O Lord" and "All the Way My Saviour Leads Me."

Born in southeast Putnam County, New York, on March 24, 1820, Fanny Crosby became blind at the age of six weeks during a sickness. As a young girl she joined the Old St. John Methodist Church in New York City. At the age of fifteen she entered the New York Institute for the Blind, where she received an excellent education. She later taught there.

"Blindness can not keep the sunlight of hope from the trusting soul," she wrote in later life. "One of the earliest resolves that I formed in my young and joyous heart was to leave all care to yesterday, and to believe that the morning would bring forth its own peculiar joy."

In 1858 she married Alexander van Alstyne, who was also blind. He was an organist in two New York City churches, and his co-operation and musical knowledge contributed greatly to her success. Their united lives made harmony for forty-four years until his death in 1902.

Fanny Crosby's "Safe in the Arms of Jesus" was one of the first American hymns to be translated into numerous foreign languages. Among others found in almost every hymnbook are: "Jesus Is Tenderly Calling Thee Home," "Saviour More Than Life," "Pass Me Not, O Gentle Saviour" and "Jesus Is Mine."

From 1865 to 1905 she produced nearly two hundred songs each year. She died in 1915 at the age of ninety-five after giving fifty-one years of her life to enriching the Christian hymnology.

FRANCES RIDLEY HAVERGAL, with whom Fanny Crosby corresponded, was born in 1836 at Astley Rectory, in Worcestershire, England. The Ridley in her name derived from Nicholas Ridley, the great bishop who was martyred at Oxford in the sixteenth century. Her father, Rev. William Havergal, and her mother were earnest Christians. He composed cathedral music and hundreds of chants, tunes and sacred songs. His daughter inherited his talent for singing and playing the piano.

When she was confirmed and the bishop put his hands on her head and prayed, "Defend, O Lord, this Thy child with Thy heavenly grace, that she may continue Thine forever," she found special meaning in the words "Thine forever." That same day she wrote a verse containing these words.

She mastered Greek and Hebrew so that she might understand the Bible better. It was her custom to pray three times a day and she kept a note giving the subject for each prayer hour in her Bible.

At eighteen she wrote her well-known hymn "I Gave My Life for Thee." Then came a bitter disappointment. During a period of illness and enforced rest, she laid her pen aside for nine years.

Her father died in 1870 and she prepared *The Ministry of Song* for the press, accepting the inspiration that came to her as a direct gift from God. Very often, she had a distinct and happy consciousness of direct answers. "I never seem to write even a verse by myself and feel like a little child writing what is dictated," she said. She lived in the spirit of her hymns and touched other lives with her words.

She died at Caswell Bay, Swansea, South Wales, in the forty-third year of her life, and was buried in a quiet English churchyard. As a memorial to her a fund was raised to support native Bible women in India, and to circulate her works.

Though the hymn writers above are among the better known in the Church, others, like the psalmists of the Bible, speak out of obscurity. One is

JEMIMA LUKE, who wrote "I Think When I Read That Sweet Story of Old." Little is known of her other than that she was the wife of Samuel Luke, an English Congregational minister. Still less is known of ANNIE S. HAWKS, who wrote "I Need Thee Every Hour" in 1872. She was born in upstate New York, and resided for many years at Brooklyn, but the facts of her life are obscure. Another, SARAH FLOWER ADAMS, author of "Nearer, My God, To Thee," died at forty-four, never knowing of the fame of her hymn. She was a native of Cambridge, England, where her father was editor of a Cambridge weekly.

Whether famous or unknown, the sacred songs of these women hymn writers continue to inspire each worshiping generation.

SECTION III

VIGNETTES OF
OTHER CHRISTIAN WOMEN
THROUGH NINETEEN CENTURIES

◆ ◆ ◆

SHE ILLUMINATED MANY BY THE WORD OF GOD

THECLA (first century) was a native of Iconium, a city in Asia Minor visited by Paul and Barnabas on their first missionary journey (Acts 13:51). Because of their preaching in her city, Thecla became a Christian. The Greeks later called her the "first martyr and equal of the Apostles." According to tradition, she founded a convent near Seleucia, which was the port of Syrian Antioch and from which Paul and Barnabas embarked for Cyprus on their first missionary journey. Thecla's religious house was one of the earliest Christian monastic retreats. Gregory of Nazianzus mentions that a meeting of bishops was to be held "in the convent of the holy and distinguished virgin, Thecla."

It was written of her: "She illuminated many by the word of God." Basil of Seleucia interprets this to mean that she baptized many whom she converted to Christ, illumination being understood as a synonym for baptism. If this interpretation is correct, she was one of the first Christian women permitted to teach and baptize.

Thecla's name occupies an important place in the apocryphal writings of the New Testament, where she is honored as a companion of Paul. *The Acts of Paul and Thecla*, which, according to Tertullian, was written by a presbyter in Asia Minor about 160 A.D., contains a fictionalized version of her story. Though it includes fantastic stories of escapes from burning, wild beasts, bulls and serpents, it undoubtedly preserves some authentic facts of early church history.

This apocryphal book relates that while Paul was speaking in the house of Onesiphorus at Iconium, Thecla sat at a window of her house listening intently to the address. Her mother, also hearing Paul's words, became alarmed and sent for Thecla's fiancé, Thamyris. She warned him that he might lose Thecla, because this stranger Paul was advocating a life of chastity.

"My daughter," she said to the young man, "tied to the window like a spider, lays hold of what is said by Paul with a strange eagerness."

Going to Thecla and kissing her, Thamyris asked: "Thecla, my betrothed, why dost thou sit thus? Turn round to thy Thamyris and be ashamed." But neither he nor her mother could persuade her to change her mind. Thamyris took his case to the proconsul, who demanded that Paul come before him. A crowd of men cried: "Away with the magician, for he has corrupted all our wives and sweethearts!" Thecla came to the defense of Paul when he was arrested.

After suffering much martyrdom for her faith, Thecla went from Iconium to Seleucia, where she lived for seventy-two years, until she was ninety. Here in a mountain cave, she attracted highborn women who desired to know more about God and to be healed.

On the mountain south of Seleucia a great church was built in Thecla's memory. It is mentioned in two books by Basil, Bishop of Selecuia. In his *De Vita S. Theclae* he also describes miraculous cures that she performed, some of which he witnessed.

In 1907 Dr. Samuel Guyer and Dr. Ernest Herzfeld explored and partially excavated the site of this ancient church at a place now called Meriamlik, near Selecuia. Only the ruined walls of the apse were standing but the outline of the ground plan indicates how splendid the great church built in Thecla's honor must have been.

A church in Rome on the Via Ostiense not far from the church of Paul outside the old Roman walls is also dedicated to her.

There is an ancient marble sarcophagus, preserved in the Church of San Stefano in Bologna, which shows Thecla side by side with Ambrosius, Bishop of Milan, and with Agricola, patron saint of the city, who suffered martyrdom in 304.

Thecla's fame continued through the centuries. She was mentioned by Epiphanius, Ambrose, Augustine and other church fathers. Gregorius speaks of Peter, Paul, James, Stephen, Luke, Andrew and Thecla as those who contended for the faith "with fire and sword, beasts and tyrants."

A CHRISTIAN CHARGED WITH ATHEISM

FLAVIA DOMITILLA (first century) a member of the imperial family of Rome, became a Christian toward the close of the first century. She is immortalized in a famous catacomb on the Via Ardeatina, outside Rome. Unlike most of the catacombs, which are in dark, underground passages reached by obscure doorways, this one has a gateway and fresco-adorned walls—indicating that it was erected for a person of note.

Flavia Domitilla was important as a niece of the Emperor Domitian. Her husband, Titus Flavius Clemens, was the emperor's cousin and was appointed consul by him. Both Flavia and her husband were accused of atheism because they refused to worship the emperor as a god. Since they rejected the state religion, and could not plead the excuse of being Jews, they were branded as atheists.

Flavia not only suffered for her faith in being a Christian but also for giving aid and shelter to the needy, for burying dead martyrs, and for reading the Bible. As soon as her husband's consulate ended in 95 A.D., Domitian ordered that he be put to death for refusing to assist in the persecution of Christians. Flavia was spared death but was forced to endure a long and lonely martyrdom on an island in the Mediterranean Sea near Naples.

Jerome, writing almost three centuries later, says that Flavia was banished to Pontia. He represents her as the niece, not the wife, of the consul Flavius Clemens. He records that when Paula, another famous Roman Christian, was on her way to Bethlehem, her vessel touched the island of Pontia (now Ponza). Paula visited the cell in which Flavia passed her long exile.

Most of the later authorities conclude that Flavia was the wife and not the niece of the consul Flavius Clemens, a first cousin to Domitian. After losing his own sons, Domitian is believed to have adopted Flavia's sons, giving them the names of Vespasian and Domitian. He was supervising their education when he was assassinated in 96 A.D. With Domitian's death the imperial authority of the Flavian household came to an end. The fate of Flavia's sons is not known.

Actually, there were three Flavia Domitillas in Roman history, the mother, daughter and granddaughter. The first was the wife of the Emperor Vespasian. The second was their daughter who was also a sister of the Emperors Titus and Domitian. The last Flavia was a niece of Domitian. It is this latter Flavia who, through her willingness to suffer for the Christian faith, greatly strengthened Christianity in the first century; and it is her name that is perpetuated in the catacomb on the Via Ardeatina.

THE PATRONESS SAINT OF CHURCH MUSIC

CECILIA (?-230 or, according to some, 176) was an early Christian martyr honored for her place in the history of church music. In 1513 Raphael painted her seated at an organ. She was made patroness of the Academy of Music at Rome, when it was founded in 1584, and after this her veneration became more widespread.

In medieval times pilgrims visiting the burial places of Roman martyrs were shown Cecilia's grave beside the Appian Way, next to the crypt containing the bodies of third-century Roman bishops. The nineteenth-century archaeologist De Rossi discovered that the property above the catacomb of Bishop Callistus of Rome probably first belonged to the family of Cecilia, later passing into the possession of the Roman Church. Cecilia's body, wrapped both in a silken robe, embroidered with gold, and in linen cloths dipped in blood, is supposed to have been found in this catacomb.

The Church of St. Cecilia in the Trastevere quarter of Rome, built in the fourth century, was dedicated to Cecila in the fifth century. It is inferred that the church is built on property given by Cecilia. It was rebuilt by Paschal I, who was Pope in the years 817-824. A marble statue of Cecilia by the artist Stefano Maderna stands beneath the high altar. She is represented not as one dead, but as lying on her right side, asleep. In this same church, a ninth-century mosaic pictures her in beautiful garments as a patroness of Pope Paschal.

Recent excavations beneath the Church of St. Cecilia have unearthed the remains of ancient Roman buildings. Under the middle aisle of the church there is a richly adorned chapel. A side chapel contains the bath in which, according to tradition, Cecilia was put to death. This is the most ancient private bath discovered in Rome.

Pious romances represent Cecilia as a Roman woman of noble birth, who is said to have suffered martyrdom under the Roman Emperor Marcus Aurelius (161-180), but these cannot be taken as factual. One legend states that while musicians played at her wedding, she sang in her heart to God. Some authorities attribute her connection with church music to this tradition.

Her name is in the Canon of the Mass, in the oldest martyrologies attributed to Jerome. Chaucer sang her praises in "The Second Nun's Tale," one of the *Canterbury Tales,* and both Dryden and Pope wrote odes in her honor. Domenichino and Dolce, as well as Raphael, used her as a subject for paintings.

THE GLORY OF WIDOWS OF THE EASTERN CHURCH

OLYMPIAS (368-408) was a deaconess in the church at Constantinople and a friend of John Chrysostom, Bishop of Constantinople. Seventeen letters that he wrote to her survive as does a treatise, prepared for her consolation on the theme: "No one is really injured except by himself."

Olympias was a daughter of Seleucus, a count of the empire and a man of illustrious birth and immense wealth. At his death Olympias became the greatest heiress in Constantinople. She was married in 384 to Nebridius, a young man of good character and high station who died twenty months after their marriage.

Her wealth and beauty attracted many suitors, all of whom she rejected. The Emperor Theodosius the Great planned to give Olympias in marriage to one of his own relatives, the Spaniard Elipidius, but she steadfastly declared that she would remain a widow. Her suitor, hoping to overcome her resistance, persuaded the emperor to deprive her of the administration of her property until she was thirty.

Her calm response reveals her character. "Your goodness toward me has been that of an emperor and a bishop, in thus relieving me from the heavy burden of my property. Add to that goodness by dividing my wealth between the poor and the church. I have long been seeking a fit opportunity to avoid the vanity of making the distribution myself, as well as of attaching my heart to perishable goods instead of keeping it fixed on the true riches." The emperor, somewhat ashamed and full of admiration, had the property returned to her.

Olympias used her money to help the sick, prisoners, beggars and exiles. She purchased hundreds of slaves and set them free. For her generosity, she became known as "the glory of widows of the Eastern Church."

When Chrysostom's long struggle with the Empress Eudoxia ended in his banishment, Olympias assembled with a number of women in the baptistry of the great church of Santa Sophia to receive his parting blessing.

After he was exiled, she and his other followers suffered greatly. She lost all of her property. The soldiers insulted her and dragged her to court. Her suffering was not in vain, for now more than fifteen centuries since her death, she is revered as one of the great women in the Eastern Church.

THE FOUNDER OF THE FIRST HOSPITAL IN EUROPE

FABIOLA (?-399) was called by Jerome "the praise of the Christians, the marvel of the Gentiles, the mourning of the poor, and the consolation of the monks." The best source of information about her is contained in Jerome's Letters 64 and 77. In a letter which he wrote at her death, he eulogizes her as "the first person to found a hospital in Europe." This hospital was in Rome.

Fabiola was a member of the great Fabian family of Rome. After an unfortunate first marriage to a man described by Jerome as "one that not even a prostitute or common slave could put up with," she took another husband. Since this was against the laws of the Church, to atone for this marriage she dedicated her wealth and energy to the Church after the death of her second husband.

Jerome says that she wore sackcloth to make a public confession of her error, discarded her jewels and sold all her property. She used the money that she received from her property to supply the wants of the poverty-stricken, distributing her alms herself. She personally cared for the sick, and because of her high social position, this action made a strong impression on both Christians and pagans in Rome.

With the help of Pammachius, a Roman senator, Fabiola set up a tent for travelers landing at Ostia. There she and the senator showed kindness to those in distress. Many who were helped at this place of refuge were reminded of another retreat on the island of Melita (Malta)—a place where Paul received help when he was shipwrecked.

Jerome writes of Fabiola's voyage to Bethlehem, where she stayed with Paula and Eustochium, and of her zeal for the Bible and the earnestness with which she studied it. Once, when he was reading the Book of Numbers, she modestly questioned him as to the meaning of the great mass of names there. He replied as best he could. Unrolling the book further, and coming to the list of the forty-two halting places of the Israelites in the wilderness, she asked him to write a treatise on this subject. After her death he wrote one dedicating it to her memory.

While she was in Jerusalem, news came that hordes of Huns were marching on Palestine. "Having no other property but what her baggage contained," Jerome records, "she made her way back to her native land."

In recounting her death, he affirmed: "As she was already ready, death could not find her unprepared." When she died in Rome in 399 the people, remembering the solicitude she had shown for them, turned out in thousands to honor her.

"Her triumph was more glorious than that accorded emperors and generals," Jerome concludes. "They had conquered physical force, she had mastered spiritual iniquities."

SHE BESTOWED MANY BENEFITS ON THE FOURTH-CENTURY CHURCH

PULCHERIA (399-453), regent and empress for forty years, ruled the Empire of the East. The English historian Gibbon says of her: "She alone, among all the descendants of the great Theodosius, appears to have inherited any share of his manly spirit and abilities." She was a devout Christian who did so much for the Church that she has been venerated as a saint since the Middle Ages. In her youth she and her sisters made a solemn vow of virginity. For the remainder of her life she dressed simply, ate frugally and kept her palace to resemble a monastery.

After the death of her father Arcadius in 408, imperial affairs fell into the hands of male regents, but in 414 Pulcheria, who was only fifteen and just two years older than her brother Theodosius, took over the regency and was proclaimed empress by the senate and made regent for her brother.

A student of Latin and Greek, and deeply interested in medicine and natural science, she helped to prepare and inspire her brother for his role. After he was made monarch, she served as a joint ruler for about ten years. Then she arranged his marriage with an Athenian girl, Athenias, whom she converted to Christianity and had baptized under the name of Eudoxia.

Under Pulcheria's Christian influence, Eudoxia composed a poetical paraphrase of the five books of Moses, Joshua, Judges and Ruth, as well as the prophecies of Daniel and Zechariah. Although Pulcheria educated Eudoxia and raised her to the status of an empress, the latter sided with Pulcheria's enemies in a clash over church doctrine. However, she was fervent in the Christian faith and journeyed to the Holy Land, bringing back to Constantinople some of the sacred relics of the Church, including the chains of Peter. Eudoxia returned to Jerusalem a second time and it was there that she died.

At her brother's death in 450, Pulcheria became sole ruler. Since it was unprecedented that a woman should rule in her own right and name, Pulcheria made Marcian, a distinguished general, her husband. She was past fifty; he was a little under sixty. After her death in 453, he continued to rule for four years.

Pulcheria's benefits to the Church were numerous. She built three magnificent churches in Constantinople, and dedicated them to Mary, Mother of Christ. She established hospitals and a home for pilgrims. In order to restore unity to the Church at Constantinople, she brought back from Pontus the body of John Chrysostom, Bishop of Constantinople. He had been banished to that Province by Pulcheria's pleasure-loving mother, Princess Eudoxia, and deliberately killed by being forced to travel on foot in severe weather.

She also brought to Constantinople relics of the forty martyred Christian soldiers of the "Thundering Legion," who in Lesser Armenia in 320 were left naked on the ice of a frozen pond at Sebaste, within sight of baths of hot water placed on the banks to tempt them to renounce their faith.

Wishing to preserve orthodoxy within the Church, she vigorously opposed the heresy of Nestorius, Patriarch of Constantinople. He was deposed in 431 by the Council of Ephesus. She favored the great theologian Cyril of Alexandria, who upheld the perpetual virginity of Mary.

Because Pulcheria condemned Nestorius, his followers attacked her, forcing her to retire temporarily to a suburb of Constantinople, where she led a monastic life. Several years later she returned to the imperial palace.

In 451, two years before her death, she was invited to the Council of Chalcedon, which was attended by six hundred bishops. She was one of the few women, if not the only one, at this ecumenical council, which drew up the historic statement of faith asserting "one Christ . . . in two natures, without confusion, without change, without division, without separation."

When Pope Leo I wrote to Pulcheria, he noted that both Nestorian and Eutychian heresies, which divided the early Church, had been overcome largely by her efforts. He also thanked her for other benefits, including the solemn burial of Flavian, Patriarch of Constantinople.

THE BELOVED PATRON SAINT OF PARIS

GENEVIEVE (422-500) had a faith that saved Paris when Attila and his Huns invaded France in 451 threatening to besiege the city. Genevieve assured the inhabitants that God would protect them if they would pray. While the men prepared for battle, she persuaded the women to pray for hours in the church. The miracle took place. Attila destroyed Orléans but did not touch Paris.

When Merovee, King of the Franks, and his son Childeric besieged and took Paris, Genevieve was at Troyes and prophesied their defeat. According to legend, she averted famine in Paris and surrounding cities by distributing miraculous gifts of bread. For twice saving Paris, once from destruction, the second time from famine, Genevieve was made patron saint of that city.

It was she who first conceived the idea of erecting in Paris a church in honor of Peter and Paul. This church was built by Clovis I and his Christian wife Clotilda, who, along with Genevieve, are buried there. It later became known as the Church of St. Genevieve. Plundered by the Normans in 847, it was partially restored in 1177. Six hundred years later it was completely rebuilt by Louis XV in the form of a Greek cross. The Revolution broke out before it was dedicated in 1791, under the name of the Pantheon. It became a burial place for distinguished Frenchmen. Scenes from Genevieve's life are pictured in several beautiful wall panels painted by Puvis de Chavannes.

SHE CONVERTED THE FRANKS TO CHRISTIANITY

CLOTILDA (474-545), whose life marks a turning point in the Christian history of Europe, was responsible for the conversion of her husband Clovis I, king of what is now modern France, to Christianity. Clotilda was the daughter of Chilperic, King of the Burgundians. Because her entire family, with the exception of one sister, were massacred, Clotilda was brought up in the Burgundian court of an uncle, Gundobald.

Clovis asked for her hand in marriage just after he had conquered Gaul. The wedding, celebrated in 493, was important to all Europe. Although Clovis was a pagan, he gave his bride freedom to practice her own religion, and to set up an oratory in the palace. As time went on Clotilda kept urging her husband to become a Christian. Clovis was shrewd enough to see that if the Church were on his side, he would rule all of the Gallo-Roman population.

When their first son was born, Clovis consented to the infant's baptism, but the child lived only a few days. Serious misgivings then arose in the king's mind as to whether he had been well advised in permitting the baptism. A second son, Clodomer, was baptized, and he too fell seriously ill. Clotilda remained at his bedside for days to pray, and the child recovered. Her husband became more receptive to Christianity.

Shortly thereafter when the whole future of the Franks was at stake, Clovis swore that if he won the battle against the Alemanni, he would be baptized if Clotilda's God would grant him victory. Clovis won the battle.

On his return home, to make sure that he would fulfill his vow while his gratitude was warm, Clotilda sent for Bishop Remigius of Rheims to make plans for the baptism. On Christmas Day in 496, Clovis was baptized in a great public ceremony in which three thousand Franks were also baptized. After this he erected the basilica to Peter and Paul near his palace. He and Clotilda also built in Paris the Church of the Holy Apostles, afterward known as the Church of St. Genevieve.

The success of Clovis was, in a great measure, attributed to his alliance with the Church. Its tenets, however, he seemed to accept in word only, for, according to the historian Gibbon, his ambitious reign was a perpetual violation of moral and Christian duties. Clotilda's faith in God was one spark of good in the darkness of the times.

Clovis died in 511 and was buried in the crypt of the unfinished Church of the Holy Apostles. Clotilda's three sons—Clodomer, who reigned at Orléans; Childebert I, at Paris; and Clotaire I, at Soissons—fought among themselves for power. Her only daughter, Clotilda, was forced to marry Amalaric, King of the Visigoths, a fanatic Arian. Her two grandsons, the children of Clodomer, were murdered by their two uncles, Clotaire and Childebert.

All this caused her such bitter suffering that she retired to the Abbey of St. Martin at Tours, where she spent her time fasting, praying and helping the poor. One of her last acts as a queen was choosing bishops for Tours. For these high positions in the Church she sought men of character, rather than of power.

In her last illness, Clotilda called her sons Childebert and Clotaire to her, and exhorted them to lead a godly life. At her death, she was buried beside her husband in the Church of the Holy Apostles in Paris.

Though she did not live to see it accomplished, her Christian faith found fulfillment in her granddaughter Bertha, who became the wife of King Ethelbert of Kent and introduced Christianity into Anglo Saxon England. Her great-granddaughter Ethelberga planted the first seed of Christianity in Northumbria.

Considered one of the greatest queens in early Christian history, Clotilda is revered as a saint.

IRELAND'S BEST-LOVED WOMAN SAINT

BRIDGET—also known as Brigid, Brigida or Bride—(453-524) was the daughter of a bondwoman, Brotseach, and a nobleman of Ulster, Dubtach. According to legend, her father took her to the King of Leinster to sell her. On reaching the king's castle, her father went inside, leaving Bridget in the chariot. When a leper approached her and begged alms, she gave him the sword her father had left in the chariot. The king came out with her father and, learning that she had given away the sword, exclaimed: "I cannot afford to buy such an extravagant slave as this!" Her father drove home in a rage and thereafter made life so miserable for Bridget that she resolved to become a nun.

Bridget founded the first nunnery in Ireland, establishing at Kildare, or Cill-dara, her "Cell of the Oak." Bridget's own cell, built of wattle and clay, was in the shelter of a giant oak tree. The little cell in the great oak became a sacred and famous landmark by the tenth century.

As the saint of Irish agricultural life, every farm in Ireland is, in a sense, her shrine. In history she has been pictured as a true farm saint, making firkins of butter, rounds of cheese and tubs of home-brewed ale. Even as the Mother Abbess of all the nuns of Ireland, she retained her rural occupations.

Bridget's hospitality and charity were unbounded, and the fame of her holiness has never died. Her name is commemorated in churches, convents, orphanages, hospitals, wells and springs in Ireland. She is a much-loved saint in England, also, where she is called St. Bride. In Scotland, a church is dedicated to her.

So many legends have grown up around Bridget that it is difficult to sift out the facts. Alice Curtayne, who presently lives in Bridget's county of Kildare, says in her biography *St. Brigid of Ireland* that "the cult of St. Brigid of Ireland is one of the most sublime offerings ever laid at the feet of mortal woman, because, with so little material aid or external symbolism of any kind, it has burned with such ardor through fifteen hundred years, fed by the Spirit only." Montalembert, a nineteenth-century French writer, notes that Ireland was evangelized by two slaves, Patrick and Bridget, that Bridget was twice sold, was flogged, insulted and subjected to the hardest labor required of a female slave. She learned mercy in the school of oppression.

Bridget was buried at Kildare, where both monastery and town testify to her influence. Later her body was removed to Downpatrick and placed beside the bodies of two of Ireland's most famous saints, Columba and Patrick.

A COURAGEOUS AND GODLY QUEEN

RADEGONDE—also known as Radegunda—(518-587), Queen of the Franks, founded at Poitiers the Monastery of the Holy Cross. It was the first of those great double monasteries that soon abounded in France and England. She inspired one of the most majestic hymns of the early Church, *Vexilla Regis Prodeunt,* written by Venantius Fortunatus in 569 and translated into English in 1851 by John Mason Neale. The hymn, still sung in the Church, especially during Lent, begins:

> The royal banners forward go,
> The cross shines forth in mystic glow.

It ends:

> To Thee, eternal Three in One
> Let homage meet by all be done:
> As by the cross Thou dost restore
> So rule and guide us evermore.

A daughter of a prince of Thuringia, Radegonde fell into the hands of the Franks when she was only twelve years old, after they had successfully invaded her country. Later she became the wife of her captor, Clotaire I, who became King of the Franks. He was the son of the Christian Queen Clotilda, but possessed none of his mother's spiritual qualities. Radegonde did not wish to marry a man of such evil character, but after being forced into the marriage, she turned to her religion for strength and was the first of many queens to become a nun.

Her husband violently opposed this, but in the end he begged her forgiveness for all the sorrow he had caused her, as well as for the massacre of many of her family, the destruction of much in Thuringia that she held dear, and later the murder of her brother. Radegonde continued to pray for her husband but she did not return to him even when he repented of his sins. The remaining thirty years of her life she spent in prayer, study and good works.

SHE BROUGHT THE LOMBARDS INTO THE CHURCH

THEODELINDA (568-628) was a Bavarian princess who became Queen of Lombardy. She intervened in the struggle between the Church and her husband King Autari. When peace was made, Pope Gregory the Great wrote her this letter of thanks: "We knew that we might reckon your Christianity for this, that you would by all means apply your labor and your goodness to the cause of peace."

In this area of northern Italy, still called Lombardy, she built many churches and monasteries. She was instrumental in turning her people back to orthodoxy from Arianism, which denied the divinity of Jesus Christ. In Pavia, capital of Lombardy, she created the cathedral at Monza, placing it under the patronage of John the Baptist, and directing that the relics of Augustine be brought there.

After her husband's death, Theodelinda married Flavius Agiluphus of the Province of Pavia and was instrumental in checking his march on Rome. At her second husband's death, she became full regent of Lombardy and used her power to endow charitable foundations, encourage and improve agriculture, and aid the poor and build up the Church. She also gave assistance to Columba, the Irish saint who became a missionary to northern Scotland.

Pope Gregory the Great dedicated his *Dialogues* to Theodelinda, and when her son Adaloald was born, he sent the child a cross containing what was supposed to be a fragment of the Cross of Christ. He also sent her relics of John the Baptist for the church at Monza. The catalogue which accompanied them, written on papyrus, is still preserved at Milan.

ENGLAND'S FIRST CHRISTIAN QUEEN

BERTHA (?-612), daughter of Charibert, King of the Franks, and granddaughter of Clotilda, went to England to become the bride of King Ethelbert of Kent. In their marriage treaty she asked for freedom to practice her religion. Her Frankish chaplain accompanied her into England. So exemplary was her life that she inspired her husband and his court with high respect for herself and for her religion.

The Pope, taking advantage of this, sent forty monks, among whom was Augustine (later known as Augustine of Canterbury), to preach the Gospel and spread Christianity in England. With the queen's help, the monks were able to approach the king and preach to him. He finally became a Christian and was baptized in a public ceremony. Thus, owing largely to the influence of pious Queen Bertha, England began to turn to Christianity.

To Bertha belongs the glory of establishing the first Christian church in Canterbury. A little way outside the walls of Canterbury the Romans had built an edifice, which Bertha had repaired and made into a church, the first church in Anglo Saxon England. Here Bertha worshiped.

Her husband later gave their own house at Canterbury to Augustine, who founded there a church that became the great Cathedral of Canterbury. King Ethelbert and Bertha are depicted in one of the windows of the nave of this cathedral. The queen stands between Augustine of Canterbury and her first chaplain, Liudhard, whom she brought with her from France.

Queen Bertha's daughter was Ethelberga, who, when she married Edwin, King of Northumbria, took a monk, Paulinus, with her to her new kingdom. This monk baptized Hilda, who became the great abbess of the monastery at Whitby. Bertha's granddaughter Aelfled, daughter of Edwin and Ethelberga, was educated by Hilda and succeeded her as abbess in 680.

A QUEEN WHO PRIZED FREEDOM

BATHILDIS (?-680) was a slave before her marriage to Clovis II of the Franks, a drunken, gluttonous and dissolute king. When he died in 657, he left his widow with three sons, the eldest of whom, Clotaire, was only five. Bathildis found her kingdom burdened with slavery and heavy taxes, and the Church dishonored by the buying and selling of church offices. She quickly took steps to end these abuses when she became regent at her husband's death.

Bathildis waged incessant war against slavery, although she was unable to abolish it completely. She bought a large number of the most oppressed slaves and set them free. She paid the debts of poor people compelled to sell themselves into bondage in order to pay the heavy taxes. In another bold step, she abolished a tax which lowered human beings to the level of cattle. She gave freedmen the right to own property and declared them citizens of the state.

One of her services to the Church was to restore the Abbey of St. George at Chelles on the Marne, about ten miles from Paris. After reigning for almost a decade, Bathildis retired in 665 to the monastery of Chelles, where she lived and worked for fifteen years, showing heroic patience during a painful illness.

A contemporary said of her: "Queen, she never forgot that she had been a slave; and nun, she never remembered that she had been queen."

SHE PIONEERED IN THE CHRISTIANIZATION OF GERMANY

LIOBA (?-779) helped her cousin Boniface to establish a settled ecclesiastical organization in Germany.

Before she was born, her mother Aebbe dreamed that she had given birth to a church bell which rang as she held it in her hand. Her old nurse foretold that she would have a daughter, whom she must give to God from her birth. Lioba's life was to be a veritable church bell, ringing a Christian message over the north of Germany.

Lioba received her early training in a monastery at Wimborne, England, under the distinguished abbess Eadburga. Boniface, known as "the Apostle of Germany," wrote to Eadburga begging for monks and nuns to go with him to Germany to help the infant church there.

Lioba's response to this call from Boniface follows in part:

I ask of your clemency that you would deign to remember the former friendship which you made long ago with my father in the west country, now dead for seven years. I commend also to you the recollection of my mother, Aebbe.

I am the only daughter of my parents: and I would that I might, though quite unworthy, take you in place of a brother; for in no man of my family do I place such confidence of hope as in thee. I send a little gift (pepper and socks) to you, not that they are worthy your looking at, but that you may retain some memory of my littleness, and not forget me by reason of distance.

She told Boniface that she had learned all she knew from her director, the abbess Eadburga, one "who gives herself to profound study of the divine law." His answer to her on this occasion has been lost but some of his letters to Lioba and the other nuns are in existence.

She journeyed to Germany in about 748, six years before the martyrdom of Boniface. He put her in charge of a large community at Bischofsheim on the Tauber, and gave her authority over all his other nunneries under the Benedictine rule. Later she went to Schonersheim near Mainz, where Boniface had established the See of Mainz.

When Boniface founded the abbey of Fulda as a center for German monastic culture, Lioba seems to have been the only woman granted admittance to the church there.

Her position was not merely that of a ruler, but of a teacher and expositor, and she sent many nuns to other convents in Germany. After the martyrdom of Boniface, she continued her work for about twenty years, and became so learned in the Scriptures and so wise in counsel that bishops often discussed church matters with her.

Her special friend was Queen Hildegarde, wife of the great Charlemagne, King of the Franks and Emperor of the West. The queen begged Lioba to leave the solitude of her convent and to come to Charlemagne's palace. Lioba did journey there but, disliking the tumult of the palace, she remained only one day.

When Boniface gave up his archbishopric at Mainz, and went to Frisia in 755, he left directions that he should be buried at Fulda. He further directed the seniors of the monastery to honor and respect Lioba, and after her death to place her body in his sepulcher. At her death, her body was taken to Fulda, but the monks, unwilling to open his grave, buried her near the altar he had built to Christ and the Twelve Apostles. As the most noteworthy woman apostle to Germany in the time of the great bishop Boniface, she rests in this place of honor.

SHE FULFILLED PSALM 128

MATILDA—also called Maud—(895?-968?), wife of Henry I ("the Fowler"), King of Germany, has been described as humble and generous. Three years before her death, when she was about seventy-five, her children and grandchildren gathered about her, and she was praised by her son Bruno, Archbishop of Cologne, as one who fulfilled Psalm 128, especially the fifth and sixth verses: "The Lord shall bless thee out of Zion: and thou shalt see the good of Jerusalem all the days of thy life. Yea, thou shalt see thy children's children, and peace upon Israel."

In addition to her son who became an archbishop, Matilda had other children who achieved rank and importance. Her son Otto I, called "The Great," succeeded his father as King of Germany and became Emperor of the Holy Roman Empire. Another of Matilda's sons was the Duke of Bavaria. Matilda's daughter Gerberga, on her second marriage, became the wife of Louis IV, King of the Franks. Another daughter, Hedwig, married Hugh, Count of Paris. Their son Hugh Capet became the first of a new line of kings of France.

Matilda was the daughter of Reinhilda and Count Theodoric, a mighty prince of Saxony, whose castle at Erfurt stood not far from the oldest Benedictine abbey in Saxony. In her infancy, Matilda was placed in the care of her grandmother. She was educated at the abbey where she was

taught the Bible and learned to read and write Latin and to sing prayers
and hymns.

Even as a queen, Matilda lived the self-denying life of the convent,
giving generously to those in need and pleading for the unfortunate and
oppressed. In the winter, she had large fires lighted where the poor might
warm themselves. She had the fullest co-operation from her husband, who
has been called "the greatest king of his time in Europe." At his death in
936 he bequeathed to her all his possessions, but she was so lavish in her
giving that her sons, Otto and Henry, accused her of impoverishing the
crown. To satisfy them she renounced the possessions left her by the king
and retired to a villa. When misfortune overtook her sons, she was called
back to the palace, and they asked her pardon.

One of Matilda's heaviest sorrows was the loss of her son Henry when
he was not yet forty. Arising from the altar after his death, she went to
her husband's grave and, laying her head on it, talked to him about their
son. She told him she was glad he had not lived to suffer such bereavement.

Among her chief foundations were monasteries at Quedlinburg, Nord-
hausen, Engern and Poehlden. She was venerated as a saint immediately
after her death.

A RELIGIOUS WRITER OF MEDIEVAL TIMES

ROSWITHA—also Hrosvit, Hrotsvitha or Hrotswitha—(935-1002) was
a German noblewoman who became a nun in the Benedictine convent at
Gandersheim in Saxony. She is known to have written eight sacred legends
in verse, two historical poems, three prefaces, several dedications in verse
and prose, a poem about the book of Revelation, and six dramas. One of
her best-known plays, *Abraham*, dramatizes the story of a woman who is
reclaimed after yielding to temptation. Conrad Celtes, Germany's first
poet laureate, who discovered her works and published them in 1501,
called her "the German Sappho."

The loftiness of her thought and the directness of her purpose have
given her works a lasting place in medieval literature. In one of her most
famous letters, she praises God, through "whose grace alone I have become what I am; and yet I am fearful of appearing greater than I am,
being perplexed by two things . . . the neglect of talents, vouchsafed to
one by God, and the pretence of talents one has not."

"She occupies a unique position in monastic life and among unmarried
women generally," Lina Eckenstein writes in her book *Woman under
Monasticism*. This author points out that the Saxon element guided the

German nation in the domain of art. Roswitha was undoubtedly the first woman north of the Mediterranean to write plays in her period. She is still admired today and is remembered by such groups as the Hroswitha Club for women bibliophiles, which has members in Philadelphia, Boston, Pittsburgh, Washington and New York.

THE HEROINE OF THE FIRST CRUSADE

ADELA OF BLOIS (1062-1137) daughter of William the Conqueror; wife of Stephen Henry, Count of Blois and Chartres; and mother of Stephen, King of England, has been called by historians "the heroine of the First Crusade" which took place from 1096-1099.

Deeply religious, she was one of the first women of France to heed the preaching of Pope Urban II at the Council of Clermont when he urged all Christians to forget their differences and unite to rescue the Holy Land from the Moslems. This Pope had received many requests from the Byzantine Emperor in Constantinople to send soldiers against the Moslems. Adela, at great personal sacrifice, wanted her husband to share this seemingly glorious enterprise. She persuaded him to join the Crusade, and he became one of the first feudal barons to raise an army. Few rulers brought so many soldiers to the standard of the Cross as did her husband.

She laid aside her needlework on the famous Bayeux tapestry, which her mother had left for her to complete, and accompanied her husband from castle to castle seeking support throughout their wide domains. She supervised the labors of her maidens, who stitched on the warriors' coats the red Cross of Christ, official badge of the Crusaders.

After bidding her husband and his soldiers good-by, she saw them depart on their journey across the Alps toward the sea route to the Holy Land. She was appointed regent in his absence.

The First Crusade ended successfully when the Crusaders stormed Jerusalem and took it from the Moslems in 1099. Stephen Henry returned home only to join another expedition in 1101 during which he was killed in battle at Ramula.

Soon thereafter a monk arrived from the Holy Land with a letter for Adela written by her husband in his dying moments. In it he confirmed his great love for her.

Left with seven children—some authorities say nine—she nobly carried on the affairs of the kingdom until her son Theobald became of age and was appointed her successor. His daughter Adela became the wife of Louis VII of France.

She saw her son Stephen, grandson of William the Conqueror, crowned King of England. She helped to turn the interest of two of her sons, Henry and Philip, to the Church. Henry became an eminent Bishop of Winchester, while Philip held the See of Chalone.

Many contemporary Norman chroniclers describe Adela as being very beautiful and equal in bravery to her father. They indicate that she was a Latin and Greek scholar, a patron of literature, and that she often tutored her own children.

Her importance was such that during Easter in 1107, she entertained Pope Paschal II. Many of the letters which Hildebert, Bishop of Le Mans, wrote to her on ecclesiastical matters are still in existence.

Adela spent her last years in a convent in the diocese of Autun, continuing to wield an important influence in churches and monasteries and settling clerical disputes. She, her mother and her sister Cecilia are buried in the Abbey of the Holy Trinity at Caen, France.

THE FIRST OF THE GERMAN WOMEN MYSTICS

HILDEGARD OF BINGEN (1098-1179), who was regarded in her time as a "tabernacle of the Divine Spirit," thought of God as Light. Many of her inspired letters begin "The Living Light Saith . . ." From this concept of Divine Light she gained ideas for her writings, gave spiritual counsel, and taught and inspired others.

In her seventieth year she wrote:

From my infancy until now, my soul has always beheld this Light and in it my soul soars to the summit of the firmament and into a different air. . . . The brightness which I see is not limited by space and is more brilliant than the radiance round the sun. . . . I can not measure its height, length, breadth. Its name, which has been given me, is "Shade of the Living Light". . . . Within that brightness I sometimes see another light. When and how I see this, I cannot tell but sometimes when I see it all sadness and pain is lifted from me, and I seem a simple girl again, and an old woman no more!

Inspired by this Light, though she was an uneducated woman, Hildegard's writings were like those more learned. Her greatest work, over which she labored for nine years, is *Know the Ways of the Lord*. In this book she shows an intimate knowledge of Paul's epistles, the Book of Wisdom, the Hebrew prophets, the Book of Revelation, and Aristotle.

She was both industrious and versatile, writing three books, as well as the words and music for sixty-three hymns. She was also skilled in medicine and interested in politics. In her letters she did not hesitate to rebuke the sins of the greatest men of her time in both Church and State, and she worked hard to infuse spiritual ardor into a lukewarm church. Living in a time of conflict, she demanded that men's minds be set on worthier things.

Hildegard's concept of the spiritual life included not only prayer but hard work. With an armed escort to protect her from the many dangers that awaited travelers in the twelfth century, she rode on horseback to visit various monasteries as far away as France. When she was nearly eighty years old she returned to Germany from this long journey.

Her father was Hildebert, Overlord of Böckelheim, a village about thirty miles south of Bingen. Her mother offered her in childhood as a tithe to the Lord. Taking a vow in her youth to renounce the world, she was trained in spiritual things by the saintly Jutta, who attracted many devout women to her church cell and who opened a convent under the Benedictine Rule in 1112. Hildegard succeeded Jutta as prioress of this convent, and multitudes of pilgrims came to visit her there.

A well-known bishop of her time described her as "a flaming torch which our Lord has lighted in His church."

In *Mirrors of the Holy*, Lucy Menzies quotes Hildegarde as saying: "The love of God created us, but the humility of God saved us."

HER BOOK WAS A LIGHT IN THE MIDDLE AGES

MECHTHILD OF MAGDEBURG (1210-1280) has been called one of the great religious figures of the Middle Ages, largely because of her book, *The Flowing Light of God* or *Streaming Light of the Divinity*. This is a collection of visions, parables, reflections, letters, poems and dialogues, in both prose and verse.

The importance of the book, however, is not in its literary style but in its spiritual content. The author wrote as if she saw God in all things and all things in God. She received many revelations. She believed that the true home of the soul is in God alone and she revealed that not only does the soul need and long for God, but God needs and longs for man's soul. She declared:

Pure, holy simplicity is the mother of all real knowledge of God; all other knowledge is born of human understanding; many misguided laymen, false clergy and foolish people are taken in by it. . . . Those who would know much and love little, will remain ever at the beginning of a godly life. . . . Simple love, with even but little knowledge, can do great things.

Mechthild pointed out that when God seeks to bestow His gift, He looks for the lowest and smallest and most unnoticed. It is not only on the high mountains, she added, that men drink of the water-springs, for God's holy spirit also flows downward to the humble valleys.

She belonged to the Béguines, a community of women who devoted themselves to religion without entering a convent or taking monastic vows. Later she found refuge in the Cistercian convent of Helfde at Rodersdorf.

Little is known of Mechthild's earliest years, except that she was born into a noble family, was well educated and lived somewhere near Magdeburg. She was about twelve when she received her first message from the Holy Spirit, and from that time on the center of her life was changed.

Mechthild of Magdeburg was a contemporary of three other women mystics: her sister, Gertrude the abbess; another Mechthild, of Hackeborn; and Gertrude the Great. Evelyn Underhill, in her book *Mysticism*, calls these mystics "the four Benedictine women of genius." Of the four, Mechthild of Magdeburg is probably the best known because of her writings, which were translated into Latin and read by Dante. Some authorities think that she was the model for the Metelda of Dante's Earthly Paradise.

A CHRISTIAN SEER AND HEALER

GERTRUDE THE GREAT (1256-1302), one of the eminent mystics and theologians of the Middle Ages, reveals in the well-known volume containing her revelations, *The Herald of Divine Love,* that she was a woman who walked with God. Her soul seemed to be as open to God as air is to sunlight.

The second part of this five-part book contains her revelations which she herself wrote. The other parts include her biography and notes, which were compiled by members of her community. This book remained in obscurity for more than two hundred years. It appeared in the vernacular in 1503, and in 1536 Lanspergius, a Carthusian monk, made it known to the world. Many editions have appeared in succeeding centuries.

The book is alive with radiant optimism. It stresses the mercy of God, telling those who sin that "the infinite tenderness of Christ will swallow up all your mistakes, if they will abandon themselves to His love."

Gertrude has been called "one of the most consoling of Christian seers since Apostolic times." In one of her best-known prayers she pleads:

O most merciful Jesus, engrave Thy wounds upon my heart with Thy most precious, precious Blood, that I may read in them Thy grief and Thy love; and that the memory of Thy Wounds may ever remain in my inmost heart to excite my compassion for Thy suffering and increase my love for Thyself.

Little is known of Gertrude's early life, but it is evident that she was well educated, for she wrote Latin with facility and grace. Her biographers say that she had the gift of miracles as well as of prophecy.

A contemporary of Meister Eckhart who has been called "one of the greatest mystics of all Christian history," she, like him, lived in a world of humility, simplicity and sublimity.

SCANDINAVIA'S MOST FAMOUS SAINT

BRIDGET OF SWEDEN (1303?-1373) founded the Brigittines, originally a branch of the Order of Augustine but eventually a separate organization. She was born in Finstad, Uppland, north of Stockholm. God seemed to be with her even before her birth. When her mother was shipwrecked on a rock in the sea, many on the vessel were drowned but her mother, who was saved, heard a voice say, "Thou wast saved from death because of the good thou bearest within thee. Bring it up therefore in the love of God, for God hath given it to thee."

Bridget's mother was of an honorable family, zealous in all good works. Her father, Birger Perssons, was one of the wealthiest landowners in Sweden and governor and provincial judge of Uppland.

At the age of thirteen, Bridget was married for political reasons to Ulf Gudmarsson, whose family was as noble as her own. She went to live in his baronial home, Ulfasa. She had four sons and four daughters. Her daughter Catherine became a well-known saint, as did her granddaughter, her namesake Bridget. Bridget saw the death of three of her sons during her lifetime. Hardest on her was the passing of her most beloved, Karl. It so happened that when Karl left his wife in Sweden to visit his mother in Rome, he had a love affair with Queen Giovanna of Naples and Sicily. Death came to him during this visit to Rome. Standing like an unshakable pillar at his deathbed, Bridget said, "Go, my son, on your pilgrimage, with God's and my blessings." Many wondered and spoke ill of her complete resignation to Karl's death, but she answered, "Let them speak ill of me; it is enough for me to do what God wills." In her heart she preferred to see her son dead than a party to adultery.

Bridget was a capable homemaker, a watchful mother and a devoted wife. In 1343, the year before her husband's death, she made a pilgrimage with him to the Shrine of St. James at Compostela in Spain.

She said of the various stages of her life: "Virginity merits the crown, widowhood draws near to God, matrimony does not exclude from heaven." Though she found happiness in marriage and motherhood, a broader world opened to her after she became a widow.

Of all her property she kept only what was necessary to live simply and dress modestly, dividing the remainder between her children and the poor. Little by little the bonds were loosened which tied her to the world.

In a two-volume definitive work, *Saint Bridget of Sweden,* Johannes Jorgensen says of the final period of her life: "The old Bridget was dead. A new Bridget had come into being in her heart. . . . The whole world was given her as a new Ulfasa, infinitely bigger than the old." She now heard a voice say: "Thou shalt hear and see spiritual things, and my spirit shall remain with thee until death."

During the second half of her life, people came to her asking her prayers and guidance. She received many revelations, which have been published under the title *Bridget's Revelations.* Like Catherine of Siena, of whom she was a contemporary, she worked for the inner reformation of the Church. She is said to have possessed the gift of healing and to have performed other miracles.

In 1346 she founded a double community of men and women known as the Order of the Brigittines. This was held in great repute during the Middle Ages, and today a few houses of the Order survive in Germany, Holland, England and Spain.

Bridget's rule for the Order contains minute directions not only for the conduct of members, but for their dress and for furnishings of the house and church. The principal house was at Vadstena, on the shores of Lake Wettern, formerly the mansion of King Magnus Errikson, a kinsman of Bridget, and Queen Blanca. In 1349 Bridget journeyed to Rome to obtain confirmation of her Order. For the next twenty years, she resided in Rome, except for occasional visits to Naples and Sicily. She supported the efforts of Catherine of Siena to return the papacy to Rome, but she died four years before Gregory XI returned to Rome in 1377 from Avignon, France.

With her in Rome was Bridget's daughter Catherine, later to become a well-loved saint. Her sons Karl and Birger also visited her there.

Both Birger and Catherine accompanied their mother to the Holy Land when she was seventy. Old and feeble, she doubted whether she should make the journey, but she heard a voice say: "Am I not the Creator of all things in nature? I am able to make ill whom I choose, and to strengthen others if it seems good to me. I will be with you and I will direct your road, and I will lead you thither and lead you back to Rome, and I will provide you more amply with what you need than ever before."

In his biography of Bridget, Jorgensen comments that "the little girl who had wept one night at home in Finsta over the Passion of Christ, now knelt, a woman of seventy, on Golgotha."

She was taken ill on the return journey and died in Rome soon afterward. A procession of mourners carried her body home to her beloved Vadstena, and everywhere multitudes came out to offer her their homage. Except for Catherine of Siena, few medieval women were so much loved, and few influenced for good so many lives as did Bridget.

THE FIRST ENGLISHWOMAN TO WRITE A SPIRITUAL BOOK

JULIANA OF NORWICH (1342-1413?) is chiefly known as the author of *Revelations of Divine Love,* a book which is described by Evelyn Underhill as "the most beautiful of all English mystical works." Juliana is far better known today than when she lived She was a contemporary of Wycliffe, who was the first translator of the Bible into English, and of the English poet Chaucer.

Four manuscripts of her book are known to exist. These copies range in date from the middle of the fifteenth to the middle of the eighteenth centuries. Three of them are in the British Museum in London, and one is in the Bibliothèque Nationale, Paris. Until recent decades, Juliana's book was known to only a few scholars, but after it was printed in 1902, a renaissance of Lady Julian, or Dame Julian as she is sometimes called, began and her work became popular.

Few in Christendom have spoken so eloquently of the love of God as she did. The keystone of her faith is: "Our soul is oned to Him, unchangeable Goodness, and between God and our soul is neither wrath nor forgiveness in His sight." She declares that God is nearer to us than our own soul, for the soul is so deeply grounded in God, and so endlessly treasured, that we do not come to know it until we have first known of God.

Revelation of Divine Love focuses faith into one point—the oneness of the soul with God. This point she makes radiant with love and bright with joy. All differences are merged into one ultimate unity. All colors are blended into their original whiteness. Juliana's picture of the majesty of the Creator, and of the creature's dependence upon Him, is almost unequaled in imaginative insight and beauty.

The revelations recorded in her book were received at Norwich, England, on May 8, 1373, after Juliana had undergone seven days of mortal sickness. The experience became as significant to her as Paul's vision on the road to Damascus. So vivid were the five-hour revelations that twenty years after they occurred she dictated a minute account of them for her book.

Juliana was a religious recluse living in a cell built on the wall of the Norman Church of St. Julian at Norwich. King Stephen gave this church to the Benedictine nuns of Carrow in the twelfth century, and it is possible that Juliana was educated there and joined their Order.

Through her cell window she could speak with those who came to her, but this was practically her sole communication with the outside world. Through another window she heard mass and received communion.

The restored church, still in use today, has traces of Juliana's fourteenth-century cell. In May of 1953, the Bishop of Norwich dedicated a new chapel and shrine "in thanksgiving for the life and work of Dame Julian of Norwich."

Juliana attained profound knowledge of God despite her cloistered life and the tragedies of her time. She lived while the Hundred Years' War with France sapped England's strength. The Black Death spread over Europe and reached England when she was a child. Within the Church there was growing spiritual unrest during her lifetime. Her book is regarded as a rare reflection of the spirit of the Middle Ages. P. Franklin Chambers points out in his book *Juliana of Norwich, an Appreciation and an Anthology,* that "she accepted the tension as part of the mystery of life, and grew in grace in consequence, witnessing to another power, less apparent at the time but more penetrating and undermining, and destined to shake and shatter the growing worldliness in Church and State."

Robert H. Thouless, author of *The Lady Julian, A Psychological Study,* calls her one of those souls who is more creative than intellectual. He observes that Juliana made religion an art rather than a science.

A WANDERING FIFTEENTH-CENTURY EVANGELIST

MARGERY KEMPE (1373-1438?) was a writer who prayed, preached and healed. Her experiences, related in her autobiography, were lost to posterity for five hundred years. They came to light in an interesting way. In 1934, in the library of Pleasington Old Hall, Lancashire, an ancient manuscript lying next to a missal of 1340 was noticed and identified by Professor Hope Emily Allen of the University of Michigan as the missing *Book of Margery Kempe.*

This book was edited and published by its owner, Lt. Col. W. Butler-Bowden. It is important both as a religious treatise and as a literary landmark, for it is the earliest known autobiography in English. In it, for the first time, an English writer gives an intimate and revealing account of her life and thoughts.

Margery Kempe began to dictate her memoirs in 1432, the year after the trial and death of Joan of Arc. She finished the book in 1438.

She was the daughter of John of Burnham, five times mayor of Lynn and alderman of the Trinity Guild. She became the wife of John Kempe, burgess of Lynn, by whom she had fourteen children. In 1413, however, she and her husband took vows of chastity before Philip Repingdon, Bishop of Lincoln.

Margery Kempe's memoirs, like Augustine's *Confessions,* are mercilessly honest in portraying her character. She writes of her early love for fine garments and how she enjoyed parading about in them, so that men would stare at her. She reveals, too, that she was a brewer for three or four years and later turned to milling. But ill luck so dogged her brewing and milling that others saw in this a call for her to leave worldly things. As she came to realize that this interpretation might be correct, she gave more time to prayer and contemplation.

Her religious enthusiasm is revealed in her autobiography. Like Joan of Arc, she heard voices. Like some of the earliest Christians, she healed the sick. One of her most remarkable healings took place when she went to a woman who lost her mind after childbirth. Margery told her at her bedside, "I behold many fair angels about you," and, praying for her, assured her that God would restore her again.

Another story about her tells how, in 1421, when there was a great fire in Lynn and the Church of St. Margaret was threatened, Margery went inside the church to pray. Although the sparks were falling about her, she did not leave until men with snow on their clothes came in to tell her that God had sent "a fair snow to quench the fire." It was characteristic that through all her trials, Margery Kempe demonstrated her striving to be closer to God.

She had many eventful journeys rarely experienced by women of her time. Once, after going from England to Italy, she had to wait in Venice for some months for a pilgrim ship to the Holy Land. She was finally able to embark in 1414. For about a month she journeyed quite unafraid through storms and among pirates and enemy vessels. On her arrival in Jerusalem, she was so eager to tread places made holy by Christ that she could scarcely stay on her donkey. At Easter time in 1415 she turned homeward, after being absent from England for eighteen months.

Her habit of asking for divine guidance increased with the years. Two years after her return from the Holy Land, she decided to go to the great Shrine of St. James at Compostela in Spain, where the saint's remains were kept.

Before her departure she heard a voice say: "Daughter, study not for any money, for I shall provide for thee." She remained at the shrine for a fortnight, and wrote that "the creature" (which she always called herself in contrast to the Creator) had "great cheer, both bodily and of the spirit."

Margery Kempe spent the next few years at Lynn. In her old age she accompanied her widowed, foreign daughter-in-law to her home in Danzig, Germany. She returned overland through a warring Germany in order to avoid the voyage across the North Sea. She then made a pilgrimage to Wilsnack, but became ill on the way. At last, impeded by age and illness, she reached Calais and crossed the English Channel to Dover. From there she went to Canterbury and finally entered London where she remained for a short time. In a curious cloth of canvas, which she wore as if it were a "sacken" apron, she attracted considerable attention. She refused to eat meat. Churches were closed to her. Many derided her. But she prayed only for more of God's love. After many persecutions and trials, she finally arrived at her home in Lynn. It had been a phenomenal journey for a woman of medieval times, especially for one in her sixties who often traveled alone.

Margery Kempe recorded that as she traveled she prayed: "Highly I thank Thee if Thou wouldst let me suffer any pain in this world in remission of my sins and increase of my merit in Heaven."

In her last years, after these eventful travels, she attempted to record her life. Since she was uneducated, she had to find someone who was willing to take down her story. Finally she persuaded a priest to act as her scribe. When the book was finished in 1438, Margery's life was drawing to an end.

Though she lived and died an eccentric, many worth-while things are attributed to her. She sought to live up to one of her best-known sayings: "Every good thought is a speech of God."

SHE LIVED IN THE WORLD BUT DID NOT CONFORM TO IT

CATHERINE OF GENOA (1447-1510), as a wife and then a widow, became a constructive mystic, a profound thinker, an original teacher and a busy and practical philanthropist. She did all this not in the cloister but in her own home and in the hospital where she served.

Catherine Fieschi was born a year after Christopher Columbus, and seventy years after Catherine of Siena, for whom she was named. She belonged to two illustrious families, her father being related to two popes, and her mother belonging to an old and noble Italian family.

In 1463, in the Cathedral of Lorenzo, she became the bride of Giuliano Adorno, who was of another ancient and wealthy family. Giuliano was undisciplined and devoted to the pleasures of the world. When Catherine tried to live the kind of life he enjoyed, she sank into spiritual stagnation.

She began to take walks through the woods to a monastery, and to use her leisure time for reading spiritual books. She found that these gave her more pleasure than anything she had enjoyed as a girl or as a young woman in the Fieschi Palace of her parents, or in the palace of her husband's parents.

Catherine was a beautiful, tall woman with a noble oval face, possessing a lofty brow, finely formed nose, winning countenance and delicate complexion. In the years during which she devoted herself to the things of the spirit she developed a radiant expression. Lucy Menzies writes of this period of Catherine's life in an excellent sketch in a book entitled *Mirrors of the Holy*. She says Catherine's "real personality was transformed and merged in God, the Supreme Spirit."

Catherine's husband squandered his fortune and had to leave his palace. Afterward, when he too had turned to religion, he gained courage to tell Catherine that he was the father of a small daughter by another woman. She was able to receive this news without reproaching him.

They lived in a simple house, and her husband became a member of the Third Order of Francis. Catherine herself never joined an order but demonstrated by her own daily life that God can reach the soul in the home just as He does in a religious order.

As evidence of this she entered upon a period of complete self-dedication. She spent six hours daily in prayer, cleansed the houses of the poor from disgusting filth, and lovingly tended the sick, ministering to their spiritual as well as to their bodily needs.

For four penitential years she sought to cleanse herself of all sin, until her mind became so clear and free and filled with God that nothing else entered it. She would say to her Lord: "I do not want that which proceedeth from Thee, I want Thee alone, O Tender Love." Her prayers strengthened and invigorated her body and soul.

Even though she practiced fasting for nearly twenty-three years, as she became more active in good works she seemed to acquire greater strength and radiance. She saw God in everything. She wrote of Him:

The glorious God is the whole essence of things both visible and invisible. He is that Infinite Perfection, that Boundless Love which gives life to the soul, without which it cannot live. . . . Every good thing belongs to God. All the sanctity of the saints is outside of them and all is God.

Through her detachment from self and her absolute confidence in God, she lost her tenseness and achieved tranquillity. In 1479 she and her husband moved from their simple home to two rooms in the hospital in Genoa. There she spent all of her time caring for the sick. Her husband died the following year but Catherine worked on. In 1490 she was elected matron of the hospital, an office she held for six years. In this capacity she managed the hospital funds and supervised its organization and details. At the same time she was spiritual mother of a large group of disciples.

When plague broke out in 1493, Catherine became the central figure in the grim fight between life and death. She organized open-air wards and filled the hospital grounds with sailcloth tents where others helped to nurse the plague-stricken people.

A practical woman as well as a visionary, she never permitted her spiritual longings to keep her from material responsibilities. After her husband's death, she successfully managed the legacies he had left, including one for his daughter and her mother.

In her last years she was stricken with a nervous illness but was able to put it bravely behind her as something to be transcended. She died in September 1510.

One of her best-known works is *The Pure Love of God,* published in her native city of Genoa in 1511. This book explains the soul's purification after death, a doctrine which she particularly stressed. Another of her writings, *Treatise on Purgatory,* has for its theme the idea that the body is the purgatory of the soul. In this, Catherine shows that she herself gladly submitted to the purifying disciplines of the world, for they alone could draw her closer to the longed-for union with God. In addition, four hundred of Catherine's letters to others have been preserved.

One of the finest modern treatments of her life and work is Baron F. von Hügel's *The Mystical Element of Religion as Studied in Saint Catherine of Genoa and Her Friends.* Evelyn Underhill has also written understandingly of Catherine of Genoa in *The Mystics of the Church* and *Mysticism.* She refers to her as a woman who was completely consecrated to the purpose of the spirit.

In 1944 Pope Pius XII proclaimed her Patroness of the Hospitals in Italy.

SHE OPENED HER HOME TO THE FIRST PROTESTANTS

ANNA REINHARD ZWINGLI (1487-1538?) was the wife of Huldreich Zwingli, the Swiss clergyman who led the Protestant Reformation in his country. The Zwingli home was a gathering place for those who openly opposed the Pope and broke with the Roman Catholic Church.

Zwingli, a priest, began preaching in 1519 against clerical celibacy, monasticism, and many other church practices. In 1522 he was privately married to Anna Reinhard, a widow with three children. This private marriage started much malicious gossip and in 1524, a year before Martin Luther married the former nun Katherine von Bora, Zwingli publicly celebrated his marriage to Anna Reinhard, thus crowning his arguments against the enforced celibacy of the clergy.

Anna was the daughter of Oswald Reinhard, landlord of the Little Horse Inn, and Elizabet Wynzuern. She has been described as a beautiful girl. Her first husband, Hans Meyer von Knonau, who belonged to a distinguished family, was disinherited for marrying Anna. At his death she was left with two daughters, Margaret and Agatha, and a son Gerrold to support. The little court in Cathedral Lane where she spent her widowhood was not far from Zwingli's church in Zurich, and she became one of his most attentive listeners. Zwingli's fatherly care of her son Gerrold prepared the way for their marriage. She was a charitable woman known in Zurich as the "apostolic Dorcas," and Zwingli saw in Anna the qualities of a good wife. Anna and Zwingli had four children: two daughters, Regula and Anna, and two sons, Wilhelm and Huldreich.

Only one short letter of those Zwingli wrote his wife survives. That was written from Berne on the birth of one of their sons. "Grace and peace from God," he says. "Dearest wife, I thank God that He has bestowed on you a happy birth. He helps us to bring up the children according to His will. Herewith I commend you to God! Pray for me and for all of us. Give my love to all your children, especially Margaret; comfort her on my behalf."

Zwingli never ceased to be interested in the children of Anna's first marriage. He dedicated to Gerrold his *Little Manual of Christian Education for Youth*, now regarded as one of the educational treasures of the sixteenth century.

In this manual Zwingli warns the lad against seeking honor and praise by wearing expensive clothes and against entering into foolish love affairs. He advises him to choose someone to love whose ways he will be able to endure forever, even in marriage. He tells the boy that "he is not a Christian who only talks a lot about God, but he who makes an effort to do great things with the help of God." He also tells him to consider that the only hallmarks of distinction are virtue, piety and honor, and that nobility, beauty and riches are not the true blessings of life, for they are subject to changes of fortune. Zwingli's final message to the boy is: "May God lead you safely through these things, so that you may never be separated from Him."

Anna no doubt rejoiced in her husband's roles both as a father and as a clergyman boldly leading in reforms within the Church. His latter role brought her many fears and cares. It also brought tragedy. On October 11, 1531, news came that an army of the Catholic states in the Swiss Confederation were approaching Zurich. Zwingli quickly assembled a Protestant army and rode forth on his horse as chaplain with his Bible under his arm. Early in the battle, he was slain. Anna's son Gerrold, her son-in-law, her brother-in-law and her brother all died in this battle.

Left with no material resources, the twice-widowed Anna and her children found lodging with Zwingli's successor as chief pastor at Zurich, Heinrich Bullinger. In his care of Anna, Bullinger has been compared to John, the disciple to whom Jesus entrusted His mother.

For seven years till her death about 1538, Anna remained in the Bullinger home. Her daughter Regula married Rudolf Gwalther, the adopted son of Bullinger and his successor in the office of chief district clergyman. During the Marian persecution in England, when many refugees came to Switzerland, Regula followed the example of her hospitable mother and opened her home to them. Regula inherited her love for people from Anna, who, after more than three centuries, is still remembered as the helpmate of the greatest Swiss reformer.

A GREAT REFORMER'S FAITHFUL WIFE

IDELETTE DE BURES (?-1549), wife of John Calvin, French reformer and theologian, was called by him "the excellent companion of my life, the ever faithful assistant of my ministry." In replying to friends who had been urging him to marry, he said:

Remember what I expect from one who is to be my companion for life. I do not belong to the class of loving fools, who, when once smitten with a fine figure, are ready to expend their affection even on the faults of her whom they have fallen in love with. The only kind of beauty which can win my soul, is a woman who is gentle, pure, modest, economical, patient, and who is likely to interest herself about my health.

Calvin found the high ideals that he sought in Idelette de Bures, widow of Jean Stordeur, who had died of the plague and left her with three children. Before Stordeur's death, Calvin had converted the family to the ideals of the Reformation and he continued to visit the widow, but with no thought of marriage. Although he admired her, it was not until after his friends suggested that he should marry that he began to court her.

Their marriage was celebrated in Strasbourg in September 1540, in a large public ceremony to which some of the Swiss and French towns sent deputies, for Calvin was already an important figure. The previous year he had published his commentary on Romans. It was followed by commentaries on most of the other books of the Bible. Four years earlier he had published *Institutes of the Christian Religion*, still considered one of the most important contributions to Christian literature.

Immediately after his marriage to Idelette, Calvin was summoned to conferences at Hagenau and Worms. He left his wife at Strasbourg. When the plague broke out there Calvin's duty to the Protestant cause prevented his return to his wife. Writing to a friend he said: "Day and night I see my wife before my eyes, who is in the midst of these dangers without help and advice because her husband is away. I make great efforts to resist my grievous anxiety. I have recourse to prayer and holy meditation." Idelette's life was spared, and he was soon able to return to her in Strasbourg.

When he was called in September 1541 to the strongly Protestant city of Geneva, the council there sent three horses and a carriage to bring his wife and her household. The council allotted the Calvin family a house with a garden on the gently sloping banks of the Lake of Geneva, with a view of the Alps in the distance. There, during Calvin's periods of stress, when he suffered with headaches and other illnesses, his wife watched by his bedside. When adverse news came, she strengthened and comforted him. When rebellious people raged through the streets, crying out against her husband—who was both civil and ecclesiastical head of Geneva—Idelette retired to her room, fell on her knees and prayed.

Her house became a sanctuary for refugees, and she cared for them so diligently that she was accused of being more solicitous of strangers than of the people of Geneva. She realized, however, that many to whom she gave aid were important members of her husband's reform movement. Some carried her husband's doctrines across Western Europe and strengthened members of the Reformed Church of Holland, the Presbyterians of Scotland, the Puritans in England and the Huguenots in France.

On July 28, 1542, their child Jacques was born. Unhappily, he lived only a few days. Writing to a friend, Calvin said:

Salute all the brethren—salute also thy wife, to whom mine sends her thanks for the sweet and holy consolation she received from her. She would write to acknowledge these with her own hand, but she had not strength to dictate a few words. In that He hath taken away our son, He hath stricken us sorely, but He is our Father. He knoweth what is meet for His children.

The Calvins had four other children, all of whom died in infancy.

Idelette was never strong. Some days before her death, which occurred April 5, 1549, a friend urged her to speak to Calvin about her children by a former marriage. Having entire confidence that he would do his duty by them, she answered:

> The chief thing is that they should live a godly life. It is not necessary to make my husband promise to bring them up in holiness and fear of God. If they be pious I am confident that he will be to them an unsought father; if they be not, they do not deserve that I should ask anything for them.

Three days before her death, Calvin assured her that he would care for the children as if they were his own. When she told him, "I have already commended them to the Lord," his reply was: "That will not prevent my caring for them." She answered: "I am sure you will not neglect the children who, you know, are commended to the Lord."

Relating this conversation later, Calvin said: "This greatness of soul will influence me more powerfully than a hundred commendations would have done."

To Benedict Textor, the distinguished physician who attended Idelette in her last illness, Calvin dedicated his *Commentary on the Second Epistle of Paul to the Thessalonians.*

Calvin never married again. Seven years later, writing to Richard de Valleville, minister of the French Protestant congregation at Frankfort, about the loss of his wife, Calvin referred to his own great distress of mind under a similar loss. His attachment to Idelette was so deep that he could never consider taking another wife.

A MINISTERING ANGEL TO REFORMATION REFUGEES

ANNA BULLINGER (1504?-1564) was a nun before her marriage to Heinrich Bullinger, the Swiss reformer who succeeded Zwingli as chief pastor at Zurich.

She won renown as a hostess to refugees during the Reformation when her husband became something of an oracle among the English higher clergy who had fled to Zurich during the reign of Mary. Celio Curione, one of the Italian members of the reform movement, wrote a letter of thanks in which he called Bullinger a bishop according to the description of a bishop given by Paul in I Timothy 3:1-7. He further commented: "Your friendliness and your Christian care for us during our stay with you obliges me to give you my inmost thanks. Greet for us very heartily your wife, who showed herself so full of kindly service and love."

Anna's maiden name was Adlischweiler, and the date of her birth was probably 1504, the same year her husband was born. She was only eight when her father died in battle. Her sick mother placed her in the cloister of Oedenbach at Zurich. Here she later became a nun. Her mother remained in the convent as a boarder.

When Zwingli was ordered by the City Council of Zurich to preach in that city, his sermons had a double effect in the convent. Some of the nuns welcomed the news of the Reformation; others became bitter. Soon Anna was the only nun left in the cloister and would not have remained had it not been for her sick mother.

One day Leo Juda, the chaplain for the nunnery, took Bullinger with him to the convent, where he met Anna. He later proposed marriage to her by letter, summing up his feelings by assuring her "the greatest, surest treasure that you will find in me, is a fear of God, piety, fidelity and love, which with joy I will show you." He also promised that he would labor earnestly in her behalf.

Ten days later Anna sent her acceptance to Bullinger but said that she wanted to delay her marriage on account of the illness of her mother. Meanwhile Bullinger prepared her for her future position as his wife by writing for her a small book entitled *Concerning Female Training, and How a Daughter Should Guide Her Conduct and Life.*

They were married in 1529, following her mother's death and after he had been licensed by the Zurich Synod to succeed his father as pastor at Bremgarten, Argau, Switzerland. Two daughters were born to them while they lived there.

After the battle at Cappel on October 11, 1531, in which Zwingli fell, Bullinger and his family were no longer safe. While Roman Catholic armies were attacking Protestant ministers, Bullinger fled from Bremgarten with his aged father and brother. They had hardly left when Catholic soldiers plundered his house and quartered thirty soldiers there. Anna escaped with her two children, one aged six months and the other eighteen months. She made her way through the city gate, wresting the key from the guard by force. She was finally able to join her husband at Zurich.

At twenty-seven, Bullinger was elected to Zwingli's place in the cathedral in Zurich. His new position brought much honor to his wife, but also many cares. Not only did her family grow by the birth of one child almost yearly until they numbered eleven, but as the wife of the chief pastor at Zurich she had to make a home for many refugees. Among these were Anna Reinhard Zwingli and her children, as well as several young men who became important in the Reformation.

Anna practiced many economies, for she had to manage on a small income. The letter Bullinger wrote to his eldest son at Strasbourg on December 20, 1553, reflects their difficulties:

Your mother makes big eyes when you already speak of needing another pair of shoes for the winter. It is hardly fifteen weeks since you left us, when you took three pairs with you, the red, the gray and black. At this rate you will need six pairs a year. I have more than enough with two. Do not let your shoes go to pieces, but get them mended in time.

Ten months later he praised his son for his economy.

Anna was aided in her household duties by a maid named Brigette, who has been called the model servant of the Reformation. In a letter of 1556 to his son Henry at Strasbourg, Bullinger wrote: "Your five sisters greet you, and especially Brigette, who sends to you a present of three groschen."

Anna died in 1564 of the plague. Her husband became ill with it first, and forgetful of herself, she nursed him back to health at the cost of her own life. Bullinger survived her by eleven years.

A FRIEND OF THE PERSECUTED DURING THE REFORMATION

RENÉE OF FRANCE (1510-1575), the second daughter of King Louis XII of France and Anne of Brittany, was born at Blois on October 25, 1510. She was married with great pomp at the age of eighteen to Hercules of Este, Duke of Ferrara, a member of one of the oldest and most powerful families of Italy. Many other noted names in European history are associated with that of Renée. Her mother-in-law was Lucretia Borgia, daughter of Pope Alexander VI. Her daughter Anna was married to François de Lorraine, second Duke de Guise and powerful enemy of the Huguenots during the Reformation. Later he was the cause of many of Renée's heartaches. Her niece by marriage was Catherine de Médicis, Queen of France. Among her close friends were Vittoria Colonna, one of the great spirits of the Italian Renaissance, and Margaret of Navarre, godmother of the French Reformation. But Renée's lasting place in history is as a friend of the great reformer John Calvin and of the persecuted Huguenots in France.

Her governess, Mme de Souboise, an Englishwoman of fine qualities, not only taught Renée to love the Scriptures from her own Wycliffe Bible, but managed to keep her from the evils of the court of Francis I of France.

After Renée's marriage, she lived in a beautiful villa on the Po River. The estate included a chapel decorated by famous artists of the day, gardens with fountains, shady walks and rare plants and birds. When her father-in-law Alfonso died, her husband became Duke of Ferrara and Renée went to live at the family court, a home filled with such works of art as paintings by Titian. Here her five children were born—two sons and three daughters.

The court became a center for those interested in religion. A translation of the Old Testament from the Hebrew into Italian was dedicated "To the Most Illustrious Lady Renée of France, Duchess of Ferrara." Among the famous literary and religious people who visited her court was Clément Marot who wrote a metrical version of the Psalms. Young Calvin resided at her court under the assumed name of Charles d'Esperville after he was exiled from France. He had just completed writing his *Institutes of the Christian Religion.* Unfortunately, Renée's husband was unsympathetic with the ideas of the Reformation. He had Calvin arrested for heresy and carried off by an armed force. Renée secretly equipped a larger group who overtook the party, recaptured Calvin and escorted him to a place of safety.

Renée's husband not only banished Calvin and his friends but finally took their children from Renée and threw her into prison. How far she humbled herself before her persecutors has not been revealed, but she did send for a Jesuit priest and received the Eucharist from him. Her husband, whose dukedom was a feudatory of the Pope, claimed to be well satisfied, but true domestic confidence was never re-established. In her heart Renée remained a friend of the persecuted.

At the Duke's death in 1559, he bequeathed a fortune to his wife on condition that she remain loyal to his Catholic faith. No longer concealing her religious views, Renée spoke out in favor of the Calvinists. Her own son gave her the alternative of becoming a Catholic or of leaving Italy. She chose the latter, amid great mourning on the part of the people of Ferrara.

When she returned to her girlhood home in France, she found the spirit of persecution even more violent than it had been in Italy. It was unsafe for her to stay in Paris and she retired to her ancestral castle at Montargis, on the edge of a forest sixty miles southeast of Paris.

Here she stood up for the persecuted Huguenots and ministers of the Reformed faith against enemies, not only protecting but feeding and encouraging them with Christian tenderness. It is said that three hundred sat at her table at one time. Her castle became known as Hôtel Dieu, or "Hotel of the Lord."

During her first year at Montargis Renée established Protestant worship in her castle, employed two Reformed ministers and built a chapel where people could worship according to the new faith.

Her position was especially difficult because her son-in-law, the Duke de Guise, headed the Catholic party in France. Renée aided his enemies, the Huguenots, during the perilous days before and after St. Bartholomew's Day, August 24, 1572, when thousands of Protestants were murdered in Paris and throughout France.

Hearing that the Duke de Guise and her nephew King Charles IX were to pass through Montargis, Renée threw open her doors to the terrified Protestants. She pleaded for them and the king promised her that not one should be molested.

The Duke de Guise called her castle "a nest of Huguenots," and as soon as the king's army had withdrawn, he deprived her of the government of Montargis and forbade her servants to hear the Reformed ministers preach.

Catherine de Médicis sent letters saying that the castle was needed for military purposes, and requested that Renée take up her abode in one of three other palaces. With queenly dignity Renée met Melicorne, the officer who brought this message, but refused to surrender the castle to him. She told him that Montargis was not a place of military importance, and that it was not for the king's service that they wished to remove her. While Melicorne was awaiting orders from Paris to destroy the castle, a courier came in haste with the news that the Duke de Guise had been assassinated. Montargis was saved in the confusion that followed.

The trials of the persecuted Huguenots were not over. Melicorne again appeared at the gates of her city, this time bringing an order from King Charles IX that the fugitives under her care leave. She asked for a few days for preparations, then bought wagons and fitted them with provisions. Commending the weeping men and women and terrified children to God's mercy, she hurried them away, bidding them leave the country as quickly as possible.

Looking behind them, the fleeing saw two hundred armed horsemen in pursuit. At the moment when all seemed lost, eight hundred armed Huguenots came from behind a hill, attacked the king's horsemen and put them to flight. Then they escorted the nearly five hundred helpless fugitives to a place of safety.

Soon Renée was virtually alone in her castle. She died there in 1575 and was buried in the castle's chapel, where she had worshiped for sixteen years.

SHE WAS BURNED AT THE STAKE BECAUSE OF HER RELIGIOUS BELIEFS

ANNE ASKEW—also Ascue—(1521?-1546), an English Protestant martyr, was burned at the stake because of her beliefs concerning the Lord's Supper. She denied the real body and blood of Jesus Christ in the sacrament at the altar, insisting that God was not actually present in the wafer and wine itself. She also declared she would rather read five lines in the Bible than hear five masses in the temple.

Anne Askew was born at Stallingborough, the second daughter of Sir

William Askew of South Kelsey, Lincoln. She became the wife of Thomas Kyme and the mother of their two children. When her husband, who was a Catholic, turned her out of their home because of her religious beliefs, she journeyed to London and made friends with Joan Bocher and other Protestants who were being persecuted by the Catholics.

She was brought before the Lord Mayor of London, who asked: "Thou foolish woman, sayest thou, that the priests cannot make the body of Christ?" And she answered: "I say so, my Lord; for I have read that God made man; but that man can make God, I never yet read, nor, I suppose, ever shall read."

Then the Lord Mayor questioned her: "After the words of consecration, is it not the Lord's body?" And she answered this time: "No, but it is consecrated bread." Finally he asked: "What if a mouse eat it after the consecration? What shall become of the mouse?" Her answer was: "Alack poor mouse!" Because she would not deny her religious beliefs regarding the Lord's Supper, she was imprisoned in the gloomy dungeon of Newgate Prison in London. Later, the authorities dragged her to the torture chamber in the Tower of London and put her on the rack in an effort to make her recant.

When her limp form, dressed in a white robe, was raised from the rack, she still would not recant. "Then I was brought to a house and laid in a bed, with as weary and painful bones as ever had patient Job," she reports. "Then my Lord Chancellor sent me word, if I would leave my opinion, I should want nothing; if I would not, I should forthwith to Newgate, and so be burned. I sent him word again that I would rather die than break my faith."

During the interval between her torture and death, she gave herself to prayer. One of her prayers at this time reveals her courage and charity:

O Lord! I have more enemies now, than there be hairs on my head; yet, Lord, let them never overcome me with vain words, but fight Thou, Lord, in my stead; for on Thee I cast my care. With all the spite they can imagine, they fall upon me, who am Thy poor creature. Yet, sweet Lord, let me not set by them that are against me; for in Thee is my delight. And, Lord, I heartily desire of Thee, that Thou wilt of Thy merciful goodness forgive them that violence which they do, and have done unto me. Open also their blind hearts, that they may hereafter do that thing in Thy sight which is only acceptable before Thee, and so set forth Thy verity aright, without all vain fantasies of sinful men. So be it, Lord.

On June 18, 1546, she was brought before a special commission without jury or witness, and was condemned, on her beliefs, to be burned. Because her body had been so crippled on the rack, she was taken to the stake in a chair, tied up in the middle with a chain and burned as a heretic at Smith-field July 16, 1546.

Her self-possession and her skill in argument during her trial had won her much support. When her own account of her life and the events leading up to her martyrdom was published by her contemporary J. Bales, the Protestant cause was greatly strengthened.

HER HOUSE WAS A CENTER OF RELIGIOUS RENAISSANCE

MME BARBE ACARIE (1566-1618) turned her Paris home into a center for those who desired to live a spiritual life. Two of the most famous men who came to her were Vincent de Paul and Francis de Sales. Mme Acarie is said to have inspired much of what Francis wrote in his *Treatise of the Love of God*.

"One may frankly say that of all the beacons of light lit during the reign of Henry IV, none equalled her in brilliance, intensity or radiance," says Lucy Menzies in her excellent account of Mme Acarie in *Mirrors of the Holy*.

It was through Mme Acarie's influence with King Henry IV and his court that the reformed Carmelites were established in France in 1604, with the assistance of nuns from Teresa of Ávila's centers in Spain.

Her father, Nicolas Avrillot, was a wealthy aristocrat; her mother belonged to one of the oldest Parisian families. At sixteen she was married to Pierre Acarie, a rich nobleman who was undisciplined, easy to anger and a squanderer of a large fortune. She worked hard to re-establish his good name and succeeded in restoring the family fortune and in educating her children.

A woman who thought deeply, she was convinced that "one must search right down into the depths of the soul to see if God is there, or at least if He will come there after religion has cultivated the soul."

During the last four years of her life, Mme Acarie became a humble lay sister at the Carmelite convent at Amiens, where her eldest daughter was Sub-Prioress. Two other daughters followed in her footsteps.

Mme Acarie died at fifty-two. For thirty-two years she had never known what it was to be without pain, and had used crutches most of that time. She said that suffering taught her that she herself was nothing, "only a small channel whose waters flowed from the Infinite Ocean of the Goodness of God."

She is an outstanding example of a woman who, living in her own home with a husband and six children, managed to preside over a large mansion, and who at the same time was able to train novices and inspire new ardor in religious orders.

THE FAITHFUL WIVES OF JOHN KNOX

MARJORY BOWES KNOX (1538?-1560), the first wife of John Knox, Scottish Reformer and Founder of Scottish Presbyterianism, was the daughter of Richard Bowes, the captain of Norham Castle, and of Elizabeth Bowes, co-heiress of Aske in Yorkshire. Their home was six miles up the Tweed from Berwick, Scotland, where Knox not only propagated Protestantism but sowed some of the earliest seeds of English Puritanism.

The mother, Elizabeth Bowes, was the earliest of that little band of faithful women who aided the Reformer both in religious ardor and with their money. Her correspondence with Knox on religious matters is an important source of information on Knox's life. Although her husband remained in the Roman Church, she gave Knox faithful support in his new Reform and he in turn became her spiritual adviser.

Marjory accompanied her mother when she first went to hear Knox preach at Berwick, the center of one of the memorable periods in the Reformer's life. However, it was not to Marjory, then in her early teens, but to her mother, a mature woman in her late forties, that Knox poured out his religious confidences. In the letters, which were always passing between them, he addressed her most often as "Dearly Beloved Mother." "In my conscience I judge," he wrote, "by the Holy Spirit of my God, I am fully certified, that ye are a member of Christ's body." In another letter to her, he declared: "There is none with whom I would more gladly speak."

Although many letters to Elizabeth Bowes survive, few to Marjory are extant. In one, a brief but dignified account, he addresses Marjory as "Dearly Beloved Sister in the common faith of Jesus our Saviour." This letter focuses entirely on "false teachers" and references to her mother's doubts and conflicts. Ending abruptly, he says: "I think this is the first letter that ever I wrote to you. In great haste, your brother, John Knox." In another letter to his "most dear sister," he writes: "Be sure I will not forget your company," adding as if he had gone too far, "so long as mortal man may remember any earthly creature."

From incidental references, it is inferred that Mrs. Bowes arranged the engagement between Knox and her daughter, who was over thirty years his junior. They were married in 1555, when she was about seventeen. The wedding seems to have taken place in the summer after he left Geneva and while he was visiting in Berwick on his way to Edinburgh. Soon after their marriage, he received a summons from his congregation at Geneva to continue his ministry with them. On the eve of his departure, he sent on before him, to Dieppe, his wife and his mother-in-law, a manservant and a pupil called Patrick. They arrived in Geneva in early September. In addition to his preaching in Geneva, Knox studied Greek and Hebrew and was in communication with Calvin and other Reformers. Here two sons, Nathaniel and Eleazar, were born to Marjory and John Knox.

In spite of poor health, Marjory appears to have supported her husband with sympathy and practical help. She died in Edinburgh in 1560, after five short years of married life. Her two sons were later educated at Cambridge, England, where in 1580 Nathaniel died. Eleazar, after an academic career of considerable distinction, became Vicar of Clacton Magna, in the archdeaconry of Colchester, in 1587. He died four years later. Neither son left children. This tribute is paid to their mother in *John Knox* by Marion Harland:

> Marjory Bowes Knox shrinks into the background of our picture, cast into insignificance by the tremendous personality of her husband, and the masterful forwardness of her mother. Yet rugged Calvin found her passing sweet, and to Knox she was superlatively dear. Her three years of patient waiting upon her father's will and upon her fiancés fortunes; her unmurmuring endurance of the agonized suspense of the two years' separation from her newly made husband, an exiled wanderer, penniless and a stranger in a foreign land, entitle her to a place upon the roll of unconsidered heroines, the crownless martyrs of whom the world is not worthy.

Four years after the death of Marjory, Knox was married to Margaret Stuart.

MARGARET STUART KNOX (1547?-1612) was a daughter of Andrew Stuart (Lord Ochiltree) and a relative of Scotland's Queen, Mary Stuart.

There is an interesting anecdote that tells how she and Knox became engaged. Again a mother played a leading role, this time Lady Ochiltree.

Knox was traveling in western Scotland, preaching to several families who were converts to the Protestant religion. Among these were Lord and Lady Ochiltree. Her ladyship kept a chamber, table, stool and candlestick in readiness for "the prophet," as Knox was known among them.

One night Lady Ochiltree suggested to Knox that he ought to marry again.

"Madame," said Knox, who was in his late fifties, "I think nobody will take such a wanderer as I."

"Sir, if that be your objection, I will make inquiry to find an answer by our next meeting."

Lady Ochiltree addressed her eldest daughter, telling her she would be happy if she could marry Mr. Knox. But she turned down the proposal, and hoped her mother would find some better husband for her than this poor wanderer.

Lady Ochiltree addressed herself to her second daughter, who answered as had the eldest. Then her ladyship spoke to her third daughter, Margaret, who was about seventeen years of age.

"Mother," she replied, "I'll be very willing to marry him, but I fear he will not take me."

To which her ladyship replied: "If that be all your objection, I'll soon get an answer."

The next evening at supper, the lady said to Mr. Knox: "Sir, I have been considering on a wife for you, and find one very willing."

"Who is it madame?" he asked.

"My young daughter sitting beside you at the table," she answered.

Addressing himself to the young lady, he said: "My bird, are you willing to marry me?" "Yes, sir," she answered, "only I fear you'll not be willing to take me."

"My bird," he said, "if you be willing to take me, you must take your venture of God's providence, as I do. I go through the country sometimes on foot, with a wallet on my arm, a shirt, a clean band, and a Bible in it. You must put some things in it for yourself, and if I bid you take the wallet you must do it, and go where I go, and lodge where I lodge." And she said: "I'll do all this." "Will you be as good as your word?" he asked. And she answered: "Yes, I will."

They were married at St. Giles' Church on Palm Sunday in 1564. There was criticism of this union not only because Geneva had spoken out against marriages in the ministry, but also because Knox was more than forty years older than his bride.

Despite criticism, the marriage seems to have been a happy one. Knox took his bride to his house in Edinburgh by the Tron Church, the house where Marjory had died and where her mother, Elizabeth Bowes, now lived with his two sons.

By Margaret, Knox had three daughters, Martha, Margaret and Elizabeth. The most vivid picture that history hands down of her faithfulness as a wife is that of her seated at his bedside as he lay dying in 1572, about eight years after their marriage. In the middle of the day he asked her to read the fifteenth chapter of the First Epistle to the Corinthians, which treats of the Resurrection. In the late afternoon he said to her, "Go read where I cast my first anchor," and she read the seventeenth chapter of John. He died following bedtime prayers.

In 1594 their daughter Elizabeth Knox married John Welsh, minister of

Ayr. This Scottish Reformer became famous for his bold resistance to the Crown's encroachments upon the church and liberties of the people. Once James VI had Welsh and six other ministers arrested. The brave Elizabeth left her children at Ayr and went to Edinburgh in mid-winter to attend her husband's trial. When James VI asked her who her father was, she replied: "John Knox."

"Knox and Welsh!" the king exclaimed. "The Devil never made such a match as that!"

She begged that her husband, now ill from his long imprisonment, might return from England to his native Scotland. The king said he would grant her request, if her husband would submit to the bishops. Arising in all her dignity, she hurled back the challenge that she had rather keep him in England than return to their native Scotland under those conditions.

Her husband, who had been one of the strong pillars of the church, died soon afterward. She returned to Scotland but survived him only two years. Three of their six children survived her, and among these was Josiah, who became one of the founders of the Presbyterian Church in Ulster. Her grandson John also followed in the footsteps of his grandfather and of his great-grandfather, John Knox, thus fulfilling God's promise to the righteous, to the third and fourth generations.

HER "DAUGHTERS" WENT ON ERRANDS OF MERCY

JANE FRANCES FREMYOT DE CHANTAL (1572-1641) and Francis de Sales founded the Order of Visitation for young girls and widows who were eager to enter religious service but were unable to endure the severe ascetic life of the religious houses of the seventeenth century. The primary service of the Order was teaching and caring for the sick.

Mme de Chantal never ceased to tell her spiritual daughters that it was necessary to die to self and live to God. "We come into the world unpolished and full of evil inclinations, which we must labor to cut away," she told them. "We must pray and love while we are at our recreation, working, speaking or resting."

She first heard Francis de Sales speak in 1604. Later he inquired: "Who was the widow who listened so attentively to the word of the Gospel?" He became her spiritual adviser and aided her in the founding of the Order in 1610 at Annecy, France. Of her he said: "I have found the Virtuous Woman whom Solomon had difficulty in finding in Jerusalem." Their long friendship, one of the most inspiring in religious history, brought into existence the ideal of the Order, which was a blend of her mysticism with his teachings. She in turn inspired him in his writing of *The Devout Life* and *The Love of God.*

The Order of Visitation, it has been said, marked a genuine forward movement in the corporate expression of Christian mysticism. "The importance of Mme de Chantal and Francis consists in the fact that they realized and gave form to this ideal," states Evelyn Underhill in *The Mystics of the Church.*

Mme de Chantal was a well-born and beautiful woman, warmly affectionate and innately religious. Her mystical genius was balanced by a touching dependence on human ties which made her very lovable.

She was married at twenty to Baron Christophe de Chantal, a religious man who died when she was twenty-eight, leaving her with three daughters and a son. She had had two other children who died in their infancy.

After her husband's death Mme de Chantal had many family perplexities, but she faced them with patience and still found time to serve the sick and needy. In her grief she sought solace in religion.

Her son engaged in so many duels that his mother feared for him, praying constantly that he might not be killed. But he was to die in battle when he entered the service of his country. He left a daughter, Marie de Rabutin-Chantal, whose education Mme de Chantal directed. This granddaughter afterward became the celebrated Mme de Sévigné, one of France's well-known literary figures in the seventeenth century.

Mme de Chantal is connected with other distinguished names in French history. Her father Benigne Fremyot was president of the Parliament of Burgundy and a leader in the Royalist Party that helped bring about the triumph of Henry IV. Her eldest daughter married the brother of Francis de Sales, the young Baron de Thorens.

At the time of Francis de Sales' death in 1622, there were nineteen houses of the Order of Visitation. When Mme de Chantal died nineteen years later, there were eighty-eight. Francis was buried with great honor in the church of the convent at Annecy, where she also was buried in 1641.

Vincent de Paul, the French churchman, said of her:

She was full of faith and yet all her life long had been tormented by thoughts against it. While apparently enjoying that peace and easiness of mind of souls who have reached a high state of virtue, she suffered such interior trials that she often told me her mind was so filled with all sorts of temptations and abominations that she had to strive not to look within herself, for she could not bear it. But for all that suffering her face never lost its serenity, nor did she once relax in the fidelity God asked of her. And so I regard her as one of the holiest souls I have ever met on this earth.

Mme Jeanne Guyon, born seven years after Mme de Chantal's death, studied her books and made a vow, in imitation of Mme de Chantal, "of ever aiming at the highest perfection, and of doing the will of God in everything."

THE FIRST SAINT OF THE NEW WORLD

ROSE OF LIMA (1586-1617), a native of Lima, Peru, was the first woman born in the Western Hemisphere to be canonized. She has been declared by the Roman Catholic Church to be patroness of South America and of the Philippines and is highly honored in Latin-American countries.

She was the daughter of a Spanish father, Gaspar de Flores, and an Inca Indian mother, Maria d'Olivia. Although christened Isabella after her grandmother, Isabella de Herrara, so great was her beauty as a child that her mother called her Rose.

She patterned her life after Catherine of Siena. Like Catherine she was the youngest of a large family and practiced prayer and penance amid family obstacles. In the family garden she created an oratory for spiritual retreat. She made it a place of beauty by surrounding it with flowers so lovely that she might well have been called the patron saint of flowers. Not only did she make them grow profusely in her garden, but with her expert needlework she made them grow on damask, silk and velvet.

As a member of the Dominican Third Order, Rose was first buried in the Dominican Convent at Lima. Later her body was removed to the Church of San Domingo in Lima.

A FAMOUS AMERICAN INDIAN CONVERT TO CHRISTIANITY

POCAHONTAS (1595-1617) was the first Indian woman to become a Christian at the English settlement of Jamestown. She was captured by the English in 1613 and held as a hostage to insure the safety of white prisoners taken by the Indians. During this time she was baptized and given the Biblical name of Rebekah. On a visit to England in the latter days of her life, she was called "Lady Rebekah."

In his *General Histories of Virginia*, published seven years after Pocahontas' death, John Smith records the story of her life. He indicates that she was the daughter of the Indian chieftain Powhatan. While John Smith was exploring the Chickahominy River, he was waylaid by Indians, taken prisoner and brought to Powhatan. He was forced to kneel down preparatory to having his head crushed with heavy clubs. At that moment

Powhatan's twelve-year-old daughter Pocahontas rushed forward and saved his life.

Pocahontas became a loyal friend to the Jamestown settlement, saving the colony more than once from starvation during famine. She was baptized by Rev. Alexander Whitaker, an Episcopal clergyman, and married in a Christian ceremony in Jamestown in April 1613 to John Rolfe, described in old records as an "honest and discreet gentleman of good behaviour."

A year later, their only son Thomas was born and they moved to a new plantation on the James River. Here John Rolfe, Governor Thomas Dale, and the minister of the settlement are said to have taught Pocahontas English and the Christian religion.

When Governor Dale returned to England late in 1616 he took Pocahontas with him, together with her husband and son and an old Indian named Tomocomo. Pocahontas was treated in England as an Indian princess and presented to James I and Queen Anne. Her portrait was painted by Simon de Passe.

Wearying of crowded London, she longed for the American forest. But she never saw it again, for she died of smallpox in England at the age of twenty-two. She was buried in the little church at Gravesend on the Thames.

Her son Thomas, educated in England, returned to Virginia. Among her descendants were John Randolph, William Henry Harrison and Edith Bolling Wilson (the second Mrs. Woodrow Wilson).

A SIXTEENTH-CENTURY PREACHER

ELIZABETH HOOTON (1598-1672) was the first convert and first woman minister of the Quakers. George Fox came to her area of Nottingham, England, in 1647, while he was a shoemaker only twenty-two years old. Elizabeth Hooton was attracted to his message and remained faithful to his teachings until her death in Jamaica twenty-five years later.

When she joined Fox she was a middle-aged woman in comfortable circumstances, the wife of Oliver Hooten and the mother of several children. She had belonged to a group of Baptists who had split up and scattered before Fox's coming. Falling away from their religious ideals, they continued their Sunday meetings "only to play at shovelboard and to be merry." In his *Journal*, Fox calls them the "shattered" Baptists.

Elizabeth Hooton, one of the few who were faithful as Baptists, found a new light in Fox's ideas. Three years after becoming his follower she was imprisoned for the faith. This was the first of many imprisonments. She was sent to Derby and then to York Castle Prison for no graver fault than exhorting the people to repentance. Later, she was committed to Beckenham Prison and then to Lincoln Castle Prison. But like Paul she regarded her prison not with shame or tears but as a place where she could draw closer to the Light Within.

After leaving Lincoln Castle Prison she made plans to go to Boston, where many Quakers were suffering for their faith. She was able to take this voyage in 1661 after the death of her husband. Though she was left with considerable farming property near Mansfield, England, and was nearly sixty years of age, she was heedless of the ease and comfort she could have enjoyed. Her heart was with the persecuted church at Boston, which she determined to aid with her newly-gained wealth and independence.

Arriving in Boston, she encountered a law forbidding any Quaker to be entertained by an inhabitant of the town. When she went to visit Boston prison where other Quakers were confined, the jailer took her to Governor John Endicott.

The governor demanded the cause of her coming. In the simple words of Scripture she answered: "To do the will of Him that sent me." The governor then asked: "What do you understand by that will?" Her courageous answer was: "To warn them of shedding any more innocent blood." When Governor Endicott boasted that he would hang more Quakers, she quietly reminded him that he was in the hand of the Lord, who could take him away first, a prophecy which was fulfilled before another five years had passed.

When Elizabeth Hooton and twenty-four other Quakers were committed to prison by the governor, she hourly expected to be executed, since Mary Dyer had died on the gallows only a few months before. Then the rumor began to circulate that the king was displeased with this and other hangings in Boston and she was finally released.

Like other Quakers she went to Rhode Island to find freedom from persecution. Then she sailed to the Quaker settlement at Barbados in the West Indies.

When Elizabeth Hooton returned to Boston in 1662, having sold her farm in England, she planned to buy a house to use as a meeting place for Quakers and a refuge for traveling preachers who were homeless because of Boston's inhospitable law. She also planned to purchase land for a cemetery for those who might be executed and, for lack of a suitable burial place, be interred under the gallows in the open field.

Mrs. Hooton found that the situation in Boston had not changed as far as the Quakers were concerned. She went into the districts of northern Massachusetts, preaching from place to place. Even there, her sufferings were almost unbearable. She was once thrown into a miserable dungeon where there was no place to sit or lie down. She received lashings on three different occasions. At Cambridge she was tied to a whipping post and given ten stripes with a three-stringed whip having three knots at the end. At Watertown she was also whipped. At Dedham she received ten cruel lashes while tied to the tail of a cart. After being beaten and torn, she was put on horseback and taken many miles into the wilderness. Toward nightfall she was abandoned in a place where there were many wolves, bears and other wild beasts, as well as many deep streams. These are among the horrors related by William Sewel in his *History of the Rise, Increase and Progress of the Christian People Called Quakers.*

Sewel adds that after the Dedham ordeal,

being preserved by an invisible hand, she came in the morning into a town called Rehoboth, being neither weary nor faint; and from thence she went to Rhode Island, where coming to her friends she gave thanks to God, for having counted her worthy, and enabled her to suffer for His name's sake, beyond what her age and sex, normally speaking, could otherwise have borne.

At this time she was nearly seventy.

Her own explanation of her suffering is a witness to her faith: "The love I bear to the souls of men makes me willing to undergo whatsoever can be inflicted on me."

Sometime before 1667 Elizabeth Hooton returned to England and the next three years seem to have passed quietly for her. The terrible persecution of Quakers drew her finally to London in 1670 to work for the relief of Quaker prisoners and to enlighten the public about their suffering.

In 1671 she journeyed with George Fox and other Quakers to the West Indies. A farewell letter written to King Charles II on the eve of her departure from England expresses the pathos of a dying testament:

King Charles—How often have I come to thee in my old age, both for reformation and safety, and for the good of thy soule, and for justice and equity. Oh that thou would give up thy kingdom to ye Lord, God of heaven and earth, whose it is, and thy strength and power to Jesus Christ, who is Lord of lords, and King of kings, and then thou wilt be more honorable than ever thou wast.

On January 8, 1672, a week after the party had landed at Jamaica, Elizabeth Hooten died and was buried there, like a weary soldier fallen at her post.

FOUNDER OF THE OLDEST NORTH AMERICAN
CONVENT SCHOOL

MARIE DE L'INCARNATION (1599-1672), a widow and mother, forsook her comforts in France to pioneer in establishing an Ursuline mission at Quebec. The city was only a trading post in what was called New France. When she arrived in the New World on August 1, 1639, she was escorted to a small hut on the riverbank. At once she took six little Indian girls to live with her and taught them cleanliness and godliness.

Commenting on her new life, she said in a letter written from Quebec: "Daily we find hairs, bits of coal and other rubbish in our soup, and sometimes we even discover an old shoe in the soup-pot, but we do not make too much of that."

Later she wrote: "What a joy it is to find oneself with a great troop of native women and girls, whose miserable coverings—a skin or an old rug —do not smell so pleasant as those of the ladies of France but whose candor and simplicity is so unspeakably attractive."

Marie first learned the Algonquin Indian dialect, and later, the Huron and Iroquois. She mastered these so well that she was able to write a simple book of Christian belief in Algonquin with a cathechism and vocabulary, and finally to compile a large French-Algonquin dictionary.

Although she experienced fire, famine, pestilence and Indian raids, Marie never lost her sense of union with God, and she continued to write and speak uplifting thoughts to those who were hungering for things of the spirit.

Of prayer, she said: "Many long for its gifts but they do not strive for that of humility and real self-giving, without which there can be no real prayer." She called simplicity the "gateway to perfection" and said "it is impossible that a soul can ever be filled with the Spirit of Christ till simplicity has emptied it of self."

She spent thirty-two years working among the Iroquois and Huron Indians, building a mission that grew and prospered. It continues today, more than three centuries later, as one of the most important missions in Canada.

She was born Marie Guyard at Tours, France, October 28, 1599. Her father was a silk merchant and her mother belonged to the aristocracy of France. At eighteen she was married to Claude Martin, a silk manufacturer. When he died three years later, Marie was left with their year-old son Claude.

After settling her husband's business affairs, she turned from temporal to spiritual matters and for several years led a life of solitude in some rooms at the top of her father's house. Later she worked for a brother-in-law, who was an agent for the transport of merchandise, and said to have had the largest establishment in the whole province. Her office was in a stable, but she describes her state as one of "continual tendency to God." This state of illumination lasted for about eight years, and the radiance of her inner life penetrated all of her later activities.

Because her spirit was bound to the Word Incarnate, she took the name of Marie de l'Incarnation when she entered the Ursuline convent at Tours on January 25, 1631. She wrote that "the Holy Word Incarnate breathes into the soul an unction past all expression and gives to its actions sincerity, straightness, frankness, simplicity." Her son, then ten years old, accompanied her into the convent but he rebelled against the cloistered life his mother had chosen. She was confident, however, that he would one day be drawn into the service of God and later he did lead a life of piety. He praised his mother in a seven-hundred-page biography, in which he recorded:

> I do not doubt that the light which made Abraham see that he must sacrifice his only son . . . was the same which made this generous soul see that she must abandon hers, after God had many times declared that such was His Will. . . . Whatever love she had for him, she had infinitely more for God who commanded her to leave him. And after all Christ gave the command to leave father, mother, and all children.

In addition to her biography, her son published her *Letters* in two large volumes, and a small book of her *Meditations*. This little book has been called more useful than twenty ordinary treatises on mysticism.

Marie never ceased to be a good mother, even after the ocean divided her from her son. Constantly sorrowing over her absence from him, she consoled him with the thought: "God has been your father beyond all hopes." When she thought that he was becoming self-condemning, she reassured him with words like these: "Do not be surprised if you see faults in your conduct; it is the state of union to which God calls you which opens your eyes to them. The more light the Spirit gives you the more you will see such impurities."

A tall, handsome woman possessing a gentle presence, she succeeded in her dual callings, that of mother and that of foundress and head of the oldest convent school in North America. The Ursuline nuns with whom she was associated were among the first to establish missions in the Rocky Mountains and to penetrate Alaska.

On the spot where Marie de l'Incarnation lived and died the Ursuline convent stands today, a striking group of buildings covering seven acres of ground in the old city of Quebec.

SHE FOUNDED THE FIRST CANADIAN SISTERHOOD

MARGUERITE BOURGEOYS (1620-1700) founded the first uncloistered Catholic missionary community for women in the New World. One of those admitted to its ranks was Lydia Longley, the first New England girl to consecrate her life to God in the service of religion. The Congregation of Notre Dame of Montreal, which spreads over Canada, parts of the United States and Japan, is the outgrowth of Marguerite's pioneering work.

Marguerite, the sixth child of Abraham Bourgeoys, was born in Troyes, France, in 1620. When she set out for the New World it was in a ship that leaked so badly it had to return to France for repairs. Fever broke out during the later crossing, and she devoted herself to nursing the sick and burying the dead.

In 1653 she arrived in Ville Marie, Canada—a fort established by the French in the area of what is now Montreal. She lost no time in making herself a servant of the new French community. On her arrival she persuaded the governor, M. de Maissonneuve, to restore a cross that had been removed from the top of a nearby mountain, and she inspired the colonists to begin work on a chapel. In time she founded the Church of Bonsecours in Ville Marie.

After establishing her school in a stone stable at Ville Marie on April 30, 1658, she returned to France in search of recruits for her community for women. Although she was able to promise them only bread and soup and hard work, she succeeded in persuading four to embark with her for Canada. One of these found the life too difficult, but three remained to assist in her pioneering work.

SHE TYPIFIED PURITANISM AT ITS BEST

LUCY HUTCHINSON (1620-?) and her family represent a seventeenth-century Puritan household in its finest form.

In Lucy's *Memoirs of the Life of Colonel Hutchinson*, written after the death of her husband John Hutchinson in 1664, she not only immortalizes this Puritan gentleman but she also gives a picture of Puritanism's contributions to the Protestant Reformation in England.

Born June 29, 1620, in a hamlet southwest of London, Lucy was the daughter of Sir Allen Apsley and his third wife, Lucy St. John. Before Lucy was born her mother dreamed that she was walking in a garden when a star from heaven came down into her hand. She took this to mean that her child would become eminent. The child's unusual beauty and talents confirmed this belief.

At the age of four she could read English perfectly. When she was seven her tutors instructed her in Hebrew, Latin, Greek and French, as well as in music, dancing and needlework.

At eighteen she married John Hutchinson. On the day of her wedding she fell ill of smallpox and was badly disfigured by it, although several years later her skin became clearer again. The early days of her married life were spent at Owthorpe, her father-in-law's estate in Nottinghamshire, where she presided over a fine old English manor house.

During the fourth year of her marriage the English Civil War began. Her husband was reluctant to oppose the king, but he finally joined the parliamentary party and was given the rank of colonel. During the war Lucy aided her husband, though if she could have had her way he would never have taken up arms at all.

Her first thought was to keep those she loved out of danger. For herself she feared nothing. Though delicate in health, she took upon herself the duties of tending sick and wounded prisoners. One day a captain came in and told her that he "abhorred to see this favor to the enemies of God." She replied that she ministered to them not as enemies but as fellow creatures, because she lived by Jesus' command: "Love your enemies, do good to them which hate you" (Luke 6:27).

At the end of the Civil War, her husband returned to his estate, which had been damaged in the conflict. He rebuilt his house, spent two thousand pounds adorning it with pictures and works of art, and here Lucy Hutchinson settled down to live the life she loved, free from politics and strife.

Her peaceful existence was short-lived. Because of having been one of those who signed the death warrant of Charles I, her husband was singled out for punishment after the Restoration. He had no thought of seeking his own safety, but his wife forged his signature to a letter in order to procure his pardon. Two years later he was arrested on a capital charge, imprisoned in the Tower of London and finally banished to an old ruined castle which had no accommodations for lodging or food. His room had five doors, one of which opened onto the bleak air of the sea which washed at the foot of the castle walls. In 1664 he became ill with a fever caused by the damp air of his prison. Lucy was permitted to minister to her husband in this unhealthy place, and as his death drew near she brought their children for a last visit. He gave her directions for the arrangement of his house and garden.

"You give me these orders," she said, "as if you were to see the place again." He replied: "If I do not, I thank God that I can cheerfully forget it."

He sent his wife this message from his deathbed: "Let her, as she is above other women, show herself on this occasion a good Christian, and above the pitch of ordinary women."

She had his body removed to the gardens of his home at Owthorpe. A stately monument in the church, supposed to have been erected by her, records his many virtues.

Lucy now dedicated herself to their children and to writing memoirs of her husband's life so that they might have a vivid portrait of their Christian father. The biography was not published until 1806, more than one hundred and twenty-five years after she had written it. In the book, Lucy defines Christianity as "that universal habit of grace which is wrought in a soul by the regenerating Spirit of God, whereby the whole creature is resigned up into the divine will and love, and all its actions directed to the obedience and glory of its maker."

During the remaining years of her life, Lucy Hutchinson lived in such obscurity that the date of her death is not known.

AN EARLY AMERICAN MARTYR

MARY DYER (?-1660), the Quaker martyr, was hanged on Boston Common June 1, 1660, for preaching the Quaker doctrine. Her witness to her faith even unto death, her fearlessness at the gallows, and her willingness that "the will of the Lord be done" helped the cause of religious tolerance in America.

She and her husband William Dyer emigrated from London to Boston and became members of Boston's First Church in 1635. In Rhode Island, where they later lived, he served as commissioner, deputy, general solicitor, secretary of the Council for the Colony of Rhode Island, and in 1649 as attorney general.

Mary was a woman of good parentage and possessed an estate of her own, which is described by Gerard Croese, a Dutch writer, as being "pretty plentiful." He says she was a woman of "piercing knowledge in many things, fit for great affairs, attractive in stature and countenance and of wonderfully sweet and pleasant conversation." These and other facts are recorded in *Mary Dyer, the Quaker Martyr* (1896) by Horatio Rogers, an associate justice of the Supreme Court of Rhode Island.

Mary was the mother of six children. One of her sons bore the Bible name of Maharshalalhashbaz (the symbolic name Isaiah wrote in a public place and later gave to his second son). Little is known about any of her children except that she gave birth to a stillborn, deformed child in Boston in 1637. Her friend Anne Hutchinson probably served as midwife. Anne tried to protect Mary Dyer from having it known publicly that the child was so badly deformed, but the information got out, and Mary's enemies declared that she had "given birth to a monster" and that this was evidence of divine displeasure.

During Anne Hutchinson's famous trial the month after this incident, Mary stood by as Anne's stanch friend. The Dyers followed the Hutchinsons to Rhode Island when Anne was banished from Massachusetts Bay in 1637. When Anne and members of her family were massacred by Indians in New York in 1643, Mary gave a moving funeral address for her in Providence, Rhode Island. Her Puritan enemies insisted that Mary Dyer, like Anne Hutchinson, was notoriously infected with errors of doctrine.

In 1652, Mary's husband accompanied Roger Williams, founder of Rhode Island, and John Clarke, pastor and founder of the First Baptist Church at Newport, Rhode Island, to England to procure a liberal charter for Rhode Island. Mary went with her husband to England and it was there that she became a Quaker convert. Her husband returned to Rhode Island the next year, but she remained in England for four more years. In the meantime the first Quakers had reached Boston and aroused the animosity of ministers and authorities by their beliefs. Various repressive measures had been adopted against the Quakers by the time Mary Dyer returned there. With her was another Quaker woman, Ann Burden, who came to settle her husband's estate. Both were arrested and put into prison.

Though Mary had intended only to pass through Boston on her way to Rhode Island, she was kept such a close prisoner that no one could communicate with her. Hearing that she was imprisoned, her husband went to Boston for her, but he could not secure her release until he promised under oath that she would not remain in any town of Massachusetts Bay nor speak with anyone on her journey.

The next year, when she went into the colony of New Haven to preach Quaker doctrines, she was expelled. Thirty days later, she returned to Boston with other Quakers, to visit Friends in prison. Again she was arrested and held for action by the authorities.

Mary Dyer and two other Quakers who had defied the unjust Puritan laws and dared martyrdom were brought before Governor John Endicott, who asked why they had returned to his jurisdiction after having been banished from it. They declared that the cause of their coming was of the Lord and in obedience to Him.

Governor Endicott pronounced the following sentence upon Mary Dyer:

"You should go from hence to the place from whence you came, and from thence to the place of execution and there be hanged till you be dead." Mary Dyer replied: "The will of the Lord be done."

Great influence was brought to bear to prevent her execution and that of the other two Quakers, but the date for the triple hanging was formally set for October 27, 1659. Mary went from prison with her men companions, thanking the Lord that He accounted her worthy to suffer for His Name.

The gallows was a great elm upon Boston Common. With her arms and legs bound and her skirt secured about her feet, she waited with a rope about her neck, ready to share the same fate as her friends. At the last minute, upon the petition of her son and a touching letter from Rhode Island from her husband, begging clemency for "My Deare Wife," an order for reprieve came. The halter was unbound, and she was told to come down from the ladder. Her husband's petition for her release is preserved in the archives of the Commonwealth of Massachusetts.

When Mary returned to prison and was told that a full reprieve depended on her promise not to preach, she refused it. The next day she wrote to the General Court: "My life is not accepted, neither availeth me, in comparison with the lives and liberty of the Truth and servants of the living God, for which in the bowels of Love and Meekness I sought you. . . ."

She escaped death but was banished once more from Massachusetts Bay and went to her home in Rhode Island. However, she did not remain there long, for she spent most of the winter on Long Island, pondering the persecution in Massachusetts. She determined to fight it.

A little more than six months after she had first been sentenced to die, she reappeared in Boston to preach. She knew this meant death but she held it to be her duty. Once more she was brought before the court and sentenced to hang on June 1, 1660.

As she mounted the scaffold, John Wilson, her former pastor at First Church in Boston, told her that she would be released if she would repent of her errors. Her reply was final: "Nay, I cannot, for in obedience to the will of the Lord God I came, and in His will I abide faithful to the death." Her body rests in an unmarked grave somewhere on Boston Common.

THE DEVOTED WIFE OF WILLIAM PENN

GULIELMA PENN (1644-1694) was described as "a woman of ten thousand" by her husband William Penn, the founder of the Commonwealth of Pennsylvania. Beginning an account of her life, he set down these words four days after her death: "[She was] wise, chaste, humble, plain, modest, industrious, constant and undaunted."

Gulielma was born in London in February 1644, the only child of Mary Proude and Sir William Springett, who together "pressed much after the knowledge of the Lord," says Mary in a letter written when she was first married. Her father died of fever while commanding as colonel on the Puritan side at the Battle of Edgehill. This was a few weeks before Gulielma was born and her mother named her Gulielma Maria (Posthuma).

Ten years later her mother married Isaac Penington, son of a former Lord Mayor of London. Together they "sought the Lord" and were among the most distinguished of early Quakers, whom they joined in 1658. They spoke of "the worthlessness of religious belief which does not bring forth holiness of life." Gulielma publicly joined the Quaker cause at the age of fifteen. She later saw her mother and stepfather robbed of their home and driven from place to place because of their belief.

Her childhood playmate and friend was the well-known Quaker, Thomas Elwood, a friend of the poet John Milton. The poet's cottage at Amersham was within easy reach of Gulielma's home. According to tradition, she cheered Milton in his blindness by going to his cottage and singing and reading to him.

From her grandmother, Mme Springett, who was famous for removing cataracts from the eyes, and for curing cuts, burns and broken limbs, she inherited her power of healing.

Well-born, religious, pretty and an heiress with a considerable estate from the Springetts, Gulielma attracted many suitors. But it was William Penn, son of Admiral Sir William Penn, and a Quaker like herself, who won her heart. "He for whom she was reserved has appeared at last," said Thomas Elwood.

They were married in a Jacobean manor house at King John's Farm, Chorley Wood, in Hertfordshire on May 4, 1672. Their first years have been called "the halcyon period of Penn's career, one of hope and cheer." They had five children, only three of whom—Springett, William and Letitita—survived infancy.

In 1676 Penn purchased for his family the Worminghurst estate in her father's county of Sussex. The property had belonged to the Shelley family, ancestors of the poet, Percy Bysshe Shelley. Records show that the Penn family assembled with the servants each morning and afternoon for worship and Bible reading.

In 1676 William and "Guli," as she was called, spent some time in the north of England, probably visiting at Swarthmoor Hall, the home of Margaret Fell Fox. When Penn, imprisoned several times as a Quaker preacher and writer, became convinced that there was to be no religious toleration in England, he made preparations to go to America.

Before he left in October 1682 on the tiny frigate *Welcome,* carrying one hundred colonists who were mostly Friends from the south of England, he made material provisions for his family, as if he were never to see them again. He wrote long epistles for their guidance. The most famous of these gives a vivid picture of "Guli," whom he left behind. The thoughts in this letter are typical of his book *No Cross, No Crown,* one of the most noble works on Christianity in the English language. The letter says in part:

My Dear Wife and Children:
May the God of my life watch over you and bless you and do you good in this world and forever....

Remember, my dear wife, thou wast the love of my youth . . . and the reason of that love was more thy inward than thy outward excellencies, which yet were many. God knows, and thou knowest it, I can say it was a match of Providence's making.

Let the fear of the Lord, and a zeal and love for His glory dwell richly in thy heart; and thou wilt watch for good over thyself and thy dear children and family, that no rude, light or bad thing be committed: else God will be offended and He will repent Himself of the good He intends thee and thine.

Be diligent in meetings for worship and business. And let meetings be kept once a day in the family to wait upon the Lord, who has given us much time for our-selves. . . . And grieve not thyself with careless servants; they will disorder thee; rather pay them and let them go, if they will not better by admonition; this is best to avoid many words, which I know wound the soul and offend the Lord. . . .

I know thou lovest plain things, and art averse to the pomps of the world—a no-bility natural to thee. . . . My mind is wrapped up in a saying of thy father's, "I desire not riches but to owe nothing"; and truly this is wealth. . . .

I need not bid thee be humble, for thou art so; nor meek and patient, for it is much of thy natural disposition; but I pray thee be often in retirement with the Lord, and guard against encroaching friendships. Keep them at arm's length; for it is giving away our power—ay, and self too, into the possession of another; and that which may seem engaging in the beginning may prove a heavy yoke and burden too hard and heavy in the end. Wherefore keep dominion over thyself, and let thy children, good meetings and Friends, be the pleasure of thy life.

And now, my dearest, let me recommend to thy care my dear children: abundantly beloved of me, as the Lord's blessings . . . breed them up in a love of one another: tell them it is the charge I left behind me. . . . For their learning be liberal. Spare no cost. . . . When grown big, have most care for them; for then there are more snares, both within and without. . . .

Yours, as God pleaseth, in that which no waters can quench, no time forget, nor distance wear away, but remains for ever, William Penn.

During his first two years in America, William Penn expected his wife to join him, but she feared making the journey with her children, and as she wrote to Margaret Fox in 1684:

> I desire not his coming merely to fetch us, as I know he has a great deal of business to attend to; and also know it is not for want of true love or the desire to see us that keeps him, but it is that he must mind first the duties of the place in which he now stands, and do that which is right and in which he has peace.

While she was writing this letter, her husband was on his way home. Four days later he wrote Margaret Fell Fox: "My dear wife relates thy great love to her in my absence. . . . I return you my tender acknowledgment."

A daughter, Gulielma Maria, was born after his return but she died in 1689. Mrs. Penn, never strong herself, died in her husband's arms in February 1694. During her last illness she called her children and servants into her room and, sitting in her chair, spoke to them:

> Let us all prepare, not knowing what Hour or Watch the Lord cometh. O I am full of Matter! Shall we receive Good, and shall we not receive All Things at the Hands of the Lord? I have cast my Care upon the Lord, he is the physician of Value and my expectation is wholly from Him: He can raise up, and He can cast down.

Penn, who survived his wife twenty years, was later married to Hanna Callowhill of Bristol, and was survived by her three sons, John, Thomas and Richard.

The best sources for the life of Gulielma are *The Penns and Peningtons* by Maria Webb, published in London in 1867, and a more recent biography, *Gulielma, Wife of William Penn,* by L. V. Hodgkin.

THE HEROIC WIFE OF THE AUTHOR OF *Pilgrim's Progress*

ELIZABETH BUNYAN (?-1692) is immortalized in her husband's writings for pleading his case when he was imprisoned for preaching without a license.

John Bunyan and Elizabeth were married in the autumn of 1659, three years after the death of his first wife and about six years after he joined a Noncomformist church in Bedford, England. He was arrested toward the end of 1660 and put in jail. During his imprisonment she cared for his four children by his first wife, including his blind daughter Mary, who was much beloved by Bunyan. In prison he gave religious instruction to other prisoners and studied the Bible and Foxe's *Book of Martyrs.* There he also wrote some of his best-known works. He was released in 1672 after spending twelve years there, only to be imprisoned again for a shorter period. During this time he wrote *Pilgrim's Progress*, described by the *Encyclopedia of Religion and Ethics* as "the greatest of allegories." This great book has been translated into more than a hundred languages and dialects. For two hundred years it was read more widely than any book except the Bible.

During his first imprisonment Elizabeth went to London to plead for her husband's liberty before the House of Lords. On three separate occasions she presented to the judges different petitions, begging that her husband might be heard in his own defense.

In his writing Bunyan compares her to the Importunate Widow in Jesus' Parable (Luke 18:3-5) who continued to plead with the unjust judge to help her. It was the righteousness of her husband's cause that gave Elizabeth her courage.

This, in brief, is the plea she made before the judges as recorded by Bunyan:

Elizabeth: My Lord, I make bold to come again to your lordship to know what may be done with my husband.

Judge: Woman, I told thee before I could do thee no good, because they have taken that for a conviction which thy husband spoke at the sessions; and unless there be something done to undo that, I can do thee no good.

Elizabeth: My Lord, he is kept unlawfully in prison. They clapped him up before there was any proclamation against the meetings. The indictment also is false. Besides they never asked him whether he was guilty or not of preaching without a license. Neither did he confess the indictment.

Another judge: Will your husband leave preaching? If he will do so, then send for him.

Elizabeth: My Lord, he dares not leave preaching so long as he can speak. . . . He desires to live peaceably and to follow his calling that his family may be maintained. Moreover, my lord, I have four small children that cannot help themselves, one of which is blind, and we have nothing to live upon but the charity of good people. I am but a stepmother to them, having not been married to my husband yet two full years. Being young and unaccustomed to such things, I became dismayed at the news of his imprisonment and fell into labor, and so continued for eight days, and then was delivered, but my child died.

Judge: Alas! poor woman, you make poverty your cloak. I understand that your husband is maintained better by running up and down a-preaching than by following his calling. What is his calling?

Some of the company: A tinker [repairman], my lord.

Elizabeth: Yes, and because he is a tinker and a poor man, therefore he is despised and cannot have justice. . . . As for preaching, he preacheth nothing but the Word of God. . . . God hath owned him, and done much good by him.

Judge: God! Your husband's doctrine is the doctrine of the devil.

Elizabeth: My lord, when the righteous judge shall appear, it will be known that his doctrine is not the doctrine of the devil.

Judge: My lord, do not mind her, but send her away.

Another judge: I am sorry, woman, that I can do thee no good. Thou must do one of three things, either apply to the King, sue out his pardon, or get a writ of error. The last will be the cheapest.

With this Elizabeth broke into tears, "not too much because they were so hard-hearted against me and my husband, but to think what a sad account such poor creatures will have to give at the coming of the Lord, when they shall there answer for all things whatsoever they have done, whether it be good or bad."

The report of the dignity and intelligence with which his wife acquitted herself inspired Bunyan with admiration. He narrates this scene with satisfaction, proud that he had a wife of more spirit than they had expected to find in the helpmate of the "tinker preacher."

Elizabeth heard no more of her case. Her husband remained in prison ten years longer, until 1672. Finally the bishop of the diocese interceded, and Bunyan was released from jail but was required to stay within the limits of Bedford. After his release he was appointed pastor of the Baptist Church until the shorter imprisonment that was made memorable by his writing of *Pilgrim's Progress.*

Ten years later, in 1688, after riding through a heavy rain on an errand of mercy to bring about a reconciliation between a father and his son, Bunyan returned home drenched. He died of a fever a few days later.

Three years before his death he had made a will giving Elizabeth his entire property. He declared that he did this because of the natural affection and love which he bore for his well-loved wife. By this act he also demonstrated his confidence in her integrity and in her maternal affection for his children.

Elizabeth Bunyan's life recalls Philip Guedalla's famous parody:

> Wives of great men all remind us
> We can make our lives sublime.

A RIGHTEOUS EXAMPLE TO THE ROYAL COURT

MARGARET BLAGGE GODOLPHIN (1652-1678), the youngest of three daughters of Colonel Thomas Blagge, was, before her marriage, maid of honor to the Duchess of York. Though she moved in the circles of the corrupt court of King Charles II, scandal never touched her reputation. The worldliness around her did not quench her spirit because she gave herself wholly to God.

The events of her life are less significant than the nobility with which she lived. At court she was given the chief role in a play performed for the pleasure-loving King Charles II. In the play Margaret wore jewels valued at twenty thousand pounds and apparel costing more than three thousand pounds. "While the whole theater was extolling her, she was then in her own eyes, not only the humblest but the most diffident of creatures," says her biographer, John Evelyn. "As soon as the play was over she took off her rich apparel, slipped like a spirit to her little oratory and thanked God she was delivered from her vanity and with her Saviour again."

From Paris, she wrote to a friend: "I have here no time for my soul. Cards we play for hours every day. I can scarce say my prayers and seldom ever read. . . . O pity, pity me, dear friend." Amid such frivolous occupations, she felt exiled from the House of God.

So eager was she to devote her life to prayer that she seriously considered whether or not it would be spiritually wise to marry. But Evelyn, who was her spiritual adviser as well as her biographer, reminded her that the mother of Jesus was also the wife of Joseph of Nazareth. He reminded her too that when Paul exalted celibacy above marriage, it was not to condemn marriage but to say that marriage was not for him, an itinerant and persecuted apostle. When she began to plan seriously for her marriage, she said: "It will be to serve God and to encourage one another daily."

Evelyn described her husband, Lord Sidney Godolphin, an English statesman and financier, as "that excellent person most worthy to possess her." After her marriage Margaret left the English Royal Court with all its pomp and glory. In this act, says Evelyn, she resembled Paula and her daughter Eustochium, who left the court of Rome for Palestine. As Lady Godolphin, she no longer attended glittering balls or the theater, nor did she care for sumptuous entertainments. God and religion became the business of her life.

In 1678, a few days after her only son, Francis, was born, she became ill with a fever. She lived only long enough to see the child baptized. Although her husband survived her by thirty-four years, he never remarried. Their son later married Henrietta Churchill, eldest daughter of John, Duke of Marlborough.

Evelyn calls Lady Godolphin a "true daughter of the Church of England, one who seemed to thirst after nothing more than to be with God." His story of her life, written in 1685-1686, remained in the hands of his family until his great-great-grandson released it for publication in 1848. It is now regarded as a little classic on the life of an English lady who, in the midst of wickedness, became a living witness to truth and right-eousness.

THE "MOTHER" OF A NEW DENOMINATION IN AMERICA

BARBARA HECK (1734-1804) arrived in New York harbor in August 1760 with her husband Paul Heck and others from a German colony in County Limerick, on the southwest coast of Ireland. She became the mother of the first Methodist congregation in America.

John Wesley records in his *Journal* that when he first preached in County Limerick in 1747 he discovered an extraordinary community composed not of native Celts but of Teutonic people who spoke German. Because they had been without German-speaking pastors for half a century, the resi-dents had become irreligious and immoral. But a devout spirit was aroused among them by the visit of the Methodists, and Wesley states that "they turned their land into a garden."

Barbara Ruckle was born into this community in 1734 at a place named after her family, Ruckle Hill, in Balligarane, Ireland. Her people had arrived there in the seventeenth century from the Palatinate on the Rhine, when nearly all of their country was laid waste by Louis XIV. Queen Anne had sent ships to convey the refugees from Rotterdam to the British Isles. Barbara Ruckle's family was in a group that went to Ireland.

In 1760, when she was twenty-six years old, she was married to Paul Heck, a devout member of the community. In that same year they departed for the New World. Among those in their party was Philip Embury, a young itinerant Methodist preacher in Ireland who emigrated with the group as their minister. On his arrival in America, Embury seems at first to have lost his zeal or to have become discouraged.

Many other members of the little immigrant group became so absorbed with the problem of making a living that their religious zeal also slackened and they became more and more worldly-minded. Barbara Heck was one of the few who continued to read her German Bible and to live by it.

One day about six years after her arrival, she came into her kitchen to find a group of men playing cards. Among these were her eldest brother, Paul Ruckle. Disturbed by the careless way in which these men were wasting their time and drifting more and more to worldly pleasures, she approached the table, indignantly swept the cards into her apron and threw them into the fire.

Putting on her bonnet, she hastened to visit Philip Embury, who had neglected his duty as minister to the little flock.

"Philip," exclaimed Barbara Heck, "you must preach to us or we shall all go to hell together, and God will require our blood at your hands!"

Diffidently he asked: "But where shall I preach?"

"Preach in your own house," exclaimed this devout woman, "and I, at least, will come to hear you."

Embury at once began holding services in his own house, but his first congregation consisted of only five hearers: Mrs. Embury, Barbara Heck and her husband, their colored servant John Lawrence and their maid Betty. These five formed the first Methodist congregation in America.

Soon others were attracted to the services, however, and the congregation grew too large for Embury's house. As a result the famous Rigging Loft in William Street, New York, was hired for meetings, says Abel Stevens in his *Women of Methodism*.

With the spirit of a prophetess, Barbara Heck seems to have anticipated the rapid growth of Methodism in New York. Out of this early congregation grew a larger group that built a stone chapel on John Street, faced with unusual blue plaster. Barbara Heck, rejoicing in the work of her hands, helped to whitewash its walls. Embury himself constructed the pulpit.

On October 30, 1768, the first service was held in the new church, named Wesley Chapel in honor of the founder. Embury preached on Hosea 10:12: "Sow to yourselves in righteousness, reap in mercy; break up your fallow ground, for it is time to seek the Lord, till he come and rain righteousness upon you."

So primitive was the interior of the new building that the congregation climbed to the galleries by a crude ladder and sat in seats that had no backs. But these inconveniences did not keep the crowds away. Soon they overflowed the church and had to stand outside. All through this period Barbara Heck was one of the faithful members of the congregation, and her zealous spirit quickened the spirit in others.

The John Street Methodist Church stands today on the very spot where Wesley Chapel was erected, a location which is now the heart of New York's busy financial district. Although the present edifice is the third built since 1768, Embury's pulpit is still in use in the prayer room. A plaque commemorates the names of Barbara Heck and Philip Embury and their work in organizing the first Methodist Society in America. The inscription reads: "Their works do follow them."

In 1774 Barbara and her husband moved to Montreal, where he enlisted as a volunteer in the British Army. In 1785, as a reward for his loyal services to the Crown, he received a grant of land at Augusta, Upper Canada, where he moved with his family. Here Barbara Heck led in the founding of another Methodist Society, believed to be the first in Canada. Philip Embury had died in New York in 1773, but his son Samuel went to Canada and served as leader of the New Methodist Church established there.

Barbara Heck's husband died in 1792 and was buried in "The Old Blue Church" graveyard in Augusta, overlooking the St. Lawrence River. Barbara Heck died in 1804 and was buried beside her husband.

Not only was Barbara Heck the mother of American Methodism in the United States and Canada but the mother of five children as well. In early stories of the Church she is frequently called "A Mother in Israel." Like Deborah in the Book of Judges, who acted when the men had become too complacent, Barbara Heck zealously stirred up the spirits of those about her.

SHE DEVOTED HER TALENTS AND POCKETBOOK TO THE NEEDY

HANNAH MORE (1745-1833) represents the eighteenth-century religious woman at her best. John Lord, in his book *Beacon Lights of History*, sums up her life by saying: "No one woman in England or the United States ever occupied such an exalted position or exercised such a broad or deep influence on the public mind in the combined character of woman of society, author and philanthropist. Her labors have become historical."

She was born in 1745, in Stapleton, near Bristol, England, the youngest of five daughters of Mary Grace and Jacob More, a schoolmaster. She received her education at Bristol in a girls' boarding school established by her sisters. In 1762 she published *A Search for Happiness*. She wrote other successful pastoral plays, and in 1772 or 1773 she went to London, where she soon became a social and literary figure, mingling with well-known leaders such as Sir Joshua Reynolds, David Garrick, Edmund Burke, Mrs. Elizabeth Montagu and Dr. Samuel Johnson, who encouraged her to publish her plays and poems.

In these days of social popularity, her spirituality lighted the path for others. When Garrick died, it was Hannah who comforted his widow. When Benjamin Kennicott, the Oxford professor of Hebrew who spent thirty years collating the Old Testament, lay dying, Mrs. Kennicott called for Hannah. When Dr. Johnson knew that his life was ending she went to him as he received his last communion. Horace Walpole addressed her in a letter as "Dear Holy Hannah."

Until she was about thirty-five, she devoted her time to literary and social pursuits, but with maturity her interests shifted from society to philanthropy and religion. Her personality also underwent a change. Her first portrait, painted by Francis Reynolds, shows a lively, pleasant girl with merry eyes and sensitive mouth. A portrait painted by John Opie about six years later shows a serious mature woman dressed in a voluminous dark silk gown with a fluffy white neckpiece.

About this time she entered a world of new friends including John Newton, author of the hymn "How Sweet the Name of Jesus Sounds," who became her spiritual adviser; William Wilberforce, opponent of the slave trade; Dr. Beilby Porteus, Bishop of Chester and later of London; and Bishop George Horne of Norwich, who spent twenty years working on his *Commentary on the Psalms.*

She met many of these people in a group of well-to-do Anglican evangelicals who lived near the London suburb of Clapham and called themselves the Clapham Sect. All believed that religion must be manifested in good works.

In 1789 Hannah accompanied Wilberforce on a visit to the Mendips, a mining district under the ridge of the Mendip Hills. She was appalled at the ignorance and lack of religious instruction in this impoverished area and determined to do something about it.

With the assistance of her sisters, she established Sunday schools at Cheddar and in the neighboring mining villages. She held her first class in an ox barn and there she distributed prayer books, Bibles, religious tracts, and also clothing. She later established a school to teach the girls household techniques, and clubs for mothers to help them take better care of their children. Neglected old folk in almshouses also came in for a share of her attention.

Through the influence of the Clapham Sect, in 1809 she anonymously published the two-volume *Coelebs in Search of a Wife,* the most widely read of her books. She also wrote a poetical dialogue on the abolition of slavery in Ceylon. This was set to music by Charles Wesley.

Finally she turned her talents to writing tracts. The best known of these, *The Shepherd of Salisbury Plain,* was translated into several languages. The Clapham Sect underwrote these tracts, which were designed to counteract the influence of the French Revolution, which had brought a flood of demoralizing tendencies. She wrote forty-nine of the first one hundred and fourteen of these Clapham pamphlets, signing them "Z."

Among her last works were *An Estimate of the Religion of the Fashionable World,* said to have had a far-reaching influence for good among people in many walks of life, including the queen; *An Essay on the Char-*

acter of Saint Paul; and *Spirit of Prayer,* a compilation of earlier works.

At her death her fortune of some thirty thousand pounds (about one hundred and fifty thousand dollars), all made from her writings, was distributed among seventy religious societies and charitable projects as well as the Church of St. Philip and St. Paul in Bristol, a parish of the Church of England, to which she remained loyal.

She and her four sisters are buried in the churchyard at Wrighton, Somerset. Hannah More never married, but used the title Mrs. during the last half-century or so of her life, because she said it gave her more dignity.

Many biographies have been written about her. All are based on the *Memoirs of the Life and Correspondence of Mrs. Hannah More* (1834) by William Roberts. An excellent recent biography is *Hannah More and Her Circle* by Mary Alden Hopkins.

THE WIFE AND MOTHER OF THE CAMPBELLS

JANE CORNEIGLE CAMPBELL (1763-1835), wife of Thomas Campbell and mother of Alexander Campbell, founders of the Christian Churches (Disciples of Christ), imparted to her husband and son the bold independence of her French Huguenot ancestry.

From the time of their marriage in 1787 she was an inspiration to her husband Thomas. He was the author of a "religious declaration of independence" for America, a new charter of unity and liberty for the Church. This document, the "Declaration and Address," in which he called divisions in the Church "anti-Christian, anti-scriptural and anti-natural," was destined to become of historic importance.

To her son, whose practical leadership and zeal as a reformer helped to develop the Christian Churches (Disciples of Christ), the first major Protestant movement nurtured in America, she gave respect for individual rights, love of liberty and dauntless courage.

Jane's forebears, the Corneigles and the Bonners, had fled to Scotland from France in 1685 when the Edict of Nantes was revoked by Louis XIV. Later they moved to North Ireland, where they settled on the border of Lough Neagh, the largest lake in the British Isles.

Jane, the only child of the Corneigles, was born in this picturesque lakeside country. She grew up to be a beautiful person, tall, slender and erect, with brown hair that framed an intelligent face. Early in her life she became devout.

In June 1787 she married Thomas Campbell, a young teacher from

County Down who was preparing for the ministry in the Seceder Branch of the Presbyterian Church. For a time the young couple made their home on the Corneigle property on the shores of Lough Neagh. There Alexander, their first child, was born on September 12, 1788. Soon afterward the family moved to County Down so that Thomas might resume his teaching in the hamlet of Sheepbridge. This work helped to defray his expenses at the University of Glasgow and later at Divinity Hall, the Theological Seminary of the Anti-Burgher Seceders at Whitburn, midway between Glasgow and Edinburgh.

When Thomas finished his divinity course and began his term as a probationer, Jane moved from place to place with her husband as he was called to minister to congregations in several areas of North Ireland. During this time she gave birth to six children: four daughters and two sons. When her next-to-youngest child was born, her husband opened a small academy so that he might supplement the meager salary which he received as a Seceder minister and thus better support his growing family.

When their children were older, Jane mothered groups of boys under the tutelage of her husband, first in Ireland and later in Pennsylvania, Ohio and Kentucky.

Thomas Campbell worshiped with his family and instructed them in religion. Jane, a woman of strong religious convictions, carried on these duties when her husband visited parishioners. In later years Alexander Campbell paid tribute to both his mother and father for having him memorize large portions of the Bible.

In 1807 Thomas set out for the New World to make a home for his family. During the months that followed, Alexander drew especially close to his mother, assisting her with the younger children and developing a sense of responsibility for them. An unusual comradeship developed between them.

On September 28, 1808, Jane and her children embarked on the *Hibernia* for America. Alexander, ever thoughtful of his mother and the other children, had obtained comfortable quarters on board where she might read and instruct the younger children. They had barely set sail when their ship was damaged off the Scottish Hebrides. Because winter had set in, they were forced to delay their voyage for many months.

This period proved to be important spiritually for Jane and her son. Following in his father's footsteps, Alexander entered the University of Glasgow and met many important people who were producing changes in the religious life of Scotland. He now had time to visit many kinds of Glasgow churches, from ancient St. Mungo's Cathedral to the newest Haldanian Tabernacle.

Finally, on August 3, 1809, Jane and her children set sail again for the New World. Alexander spent his twenty-first birthday on board ship. When they disembarked in New York they made their way by wagon to their new home near Washington, Pennsylvania.

Jane discovered that her husband Thomas had developed new spiritual insights during the two years of their separation. He had completed writing his "Declaration and Address." Thomas Jefferson had challenged the American colonies to cast aside Old World political tyrannies; in religious matters Thomas Campbell challenged the people of the New World to throw off their bondage to the outworn creeds of Old World church councils.

By the time young Alexander had read the last page of his father's long document, he began to dream of a ministry of reform within the churches of America.

Jane's husband established the Christian Association of Washington, Pennsylvania, in 1809. In 1812 she was baptized by immersion with her son, her husband and others. In 1813 a working unity with the Redstone Baptist Association was established and this lasted nearly ten years. The two groups were separated by 1830 and the followers of the Campbells became known as the Christian Churches or Disciples of Christ. The movement had for its purpose the restoration of primitive Christianity as the way to union of all Christians.

During her wanderings with Thomas, Jane knew many homes: first in Washington, Pennsylvania; afterward in Guernsey County, Ohio where her husband opened an academy; then in Pittsburgh, where he opened a seminary; after this, in Burlington, Kentucky, where he opened another seminary; and finally in 1819 in Upper Brush Run Valley near West Middletown, Pennsylvania, a town about seven miles from Bethany, West Virginia. She remained in this vicinity for the remainder of her life. She died in 1835 at the home of her daughter and son-in-law, Jane and Matthew McKeever, who lived near West Middletown. Jane was buried in the family hilltop cemetery which her distinguished son Alexander had laid out. It overlooked his farm and the waters of the Buffalo. It is near Bethany College, which her son founded and where he served as president until his death in 1866. Her husband was buried beside her in 1854.

Her son Alexander wrote of her:

As a helpmate of my father in the work of the Christian ministry, I think I never saw her superior, if I ever did her equal.

He was frequently called from home on protracted tours in his public ministry of the Gospel; but though her cares and solicitudes were always on such occasions more or less augmented, I never heard her complain; but rather to sympathize with him in his works of faith and in his labors of love. She, indeed, cheerfully endured the privations of his company, in the full assurance that his absence from home and labors in the Gospel would ultimately redound more to the glory of God and to the happiness of man, than his confinement to any one particular locality. . . .

In all the trials and vicissitudes of her protracted life, and especially during the conflicts of her husband with the opposition, the enmity and the envy he had to encounter for duty and conscience' sake, while endeavoring to effect a reformation in his own Synod and its Presbyterian territories, both in the Old World and the New, she stood by him in faith, hope, and love, and most cheerfully became a partaker with him in all the trials and consequences incident to, and resulting from, his advocacy of primitive and apostolic Christianity. . . .

She made a nearer approximation to the acknowledged beau ideal of a truly Christian mother than any one of her sex with whom I have had the pleasure of forming a special acquaintance. . . .

Mother Campbell, in sympathy with the afflicted, the poor, the orphan, and the friendless, was, in my area of observation rarely equaled, and seldom, if ever surpassed.

Her son also added that "woman, next to God, makes the living world of humanity. She makes man what he is in this world, and very frequently makes him what he shall hereafter be in the world to come." Such a mother was Jane Corneigle Campbell.

AN EARLY MISSIONARY TO INDIA

HANNAH MARSHMAN (1767-1847) was a stanch influence behind the early Serampore Missionaries who were sent to India under the auspices of the Baptist Missionary Society which William Carey had helped to organize. At her death at the age of eighty, she was the last survivor of those who had worked with her husband Joshua Marshman, William Ward and William Carey to form the mission forty-seven years before. What she gave to its support "fell little short of the contributions of her husband," wrote her son John Clark Marshman, in *The Life and Times of Carey, Marshman and Ward.* This two-volume history of the Serampore Mission is the main source of information about his mother's life.

The Serampore missionaries were pioneers in modern missions. They produced the first editions of the New Testament in more than thirty Oriental languages and dialects. They printed the first books in Bengali. They were the first to insist that the caste system be excluded from the native Christian community and church. They established the first schools for children in North India, and Hannah Marshman was among the first to teach in them.

Hannah was the first woman to leave England for missionary work in India. Her husband's associate, William Ward, was not married until three years after the group arrived, while William Carey—actually the first to reach India—was married to a woman who had no sympathy with his work. When Mrs. Marshman set out on the perilous voyage in 1799, she committed herself steadfastly to God and gave strength to others both on the voyage and for years after their arrival in India. All needed her womanly courage. William Carey had been laboring in the barren soil of the Malda district for five and a half years, and wrote to Marshman and Ward before their departure:

I feel as a farmer does about his crop; sometimes I think the seed is springing up, and then I hope; a little time blasts all, and my hopes are gone like a cloud. They were only weeds which appeared; if a little corn sprung up, it quickly died, being either choked with weeds, or parched up by the sun of persecution. Yet I still hope in God, and will go forth in His strength.

In Serampore, about sixteen miles north of Calcutta, the English missionaries lived as one family with meals in common and with domestic duties shared by the women. Like Hannah of the Bible, Hannah Marshman was a good mother. Nine of her twelve children were born in India. She endured many hardships and became what William Carey called "A Prodigy of Prudence," which indicated that her wisdom was practical.

Hannah was the granddaughter of Rev. John Clark, pastor for sixty years of the Baptist Church at Crockerton in Wiltshire, England, where he preached his last sermon in 1803, in his ninety-first year. Since her parents had died while she was young, she was reared by this grandfather.

She was baptized in her teens, and soon after this event she met and married Joshua Marshman, a young weaver with little schooling. He eagerly seized every opportunity to educate himself, often having a book before him on the loom. In 1794 he gave up weaving to become master of the Baptist School at Broadmead, Bristol. When he read of William Carey's missionary work in India he became inspired to offer himself to the Baptist Missionary Society. His wife, already the mother of three, willingly set out with him for India.

On their arrival, she asked in bewilderment: "Where are the women?" By 1800, thanks to her efforts, many women who formerly did not leave their homes were going forth to study the Gospel. She started free schools for the children and trained her older pupils to teach in them. In 1819 she worked in Calcutta, with the Society for the Education of Native Females— the first serious attempt to educate Indian women.

In 1820, after twenty years of managing a large school which helped support the mission, she returned to England because of ill health. Through her dedicated personal service, going far beyond the line of duty, the mission was able to save many thousands of pounds. As soon as she regained her strength in England, she returned to Serampore. Two years later her eldest daughter died. Her husband died in 1837.

Hannah Marshman's name is outstanding not only because she and her husband did much in the India mission field, but also for the achievements of her distinguished son, John Clark Marshman. With his father, John founded the first paper mill in India, published the first English magazine there, established Serampore College and published a series of lawbooks. One of these was the *Guide to The Civil Law,* which for years was the civil code of India and probably that country's most useful lawbook.

John Clark Marshman paid his mother this tribute:

A woman of feeling, piety, and good sense, of strong mind . . . , fitted in every respect to be an associate in the great undertaking to which the life of her husband was devoted—and withal so amiable a disposition that nothing was ever known to have ruffled her temper.

SHE GAVE ALL SHE HAD

SALLY THOMAS (1769-1813) was a servant girl in Cornish, New Hampshire who, like the New Testament widow with the two mites, gave all she had to the Christian cause. Her wages never exceeded fifty cents a week, yet because she was industrious and thrifty she managed to save the remarkable sum of $345.83, which she gave to missions. This was the first gift actually paid to the treasurer of the American Board of Commissioners for Foreign Missions.

Little is known of Sally Thomas' life except the facts on her gravestone in Cornish, where she lived and worked for twenty-three years with the family of Daniel Chase, one of the first settlers in the town. Her gravestone reads:

In memory of Miss Sally Thomas, who died October 1, 1813, Aged 44. By the labor of her hands she had acquired property amounting to about $500; which by her last will; excepting a few small legacies, she gave for the spread and support of the Gospel among the heathen.

Thirty-six years after her death, her pastor's son, Rev. Joseph Rowell, prepared a statement about her gift and her life for the *Missionary Herald* of October 1878. In this article, the author tells of her membership in the Congregational Church in Cornish during the ministry of his father. He speaks of the family for whom she worked and how from them and their friends Sally caught the religious spirit of the time and willingly gave all she had to further the work of the Church overseas.

The fact that she gave so much when she had so little has placed her among the immortals in the records of foreign missions. Though she lived a century and a half ago, her gift still inspires churchwomen everywhere.

SHE FOUNDED THE FIRST RELIGIOUS SISTERHOOD IN THE UNITED STATES

ELIZABETH BAYLEY SETON (1774-1821), who was born during the American Revolution and was fifteen when George Washington was inaugurated President, made lasting contributions to the charitable work of both the Protestant and Roman Catholic Churches.

In 1797 she founded in New York the Society for Relief of Poor Widows with Small Children and became known thereafter as "The Protestant Sister of Charity." In 1804 she joined the Roman Catholic Church and four years later founded the American Sisters of Charity, the first sisterhood in the United States. This event has been called a milestone in the work of the Catholic Church. Mother Seton—as she came to be called—served as the first Superior of the Order from 1809 to 1821. She was also the founder of the first free parochial school in the United States.

The mother of five children, her name is carried on in her descendants as well as in the institutions she founded. A grandson, Robert Seton (1839-1927), was consecrated Titular Archbishop of Heliopolis in 1903. Another grandson, William Seton (1835-1905), a writer, served with the Union Army in the Civil War.

Elizabeth's father, Dr. Richard Bayley, was the first governmental inspector of the Quarantine in New York and also the first professor of anatomy at the medical school of King's College (now Columbia University). Her mother, Catherine Charlton Bayley, was the daughter of Rev. Richard Charlton, rector of St. Andrew's Episcopal Church, Staten Island, New York. Her mother died when Elizabeth was three years old. She was raised by her stepmother, Charlotte Barclay, daughter of Andrew Barclay and Helen Roosevelt, described by Elizabeth as "a woman of rare and sweet attainments."

One of her stepmother's blood descendants was President Franklin D. Roosevelt. "In my childhood my father often told me of Mother Seton," wrote Franklin Roosevelt about Elizabeth in 1931, when he was Governor of New York. "Her distinguished nephew, Archbishop Bayley, was a first cousin of my father, James Roosevelt, and they were very close friends. In our family we have many traditions of the saintly character of Mother Seton."

Elizabeth was married to William Seton on January 25, 1794, by Samuel Provost, Episcopal Bishop of New York. Her husband, a young merchant and a member of one of New York's oldest families, had been educated in England. Elizabeth and William had two sons and three daughters. Their marriage was a very happy one.

With her husband and one child, Anna Maria, she went to Italy in 1803 to visit William's old friends, the Filicchis, in whose banking house he had served an apprenticeship as a boy. On December 27, 1803, William died of tuberculosis and was buried in a Protestant cemetery in Leghorn, Italy.

The once wealthy Setons had suffered business reverses, and so Elizabeth, widowed at twenty-nine, went back to the United States to face financial problems. But she declared her trust in God's care for herself and her children: "Thou art my Father and doubly theirs."

It was a year after the death of her husband that she was converted to Roman Catholicism. She and her children went to Baltimore, where they were received in St. Mary's Seminary. In Baltimore she started a little school out of which was born the American Sisters of Charity. The new Order adopted a black dress made with a short cape, and a headdress of white muslin with a crimped border and a black crepe band which fastened under the chin.

Some time later Elizabeth, her daughter Anna Maria, and her sisters-in-law, Harriet and Cecilia Seton, made their way in a canvas-covered wagon from Baltimore to Emmitsburg, Maryland, a distance of about fifty miles. Here in 1810 her Order was established in a two-story log house. She decided to model her institution on the Sisters of Charity founded in France in the sixteenth century by Vincent de Paul.

In 1814 the Sisters established an orphans' home in Philadelphia, and in 1817 a second home was set up in New York City. The following year they founded a school for children of the German church in Philadelphia. This school is the basis for the claim of many historians that Elizabeth Seton organized the first parochial school in America.

Less than a score of years after her death, four of her spiritual daughters braved the dangers of the Allegheny Mountains, went down the Ohio to the Mississippi, and in 1828 opened in St. Louis the first Catholic Hospital in the United States.

Mother Seton laid the foundation for charities that exclude no one. In America today more than nine thousand nuns direct and conduct institutions fostered under her inspiration: colleges, academies and high schools; general hospitals and maternity hospitals; homes for lepers, convalescents, the aged, deaf-mutes and working girls; day nurseries, Indian schools and retreats for those with nervous and mental diseases.

In 1958 Pope John XXIII approved the continuation of her beatification which was begun in 1911. *Mother Seton—An American Woman*, written in 1852 by Rev. Charles I. White, was revised by a committee of the Sisters of Charity in 1949. Another well-known biography is *Mother Seton— Mother of Many Daughters*, by Leonard Feeney.

THE "MOTHER" OF AMERICAN MISSIONS IN HAWAII

LUCY G. THURSTON (1795-1876) went with her husband Asa G. Thurston to Kailua, chief town and port of the old Kona district in Hawaii, in 1820, eight years after Ann and Adoniram Judson, the first missionaries from the United States, went to Burma. Hawaii had been discovered by the Western world only thirty-two years before the Thurstons went there.

Lucy was the daughter of Abner Goodale, a prosperous farmer who was a deacon in the Congregational Church of Marlboro, Massachusetts. After graduating from Bradford Academy she married Asa Thurston, a native of Fitchburg, Massachusetts, and a graduate of Yale College and Andover Theological School. With him she went to Hawaii as a bride.

They set out on the trip in a small trading vessel with fifteen other people who six days earlier in Boston had formed a missionary church to be transplanted to the islands of the Pacific. "We set our faces beyond the pale of civilization, arriving on Kona 157 days later," Lucy Thurston wrote after landing.

She did not return to America for twenty years and then only to enter her older children in college. Ten years after this she returned to America a second time, "to be repaired like a worn shoe," as she put it.

On first landing at Kailua, she entered a filthy village of thatched huts built upon beds of lava on which the sun poured its furnacelike heat. She discovered the men and women to be like volcanoes, in which "raging fires of wickedness within broke out ever in desolating flows." She found them worshiping volcanoes, sharks, wood and stone. They had no written language and no organized government.

Lucy Thurston was adventurous to have come to this wild land. Japan was still wrapped in seclusion. On the Pacific Ocean there were no passing ships, no defined commerce, no regular mail. A Christmas box sent to her in Hawaii during her first year there traveled about the Pacific for ten years before it reached its destination.

Her first house was a thatched hut consisting of one room. Here she and the little band of missionaries to which she belonged stood in a circle to sing hymns and read the Bible. As she explained later, theirs was the first altar erected to God in the Hawaiian Islands. Later a wooden house was sent out from the United States, and was, as she said, "like a great rock in a weary land."

First the Thurstons spent nine months in Kailua, then they went to Honolulu, finally returning to Kailua. In Hawaii Lucy gave birth to six children. She had to fight hard to protect them against the pagan vices which "enthroned every hut and stalked every village." She often asked herself the question: "Are missionaries with their eyes open to the dangers of their situation to . . . give over their own children to Satan?"

Lucy Thurston assisted her husband in all his missionary work for forty-eight years. She and the pioneer missionaries of her group built houses, made their own furniture, constructed schools and churches. They printed leaflets and books and taught the natives to read, write, print and sing.

In addition to attending to her own domestic duties, Lucy showed the women how to sew and taught them the fundamentals of right living—all in the face of hostile neighbors who were exploiting the natives. She managed her household on her husband's salary of four hundred dollars a year, plus an allowance of fifty dollars a year for each child.

In the first years because of the climate and the insects she was threatened with tuberculosis and suffered partial paralysis. Finally she was operated on for breast cancer, and was advised against taking an anesthetic because of her recent paralysis.

For the operation, she lay on a couch with her Bible and hymnbook beside her. Though she was conscious of everything the surgeon did, she did not complain but kept affirming: "God's left hand is underneath my head. His right hand sustains and embraces me. I am willing to suffer." The pain was intense and unremitting. She was so weak for days afterward that she had to be fed with a spoon.

Four weeks later, however, in a letter to her daughter Mary she said: "Here is again your mother, engaged in life's duties and life's warfare." She lived twenty-one years after her operation, surviving all of the original missionaries with whom she had gone to Hawaii.

When her husband died in 1868 at the age of eighty, Lucy comforted herself that he walked no longer "under the fierce heat of the tropical sun." He had not left his post in forty-eight years. She had shared his trials, made long missionary tours with him on foot and equaled him in heroism.

Two years after her husband's death, when she was seventy-five, she made a stirring address of an hour and a half in the First Street Church in Honolulu, the first woman to speak in a pulpit there.

She died in 1876, lacking sixteen days of being eighty-one years old. She had enjoyed many triumphs and her children "rose up and called her blessed." Her grandson, Lorrin Andrews Thurston, became Minister of the Interior in the new constitutional government of Hawaii and an envoy to the United States from Hawaii. He also aided in framing the constitution of the Republic of Hawaii, headed the commission that negotiated the treaty of annexation to the United States (1897), and became chief owner of the *Honolulu Advertiser*. In 1934 he reprinted his grandmother's story, *Lucy G. Thurston, Pioneer Missionary in Kona Hawaii*, which has been regarded as a Hawaiian classic since it was first written and issued by her in 1872.

A SAINT IN MEDICINE AND PHILANTHROPY

DOROTHEA LYNDE DIX (1802-1887) has been compared to Florence Nightingale of the Crimean War for her work as superintendent of nurses in the Union Army during the Civil War. For her work among the imprisoned and mentally ill, she has been compared to Elizabeth Fry.

Her letters to Horace Mann, John Greenleaf Whittier, three Presidents —Polk, Fillmore and Lincoln—and to many others, reveal that her humanitarian efforts were an expression of the Christian way of life at its best.

Born at Hampden, Maine, she was the daughter of Mary Bigelow and Joseph Dix, an itinerate Methodist preacher. Dorothea's father was twenty years younger than her mother—a fact that cast a shadow over her girlhood. From her grandfather, Elijah Dix, Dorothea inherited an interest in healing; from her grandmother, Dorothy Lynde, she inherited her love for philanthropy. Her grandmother sent a Bible to every newly married couple in the two villages of Dixfield and Dixmont, and she also gave land for a meetinghouse at Dixmont. Dorothea's first efforts to aid the needy were in Grandmother Dix's barn, where she had a school for charitable and religious purposes.

In her early twenties she became a teacher. At about the same time she joined the Unitarian Church, for she was attracted by the message of the minister, William Ellery Channing, "who made human beings care about goodness with a passion," as Gladys Brooks writes in her chapter on Dorothea in *Three Wise Virgins*.

Dorothea not only went to Channing's church, but when she was twenty-five she became governess to his children at his home at Portsmouth on Narragansett Bay. Later he was instrumental in introducing her to people in England who played a vital part in her life.

"Unconsciously she built up a great spiritual reserve," Helen E. Marshall indicates in her biography, *Dorothea Dix, Forgotten Samaritan.* "In young womanhood her study of the Bible brought her hope, in old age, consolation. Through the Scriptures and through self-culture, she hoped to attain the highest moral and spiritual development."

When she was quite young Dorothea wrote: "I have little taste for fashionable dissipations, cards and dancing; the theater and tea parties are my aversion and I look with little envy on those who find their joy in transitory delights, if delights they must be called."

A tall, slight but well-proportioned woman with regular features, she had an abundance of red-brown hair, which she combed flat over the ears and coiled at the back. Her voice was well modulated and her expression was bright and intelligent. She commanded attention wherever she went. With the years her face, contemporaries say, developed rare spiritual beauty.

At the age of twenty-two she wrote her *Conversations in Common Things,* which has been issued in sixty printings. In 1825 she compiled a book of *Hymns for Children.* She also wrote *Meditations for Private Hours.*

By the late 1830's Boston, where she then lived, was full of persons who wanted to serve humanity and Dorothea was among those with a keen social consciousness. In 1841, hearing that a Sunday-school teacher was needed in the East Cambridge House of Correction, she volunteered to teach a class of twenty women who were criminals and drunkards.

When she visited the jail and found some mentally ill persons confined in an unheated room, she brought the matter into court. Armed with a shocking array of facts, she petitioned the legislature "in behalf of the insane paupers confined within the Commonwealth in cages, closets, cellars, stalls, pens; chained, naked, beaten with rods and lashed into obedience." Owing to her efforts, these abuses were largely corrected in Massachusetts. This encouraged her to undertake reform in other states.

In New Jersey, her next field of labor, she again won victories for the mentally ill and the imprisoned. In the next four years she visited prisons in eighteen states, as well as three hundred county jails and houses of correction, and more than five hundred almshouses. Everywhere she met sickening and horrible sights. Although she was weak in body and often ill, her awareness of human suffering seemed never to leave her and she toiled on, financing many of her first efforts with money she had saved from teaching, from royalties on her books, and from annuity left by

Grandfather Dix as well as the income from Grandmother Dix's estate.

Wearing a little bonnet, a tight-waisted coat with flowing skirt, a cashmere shawl, and carrying her portmanteau, Dorothea traveled by train, by carriage and by hansom cab more than sixty thousand miles in the United States, arousing people everywhere to the plight of the mentally ill. All the while she realized that "a leading Providence defines my path."

Deeply moved by all suffering, she was among the first to take up the cause of the mentally retarded child. She appealed to the Federal Government for an appropriation of five million acres of land to finance a fund for these neglected children. When Dorothea Dix appeared before Congress, Horace Mann wrote that she had a "divine magnetism." The Swedish novelist Frederika Bremer called her "a divine spinner for the House of God." She answered such comments by saying that what she had done was merely an act of simple obedience to the Voice of God. Her land bill was defeated, but she did not let this end her efforts. She began a tour of hospitals and workhouses abroad, helped to form a commission for the mentally ill of Scotland, instituted reforms in the Channel Islands, and alleviated misery wherever she found it—in the British Isles, Turkey, Russia, the Scandinavian countries, Greece and elsewhere. Her conviction that her cause was right and that God would help her carried her through seventeen years of labor for the mentally ill.

At the outbreak of the Civil War, she offered herself without pay as a nurse in the Union Army and was made chief of army nurses. She obtained the first lint, bandages and hospital shirts, and aroused the interest of thousands of women all over the North who not only made havelocks, bandages and hospital garments, but also offered to come to Washington to nurse the sick and wounded.

Twenty years' experience in public life and a passion for efficiency and humanity fitted Dorothea Dix for her work in the Army. She converted warehouses and lodge rooms into sewing rooms, and turned schoolhouses, depots, warehouses, hotels and cotton presses into hospitals. She pleaded before women's aid societies for a change in the soldiers' diet, saying that they must have more green vegetables and fruits. Great horse-drawn vans bearing these items began to arrive at her headquarters.

She purchased an ambulance out of her own personal funds, and worked for thirty months without pay or rest. Although it was difficult to find anything good in the war, she tried to see the hand of God at work in all that she could not understand.

She was sixty-three and weighed only ninety-five pounds when the war was over. She remained in Washington during the heat of the summer to visit hospitals and carry on a vast correspondence in her attempt to locate missing sons, fathers, husbands and sweethearts. She worked at this until the last weeks of 1866.

For the next fifteen years she traveled back and forth between New York and California and between Maine and Florida, working in behalf of the mentally ill. Many of the institutions she had helped to establish suffered neglect during the war, prompting her to say: "It would seem all my work is to be done over."

In her seventies she continued to devote her time to a wide range of philanthropies—inspecting almshouses, prisons and hospitals. When she was seventy-eight she could point to one hundred and twenty-three asylums and hospitals that had been built through her efforts.

For the last fifty years of her life Dorothea Dix had no home and often lived in the quarters of the hospitals she had founded. She who had revolutionized the status of the insane was uplifted by the thought, "I must work the work that is given me to do, and how is my soul straightened out until it is accomplished?"

In 1882, when John Greenleaf Whittier learned that she was ill in a hospital in Trenton, New Jersey, he wrote her: "He who has led thee in thy great work of benevolence will not forsake thee." She died in her eighty-fifth year, and Whittier's poem "At Last" was read at her funeral. The Scriptural text was: "I was an hungered, and ye gave me meat: I was thirsty, and ye gave me drink: I was a stranger, and ye took me in: Naked, and ye clothed me: I was sick, and ye visited me: I was in prison, and ye came unto me" (Matt. 25:35-36). She was buried in Mount Auburn Cemetery near Boston.

THE UNTIRING SERVANT OF MISSIONS

SARAH PLATT HAINES DOREMUS (1802-1877) was the first president of the Woman's Union Missionary Society of America for Heathen Lands, organized in November 1860 in Boston by Ellen H. B. Mason and nine other women. The society was formed when a Baptist missionary in Burma stressed the need for women in the foreign mission field. The Boston society was followed by one in Philadelphia and another in New York in Mrs. Doremus' home. When the society received its charter on April 11, 1861, Mrs. Doremus became its president. The first missionary sponsored by the group was Sarah H. Marston, who sailed for Toungoo, Burma, in November of the same year that the society was chartered.

Mrs. Doremus' home soon became a Bethel for departing and returning missionaries, and she was known as the "Mother of Missions." Her New

York home also served for fifteen years as headquarters for various other activities of the society.

Born August 3, 1802, she was the daughter of Elias Haines and Mary Ogden, and the granddaughter of Sarah Platt and Robert Ogden, who had given liberally to the Church. She grew up in the town and country homes of her parents. She had clear, cameolike features, delicate skin, hair of a soft color, and deep blue eyes. She retained her beauty to old age.

She was married on September 11, 1821, to Thomas C. Doremus, who achieved wealth and influence. He encouraged her in every Christian work. Mrs. Doremus took a deep interest in the establishment of a mission in the Hawaiian Islands. Once when her husband bought her an expensive shawl, she asked him to return it and give her the money instead. With this she purchased materials for the delicate fancy work and embroidery in which she excelled, and prepared articles which she sold for five hundred dollars. She donated this sum to missionary work in the Hawaiian Islands.

In 1834 Mrs. Doremus responded to the appeal of Rev. David Abeel, an American missionary in China and a member of the Dutch Reformed Church, to which she belonged. Speaking at a tea for a group of women of several denominations, he repeated the plea of Chinese women: "Are there no females who can come to teach us?" The formation of the Society for Promoting Female Education in the East was formed as a result of his talk.

Mrs. Doremus was the mother of eight daughters but only one son—Dr. Robert Ogden Doremus, professor of chemistry, toxicology and medical jurisprudence at the New York Medical College, and professor of chemistry and physics of the New York Free Academy, now the City College of New York.

Her many philanthropies were a witness to her Christian spirit. In 1828 she did benevolent work for the Greeks who were suffering under the Turks. In 1835 she became president of a society to promote the Grande Ligne Mission in Canada, conducted by Mme Henrietta Feller of Geneva, Switzerland. In 1840 she began serving in the women's ward of the New York City prison called "The Tombs." This work led to the formation of the Women's Prison Association, a society to aid discharged women prisoners. She labored in this association for thirty-two years, part of the time as its president. She personally helped many discharged women prisoners to return to useful and honorable living.

In 1841 she was appointed manager of the City and Tract Society, a group which was organized to evangelize among the poor. She served in this capacity for thirty-six years. In 1849 she joined the City Bible Society of New York, which gave Bibles to the destitute. She was one of the founders of the House and School of Industry (1850), and served as its manager for eight years and as its president for ten. She helped to establish the Nursery and Child's Hospital (1854) and the Woman's Hospital of New York State (1855). During the Civil War she aided in distributing supplies to all the hospitals in and around New York City.

What was the secret of her interest in many philanthropies? Helen Barrett Montgomery, in her book *Western Women in Eastern Lands,* says of her: "Perfectly consecrated to Christ's service, she yielded her life into His control, and the fullness of His power flowed through her life unhindered. A heart at leisure from itself to soothe and sympathize was hers. Her powers were not frittered, but directed."

A friend once met her at a Dwight L. Moody meeting in New York and greeted her: "Are you here alone?" She answered: "No, I am never alone." Her power was an evidence of her continual companionship with God.

She died on January 22, 1877, as the result of a fall in her own house. Dr. E. P. Rogers, pastor of the South Dutch Reformed Church in New York, adapting words from I Timothy 5:10, said this of her: "Well reported of for good works, she hath brought up children, she hath lodged strangers, she hath washed the saints' feet, she hath relieved the afflicted, she hath diligently followed every good work."

THE SELFLESS SECOND WIFE OF ADONIRAM JUDSON

SARAH HALL BOARDMAN JUDSON (1803-1845) translated religious tracts into Burmese as well as into the Peguan language of the central and coastal regions of Burma. She also wrote twenty hymns and other religious materials in Burmese. She was the mother of eleven children, eight by Adoniram Judson, American Baptist missionary to the Burmese, and three by her first husband, George Dana Boardman. At the time of her death she was translating Bunyan's *Pilgrim's Progress* into Burmese.

One of Sarah's contemporaries described her as a woman of "faultless features, molded on Grecian lines, having beautiful transparent skin, warm, meek blue eyes, and soft hair, brown in the shadows and gold in the sun."

She was born in Alstead, New Hampshire, the eldest of thirteen children of Ralph and Abiah Hall. Her early life was interwoven with that of the Judson family. At thirteen she wrote a poem on the passing of eight-month-old Roger William Judson, first child of Adoniram and his first wife, Ann. She read another of her poems to an audience that gathered to honor Ann when she visited New England in 1823.

After Sarah and George Dana Boardman were married in the First Baptist Church of Salem, Massachusetts, on July 3, 1825, they left for Burma to pioneer with Adoniram Judson at Moulmein. Later they went to Tavoy, to live among the Karens, a wild mountain tribe. There Sarah established a girls' school.

Her eldest child, Sarah Ann, died during a rebellion of the Tavoyans. The Boardman family escaped and found refuge on the Tavoy wharf, from which they were rescued by a steamer. When her husband died in 1831, Adoniram wrote to Sarah, saying: "You are now drinking the bitter cup whose dregs I am somewhat acquainted with. And though, for some time, you have been aware of its approach, I venture to say that it is far bitterer than you expected."

The widowed Sarah stayed on alone for three years as a missionary among the Karens, teaching and making missionary journeys into the hill country. She was accompanied by her son George, whom the Karens called "Little Chief." They admired this friendly white woman who braved many dangers in order to bring them the Christian Gospel.

Sarah Boardman and Adoniram Judson were married in Tavoy, April 10, 1834, when he was forty and she was thirty. She, like Ann Judson, made new translations into the Burmese language and assisted in other missionary duties. But her cares as a mother soon became heavy. She gave birth to eight children in ten years.

Exhausted by childbearing and ill with dysentery, Sarah embarked in June of 1845 from Calcutta with Adoniram and three of their six surviving children. Their ship developed a leak and put in for repairs at Port Louis, Isle of France on July 5. Here Sarah experienced a relapse. They boarded another ship for Boston, but shortly after it anchored at the island of St. Helena, she died on August 31, 1845.

She was buried beneath a banyan tree beside a Mrs. Chater, a missionary who had died on the voyage from Ceylon. The bereaved Adoniram continued his journey to America with his three motherless children. Edward, the best known, served as pastor of the Judson Memorial Church in New York City from 1895 to 1914. He also wrote the first biography of his father.

A PIONEERING SUPPORTER OF RELIGIOUS TRAINING

ELIZA CLARK GARRETT (1805-1855) gave two hundred and fifty thousand dollars in 1855 to start the Garrett Biblical Institute, a graduate school of theology of the Methodist Church, which occupies a central position on the campus of Northwestern University at Evanston, Illinois.

Abel Stevens, an early historian of Methodism, said of Mrs. Garrett in 1866: "She has the honor of having made the largest pecuniary benefaction to Methodism of any woman in its history, if not, indeed, of any woman in the history of Protestantism." Up to that time hers was the largest single gift in America, though a century earlier Lady Huntingdon of England gave more to churches in the British Isles but over a period of many years.

Born at Newburg, New York, on March 5, 1805, Eliza Clark had Christian training in her youth. She experienced personal sorrow and business reverses which gave her a new concept of the use of money. Even when fire reduced her income greatly, she continued her practice of giving half of it to religious causes. While sailing down the Mississippi River to New Orleans, she lost her first-born, a four-year-old daughter who became a victim of cholera. At Natchitoches, Louisiana, she lost a son, her last surviving child. In 1824 she and her husband moved to Chicago, and in the winter of 1839 they joined the Clark Street Methodist Episcopal Church, which became paramount in her life.

When Mrs. Garrett's husband Augustus, one of the early mayors of Chicago, died in 1848 without a will, Mrs. Garrett inherited half of his large fortune in real estate. Desiring to use her money in the right way, she devoutly considered how it could accomplish the greatest possible good and open a new channel for larger Christian living.

Realizing the demands of the church for an educated ministry, she gave two-thirds of her estate to found the Garrett Biblical Institute. To accomplish this, she went before the Illinois State Legislature and received an enactment safeguarding the terms of her will.

Dr. John Dempster, who had failed to establish a Biblical institute at Concord, New Hampshire, because of prejudice against technical schools of theology, was placed in charge of the Garrett Biblical Institute when the General Conference accepted her gift. The Ladies Centenary of Methodism gave fifty thousand dollars in October 1866 to build Heck Hall at the Institute, in honor of Barbara Heck, the founder of American Methodism.

Before the first cornerstone was laid, Mrs. Garrett died after a short illness. The Garrett Biblical Institute, still growing after her original gift to it more than a century ago, is a lasting memorial to her enlightened generosity.

THE VALIANT THIRD WIFE OF ADONIRAM JUDSON

MILY CHUBBUCK JUDSON (1817-1854), third wife of Adoniram dson, like the two other Mrs. Judsons, Ann and Sarah, served with him Burma under extremely difficult circumstances.

She was born in Eaton, New York, August 22, 1817, the fifth child of Lavinia Richards and John Chubbuck. At eleven she worked in a woolen factory twelve hours a day, earning one dollar and twenty-five cents a week. Later she taught in various schools of her area for seventy-five cents a week, with room and board included. When her first book was published, she received an advance of fifty-one dollars from her publishers. Out of her small earnings from teaching and writing she later invested four hundred dollars in a home for her ill parents.

Her valiant qualities attracted the attention of Dr. Judson. She was already well established as a writer under the pen name of "Fanny Forrester." When he read her most recent book he told a friend that it had great power and beauty. He approached her about writing a biography of his second wife, Sarah. As they worked on this book their friendship soon grew into a romance in spite of considerable difference in their ages. They were married June 2, 1846, about nine months after he and his three motherless children had arrived in Boston after Sarah's death.

He and Emily sailed about a month later from Boston for Burma, in a ship that stopped at St. Helena, where Sarah was buried. Dr. Judson poignantly recalled her burial there the previous August and, looking back as the boat departed, said: "Farewell, rock of the ocean! I thank thee that thou hast given me a place where I might bury my dead." Emily wrote a poem about her own experiences, calling it "Lines Written off St. Helena."

After Emily's arrival in Burma, she completed her biography of Sarah, published in 1848 under the title *The Memoir of Sarah B. Judson, Member of the Mission to Burma.* Emily wrote home: "Dr. Judson is pleased and I care little whether anyone else likes it or not." Many, however, did like the biography, and it sold twenty-eight thousand copies. It took its place beside the biography of Adoniram's first wife, Ann Judson, written by Rev. James D. Knowles, pastor of the Second Baptist Church in Boston and published in 1829. Emily herself was to have a biography written six years after her death by A. D. Kendrick, professor of Greek Literature in the University of Rochester, entitled *Life and Letters of Mrs. Emily C. Judson.* In 1859 *The Lives of the Three Mrs. Judsons* was written by Mrs. Arabella M. Wilson.

From Moulmein Emily wrote soon after her arrival: "Frogs hop from my sleeves when I put them on, and lizards drop from the ceiling to the table when we are eating; and the floors are black with ants." She also had to contend with bats, as well as cockroaches, beetles, spiders, rats, mosquitoes and bedbugs.

At the birth of Emily's first child, Emily Frances, on December 24, 1847, Dr. Judson wrote to his sister that "Emily Frances is the sweetest little fairy you ever saw." A few months after the child's second birthday, her father became ill and his physicians urged him to take a sea voyage in the hope of recovery. He died on board ship on April 12, 1850. Emily did not learn of his death until four months later. In the meantime she had lost their second child, Charles, on the day of his birth, which was ten days after his father's death.

Of her husband's death, Emily wrote:

His body was committed to the unquiet sepulchre of the sea. Though it is drifting on the shifting currents of the restless main, nothing can disturb the hallowed rest of the immortal spirit. Neither could he have a more fitting monument than the blue waves which visit every coast; for his warm sympathies went forth to the ends of the earth, and included the whole family of men.

A few months later she left Burma for America, arriving there in October 1851 after an absence of five years and three months. Her life was not easy, with four fatherless children—Sarah's three and her own Emily Frances—to look after.

On June 1, 1854, she died of tuberculosis, at the age of thirty-seven. A simple headstone marks her grave at Hamilton, New York.

THE FIRST AMERICAN WOMAN TO BE ORDAINED A MINISTER

ANTOINETTE L. BROWN (1825-1921) was the first regularly ordained woman minister in America, and probably in the world. She was twenty-eight at the time of her ordination ceremony in the Congregational Church of South Butler, New York, September 15, 1853. Rev. Luther Lee preached from the text, "There is neither male nor female; for ye are all one in Christ Jesus" (Gal. 3:28) and Rev. Gerrit Smith discoursed on *Woman's Right to Preach the Gospel.*

In this small church, with neither steeple nor bell, Antoinette Brown stood in her dress with its hooped skirt and faced her first congregation somewhat timidly. Two months after her ordination she wrote in her diary:

This is a very poor and small church, and my salary is three hundred dollars a year, ample I believe for my needs in this small community. My parish will be a miniature world in good and evil. To get humanity condensed into so small a compass that I can study each individual, opens a new chapter of experience. It is what I want, although it rolls upon the spirit a burden of deep responsibility. Perhaps I shall know some of the feelings with which an Infinite Mind watches the universe.

Antoinette was born in a log cabin at Henrietta, New York. She had joined the Congregational Church when she was nine and began to take part in prayer meetings at an early age. She was graduated from Oberlin College in Ohio in the class of 1847. When she returned to the college a year later to take a three-year course in theology, there was consternation among the faculty, for no woman had ever studied theology at Oberlin before.

Not only the college, but also her family was unco-operative. Her father and brother ceased to send her money for her expenses. She was even denied the right to continue as a teacher of drawing in the college's preparatory department. A woman professor came to her rescue, however, and organized a private drawing class for her. Antoinette was so successful in this that she was able to meet all of her expenses.

She had one colleague in the study of theology, Lettice Smith, who did not intend to preach. At the conclusion of their theological course they were given no part in the commencement and for many years their names did not appear in the alumni catalogue as graduates of the theological class of 1850. Years later, Oberlin inscribed their names on the list of graduates and gave Antoinette the honorary degree of Doctor of Divinity.

For several years before her ordination she lectured with success. But when she was sent as a delegate to the World's Temperance Convention in New York City in 1853, she was not allowed to speak. This incensed Horace Greeley, founder of *The New York Tribune,* and he wrote in his newspaper:

This convention has completed three of its four business sessions, and the results may be summed up as follows: First Day—Crowding a woman off the platform. Second Day—Gagging her. Third Day—Voting that she shall stay gagged. Having thus disposed of the main question, we presume the incidentals will be finished this morning.

As a result of Greeley's words Antoinette immediately received a wide hearing.

Greeley and Charles A. Dana, editor of *The New York Sun,* were so impressed with her ability that they invited her to preach regularly in New York City, promising to pay her one thousand dollars a year and board—a large salary for a woman before the Civil War. But she considered herself too inexperienced for a metropolitan pulpit and accepted the call of a struggling little Congregational Church at South Butler, New York.

She was acclaimed on every side. A few days before her ordination, her Oberlin college classmate Lucy Stone, a pioneer woman suffragist, declared at the Fourth National Woman's Rights Convention:

It is said that women could not be ministers of religion. Last Sunday, at Metropolitan Hall, Antoinette L. Brown conducted divine service and was joined in it by the largest congregation assembled within the walls of any building in this city [hisses]. Some men hiss who had not a mother to teach them better. But I tell you that some men in New York, knowing that they can hear the word of God from a woman as well as from a man, have called her to be their pastor, and she is to be ordained this month.

Antoinette's friendship with Lucy Stone was bound very close when they married brothers in 1855. Lucy became the wife of Henry B. Blackwell and Antoinette the wife of Samuel. Antoinette's husband was a well-to-do hardware merchant. Their sisters-in-law were Elizabeth Blackwell, first woman doctor of medicine in the modern era, and Emily Blackwell, who founded the New York Infirmary for Women and Children—the first hospital for women in America.

The year before her marriage during a period of religious doubt, Antoinette retired from pastoral duties and worked in New York slums and prisons with Abby Hopper Gibbons. For several months of the year 1855, she worked with Mrs. Gibbons in charitable work, and afterward said of this experience:

It became our custom to spend one day in the week together, seeking out the most pitiable and forsaken . . . in the slums and institutions of New York. This was before the days of many organized charities. We went wherever the way seemed prepared for rescue work. Now, it was down into the heart of darkest New York, in search of some suffering family or a stray girl . . . again, over to Randall's Island with some mission to strangers in a strange land . . . or perhaps to the Hospital, the workhouse, the Insane Asylum, or the Penitentiary on Blackwell's Island with some message of good will or moral tonic.

Later Antoinette Brown became a member of the Unitarian Church, along with Lucy Stone, who was expelled from the Congregational Church at West Brookfield, Massachuetts, because of her antislavery stand.

Antoinette had six daughters. She wrote ten books, and continued to preach after her marriage. In 1902 she delivered the funeral oration of Elizabeth Cady Stanton, at whose home the first Woman's Rights Convention had been held in 1848. In 1903, when Antoinette was seventy-eight, she journeyed to the Holy Land and brought back water to christen her grandchildren. Two years later she visited Alaska.

It was in 1908 that Oberlin College conferred on her the Doctor of Divinity degree. At the age of ninety she preached her last sermon in Elizabeth, New Jersey, at the Unitarian Church, which she served as pastor for fifteen years.

She was ninety-six years old when she died. By this time, sixty-eight years after her ordination, the census showed there were more than three thousand women ministers in the United States.

SHE KNEW THE CHRISTIAN'S SECRET OF A HAPPY LIFE

HANNAH WHITALL SMITH (1832-1911) wrote the religious classic, *The Christian's Secret of a Happy Life*, which has been translated into many languages since it first appeared in 1875 and is still in print.

In the last chapter, "The Life on Wings" based on Isaiah 40:31, she writes: "The soul that waits upon the Lord is entirely surrendered to Him, and trusts Him perfectly. Therefore we might name our wings the wings of Surrender and Trust." Asking the question, "How is it that all Christians do not always triumph?" she answers, "It is because a great many Christians do not mount up to this higher plane. The religion of Christ might be and was meant to be to its possessors not something to make them miserable, but something to make them happy."

As the daughter of a Philadelphia Quaker and wealthy glass manufacturer, John M. Whitall, and Mary Tatum, Hannah had a happy childhood. As she grew older, nature's marvels, the things of the spirit and other intangibles became fountains of ecstasy to her.

She grew into a young lady of "amazing beauty." In June 1851 she and Robert Pearsall Smith, also a Quaker, were married. In 1865 they moved from Germantown, Pennsylvania, to Millville, New Jersey, where he became manager of the glass factory owned by her family. Dissatisfied with the "spiritual deadness of nineteenth-century Quaker doctrine," she and her husband welcomed the new outburst of revivalism they found in Millville. Their evangelical activities formed for many years the absorbing interest of their lives. Both preached, wrote tracts and converted souls.

Robert's health was affected by the strain of his combined mercantile and evangelical activities. He was also injured in a fall from a horse. In 1874 he and his family embarked for England, where he and Hannah preached to large gatherings. They returned in the late seventies to Philadelphia, where Robert lost heavily in worthless silver mines, financed largely by her family. In 1886 they went back to England to settle permanently.

The Smiths had five children: Nelly, whose death at the age of five hastened her mother's conversion; Logan Pearsall Smith, the well-known English essayist; Franklin, who died of typhoid at the age of eighteen and inspired his mother to write *The Record of a Happy Life: Being Memorials of Franklin Whitall Smith* (1873); Mary, who became the wife of Bernard Berenson, the author and critic; and Alice, later the wife of Bertrand Russell, the English mathematician and philosopher.

"My father was an acceptable preacher," says Logan Pearsall Smith in his book *Unforgotten Years*, "but my sincere simple-minded mother, beautiful in her Quaker dress, with her candid gaze and golden hair, was given the name of 'the Angel of the Churches,' and her expositions of the Gospels . . . made those gatherings famous in the religious world."

He says that his mother preached in order to help others to a true knowledge of the Gospel, but his father "was immensely delighted by his sanctified success among the great ones of the earth." He fell into religious fanaticism, and at the time of his death in 1898, he was a bitter, disappointed, unhappy man. Hannah did not let disaster or her husband's downfall destroy her capacity for happiness. She continued to live in England after his death.

To her children she always tried to impart something of her own Christian faith. This is typified in a note that she wrote her son Logan: "Life has not contained much trouble for thee, yet, darling son, but when it comes, remember that thy Mother has assured thee that there is comfort and ease in the grand fact that GOD IS."

About this time, Hannah made a momentous discovery described in her spiritual autobiography and reflected in its title: *The Unselfishness of God and How I Discovered It* (1903).

During the last years of her life, she reared two grandchildren, daughters of Frank Costelloe, her daughter Mary's first husband. In his will he specified that his daughters must be brought up as Roman Catholics. She adhered strictly to his wishes, regarding her role of grandmother as a "divine relationship."

She spent her last years at "Friday Hill," the home of her son Logan at Iffley, on the Thames in Sussex, England. From this gray eighteenth-century farmhouse, set amid great trees and meadows, she wrote in 1907:

Although I am confined to my wheel chair and cannot get out much, yet the views out of our windows are so lovely, and the river is so shining, and the grass is so green, that I feel the lines have indeed fallen to me in a pleasant place. I often have a feeling as if I were living in a novel.

She wrote in *Philadelphia Quaker, The Letters of Hannah Whitall Smith,* that "the world was a place for brief abiding." She began to look on death as an eternal reality.

In one of her last letters, written not long before she died in 1911, she said: "I am very happy and content in my narrow life, and with my lessening capabilities, and can say, 'Thy will be done' to my Divine Master from the very bottom of my heart." Although rich in nothing of her own, she could still declare: "I am rich beyond words in the wisdom and goodness and love of our God. Thou, oh God, art all we want, more than all in Thee we find. This God is our God and He is enough."

THE FIRST MEDICAL MISSIONARY TO WOMEN AND CHILDREN OF INDIA

CLARA SWAIN (1834-1910) for thirty years built hospitals, taught nurses, trained native midwives in Western methods and introduced Christianity wherever she could in India.

Clara was the youngest of John and Clarissa Swain's ten children. The family lived in Castile, New York. As a young woman, Clara received her first medical training in her home town from Dr. Cornelia Greene, who had established a sanitarium at Castile.

After Clara was graduated from the Woman's Medical College of Philadelphia, she was sent to India in 1870 by the Woman's Foreign Missionary Society of the Methodist Church. She is recognized as the first woman missionary-physician to minister to women and children in non-Christian lands.

She started a medical class with fourteen native girls, thirteen of whom three years later passed examinations and were admitted to practice "in all ordinary diseases." She also treated women and children at Bareilly, India, her first mission post. In 1873 she helped establish the first woman's hospital in India on a forty-acre site containing an immense brick house, trees, two fine old wells and a garden. The estate joined her mission and was the gift of a Mohammedan prince who had once bitterly opposed Christianity. She and three others made a journey to see the owner in Rampore, traveling in a fine carriage with coachmen, two grooms and outriders and twenty-four horses, all of which he sent for them. The horses were changed every six miles, four doing duty at a time. As the prince was in prayer the day they arrived, he sent them two music boxes, and some trained athletes to perform some wonderful feats for their entertainment. Much to their surprise, when they asked him about the land the next day, he said: "Take it, take it. I give it with pleasure for such a purpose."

Clara Swain wrote afterward: "We accepted the gift with gratitude not to this prince alone, but to the King of the Universe, who, we believe, put it into his heart to give it to us."

She used the house for herself and her staff; built native dormitories where the women being treated could be housed. In the front of the enclosure was a large well where "each modern Rebecca who comes to us can draw water for herself, with her own bucket and rope as is the custom of people of caste in India," she wrote. "The grounds are tastefully laid out and in due time will be beautified with some of India's lovely roses, flowers and shrubbery."

Because of ill health, Clara went home to the United States in 1876. She was able to return to India in 1879 to devote herself to active service in the hospital.

In 1885, at the request of the Rajah of Khetri, Rajputana, Clara Swain became physician to his wife, the Rani, and other ladies of the palace. The Rajah provided her mode of travel and she departed in great state with a native Christian teacher, a companion, an English nurse, a cook and two other servants. Their entourage consisted of a camel chariot for her, two palanquins carried by seventy men each, riding horses and elephants, and a rath drawn by beautiful white oxen. Two servants rode in the latter. An escort of one hundred menservants protected her party on the journey.

The twenty-two-year-old Rani improved so greatly under her care that the Rajah asked Clara to open a dispensary for the women of the surrounding country. She decided to remain in Rajputana with its millions of people to whom God had so strangely led her.

She first set about to teach Christianity and the Bible to the Rani and to her little daughter. She also moved in and out of the market place, ministering to the sick and distributing copies of the Bible.

In 1896 Dr. Swain retired from active service and returned to Castile, New York. During the Jubilee celebration of the founding of the Methodist mission in India (1907-1908) she revisited India. A collection of her letters entitled *Glimpses of India,* published in 1909, tells the story of her work.

Clara Swain died in Castile in 1910, the same town where she was born.

THE FIRST WOMAN MISSIONARY TO ALASKA

AMANDA McFARLAND (1837?-1898?) served with her husband, D. F. McFarland, as a missionary among the Indians in Sante Fe, New Mexico, and the Nez Percés Indians in Lapwai, Idaho, until his death in 1875. In 1877 she was sent to Alaska by the Presbyterian Board as the first woman missionary there.

Her post was at Fort Wrangel, where she rented a house and sheltered a group of girls who were fleeing from the white traders, to whom they had been sold by their parents for a few blankets. Being practical-minded, Mrs. McFarland taught the girls to sew as well as to study the Bible. She also trained them in the ways of civilized people. Soon more than one hundred girls were living in her house.

The first winter she wrote to Sheldon Jackson, Rocky Mountain superintendent for the Presbyterian Board: "The father of a bright little thirteen-year-old girl sold her to Mr. Froman the storekeeper, for twenty blankets. I had a hard time to rescue her, but I succeeded. Now, Mr. Froman is angry at me." Mrs. McFarland frequently became involved in trying to settle quarrels between husbands and wives, and in fighting the problem of liquor, which was home-brewed in large quantities on the Alaskan frontier.

For a long time no denominational funds were available for the mission, and so she used her own money for its support. After funds were allotted, her first requests were for drugs, a set of carpenter tools, a sewing machine, a barrel of fire paint for the roof and two stiff paint brushes.

Having been born in Virginia, she suffered much from the cold. She spent eleven dollars of her own money—a large sum in those days—for a stove, in an attempt to keep her household warm.

Fort Wrangel was a difficult place for a woman alone, for there was neither law nor order, church nor doctor. Whenever she was tempted to give up, she thought of her girls, who without her protection would soon be swept into slavery.

After three years of hard work, she found a larger house and moved into it with twenty-one girls. Three years later, a fire destroyed this home and everyone's possessions.

They then moved into an old garrison house at the fort, and finally to Sitka where the school later became the Sitka Training School, now known as Sheldon Jackson Junior College. Mrs. McFarland's last teaching post was at Hydah, Alaska.

Little is known of her youth beyond the fact that she was born in Brooke County which is now in West Virginia. No official records exist of her birth or death. *Letters of Amanda McFarland,* edited by Charles A. Anderson, executive secretary of the Presbyterian Historical Society, appeared in the June and December 1956 *Journal of the Presbyterian Historical Society.* These letters are filled with enthusiasm, courage and heartache. They reveal this devoted woman's power to guide people on the Alaskan frontier toward Christian living.

A PIONEER IN CHRISTIAN EDUCATION IN INDIA

ISABELLA THOBURN (1840-1901) opened the first mission school for girls and the first Christian college for women in India. In 1870 she was sent as the first missionary of the Woman's Foreign Missionary Society, Methodist Episcopal Woman's Board, organized in Boston March 23, 1869.

Born at Clarksville, Ohio, of Scotch-Irish parentage, she was graduated from Wheeling Female Seminary in Ohio and from an art school in Cincinnati. During the Civil War she ministered to sick and dying soldiers. When her young brother, Bishop James Thoburn, first went to India, he came face to face with the oppression endured by Hindu women. Realizing the importance of educating them, he sent for his sister to undertake the work.

On reaching India, she found that not even her missionary brother fully comprehended the magnitude of the task. He asked her to copy a few letters for him, and after she cheerfully did so, he later repeated the request. This time she quietly reminded him that a copyist would be a great assistance to her as well as to himself.

"I discovered I had been putting a comparatively low estimate on all work which the missionaries were doing, and that her time was as precious, her work as important, and her rights as sacred as those of the more conventional missionaries of the other sex," he later remarked.

Fighting apathy and antagonism, Isabella Thoburn opened a school for girls in Lucknow. Her first pupils were seven timid little maidens. A year later, she needed larger quarters, and while searching for them heard of a beautiful house called "Lal Bagh" ("Ruby Garden") built by a rich Moslem, in a garden of seven acres. It was surrounded by amalta, babool, banyan and palm trees, and red pomegranate bushes. Begonia and other climbers clung to the portico, old trees and trellises, and roses and passionflowers lent their fragrance. She was able to buy the property for seven thousand dollars, and she moved into the house.

There, in 1887, she started "The Ruby Garden for Girls." It was later to become the Isabella Thoburn College, affiliated with Calcutta University. She courageously began the college without reference books, microscopes, telescopes, library or encyclopedias. Her faith and a donation of five hundred rupees from a Christian mother who wanted her daughter to continue her education in a Christian atmosphere were her securities.

Isabella Thoburn trained her girls for responsibility. One of them, Lilavati Singh, succeeded her as president of the college. In 1900 the two of them went to the Ecumenical Missionary Conference in New York. On this and other trips they raised twenty thousand dollars for a new building and equipment.

At Lucknow, Isabella lived and toiled for thirty-one years. Her strenuous activities lowered her resistance, and there in September 1901 she died of cholera. In her last moments her words were all in Hindustani, the language of her adopted country.

THE INSPIRING WIFE OF DWIGHT L. MOODY

EMMA REVELL MOODY (1842-1903), the Civil War bride of the American evangelist Dwight L. Moody, was affectionately referred to by religious people of the last century as "Mrs. D. L." One of the Moodys' nieces said of them: "Aunt Emma and Uncle Dwight were so perfectly one that nobody could possibly tell which was the one." Moody found in her what he termed "my balance wheel."

Their son Paul, a Presbyterian clergyman and the president of Middlebury College in Vermont (1921-1942), in writing of his mother, said:

My father's admiration for her was as boundless as his love for her. Till the day of his death he never ceased to wonder two things—the use God had made of him despite what he considered his handicaps, and the miracle of having won the love of a woman he considered so completely his superior. . . .

He said that in thirty-seven years of their married life she was the only one who had never tried to hold him back from anything he wanted to do and was always in sympathy with any new venture.

She made a home-away-from-home for him, shielding him from interruptions, bores and cranks always in abundance; writing his letters; handling all his money; paying his bills; and doing all in her power to set him free for the work he was doing, in which she took the greatest pride and interest. Only the closest and oldest of his associates knew the extent to which he leaned upon her. She did not intend that they should. . . .

To my mother, I am very sure, belongs the credit of having by precept and example made my father what he was in one respect, the most courteous man I ever knew.

Her other son, W. R. Moody, paid her this tribute: "To you, father owed such an education as no one else could have given him."

Married to a man who worked so intensely, spoke so passionately and traveled across Britain and America, Emma played no easy role. She raised their three children under the most difficult circumstances. Her daughter Emma said: "She deserved a beautiful, permanent home but she never had it." She spent years in hotels and in the homes of strangers both here and abroad. Finally she and her husband decided to restore his family home at Northfield, Massachusetts. She returned to live in it during her last years.

Emma was born in London in 1842, the daughter of Emma Manning and Fleming Revell. Her family left London in 1849 and came to America to live in Chicago. Emma was a Sunday school teacher at fifteen, a public school teacher at seventeen and the loving instructor of her husband after they were married in 1862. Dwight L. Moody saw her first when she was about seventeen. A short time later she went to a little class in a mission Sunday school where he was working, and she became a recruit teacher in his organization. Emma was a Baptist and Mr. Moody belonged to the Congregational Church. His evangelistic career was supported by clergymen of many denominations.

She was a beautiful woman with dark hair, queenly and dignified. Over the family mantel hung her portrait painted about the time she and Moody met. In this she wears a dress with a dainty, soft neckline and a silk bonnet with enormous wide ribbons hanging down over her shoulders.

From the time Emma was seventeen until her death at sixty-one, she loved teaching her own children and those of other parents. Neither she nor her only daughter Emma went to college, but they received their education from extensive travels, a wide range of reading and their contacts with every conceivable type of human being. Her son Paul, in becoming a college president, followed in the footsteps of his father, who founded Northfield Seminary for girls (1879), Mount Hermon School for boys (1881) and the Chicago Bible Institute (1889), now the Moody Bible Institute.

"Mrs. D. L." survived her husband by almost four years. After his death she must have been comforted many times by his famous lines:

Some day you will read in the papers that D. L. Moody of East Northfield, is dead. Don't you believe a word of it! At that moment I shall be more alive than I am now. I shall have gone up higher, that is all; out of this old clay tenement into a house that is immortal—a body that death cannot touch; that sin cannot taint; a body fashioned unto His glorious body. I was born of the flesh in 1837. I was born of the Spirit in 1856. That which is born of the flesh may die. That which is born of the Spirit will live forever.

Emma Moody died at Northfield in 1862. Her life is memorialized in a biography, *Heavenly Destiny,* written by her granddaughter Emma Moody Powell and based on Wordsworth's words: "And stepping westward, seemed to be a kind of heavenly destiny."

HER FAITH IS ENSHRINED AT LOURDES

BERNADETTE OF LOURDES (1844-1879) was a humble, neglected and untaught French peasant girl, to whom Mary, the Mother of Jesus, is said to have appeared eighteen times in a grotto at Lourdes. Mary told her to make known the healing power of the waters of the Gave River, which flows from rocks high up in the mountains to the bottom of a valley in one of the loveliest parts of the country near the Pyrenees.

The story goes that on February 11, 1858, Bernadette went to the valley with playmates to gather firewood. While the others ran ahead, she paused in a rocky grotto to pray. A lovely Lady appeared, and talked with her.

Bernadette said the Lady came forth heralded by sounds "like a sudden rush of wind." The next day she appeared to her again and then a third time on February 18, and finally for fifteen successive days she came to this young peasant girl who was so simply attired in a long dress with a black shawl around her shoulders, pinned together over her breast and falling down her back to a point. She also wore a kerchief tied at the side, and a white coat. It was on the thirteenth day that the Lady told Bernadette that a chapel should be built and a procession formed.

Bernadette visited the grotto eighteen times, and each time more and more people from Lourdes and eventually from other parts of France went with her. They could see nothing but a small girl who prayed and appeared to be in ecstasy. But Bernadette vowed that she saw and talked with a Lady lovelier than any she had ever seen before.

One day the Lady asked her to drink from the waters of the spring. Bernadette said she saw no spring. While hundreds watched, the girl scratched her hand in the sand of the grotto, and water began to trickle forth. The spring grew larger and larger.

The young peasant girl's background was very simple. She was born in Lourdes on January 7, 1844, the first child of François and Louise Soubirous. At the time of her birth, her father was a miller, but the mill had to be forfeited for debts and François became an odd-job man, picking up a day's work wherever he could. To escape from his problems and responsibilities, he began to drink.

His harassed wife went out to work by the day, doing laundry and other heavy tasks, even helping to harvest grain. A peasant woman of the region told of seeing Bernadette, then about twelve, carry the youngest baby to her mother in the field, to be nursed at noon.

Although Bernadette suffered from constant ill health, she made herself useful at home and in the field. When she was thirteen, she was sent to the neighboring mountain hamlet of Bartres to the home of Marie Arevant, who had nursed her when she was an infant. One of her duties there was to tend a small flock of sheep that grazed on the hillside. This brief phase of her life has inspired artists to paint her as a shepherdess.

Bernadette's childhood was careworn and poverty stricken. Her family moved from one poor location to another. When she was fourteen, the year she saw the Lady, the family was living in a single room of a dilapidated structure at Lourdes. This damp, unwholesome place had once served as a jail. Above it loomed an ancient fortress.

In 1864, at the age of twenty, Bernadette took the habit as Marie Bernard. In the convent she met all her tests with humility, cheerfully performing any menial tasks in kitchen or field.

She died on April 16, 1879. Cures from the waters of Lourdes had begun in Bernadette's lifetime. On March 3, 1858, a blind quarryman of Lourdes, named Bourriette, bathed his eyes in the water and was miraculously healed of his blindness. Others began to find healing in the springs, and cures have continued ever since. The sick, the lame and the blind go to this place by the thousands every year. In 1958 it was estimated that some five million pilgrims came to Lourdes. In the last one hundred years, the waters have been credited with thousands of miraculous cures. The shrine of Lourdes has become one of the most famous in Christendom.

The first chapel, actually a basilica, was built in 1876, with four million dollars contributed by Catholics the world around. Another church was constructed at the base of the basilica in 1901. The most recent structure is a huge underground basilica, with the roof at ground level. It is designed in the shape of a fish, the symbol widely used by early Christians as a symbol of Christ. This new building is air conditioned and its nave accommodates twenty thousand people. The altar is in the center of the nave and there are no pillars to obstruct the worshipers' view of it. This new building was dedicated on March 25, 1958, the one hundredth anniversary of the day on which the Lady is said to have told Bernadette Soubirous that she was the Immaculate Conception.

Considerable literature has been based on the story of Bernadette. *The Song of Bernadette* by Franz Werfel—a Jewish writer—has been published in many languages and read by millions of people. It was also made into a popular motion picture. Another well-known story of her life is *Bernadette and Lourdes* by Michel de Saint-Pierre.

THE FIRST AMERICAN CITIZEN TO BE DECLARED A SAINT

FRANCES XAVIER CABRINI (1850-1917) was born near Lodi, Italy, July 15, 1850. She was the thirteenth child of Augustine and Stella Cabrini. She is also referred to as Francesca. On the day of her birth, doves, never before seen at Lodi, flew and hovered about the roof and windows of the Cabrini home situated on the peaceful Lombard plains. Frances came to New York in 1888 and became a citizen of the United States in 1909. She died in Chicago December 22, 1917, but her body lies in the chapel of the Cabrini High School in New York. In 1947 she was declared a saint by the Roman Catholic Church and canonized by Pope Pius XII in 1950.

Through her work in hospitals, schools and orphanges, Frances helped to change the status of Italian immigrants in the United States, and because of this Pope Pius XII named her patron saint of immigrants.

She founded the Missionary Sisters of the Sacred Heart of Jesus in Codogno, Italy, in 1877, and afterward institutions in Peru, Chile, Argentina, Brazil, Nicaragua, France, England and Spain, as well as in the United States, where her sisterhood has had its greatest development. She founded Columbus Hospital in New York in 1892 and Columbus Hospital in Chicago in 1905.

She frequently inspired her nuns to be prepared for the performance of impossibilities, saying: "Nothing is ever to daunt you. You are to press on, not of yourselves but under obedience. I have already learned that whenever I failed in any undertaking it was because I trusted too much in my own powers. None of us will fail if we leave everything in the hands of God. Under Him the question of possible and impossible ceases to have any meaning."

"To become perfect," she admonished, "all you have to do is to obey perfectly. When you renounce your personal inclinations you accept a mortification countersigned with the cross of Christ."

"Put on wings," she counseled her nuns. "The road to heaven is so narrow, rocky, thorny, that only by flying can one travel over it."

AN EXPONENT OF THE MYSTICAL LIFE

EVELYN UNDERHILL (1875-1941), one of the most influential women in the field of mystical religion in recent times, is best known for her classic works entitled *Mysticism* and *Worship*. For many people she was a loved and trusted personal guide in things of the spirit.

She was born in December 1875 at Wolverhampton, the daughter of a distinguished barrister, Sir Arthur Underhill, and Alice Lucy Ironmonger. The family home in London was a pleasant Tory house. Evelyn was educated in London until she was sixteen and was then sent to a private school at Folkestone. Afterwards she went to King's College for Women in London.

Many members of her family were religious, and her uncle was a priest. Her parents, however, though members of the Church of England, were not churchgoing people. Her father, an enthusiastic yachtsman, frequently took her on trips in his yacht, the *Amoretta,* and she became an excellent boat-racer. The Stuart Moores, whose yacht often sailed with theirs, were neighbors and friends. Evelyn married Hubert Stuart Moore in 1907 and they enjoyed a happy life together. Their London house at 50 Campden Hill Square, a short walk from her parents' home, became in a very special sense the place of her ministry. It was there that she wrote her books. Her upstairs study became a place of prayer. It was a friendly house, where many distinguished people gathered, "though you didn't need to be distinguished to be welcome there," says Margaret Cropper in a biography, *Life of Evelyn Underhill*.

Both before and after Evelyn's marriage, she traveled widely—especially in Europe. From Florence, where she often went, she wrote: "This place has taught me more than I can tell you; it's a story of gradual unconscious growing into an understanding of things." She was then twenty-two, and she loved the Florentine art galleries and churches.

In 1907, about the time of her marriage, Evelyn experienced a religious conversion, and began to study the lives of the mystics. The first fruit of her newly awakened interest was *Mysticism*, on which she worked from 1907 to 1911. This book has gone into many editions since its original publication in 1911.

The publication of this book brought her the friendship of the noted theologian and philosopher Baron von Hügel, who had a strong influence on her as long as he lived. Although she had studied the mystics and lived with their thoughts, she had heretofore not found a living master to whom she could turn for counsel and instruction.

Baron von Hügel taught her how to take Holy Communion, saying to her that "this devotion has formed Saints and great Saints." Although she "struggled between Roman allegiance and Anglican communion, she learned to accept Anglican communion as a part of the Holy Catholic Church," her biographer explains.

Baron von Hügel continually advised her to visit the poor, telling her "you badly want de-intellectualizing." He told her that such experiences would "discipline, mortify, deepen and quiet" her. Later she wrote him of visiting "a woman living in a basement with six restless children, poor health, endless difficulties, and a drunken cruel beast of a man to whom she is not even married." And she also wrote of her visits to the poor:

I should go completely to bits. It all makes one feel, religiously, as well as physically, rather pampered. I think more and more unless one can stretch out one's own devotional life to make it avail for them it remains more or less a spiritual luxury. . . . Of course it is taxing and a bit of an effort, but on the whole a source of real happiness, not mortification. The queer thing is the tranquillizing effect they have. However jangled one may be when one goes to them, one always comes away mysteriously filled with peace and nearer God. You were absolutely right; they give one far more than one can ever give them, and I feel I ought to give them a much greater love and compassion than I do. Of course, the temptation is to concentrate on the most attractive, but I try not to do that. . . . I can not tell you what a sense of expansion and liberation I have got from this.

Baron von Hügel also taught her to pray at least an hour a day and at most an hour and a half, and to practice the Presence of Christ. After following these and other methods suggested by him, she wrote him:

My old religious life now looks too thin and solitary; this is more various, contemplating, Holy Communion, the felt presence of God, struggles to behave properly, and love for my poor people—all seem articulated points of it. All sense of contact departs abruptly the minute I become critical or horrid or fail in love and patience, or otherwise fall below my none too high standard.

She grew in spiritual wisdom and stature with the passing years. From 1924 on, she was much sought after to conduct retreats. Her favorite retreat was at Pleshay. There she and one of her closest friends, Lucy Menzies, author of *Mirrors of the Holy,* added many beautiful touches to the retreat house and to the chapel, which now contain memorials to both of them. It was a new step in the Church of England for a woman to conduct a retreat, but during her later years she led seven or eight retreats a year. "She always wore her Anglicanism with a difference," says her biographer, Mrs. Cropper. "It was tremendously enriched by her having companioned so long with saints and thinkers from every century."

Evelyn Underhill was also in demand as a speaker, and her words had the authority of one who lived with the great souls of the ages.

Besides giving countless lectures, she wrote fourteen books in fourteen years, as well as other later books. *Worship* was published in 1936. Among her other works are *The Path of Eternal Wisdom* (1911), *The Spiral Way* (1912), *The Mystic Way* (1913) *Practical Mysticism* (1914), *The Essentials of Mysticism* (1920) and *The Life of the Spirit* and *The Life of Today* (1922). Among her translations and editions are *The Cloud of Today* (1912), *Walter Hilton's Scale of Perfection* (1923) and *Eucharistic Prayers from Ancient Liturgies* (1939). She published *The Path of Eternal Wisdom* and *The Spiral Way* under the pseudonymn "John Cordelier." She also wrote a study of Jacopone da Todi (1919).

In 1927 she was made a Fellow of King's College. The first woman to be appointed an outside lecturer at Oxford University, she was chosen largely because she had a vital religious message for young men and women.

Evelyn Underhill could be many people—writer, lecturer, scholar, bird watcher, gardener, a delightful hostess, devoted friend and loving wife and daughter. A pacifist at heart, she suffered much in World War I and during the early months of World War II, shortly before her death. About this time she wrote:

If she remains true to her supernatural call, the Church can not acquiesce in War —for War, however camouflaged or excused, must always mean the effort of a group of men to achieve their purpose . . . by inflicting destruction and death on another group of men.

Finally exhausted with the ceaseless pressure of work and frail health— she was never strong—she suffered from asthma during 1940 and the early part of 1941. She grew to look even frailer than usual, but, as one of her friends said, "the light simply streamed from her face, illuminated with a radiant smile." Although she suffered, she seemed to have attained a serenity that made one forget she was suffering. One who worked with her constantly described her as "a thin creature with a pale face and dark eyes, a face that when she was truly interested would look like alabaster with a light behind it." One of her last photographs suggests Whistler's painting, "Mother."

She died on June 15, 1941, and was buried at St. John's Parish Church, Hampstead. Her fame grows with the passing of time, and her words, such as these, continue to inspire those who want to learn more of the things of the spirit:

We should think of the whole power and splendor of God as always pressing in on our small souls . . . but that power and splendor mostly reach us in homely, inconspicuous ways; in the Sacraments, and in our prayers, joys, and sorrows and in all opportunities of loving service. This means that one of the most important things in our prayer is the eagerness and confidence with which we throw ourselves open to His perpetual coming. There should always be more waiting than striving in a Christian prayer.

BIBLIOGRAPHY

• • •

The books selected for this list have been of special value in the author's research. References to other important works consulted will be found within individual biographies.

GENERAL REFERENCE BOOKS

Andrews, Edward Deming. *The People Called Shakers*. Toronto: Oxford University Press, 1953.

Barnhart, Clarence L., and Halsey, William D. *The New Century Cyclopedia of Names*, 3 vols. New York: Appleton-Century-Crofts, 1954.

Butler, Alban. *The Lives of the Fathers, Martyrs and Other Principal Saints*, 2 vols. London: Henry and Co.

Cross, F. L. (ed.). *The Oxford Dictionary of the Christian Church*. New York, Toronto: Oxford University Press, 1957.

Garrison, Winfred E., and Hutchinson, Paul. *Twenty Centuries of Christianity*. New York: Harcourt, Brace and Co., 1959.

Jackson, Samuel McCauley (ed.). *New Schaff-Herzog Cyclopedia of Religious Knowledge*. Grand Rapids: Baker Book House, 1949.

Johnson, Allen (ed.). *Dictionary of American Biography*. New York: Charles Scribner's Sons, 1928.

Latourette, Kenneth Scott. *A History of Christianity*. New York: Harper & Brothers, 1953.

Nigg, Walter. *Great Saints*. Chicago: Henry Regnery Company, 1948.

Schaff, Philip (ed.). *New Schaff-Herzog Encyclopedia*. New York: Frank Wagnall, 1894.

Stephen, Sidney Lee. *Dictionary of National Biography*. London: Oxford University Press, 1919.

Underhill, Evelyn. *The Mystics of the Church*. London: James Clarke & Co.

Vann, Joseph (ed.). *Lives of Saints*. New York: John J. Crawley & Co., 1954.

Webster's Biographical Dictionary. Springfield, Mass.: G. & C. Merriam Co., 1948.

Yust, Walter (ed.). *Encyclopaedia Britannica*. Chicago, London, Toronto: 1954.

GENERAL BOOKS ON OUTSTANDING WOMEN OF HISTORY

(These titles are in the author's private collection on the role of women in history.)

Abbott, Willis J. *Notable Women in History*. Philadelphia: John C. Winston Co., 1913.

Anderson, James. *Ladies of the Reformation.* Glasgow: Blackie and Son, 1856.

———. *Memorable Women of the Puritan Times.* Glasgow and Edinburgh: Blackie and Son, 1862.

Bloss, C. A. *Heroines of the Crusades.* Rochester: Alden, Beardsley and Co., 1853.

Brailsford, M. R. *Quaker Women.* London: Duckworth & Co., 1915.

Buoy, Charles Wesley. *Representative Women of Methodism.* New York: Hunt and Eaton, 1803.

Burden, Samuel. *Memoirs of Eminently Pious Women of the British Empire.* Ogel, Duncan, and Co., 1823.

Code, Joseph B. *Great American Foundresses.* New York: The Macmillan Company, 1929.

Coles, George. *Heroines of Methodism.* New York: Carlton & Porter, 1857.

Dunbar, Agnes B. C. *A Dictionary of Saintly Women,* 2 vols. London: George Bell & Sons, 1904.

Eckenstein, Lina. *Women under Monasticism.* Cambridge: Cambridge University Press, 1896.

———. *The Women of Early Christianity.* London: The Faith Press, Ltd., 1935.

Foster, Warren Dunham. *Heroines of Modern Religion.* New York: Sturgis and Walton, 1913.

Good, J. I. *Famous Women of the Reformed Church.* Heidelberg Press, 1901.

Gould, S. Baring. *Virgin Saints and Martyrs.* London: Hutchinson & Co., 1900.

Hare, Christopher. *The Most Illustrious Ladies of the Italian Renaissance.* New York: Charles Scribner's Sons, 1907.

Kavanagh, Julia. *Women of Christianity.* New York: D. Appleton & Co., 1851.

Lord, F. Townley. *Great Women in Christian History.* London: Cassell and Co., 1949.

Mathews, Winifred. *Dauntless Women.* New York: Friendship Press, 1947.

Menzies, Lucy. *Mirrors of the Holy.* London: A. R. Mowbray & Co., Ltd., 1928.

Mossman, Samuel. *Gems of Womanhood.* Edinburgh: Gall and Inglis, 1870.

Richardson, Mrs. Aubrey. *Women of the Church of England.* London: Chapman and Hall, 1908.

Rolt-Wheeler, Ethel. *Women of the Cell and Cloister.* London: Methuen and Co., Ltd., 1913.

Schmidt, Minna M. *400 Outstanding Women of the World.* Chicago: Minna Moscherosch Schmidt, 1933.

Smith, Eva Munson (ed.). *Woman in Sacred Song.* Boston: D. Lothrop and Co., 1885.

Spencer, J. A. (ed.). *The Women of Early Christianity.* New York: D. Appleton & Co., 1851.

Stenton, Doris Mary. *The English Woman in History.* New York: The Macmillan Company, 1957.

Stevens, Abel. *Women of Methodism.* New York: 1866.

Walsh, Walter. *The Women Martyrs of the Reformation.* London: The Religious Tract Society.

White, E. M. *Woman in World History.* London: Herbert Jenkins.

BIBLIOGRAPHY

Wittenmyer, Annie. *The Women of the Reformation*. New York: Phillips and Hunt, 1885.

Zahm, J. A. *Great Inspirers*. New York: D. Appleton & Co., 1917.

———. *Woman in All Ages and in All Countries—Women of Early Christianity*, 10 vols. Philadelphia: George Barrie and Son, 1905.

BIOGRAPHIES AND AUTOBIOGRAPHIES

Anderson, Courtney. *To the Golden Shore*. Boston: Little, Brown and Co., 1956.

Anderson, Mary. *Audentia Smith, Life of Joseph Smith III*, condensed by Bertha Audentia Hulmes. Independence, Mo.: Herald House, 1952.

Bolton, Reginald Pelham. *A Woman Misunderstood: Anne, Wife of William Hutchinson*. New York: The Schoen Printing Co., 1931.

Booth-Tucker, F. DeL. *Memoirs of Catherine Booth*, 2 vols. Chicago: Fleming H. Revell Co., 1892.

Bowden, W. Butler. *The Book of Margery Kempe*. New York: Devin-Adair Co., 1944.

Brailsford, Mabel R. *Susanna Wesley: The Mother of Methodism*. London: Epworth Press, 1938.

Canton, William. *The Story of Saint Elizabeth of Hungary*. London: Herbert and Daniel, 1912.

Clark, Elmer T. *The Chiangs of China*. Nashville: Abingdon Press, 1943.

Cropper, Margaret. *Life of Evelyn Underhill*. New York: Harper & Brothers, 1958.

Crosby, Fanny. *Fanny Crosby's Life Story*. New York: Everywhere Publishing Co., 1903.

Doughty, W. L. *The Prayers of Susanna Wesley*. New York: Philosophical Library, 1956.

Doyle, Sister St. Ignatius. *Marguerite Bourgeoys and Her Congregation*. New York: Garden City Press, 1940.

Drury, Clifford. *Marcus Whitman, M. D., Pioneer and Martyr*. Caldwell, Idaho: Caxton Printers, Ltd., 1937.

Dyer, Helen S. *Pandita Ramabai, The Story of Her Life*. London: Morgan and Scott, 1909.

Evelyn, John. *Life of Mrs. Godolphin*. London: William Pickering, 1848.

France, Anatole. *The Life of Joan of Arc*, 2 vols., translation by Winifred Stephens. New York: John Lane Co., 1909.

Freer, Martha Walker. *The Life of Jeanne D'Albret, Queen of Navarre*. London: Hurst and Blackett.

———. *Life of Marguerite of Navarre*. Cleveland: The Burrows Brothers, 1895.

Hodgkin, L. V. *Gulielma: Wife of William Penn*. London: Longmans, Green & Co., 1947.

Jerrold, Maud F. *Vittoria Colonna*. London: J. M. Dent & Co., 1906.

Jones, M. G. *Hannah More*. London: Broadwater Press, 1952.

Jorgensen, Johannes. *St. Bridget of Sweden*, 2 vols. New York: Longmans, Green & Co., 1954.

————. *St. Catherine of Siena.* New York: Longmans, Green & Co., 1938.

Judson, Emily Chubbock. *Memoir of Sarah B. Judson, Member of the Mission to Burmah.* New York and Cincinnati: 1848.

Kirk, John. *The Mother of the Wesleys.* New York: Hunt and Eaton.

Knowles, James D. *Memoir of Mrs. Ann H. Judson.* Boston: Lincoln and Edmands, 1829.

Lawrence, Una Roberts. *Lottie Moon.* Nashville: Sunday School Board of the Southern Baptist Convention, 1927.

Livingstone, W. P. *Mary Slessor of Calabar.* London: Hodder and Stoughton, 1915.

Marshall, David Conwell. *Dorothea Dix.* Durham, N. C.: The University of North Carolina Press, 1937.

Maynard, Theodore. *A Fire Was Lighted: The Life of Rose Hawthorne Lathrop.* Milwaukee: Bruce Publishing Co., 1948.

Miller, Basil. *Pandita Ramabai, India's Christian Pilgrim.* Grand Rapids: Zondervan Publishing House, 1949.

Moffat, John S. *The Lives of Robert and Mary Moffat.* New York: A. C. Armstrong and Son, 1885.

Montgomery, Helen Barrett. *Helen Barrett Montgomery: From Campus to World Citizenship,* with tributes by her friends. New York, London, Edinburgh: Fleming H. Revell, 1940.

Muncey, R. Waterville. *The Passion of St. Perpetua.* London: J. M. Dent and Sons, 1927.

New, A. H. *The Coronet and the Cross.* London: Partridge & Co., 1858.

Peers, E. Allison. *Complete Works of St. Teresa,* 3 vols. London: Sheed & Ward, 1946.

Powell, Emma Moody. *Heavenly Destiny.* Chicago: Moody Press, 1943.

Roderick, Stella Virginia. *Nettie Fowler McCormick.* Rindge, N. H.: Richard R. Smith, 1956.

Ross, Isabel. *Margaret Fell, Mother of Quakerism.* London: Longmans, Green & Co., 1949.

Seaver, George. *David Livingston, His Life and Letters.* New York: Harper & Brothers, 1957.

Seesholtz, Anne Geroh. *Saint Elizabeth, Her Brother's Keeper.* New York: Philosophical Library, 1948.

Smith, Amanda. *Amanda Smith's Own Story.* New York: Meyer and Brothers, 1893.

Smith, Logan Pearsall. *Philadelphia Quaker: Hannah Whitall Smith.* New York: Harcourt, Brace and Co., 1950.

Thurston, Lucy G. *Life and Times of Lucy G. Thurston.* Ann Arbor: S. C. Andrews, 1882 and 1934.

Undset, Sigrid. *Catherine of Siena.* New York: Sheed & Ward, 1954.

Upham, Thames C. *The Life of Madame Guyon.* London: Allenson & Co., 1905.

Walsh, William Thomas. *St. Teresa of Avila.* Milwaukee: Bruce Publishing Co., 1943.

White, Charles I. *Mother Seton.* New York: Doubleday & Co., 1949.

BIBLIOGRAPHY

Whitney, Janet. *Elizabeth Fry*. Boston: Little, Brown & Co., 1936.

Wilson, P. W. *General Evangeline Booth*. New York: Charles Scribner's Sons, 1948.

Willson, Arabella M. *The Lives of the Three Mrs. Judsons*. New York: C. M. Thaxton, 1859.

INDEX

• • •

INDEX

Bayly, William, 129
Bede, the Venerable, 37
Beguines, 312
Benedictine nunneries, in charge of Lioba, 306-7
Berguswida, 36
Bernadette of Lourdes, 386-88
Bertha, Queen of Kent, 36, 304-5
Berwick, 331
Bethlehem
  Church of the Holy Nativity founded by Helena in, 10
  Fabiola's voyage to, 298
  Paula and Eustochium in, 32-33
  religious houses built by Paula in, 30
Bible
  Basque translation sponsored by Jeanne d'Albret, 86
  Burmese translation of Adoniram Judson and his wives, 174, 175, 178, 373
  Caedman's paraphrases, 35
  classes of Jerome on, 18
  comfort and example to Emily H. Tubman, 182
  commentary on by Mme Jeanne Guyon, 132
  delight of Marcella in, 19-20
  German translation by Luther, 91
  guide to Dorothea Dix, 368
  Latin translation of Jerome, 18, 28-29
  love of John Chrysostom for, 27
  Marathi translation of Pandita Ramabai, 259, 266, 267-68
  polyglot, published in Spain, 73
  read in prison by Elizabeth Fry, 165-66
  Sechwana translation of Robert Moffat, 189, 190
  translation of Helen Barrett Montgomery, 268-69
  translation of Joseph Smith, 202, 203
  use in Christian Science, 206
  Vulgate, 18
Bidamon, Lewis Crum, 202
Black Death, 51, 54-55, 316
Blackwell, Elizabeth, 216
Blaesella, 20, 30, 31
Blagge, Thomas, 351
Blindness, of Fanny J. Crosby, 384, 387-88
Boardman, George Dana, 372
Boardman, Sarah Hall; see Judson, Sarah Hall Boardman
Bodley, Rachel, 264
Boniface, 306-7
Booth, Ballington, 222
Booth, Catherine, 218-26
Booth, Evangeline, 222, 223
Booth, Florence Soper, 222
Booth, Herbert Henry, 222
Booth, Marian Billups, 222
Booth, Maude Charlesworth, 222
Booth, William, 219-26
Booth, William Bramwell, 222
Booth-Clibborn, Catherine and Arthur, 222
Booth-Hellberg, Lucy and Emmanuel, 222
Booth-Tucker, Emma and George, 222
Bora, Katherine von, 90-98
Borgia, Lucretia, 326
Bourgeoys, Abraham, 342

Bourgeoys, Marguerite, 342
Bowes, Elizabeth, 331-32
Bride; see Bridget
Bridget (of Ireland), 302-3
Bridget of Sweden, 313-15
Brigid; see Bridget
Brigida; see Bridget
Brigittines, Order of, founded, 313, 314
Brittany, Anne of, 326
Brother-and-sister communities, 12
Brotseach, 302
Brown, Antoinette L., 376-78
Bullinger, Anna, 324-26
Bullinger, Heinrich, 322, 324, 345
  succeeds Zwingli, 325
  wife of, 324-26
Bunyan, Elizabeth, 349-51
Bunyan, John, 349-51
  wife of, 349-51
  imprisonment of, 349-51
  writings of, 350-51
Burden, Ann, 325
Bures, Idelette de, 321-24
Burma, Judson family in, 372-73, 374-76
Burnham, John of, 317

Cabrini, Augustine and Stella, 388
Cabrini, Frances Xavier, 388-89
Caedmon, 35
Caesarius, 15
Callowhill, Hanna, 349
Calvin, Idelette; see Idelette de Bures
Calvin, John, 322-24
  protected by Renée of France, 327
  wife of, 322-24
  writings of, 323
Calvinism
  founder of, 322-24
  Jeanne d'Albret adopts, 86
  Lady Huntingdon's Connexion, 150, 156
Campbell, Alexander, 179, 180, 184
  in New World, 359-60
  in Scotland, 358
  mother of, 357-60
Campbell, Thomas, 357-60
  "Declaration and Address," 359
  in Ireland, 357-58
  wife of, 357-60
Cancer, work of Rose Hawthorne Lathrop for patients with, 256-59
Canonized women; see Saints
Canterbury, Cathedral of, 305
Capet, Hugh, 307
Cappel, battle at, 325
Carmelites
  Acarie, Barbe, 330-31
  Teresa of Ávilla, 98-107
  Teresa of Lisieux, 280-83
Carthage, 3, 4
Cary, William, 350, 351
Catacombs, Flavia Domitilla immortalized in, 284
Catherine of Aragon, 74
Catherine of Genoa, 318-20
Catherine de Médicis, 86, 87, 88, 89

INDEX

INDEX

INDEX

INDEX

Penn, William, 119, 121, 124
  first wife of, 346-49
  in America, 348
  second wife of, 349
Perpetua, daughter of Monica, 21
Perpetua, Vibia, 3-7
Pescara, Marchesa of; see Colonna, Vittoria
Peter, Bishop of Sebaste, 11-12
Philanthropists; see Occupations of women
Physicians; see Occupations of women
Piagenti, Lapa, 51
Pilgrims
  in India
    Pandita Ramabai, 261-62
    Pandita's parents, 260-61
  to Holy Land
    Helena, 7, 9-10
    Paula and Eustochium, 28, 31-32
Pius XII, Pope, 42, 320, 388
Pleshay, 391
Pocahontas, 336-37
Pontus, 11
Poor Clares, 38-43
Porteus, Beilby, Bishop of Chester and of
    London, 356
Prayer
  Marie de l'Incarnation quoted on, 340
  mental, of Teresa of Ávila, 100-101
  Method of Prayer, by Mme Jeanne Guyon,
    132-33
Prayer, reliance on
  Catherine of Siena, 52
  Catherine of Genoa, 319
  Isabella of Castile, 67-69
  Judson, Ann, 177
  Monica, 21, 23
  Pandita Ramabai, 259
  Slessor, Mary, 250
  Smith, Amanda, 233, 235-37
  Soong, Mrs. Charles Jones, 275-79
Prayers of women
  Askew, Anne, 329
  Catherine of Siena, 59
  Clare of Assisi, 41-42, 45
  Colonna, Vittoria, 81
  Elizabeth of Hungary, 48
  Fry, Elizabeth, 166
  Gertrude the Great, 312-13
  Isabella of Castile, 69
  Judson, Ann, 171
  Luther, Katherine, 99
  Macrina, 13-14
  Wesley, Susanna, 144, 148-49
Preaching by women
  Booth, Catherine, 219, 220
  Brown, Antoinette L., 377-78
  Dyer, Mary, 345, 346
  Fisher, Mary, 126
  Fry, Elizabeth, 169
  Hooton, Elizabeth, 339
  Howe, Julia Ward, 286
  Hutchinson, Anne, 108-16
  Slessor, Mary, 249, 253
  Smith, Amanda, 232-39

Prentiss, Elizabeth, 284, 286-87
Presbyterian women
  Knox, Margaret Stuart, 332-34
  Knox, Marjorie Bowes, 331-32
  McCormick, Nettie Fowler, 229-32
  McFarland, Amanda, 382-83
  Slessor, Mary, 247-54
  Whitman, Narcissa, 204-13
Principia, 19, 20
Prison reform; see Reformers
Prophetess
  Gertrude the Great, 313
Protestant Sisters of Charity, 363
Pulcheria, 298-300

Quakers, Shaking; see Shakers
Quaker women
  Dyer, Mary, 344-46
  Fisher, Mary, 125-29
  Fox, Margaret Fell, 116-25
  Fry, Elizabeth, 164-71
  Hooton, Elizabeth, 337-39
  Penn, Gulielma, 346-49
  Smith, Hannah Whitall, 379-80
Queens
  Bathildis, 305-6
  Bertha, 36, 304-5
  Clotilda, 300-2
  Ethelberga, 36
  Isabella of Castile, 67-74
  Jeanne d'Albret, 82, 85-90
  Margaret of Navarre, 82-85, 87, 89
  Radegonde, 303-4
  Theodelinda, 304
Quietism, 130-32

Radegonde, 303-4
Radegunda; see Radegonde
Ramabai; see Pandita Ramabai
Randolph, John, 166, 337
Raymond of Capua, 55, 56, 57
Recluse, Juliana of Norwich, 315-16
Redstone Baptist Association, 359
Reformation, women of the
  Bullinger, Anna, 324-26
  Bures, Idelette de, 322-24
  Jeanne d'Albret, 85-90
  Knox, Margaret Stuart, 332-34
  Knox, Marjory Bowes, 331-32
  Luther, Katherine, 90-98
  Margaret of Navarre, 82-85
  Renée of France, 326-28
  Zwingli, Anna, 320-22
Reformers
  church (*see also* Reformation, women of
    the)
    Acarie, Barbe, 330-31
    Catherine of Siena, 50-60
    Teresa of Ávila, 98-107
  prison
    Dix, Dorothea, 369-70
    Fry, Elizabeth, 164-71
  social
    Dix, Dorothea, 367-70
    Pandita Ramabai, 258-68